SPREADSHEET SOFTWARE

Qualifications and Credit Framework

AQ2013 Level 3 Diploma in Accounting

British Library Cataloguing-in-Publication Data

A catalogue record for this book is available from the British Library.

Published by
Kaplan Publishing UK
Unit 2, The Business Centre
Molly Millars Lane
Wokingham
Berkshire
RG41 2QZ

ISBN: 978-1-78415-397-7

The text in this material and any others made available by any Kaplan Group company does not amount to advice on a particular matter and should not be taken as such. No reliance should be placed on the content as the basis for any investment or other decision or in connection with any advice given to third parties. Please consult your appropriate professional adviser as necessary. Kaplan Publishing Limited and all other Kaplan group companies expressly disclaim all liability to any person in respect of any losses or other claims, whether direct, indirect, incidental, consequential or otherwise arising in relation to the use of such materials.

Printed and bound in Great Britain

We are grateful to the Association of Accounting Technicians for permission to reproduce past assessment materials and example tasks based on the new syllabus. The solutions to past answers and similar activities in the style of the new syllabus have been prepared by Kaplan Publishing.

We are grateful to HM Revenue and Customs for the provision of tax forms, which are Crown Copyright and are reproduced here with kind permission from the Office of Public Sector Information.

CONTENTS

INTRODUCTION

HOW TO USE THESE MATERIALS

These Kaplan Publishing learning materials have been carefully designed to make your learning experience as easy as possible and to give you the best chance of success in your AAT assessments.

They contain a number of features to help you in the study process.

The sections on the Unit Guide, the Assessment and Study Skills should be read before you commence your studies.

They are designed to familiarise you with the nature and content of the assessment and to give you tips on how best to approach your studies.

WORKBOOK

This workbook has been specially prepared for the revised AAT qualification introduced in July 2013. It uses a slightly different format to other Kaplan study texts at this level due to the nature of the syllabus content.

The screen shots for this text are based around Excel 2010. However, the techniques explained should also be applicable to other versions of spreadsheet software, although the screens will look slightly different.

There are also 'tips and shortcuts' that will highlight quick ways in Excel to navigate to the correct function.

Throughout the workbook, there will be opportunities to test your knowledge through the activities. For some of these activities you will need to access pre-populated spreadsheets that you can view inside your MyKaplan account. The login details for this account can be found on the insert contained within the workbook.

This workbook is predominantly designed as a study aid used within the classroom or as a distance learning student aid.

Please note that suggested answers to all the activities you encounter in the workbook can be accessed through your MyKaplan account.

Quality and accuracy are of the utmost importance to us so if you spot an error in any of our products, please send an email to mykaplanreporting@kaplan.com with full details.

Our Quality Co-ordinator will work with our technical team to verify the error and take action to ensure it is corrected in future editions.

UNIT GUIDE

Spreadsheet Software

6 credits

Purpose of the unit

This unit has been designed by e-skills to describe the skills and competencies of an intermediate spreadsheet user. The use of spreadsheet software tools and techniques are defined as 'intermediate' because:

- the range of data entry, manipulation and outputting techniques will be multi-step and at times non-routine or unfamiliar
- the tools, formulas and functions needed to analyse and interpret the data requires knowledge and understanding (for example, mathematical, logical, statistical or financial)
- the user will take some responsibility for setting up or developing the structure and functionality of the spreadsheet.

These skills are important to accounting organisations, as they allow users to perform complex calculations quickly and efficiently; and most organisations use spreadsheets to manipulate large amounts of data on a daily basis.

Learning outcomes

On completion of these units the learner will be able to:

- Use a spreadsheet to enter, edit and organise numerical and other data.
- Select and use appropriate formulas and data analysis tools and techniques to meet requirements.
- Use tools and techniques to present, format and publish spreadsheet information.

Knowledge

To perform this unit effectively you will need to know and understand the following:

		Chapter
1	**Use a spreadsheet to enter, edit and organise numerical and other data.**	
1.1	Identify what numerical and other information is needed in the spreadsheet and how it should be structured.	1,3,15
1.2	Enter and edit numerical and other data accurately.	2
1.3	Combine and link data from different sources.	7,11
1.4	Store and retrieve spreadsheet files effectively, in line with local guidelines and conventions where applicable.	1, 16, 17, 18
2	**Select and use appropriate and data analysis tools and techniques to meet requirements.**	
2.1	Explain what methods can be used to summarise, analyse and interpret spreadsheet data and when to use them.	10
2.2	Select and use a wide range of appropriate functions and formulas to meet calculation requirements.	4, 6, 7, 12
2.3	Select and use a range of tools and techniques to analyse and interpret data to meet requirements.	19, 20, 22, 23
2.4	Select and use forecasting tools and techniques.	22
3	**Use tools and techniques to present, format and publish spreadsheet information.**	
3.1	Explain how to present and format spreadsheet information effectively to meet needs.	3, 8
3.2	Select and use appropriate tools and techniques to format spreadsheet cells, rows, columns and worksheets effectively.	3, 8, 9
3.3	Select and use appropriate tools and techniques to generate, develop and format charts and graphs.	14, 20

		Chapter
3.4	Select and use appropriate page layout to present, print and publish spreadsheet information.	5
3.5	Explain how to find and sort any errors in formulas.	13
3.6	Check spreadsheet information meets needs, using IT tools and making corrections as necessary.	13
3.7	Use auditing tools to identify and respond appropriately to any problems with spreadsheets.	23

Delivery guidance

The AAT have provided delivery guidance giving further details of the way in which the unit will be assessed.

The student should be able to design a suitable spreadsheet format using a blank worksheet, use existing spreadsheets, use spreadsheet templates, and also produce individual spreadsheets to meet certain requirements. Therefore they should be able to identify and select data (numerical and text) to include in a spreadsheet and to be able to show how the spreadsheet should be structured, in terms of both layout and format including appropriate titles and data display formats.

Designing a suitable spreadsheet structure involves using a blank worksheet to develop a logical structure and format to display prescribed information for a specific purpose. The designs should ensure that the information is easily understood by the users of that information. The design and manipulation of data/workbooks covers the use of spreadsheet templates for routine work and also the production of a spreadsheet for a particular reason. There should be a planned structure to the spreadsheet and the design and layout should be appropriate to the task. Students should know and be able to work with all component parts of spreadsheets (cells, rows, columns, tabs, pages, charts, workbooks, worksheets and windows).

The student should be able to enter and edit data accurately. This will include both numerical and textual data. They should be able to insert data into single and multiple cells, clear cells, edit cell contents, replicate data, cut, copy, paste, find and replace, add and delete rows and columns; use absolute and relative cell references and add data and text to a chart. They should also be able to hide and protect cells, and link data.

Students must be able to store and retrieve spreadsheets – therefore they could be assessed on using folders (for example, create and appropriately name) and files (for example, create, name, open, save, save as, print, close, find, share). They should also be able to use version control; import/export files into other documents and also archive information (backup and restore).

Students must be able to use font, alignment, styles, page layout, headers and footers to ensure data and information is displayed clearly and meets the specified requirements. Students should be able to proof read information and check formulae to identify and correct any errors.

Students should be able to use a wide range of formulas and functions to complete calculations; they should be able to use the design of formulas to meet calculation requirements. These could include mathematical, statistical, financial, conditional, look-up, and logical functions.

Students should be able to use a range of techniques to summarise data and then analyse and interpret the results. Assessable summarising tools include: totals and sub-totals; sorting of a cell range, rank, conditional formatting; filter rows and columns; data restriction; tables, graphs and charts; histograms, simple pivot tables and charts. The student can be assessed on their judgment of when and how to use these methods.

Students may be assessed on using the tools, formulas and functions (for example, data restrictions, data validation using formula and pivot tables and charts) needed to analyse the information within a spreadsheet.

The student should then be able to develop the spreadsheets by using forecasting techniques. What-if scenarios, goal seek and data tables may be assessed.

Students need to be able to use different formats and link data in spreadsheets and worksheets using functions such as look-up (V and H), data sort and filter and concatenate.

Spreadsheets should then be prepared for publication or sharing with others. The student should be able to format spreadsheet contents (cells, rows and columns) to ensure that they meet a competent standard and are easy to read. This may include height and width and shading for rows and columns; and for cells, formatting for numbers or text, currency, percentages, number of decimal places, dates, font, bold, underline and italic, alignment, text and cell colour, shading and borders, and alignment of cell content.

Students should be able to produce the information within the spreadsheet in different formats. They may be assessed on choosing the most appropriate way to display information. The charts should be correctly labelled (chart title, axis titles, axis scale and include a legend, data label or data table). All chart types may be assessed (2D, 3D, clustered, stacked, column, bar, pie, bubble, doughnut, line and scatter graphs). Students should be able to change the chart type; move and resize a chart and annotate the chart as needed.

To present print and publish information, the student should be able to ensure that spreadsheet is displayed in the best possible way and adjust the page set up or scale to fit, if necessary, for printing. This could include choosing the font size, the orientation (portrait or landscape), margins, header and footer, page breaks, page numbering and including a date/ time stamp.

Students should be able to check the spreadsheets for any errors. This could include accuracy of numbers and any text, accuracy of results, correcting errors in formulas; checking the layout and format validity; using formulas to determine valid entries for cells, the validity, relevance and accuracy of analysis and the interpretation of calculations and results.

Errors, once identified, should be corrected and the student's ability to do this may be assessed. The student should be able to use the help facility; identify and correct errors in formulas (use audit formulas to check for errors). Identify and correct errors in circular references, calculations and results; they should also be able to validate data and locate and remove invalid data.

Students will be assessed on the most common tasks used in the workplace. No accounts specific knowledge is required. Where accounts specific calculations are required guidance will be provided as to how to calculate these figures. This will ensure that whatever the student's prior experience/knowledge they will be able to calculate figures as they will be provided with the necessary information to perform the spreadsheet tasks.

Examples

The AAT has also provided examples as to what could be assessed within each learning outcome. Please note this list is not exhaustive.

1 Use a spreadsheet to enter, edit and organise numerical and other data

The student should be familiar with the component parts of a spreadsheet including - workbook, worksheet, column, row, cell, active cell, tab, page and panes/windows and be able to edit and label these.

The student should be able to use the following functions – open, save, save as, file name/rename, folder name, rename tab, order worksheets, password protect files, backup and archive information

The student should be able to use the following functions in editing and entering data across single or multiple cells - insert, delete, justify, input/amend text and numerical data, copy, cut, paste, paste special, clear and find and replace.

The student should be able to reorganise data in different formats and link spreadsheets and data including using functions such as data sort and filter, v and h lookup and concatenate.

2 Select and use appropriate and data analysis tools and techniques to meet requirements

The student should be to use the following functions in analysing and interpreting data - addition, subtraction, multiplication, division, sum, percentages, parentheses, pivot table, pivot charts, consolidation, sort data, filter data, data restriction, data validation, find and replace, look up, if, and, auto sum (count, max, min, sum, average), relative references, absolute references and date (today, now, day/month/year).

The student should be able to lock and hide cells, columns and rows.

The student should be able to use the analysis tools within the spreadsheet. This may include histograms, rank and percentile and moving averages.

The student should be able to forecast using trend lines within the spreadsheet.

The student should be able to display formulas on the worksheet

3 Use tools and techniques to present, format and publish spreadsheet information

Students should be able to title a spreadsheet, insert headers and footers and tab names.

Students should be to use the following formatting tools: currency, date, fixed decimal, 1,000 separator, '£', formatting percentages, applying the double underline border to cells, text alignment (including wrap text, shrink to fit, merge cells and orientation), font and font size, cell justification, borders, shading, merge cells, underline, use italics, conditional formatting, page setup (margins, orientation, print area) and be able to print formula.

Students should be able to insert and delete columns, rows, cells and to change the row height, column width.

Students should be able to hide and unhide cells, columns and rows and protect spreadsheets/cells. They should be able to print with or without gridlines visible or invisible.

Student should be able to produce, title and label all elements and graphs (column, bar, line, pie, scatter, doughnut, bubble) and be able to show different views of these (2D, 3D, clustered, stacked, exploded, combined)

Student should know how to use page layouts to present data and scale information for printing purposes.

Students should be able to use passwords, both to open and protect documents.

Students should be able to check spreadsheets for errors in content and in formulas using the following functions - error checking, trace error and formula editing.

Student should ensure that the information contained within the spreadsheet meets the needs of the recipient.

THE ASSESSMENT

The format of the assessment

This is a skills unit where students are required to demonstrate they have the skills to be able to use spreadsheet software competently to create spreadsheets and enter, edit and manipulate data to meet organisational requirements. They will have to show competence in using techniques for data analysis and auditing tools.

Students can be assessed by computer based project (CBP) using an AAT case study assessment – students will be required to complete a series of tasks, based upon a case study, provided by the AAT, which will cover all three learning outcomes.

In the assessment students will have to demonstrate their competence in:

LO1 – Use a spreadsheet to enter, edit and organise numerical and other data. This will be assessed by the student designing and using a spreadsheet and identifying what numerical and other information is needed in the spreadsheet and how it should be structured. Students must be able to store and retrieve spreadsheets – therefore they could be assessed on using folders (for example create and name) and files (for example, create, name, open, save, save as, print, close, find, share); or on their ability to import/export files into other documents and archive information (backup and restore).

LO2 – Select and use appropriate formulas and data analysis tools and techniques to meet requirements. The assessment should ensure that students are able to summarise information in a variety of ways, and can identify the most appropriate method. The assessment should cover the use of a range of functions, the use of formulas and forecasting tools. Students will also be assessed on their ability to identify and use the correct technique to analyse and interpret data to meet organisational or other given requirements and identify and use the most appropriate formulas for specific purposes. Short answer questions may be used to assess student's ability to choose appropriate techniques if necessary.

LO3 – Use tools and techniques to present, format and publish spreadsheet information. The ability to check information for accuracy and present information suitable for a range of users is an important skill. The assessment should cover the presentation of spreadsheet information in different ways. Students should be able to produce spreadsheets which are of a publishable standard, including charts and graphs. The assessment should allow students to demonstrate an ability to use appropriate formatting, for cells, rows, columns and worksheets on their evidence. Students will also be assessed on their ability or knowledge of how to check spreadsheets for problems or errors. This can be evidenced by finding errors within spreadsheets or the use of short answer questions.

The AAT case study assessment will be assessed by a qualified assessor employed by the training provider. Therefore, it will not be an instant result received on the day you take the test.

Task	Learning outcome	Assessment criteria	Task topic
1	1 2 3	1.1 1.2 1.3 1.4 2.2 3.1 3.2 3.4 3.6	Design a spreadsheet
2	1 3	1.1 1.2 3.1 3.2 3.3 3.4	Produce a chart or graph
3	1 2 3	1.3 1.4 2.2 2.3 2.4 3.2 3.5 3.6	Use techniques to calculate data
4	1 2 3	1.4 2.1 2.3 3.2 3.3	Use analysis tools
5	2 3	2.1 3.1 3.5 3.7	Spreadsheet knowledge questions

Please contact the centre you wish to take the exam at to confirm which version of Excel is available for the assessment.

Time allowed

The time allowed for this assessment is:

Scenario 1 - 2 hours and 30 minutes

Scenario 2 - 3 hours

STUDY SKILLS

Preparing to study

Devise a study plan

Determine which times of the week you will study.

Split these times into sessions of at least one hour for study of new material. Any shorter periods could be used for revision or practice.

Put the times you plan to study onto a study plan for the weeks from now until the assessment and set yourself targets for each period of study – in your sessions make sure you cover the whole course, activities and the associated questions.

If you are studying more than one unit at a time, try to vary your subjects as this can help to keep you interested and see subjects as part of wider knowledge.

When working through your course, compare your progress with your plan and, if necessary, re-plan your work (perhaps including extra sessions) or, if you are ahead, do some extra revision/practice questions.

Effective studying

Active reading

You are not expected to learn the text by rote, rather, you must understand what you are reading and be able to use it to pass the assessment and develop good practice.

A good technique is to use SQ3Rs – Survey, Question, Read, Recall, Review:

1 **Survey the chapter**

Look at the headings and read the introduction, and content, so as to get an overview of what the chapter deals with.

2 **Question**

Whilst undertaking the survey ask yourself the questions you hope the chapter will answer for you.

3 **Read**

Read through the chapter thoroughly working through the activities and, at the end, making sure that you can meet the learning objectives highlighted on the first page.

4 **Recall**

At the end of each section and at the end of the chapter, try to recall the main ideas of the section/chapter without referring to the text. This is best done after short break of a couple of minutes after the reading stage.

5 **Review**

Check that your recall notes are correct.

You may also find it helpful to re-read the chapter to try and see the topic(s) it deals with as a whole.

Note taking

Taking notes is a useful way of learning, but do not simply copy out the text.

The notes must:

- be in your own words
- be concise
- cover the key points
- well organised
- be modified as you study further chapters in this text or in related ones.

Trying to summarise a chapter without referring to the text can be a useful way of determining which areas you know and which you don't.

Three ways of taking notes

1 **Summarise the key points of a chapter**

2 **Make linear notes**

A list of headings, subdivided with sub-headings listing the key points.

If you use linear notes, you can use different colours to highlight key points and keep topic areas together.

Use plenty of space to make your notes easy to use.

3 Try a diagrammatic form

The most common of which is a mind map.

To make a mind map, put the main heading in the centre of the paper and put a circle around it.

Draw lines radiating from this to the main sub-headings which again have circles around them.

Continue the process from the sub-headings to sub-sub-headings.

Highlighting and underlining

You may find it useful to underline or highlight key points in your study text – but do be selective.

You may also wish to make notes in the margins.

Further reading

In addition to this text, you should also read the "Student section" of the "Accounting Technician" magazine every month to keep abreast of any guidance from the examiners.

Introduction to spreadsheet basics

1

1.1 Introduction

This chapter will guide you through how to open and close spreadsheets, guide you how to change names of workbooks/worksheets, and also how to save your work.

KNOWLEDGE

1.1 Identify what numerical and other information is needed in the spreadsheet and how it should be structured.

1.4 Store and retrieve spreadsheet files effectively, in line with local guidelines and conventions where applicable.

1.2 Different Spreadsheet Software Applications

There are many different spreadsheet applications available. Microsoft Excel is by far the most commonly used, and this guide is written specifically for Microsoft Excel 2010. There are 3 other versions of Excel in common use – the key differences between these and Excel 2010 are explained below, along with Open Office, a spreadsheet application which is freely available online:

Excel 2003

This looks very different to 2010 – a major overhaul to the menu system was introduced in 2007. As a result, many of the explanations for methods in this text will not apply. However, all of the formulas and techniques are the same.

Conditional Formatting has also been updated since 2003, although the basics required for this course are the same in 2003.

Excel 2007

This version, as mentioned earlier, underwent a huge cosmetic change from Excel 2003. Many features were improved in terms of functionality, although the underlying basics remained the same.

The number of rows and columns available were greatly increased, however from a practical point of view this will make no difference to your studies – no spreadsheet example would ever be big enough to fill up all the space on either version!

There are actually very few differences between Excel 2007 and 2010 – the only important one is that 2007 has the 'Office button' in the top-left of the spreadsheet, which is the equivalent of the 'File tab' in 2010. The File tab is discussed later.

The Excel 2007 'Office button'.

Excel 2013

The newest version of Excel. Again, some cosmetic changes have been made, meaning that the menu layout may not be the same as the examples shown. However, the functionality has not changed significantly enough for this to pose too much of a problem.

Open Office

As mentioned earlier, this software has the enormous advantage of being free. Its appearance is closer to Excel 2003, with a less visual menu system. The formulas are largely the same, although there are slight differences in the way some formulas are entered.

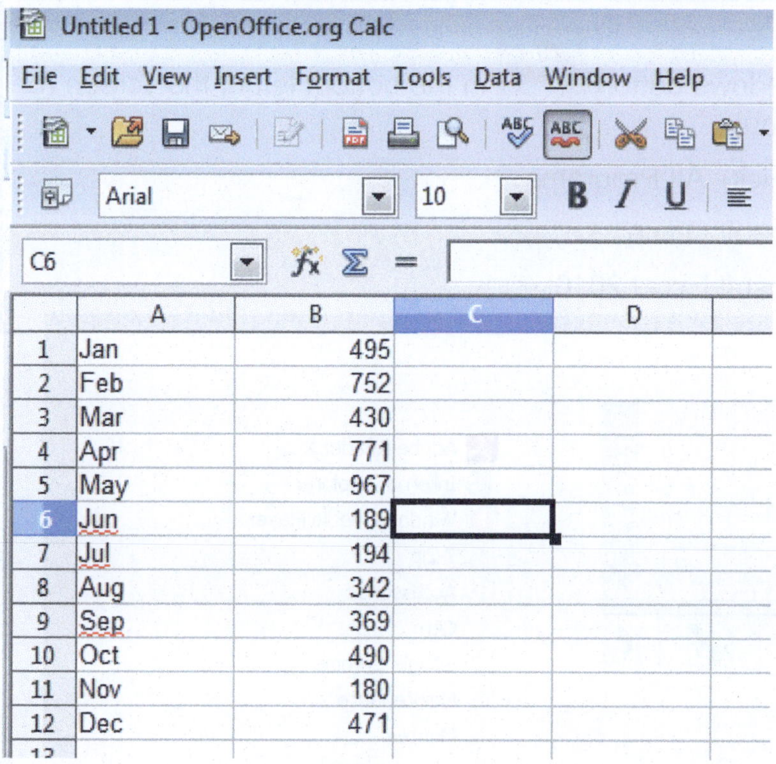

Most of the features are the same, although the appearance is different.

If you are having any problems with any spreadsheet software other than Excel 2010, the internet contains vast resources on all available software, and a quick search should be able to find the correct method.

1.3 Opening the application

There are numerous ways to open the application and the way that you do it will depend on the version of Excel that you are using and personal preference. We will follow the full path. From the bottom left hand corner of the screen:

- Click the Windows button  in the bottom left of the screen (or the Start Menu)
- Select (left click) 'All Programs'
- Select 'Microsoft Office'
- Select 'Microsoft Excel 2010'

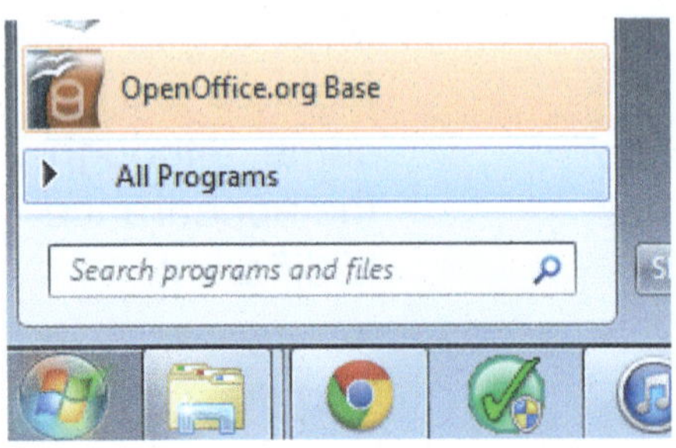

Excel will open.

1.4 Workbooks and worksheets

When Excel opens, a new, blank spreadsheet will be shown. The following terms will be used throughout this material:

A **WORKSHEET** is a single page or sheet in the spreadsheet. A new spreadsheet will have 3 of these by default (called 'Sheet1', 'Sheet2', 'Sheet3'), but this can be changed, and worksheets can be added or deleted, as well as renamed. The term worksheet is often abbreviated to **SHEET**.

A **WORKBOOK** is the spreadsheet file, made up of one or more worksheets. The default blank workbook is made up of 3 worksheets. The workbook name is the filename of the spreadsheet.

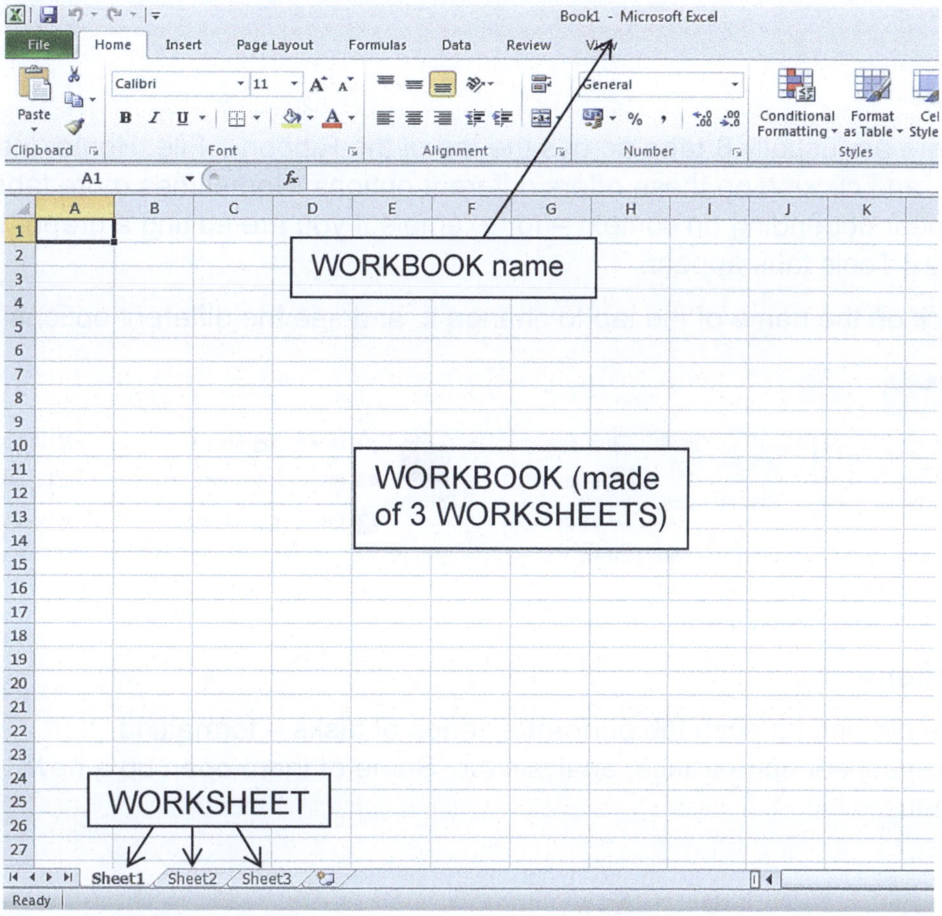

1.5 The Ribbon

The 'Ribbon' is Excel's menu system. It is made up of various tabs and buttons, allowing you access to all of Excel's features. There are many, many options within the Ribbon – the good news is that most people only use a few of them. This guide will concentrate on the key features only.

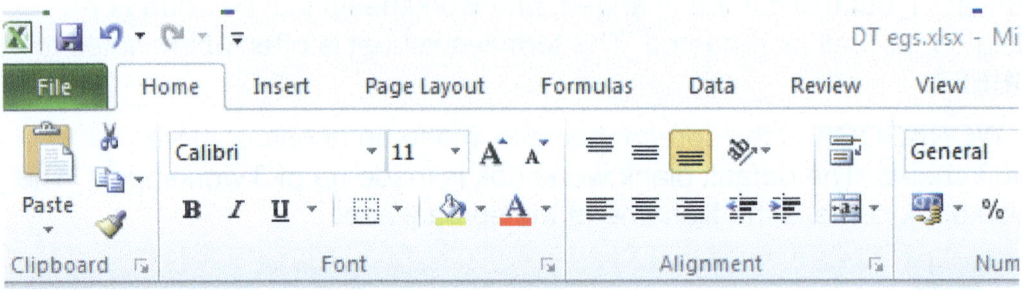

Tabs

There are usually 8 **tabs** across the top of the Ribbon – File, Home, Insert etc. and clicking on these offers different options. Sometimes more tabs appear depending on context – for example if you are editing a graph, the Chart Tools tabs appear.

Click on the name of the tab to change it, and see the different options.

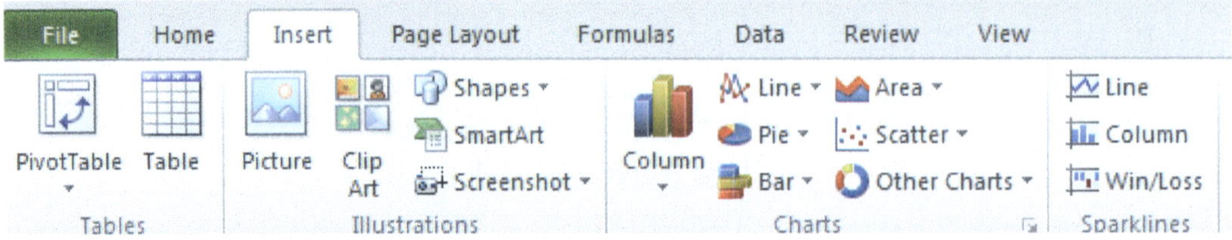

This is the Insert Tab.

Buttons

The buttons on each tab perform a series of tasks – formatting, spreadsheet appearance, analysis etc. Some of them open up a new menu.

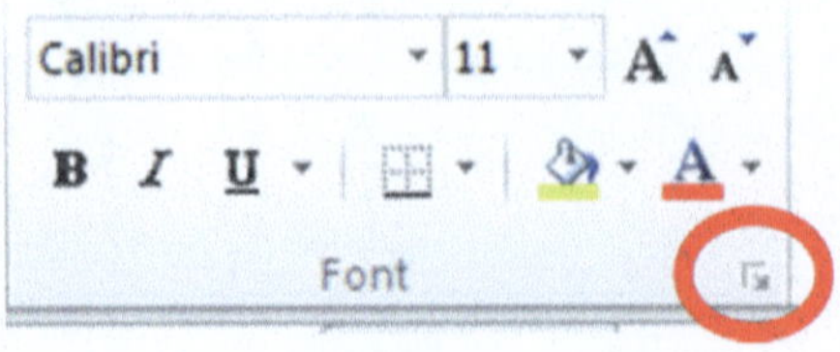

Many of the menu items on the ribbon have the above button. This opens up a specific menu – usually the 'classic' menu from previous versions of Excel, which some people are more used to.

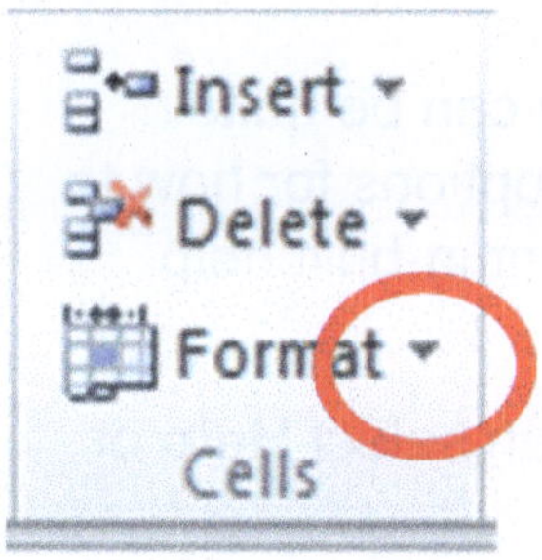

Other buttons have a small down arrow next to the name. Clicking on this opens brings up more options.

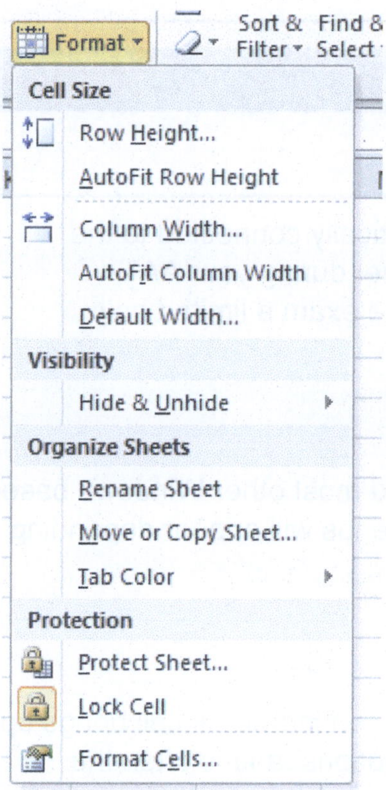

Although it seems like a lot to take in, the more you use these menu options, the more familiar with them you will become. Also, due to the way they are grouped with similar commands, you can often find what you need by looking in these menus.

Note that if you are not sure what a particular option does, hover the mouse pointer over it for a second or two and more information will be shown.

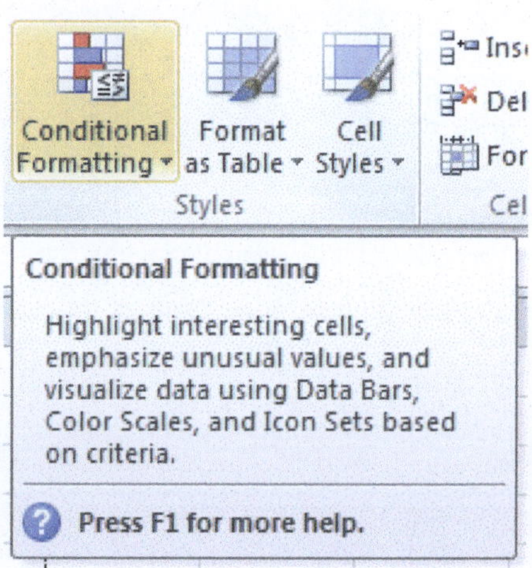

Further information about Conditional Formatting is shown by hovering over the button.

1.6 Help is at hand!

If you are not used to dealing with spreadsheets, they can be quite daunting – there are often lots of numbers and many options for how to deal with your data. Fortunately, Excel has an excellent in-built help function to help you.

The Help Function is in the **File** tab – click on **File**, then select **Help** or click on 

> **Shortcut**
>
> Press **F1** to bring up the Help menu

Important note – the help function is automatically connected to the Internet. You are not allowed to use the Internet during your AAT assessment. However if you click '?' during the exam a limited help function will be launched.

1.7 Right-click

Using the right mouse button within Excel (and most other Windows based programs) is very useful. Context-sensitive menus will appear depending on where you click.

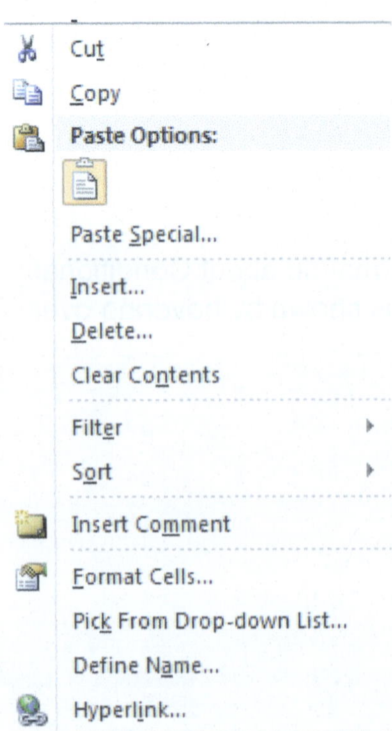

Right-clicking on an individual cell brings up several useful options, and is often the quickest way of completing a task.

1.8 Undo and Redo

Probably the most frequently used command within Excel. Undo, as the name suggests, cancels the last thing you did. The most useful thing about this is that it means you should not be afraid to experiment – if you are not sure what something does, try it. If it did not do what you wanted, undo.

Redo allows you to cancel an undo, if you decide that is what you did want!

The Undo button (the left arrow) is located in the top-left corner of the file. It is always visible, whichever tab you have clicked on in the ribbon.

The Redo button (the right arrow) is greyed out as there are currently no commands to redo.

Clicking on the blue arrow will undo the last command. Clicking on the small triangle will allow you to undo more than one recent command.

After clicking Undo, the 10 which had been typed in has gone – this has been 'undone'. Note that the redo button has now turned blue – if we click on that, the command (typing 10 into cell A1) will be 'redone'.

Remember, formatting, data entry and formula entry can all be 'undone', so if things start to look wrong, undo what you have done. If you realise you were right, simply redo!

Shortcut

- **Ctrl-z** (hold Ctrl, then press z) will undo the last command
- **Ctrl-y** will redo the last undone command

1.9 Opening a new workbook

If you wish to open a new workbook:

- Select the **File** tab
- Select '**New**'
- Select '**Blank workbook**' from Available Templates.

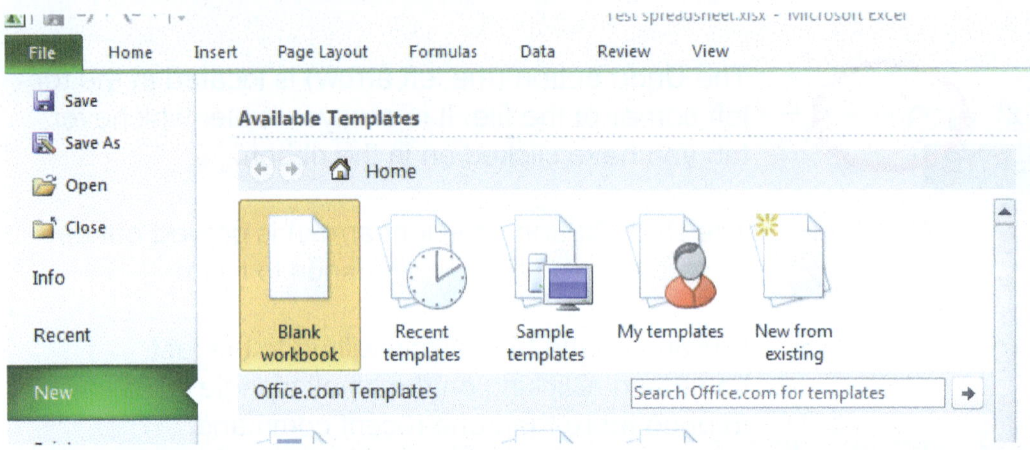

Shortcut

Ctrl-n

Opens a new workbook automatically.

1.10 Saving the workbook

Saving the workbook allows you to give it a more appropriate name, as well as keeping it for future use. To save a file:

- Select the File tab
- Select Save to save the file as it is, or Save As to give it a new name
- The 'Save As' Dialogue Box will open. Navigate to the directory in which you wish to save the file
- Type the name of the spreadsheet in the File name box
- Click 'Save'.

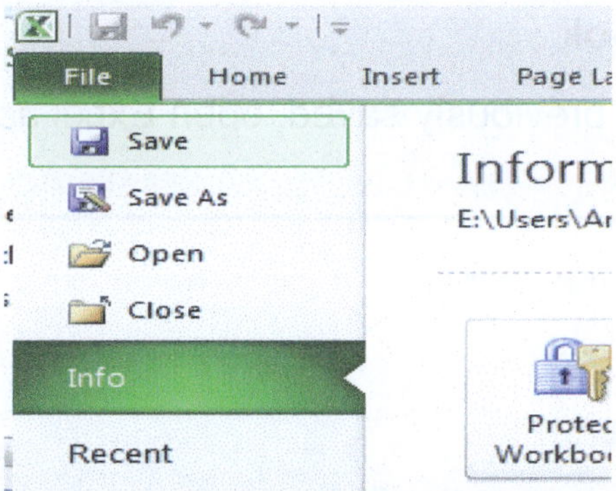

The File tab allows you to save (as well as open and close files).

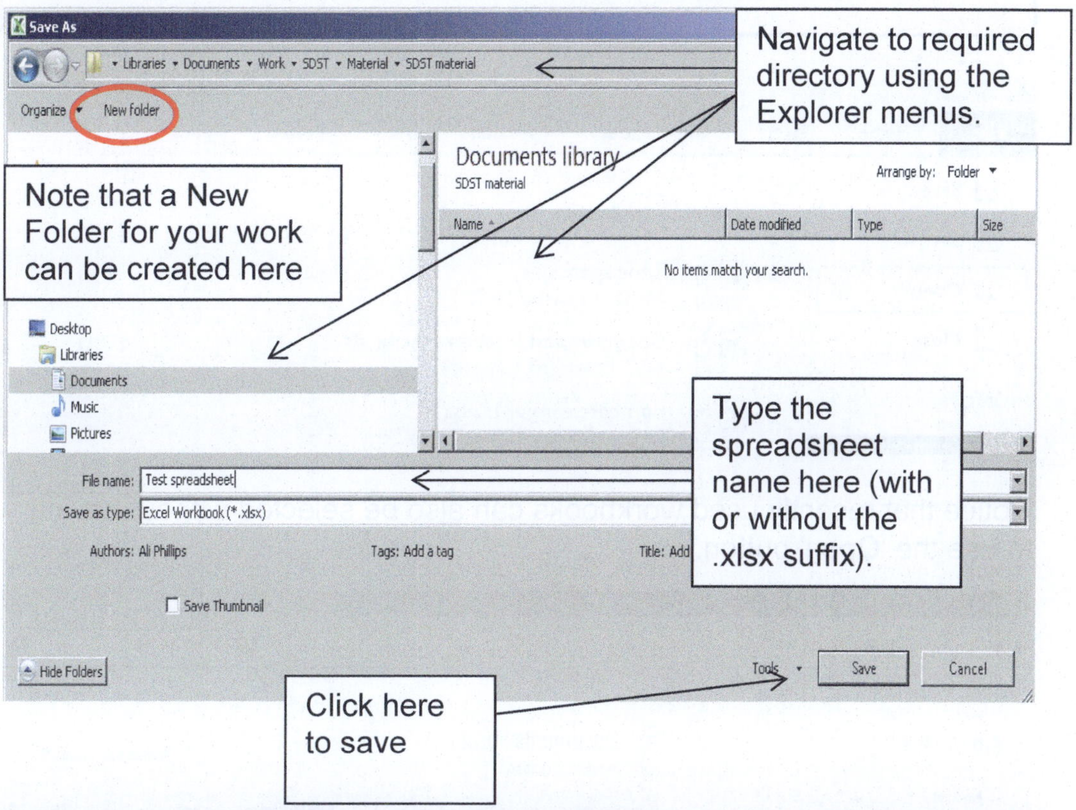

Shortcut

Ctrl-s

Will reveal the 'Save' dialogue box if a file hasn't been saved yet. It will save a file that already has a name.

1.11 Opening an existing workbook

To work on a spreadsheet that has been previously saved, open Excel as before, then:

- Click the 'File' tab in the top left of the screen
- Click the 'Open' button
- Navigate to the file you wish to open
- Click the 'Open' button, or double click on the file.

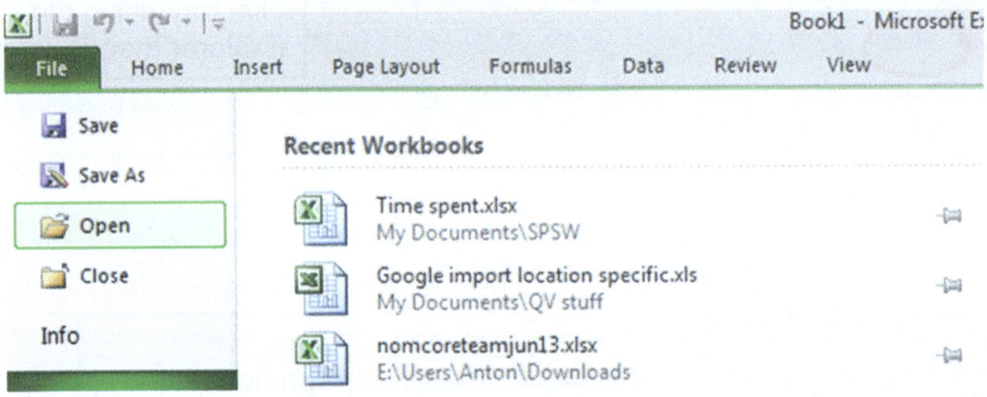

Notice that recently used workbooks can also be selected without having to use the 'Open' button.

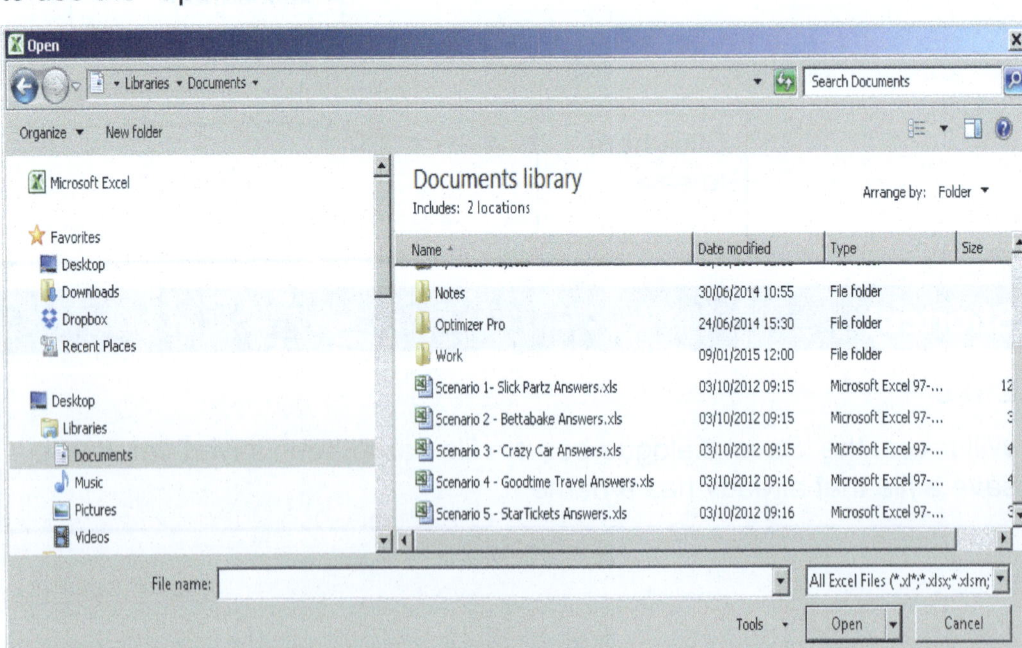

You can navigate to the folder/file you need by selecting the appropriate directory from the dialogue box shown.

Shortcut

Ctrl-o

Will reveal the 'Open' dialogue box.

1.12 Closing the workbook

Having saved your workbook you can then close it. There are 2 basic options:

1 Click the 'X' in the top right hand corner of the screen – the lower one of the two (the top one closes Excel completely). If you have multiple worksheets open then you get the option to close just the one you are working on.

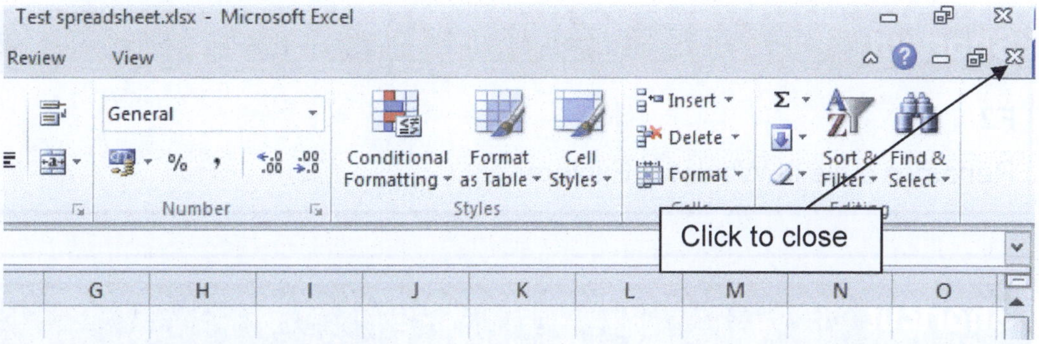

2 Select the File tab, and then Close.

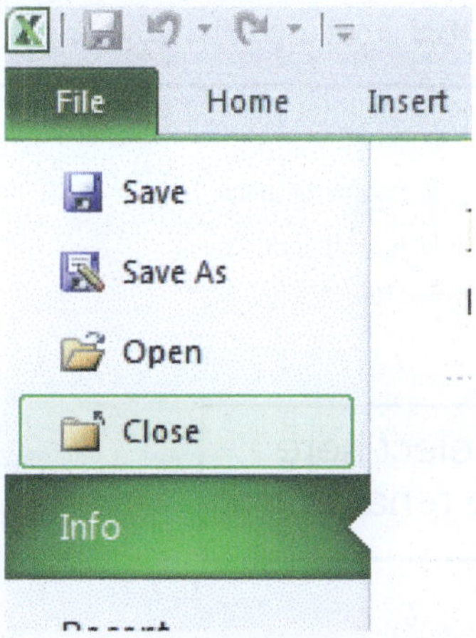

If you haven't already saved the workbook you will be prompted to do so when you click 'Close'. You can then follow the procedure above.

1.13 Renaming the workbook

To 'Rename' your workbook you could:

(a) Save the file using a different name, using Save As (note that this will keep a copy of the original file)

(b) Or with the workbook closed

- Locate the File using Windows Explorer (or My Computer)
- Right Click on the file and select 'Rename'
- Type the new name
- Press Enter.

Shortcut

F2

Renames a file in Windows Explorer.

Shortcut

On your keyboard you have a key with the 'Windows' icon

Press '**Windows-e**' to open Windows Explorer.

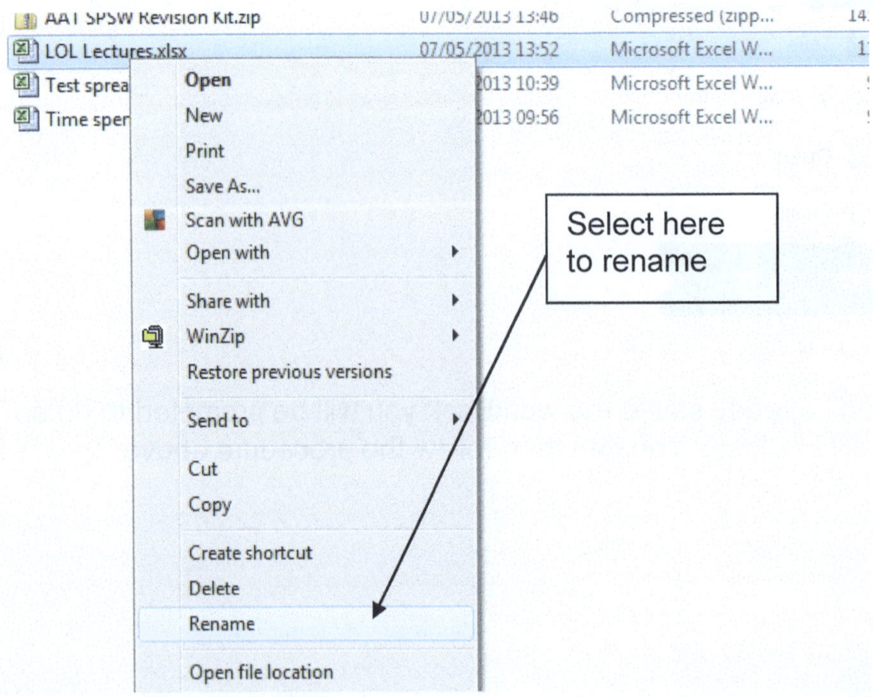

1.14 Renaming a worksheet

To 'Rename' a particular **worksheet** within a **workbook** you should do the following:

- Select the Home tab
- Select Format
- Select Rename Sheet
- The Sheet name will then be highlighted. Type the new name to overwrite it.

OR

- Right click on the worksheet name at the bottom of the page
- Select rename
- The Sheet name will then be highlighted. Type the new name to overwrite it.

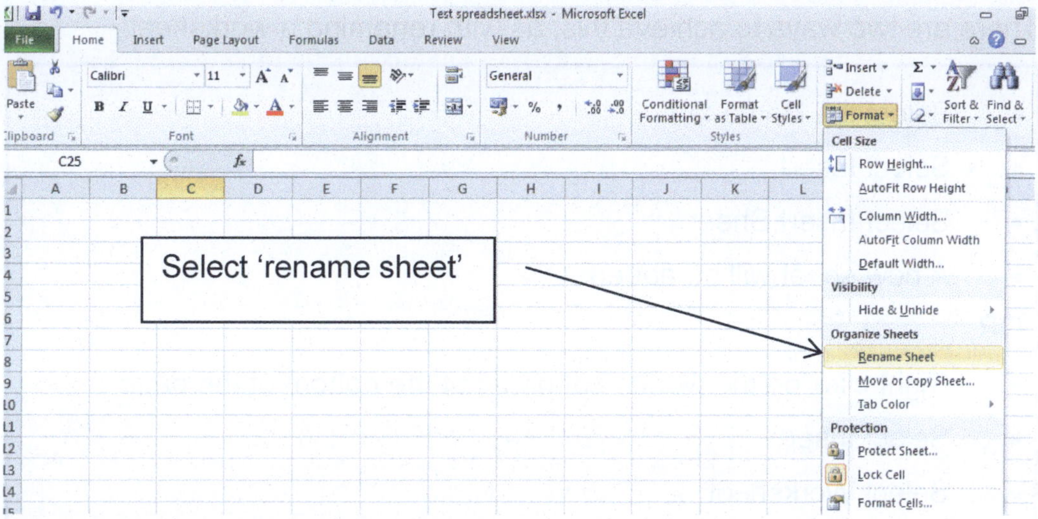

Or

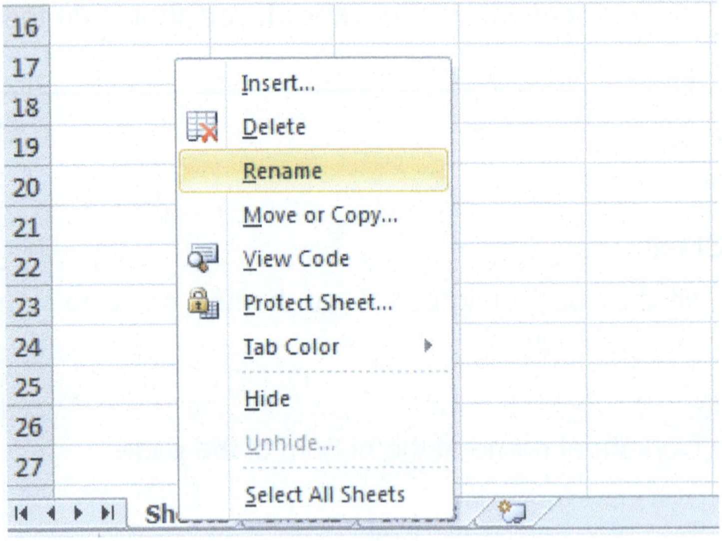

The quickest way is just to **DOUBLE CLICK** on the sheet name to edit it.

1.15 Adding worksheets

There are two ways to achieve this, as with renaming a worksheet:

- Select the Home tab
- Select Insert
- Select Insert Sheet
- A new sheet will be added

OR

- Right click on the worksheet name at the bottom of the page
- Select Insert
- Select Worksheet
- A new sheet will be added

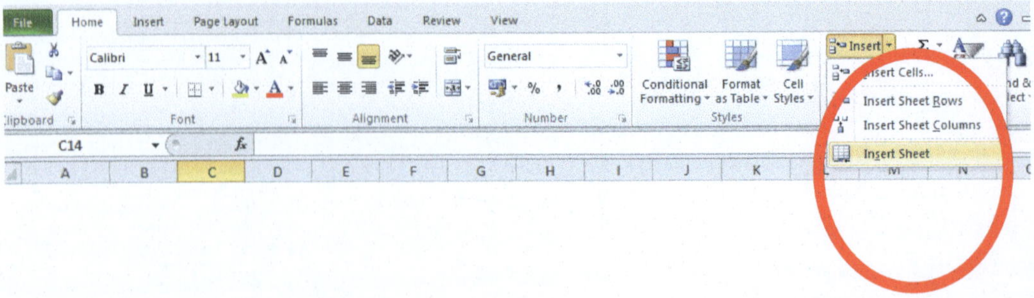

OR

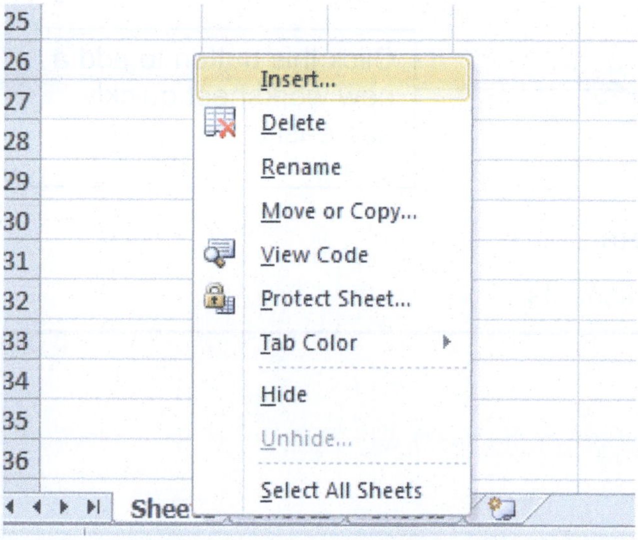

Then select Worksheet to add one.

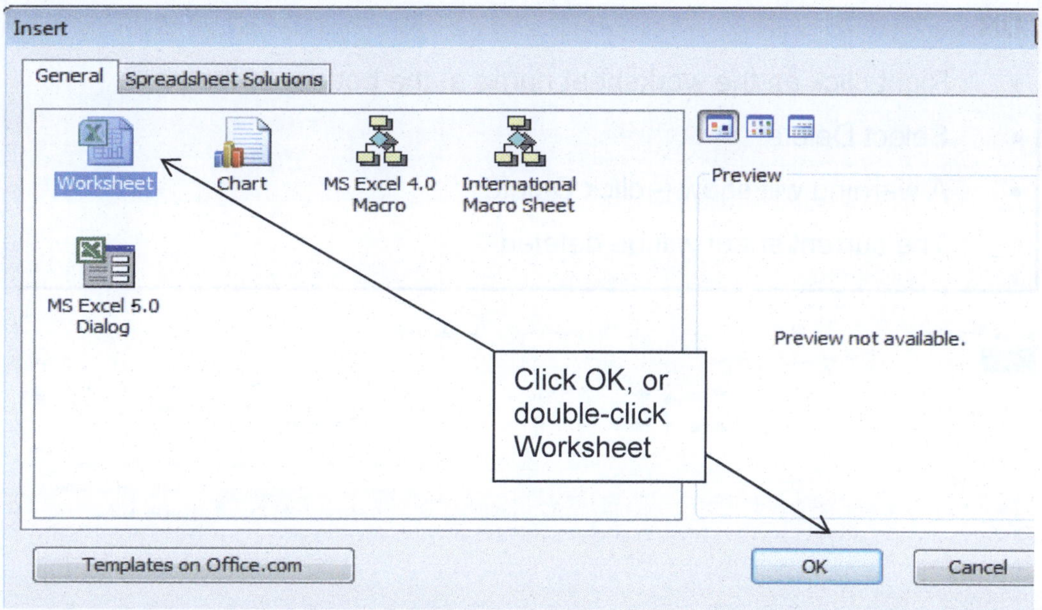

Shortcut

Shift+F11

Inserts a new worksheet

Or

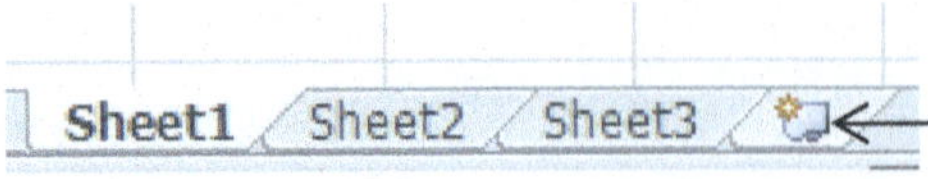

Click this button to add a new worksheet quickly and easily!

1.16 Deleting worksheets

Similar method to adding worksheets:

- Select the Home tab
- Select Delete
- Select Delete Sheet
- A warning will show – click Delete
- The current sheet will be deleted.

OR

- Right click on the worksheet name at the bottom of the page
- Select Delete
- A warning will show – click Delete
- The current sheet will be deleted.

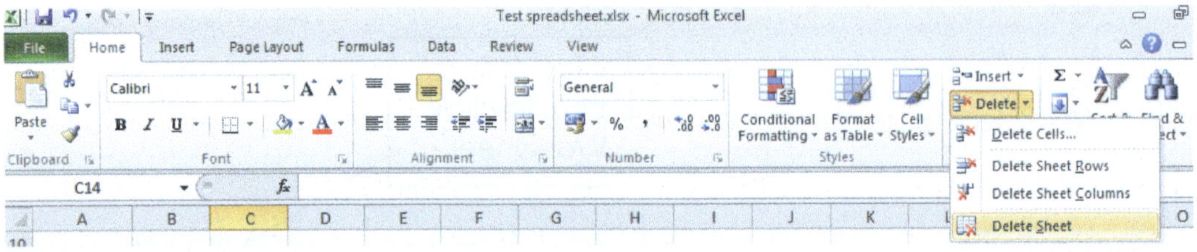

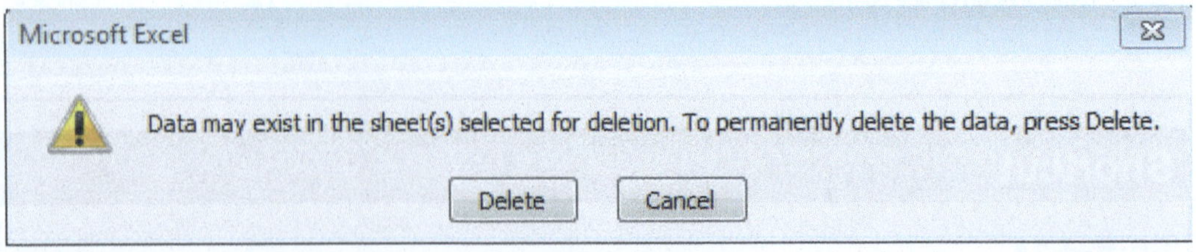

Warning message – take note, once a sheet has been deleted this action **CANNOT** be undone.

1.17 Moving/Copying worksheets

The order of your worksheets can easily be changed in Excel, and you can also quickly copy a sheet to get a duplicate version.

- Select the Home tab
- Select Format
- Select Move or Copy Sheet
- A Dialogue box will open – select where you want the current sheet to be located
- Click OK when complete.

OR

- Right click on the worksheet name at the bottom of the page
- Select Move or Copy
- The same dialogue box will be displayed.

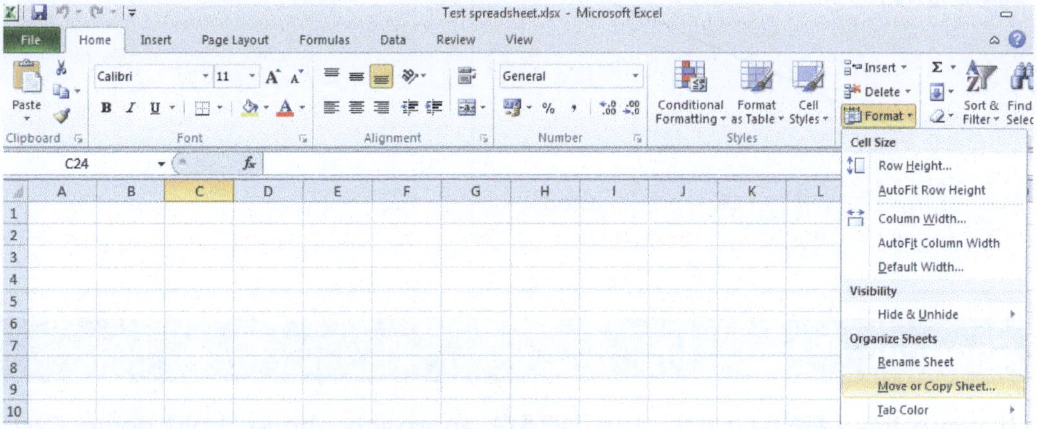

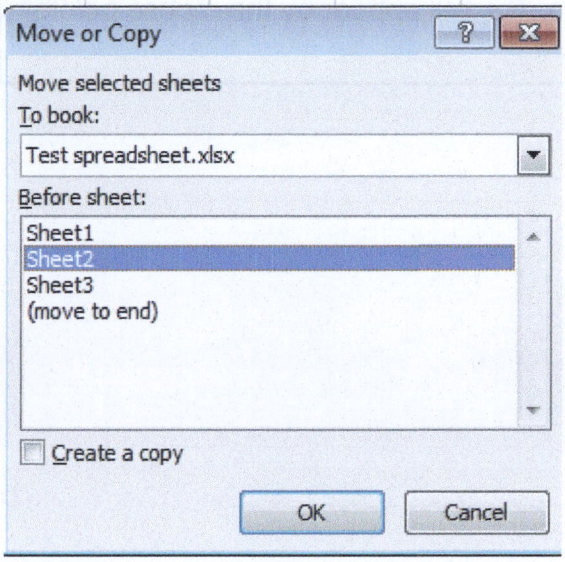

Shortcut

Simply **LEFT CLICK** and **HOLD** the button down while pointing at the sheet name – then **DRAG** the sheet to the position you require

Note that a worksheet can be moved within the existing workbook, or to another workbook you have open.

To copy a worksheet, follow exactly the same steps, but tick the 'Create a copy' box before clicking OK.

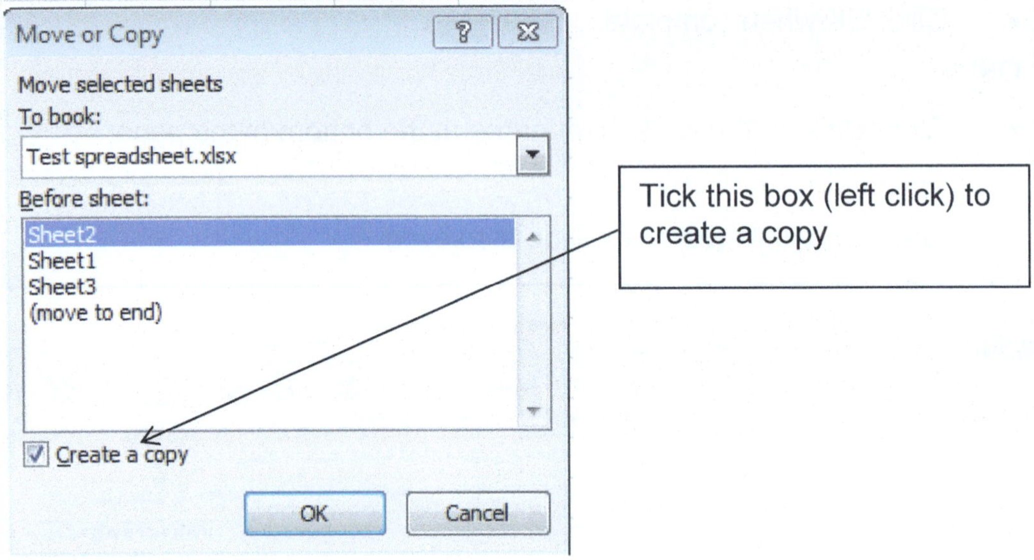

Shortcut

If using the **LEFT-CLICK** and **DRAG** approach above, hold down **Ctrl** before releasing the mouse button. A + will appear by the mouse pointer, and a copy made of the worksheet.

1.18 Activities

The activities in this guide are designed to test your knowledge on the techniques shown in this chapter. They may also use techniques used in previous chapters, to build on your knowledge. Suggested answers are available on MyKaplan, although it is better to refer to the notes and try to understand the methods than look straight at the answers.

Activity 1-1

Aim – to practice opening, closing and saving spreadsheets, as well as renaming worksheets.

(a) **Open** your spreadsheet application.

(b) If no spreadsheet is open, **Open** a blank workbook.

(c) **Rename** the worksheet **Sheet1** – call it **Data**.

(d) **Delete Sheet2** and **Sheet3**.

(e) **Save** the file in a **New Folder** called **Solutions**, filename **Test**.

(f) **Close** the file.

(g) **Rename** the file **Activity 1-1**.

(h) **Open Activity 1-1**.

(i) **Add** a new **worksheet**.

(g) **Rename** the worksheet – call it **Analysis**.

(k) **Move** the Analysis worksheet to the **left** of the Data worksheet.

(l) **Save** and **Close** Activity 1-1.

Getting started on your worksheet 2

2.1 Introduction

This chapter will guide you through the structure of the worksheet and how to enter and amend data. You will also learn how to copy, paste, and merge data and how to insert and delete rows and columns.

KNOWLEDGE

1.2 Enter numerical and other data accurately.

2.2 Spreadsheet structure

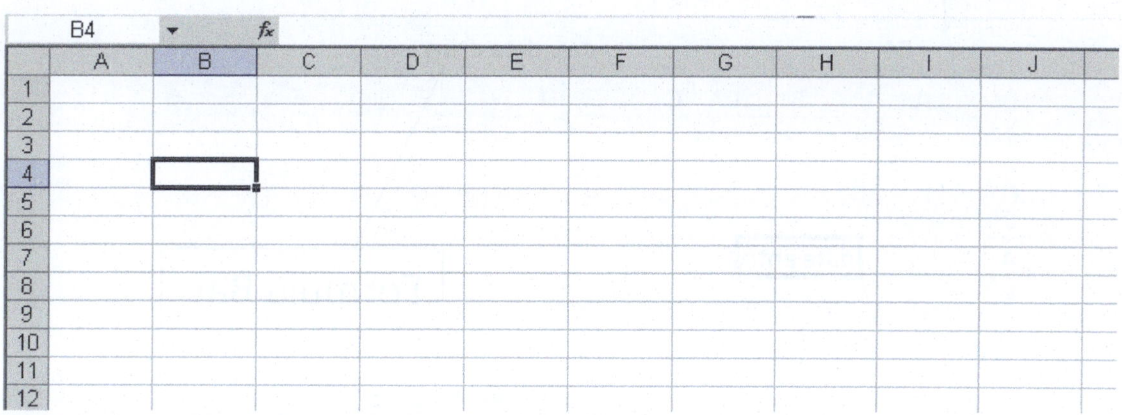

The spreadsheet (worksheet) shown above is made up of 'Rows', 'Columns' and 'Cells:

- The 'Rows' are numbered down the left hand-side from 1 onwards.
- The 'Columns' are lettered along the top from A onwards.
- The 'Cells' are the junction of columns and rows [example cell A1 is the junction of Column A and Row 1].
- The 'Active' cell is where you are be able to enter data and is highlighted with a bold border [See B4 above]. Both the column letter and the row number are also highlighted.

Shortcut

Ctrl-Home takes you to cell A1.

Ctrl-End takes you to the cell furthest into the worksheet that has been active (even if the content has been removed).

2.3 Entering data into your worksheet

Selecting cells

To select a cell, left-click on the cell you wish to select. This is now the Active Cell. The value or formula in the Active Cell will be shown in the Formula Bar, and the Cell Reference will be shown in the Name Box.

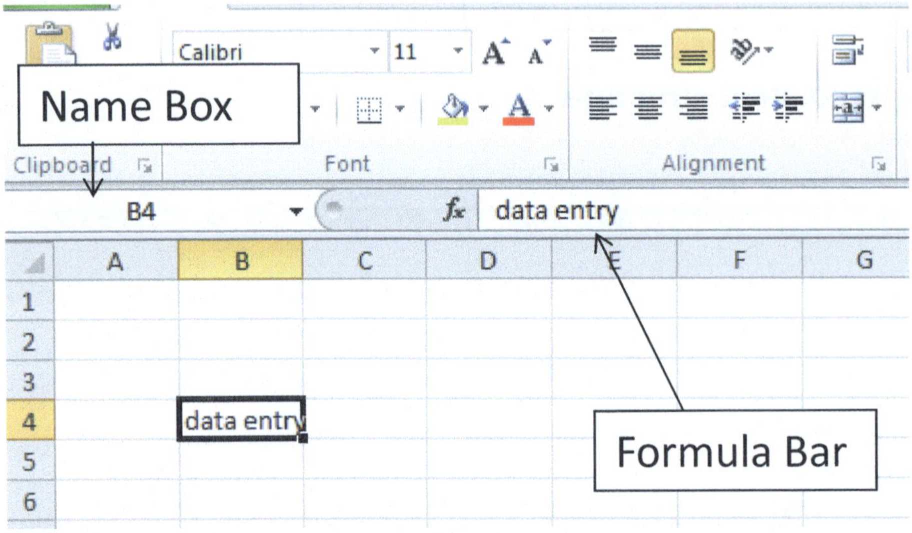

You can also change the selection by using the arrow keys to move the Active Cell Box around the screen until you reach the cell you require, or by typing the cell reference you require into the Name Box, and pressing 'Enter'.

Selecting multiple cells

Selecting several cells at once is easiest using the mouse.

- Using the mouse, **Left-Click** on a cell to select it, but **HOLD DOWN** the mouse button
- **DRAG** the mouse pointer to select neighbouring cells.

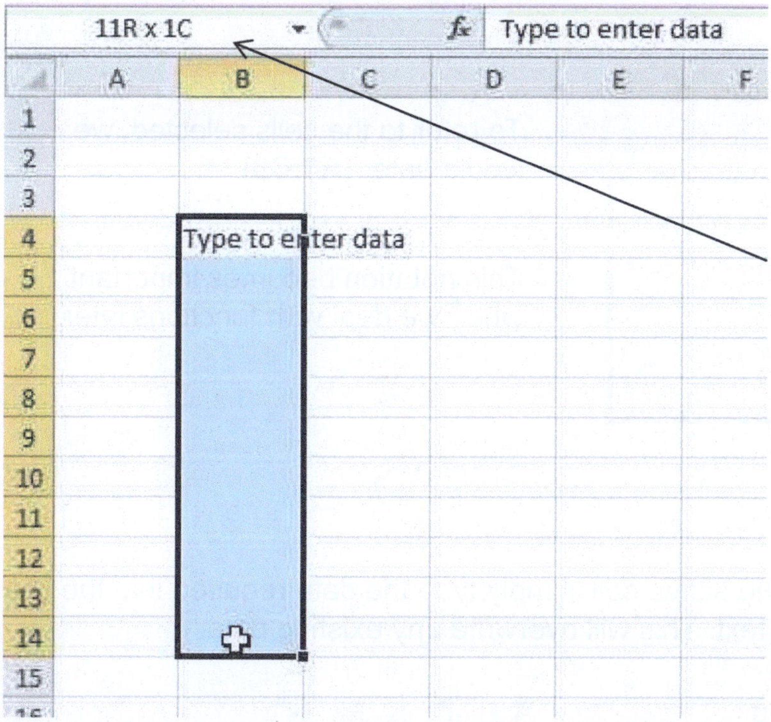

While the mouse button is held down, the dimensions of the box chosen will be shown in the Name Box – this will disappear when the mouse button is released.

If you wish to select non-contiguous (not neighbouring) cells, press the Ctrl key while selecting individual cells.

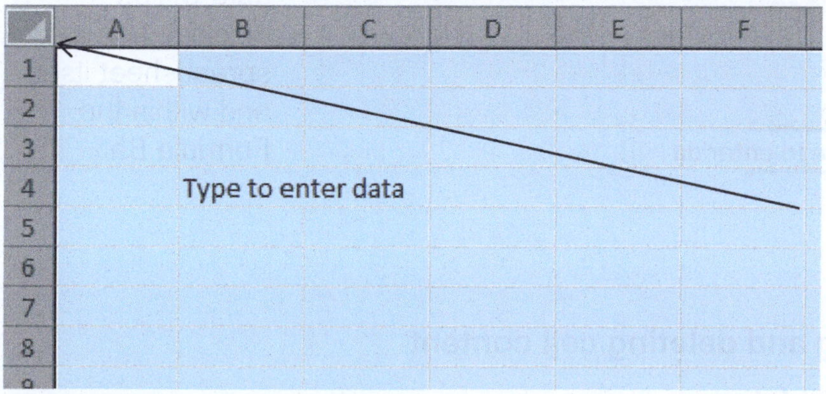

To select **ALL** cells in a worksheet, click on the box in the top-left of the sheet.

Cell ranges

As we have seen, each cell in Excel has a name (A1, B7 etc). If you select multiple cells, this is a **RANGE** of cells. If you select 2 separate cells, for example C2 and E5, the cells would be separated by a comma, so this would be displayed as **(C2, E5)**. If, as is more common, a **BLOCK** of cells is selected, these are displayed as:

(Top left cell:Bottom right cell)

For example:

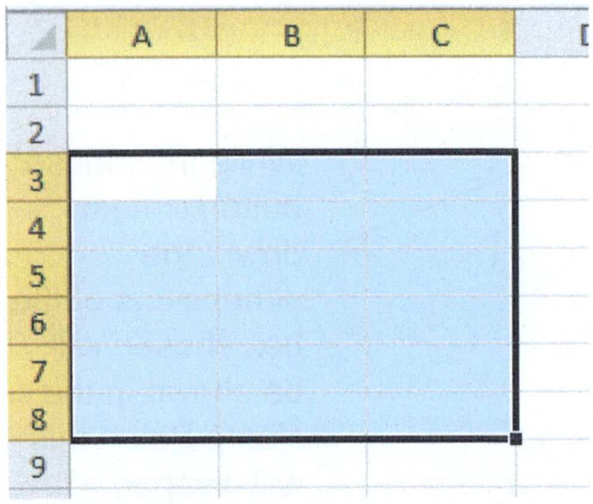

To refer to the cells selected, we would enter **(A3:C8)**.

This notation becomes important when we deal with functions later.

Entering data

To enter data into the active cell, simply type the data required into the cell – either numeric or text. This will overwrite any existing data.

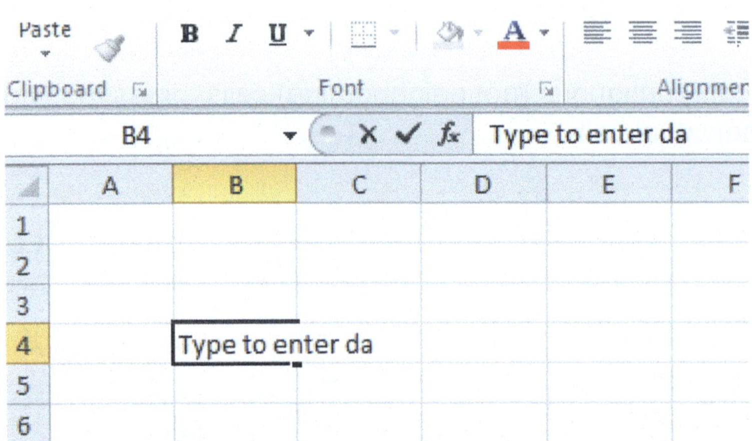

As you type, the data will be displayed on the spreadsheet itself and within the Formula Bar.

2.4 Editing and deleting cell content

Editing existing data

If a cell already contains data and you wish to edit it without overwriting, there are two ways to do this, via the Formula Bar or directly in the cell:

- **Double Click** on a cell to edit it

Or

- With the cell selected, **Left-click** in the **Formula Bar** to edit its contents.

Shortcut

Press **F2** to edit the Active Cell

Deleting data

To **delete** cell content you can do the following

1 Go to the cell you wish to delete. Press the delete key. You can highlight multiple cells and delete in the same way.

2 'Right-Click' in the active cell and then 'Left-Click' **clear contents.** You can highlight multiple adjacent cells and delete in the same way.

CAUTION!!!

If you 'Right-Click' a cell (or cells) and then click 'delete' Excel thinks you want to delete the cells completely. You will be offered a dialogue box asking you which way you want to shift the cells. This is a useful tool if it is your intention to shift data, but proceed with caution. You can always click 'Edit, Undo' or the undo icon on the toolbar if you change your mind.

2.5 Inserting and deleting rows and columns

You can insert both rows and columns into your 'Worksheet'. Doing so will not increase or decrease the number of rows and columns in your worksheet. Excel will merely insert a blank row(s) or column(s) where it is told to do so and shift the other rows or columns down/right. Excel cannot insert when all rows or columns are in use – a very unlikely event – and it cannot insert if the last row or column are in use. You would need to delete a row or column from elsewhere first.

To add a row to your worksheet

- Select the **'Home'** tab
- Select **'Insert'**
- Select **'Insert Sheet Rows'**

A row will be inserted, and the row with the Active Cell in it will be shifted **DOWN**.

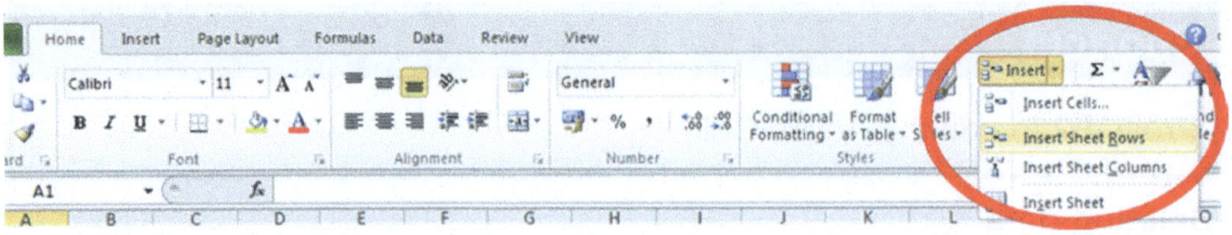

To add a column to your worksheet

- Select the **'Home'** tab
- Select **'Insert'**
- Select **'Insert Sheet Columns'**

A column will be inserted, and the column with the Active Cell in it will be shifted **RIGHT**.

Shortcut

'Right-Click' the row number or column letter where you wish to insert, then click **'Insert'**

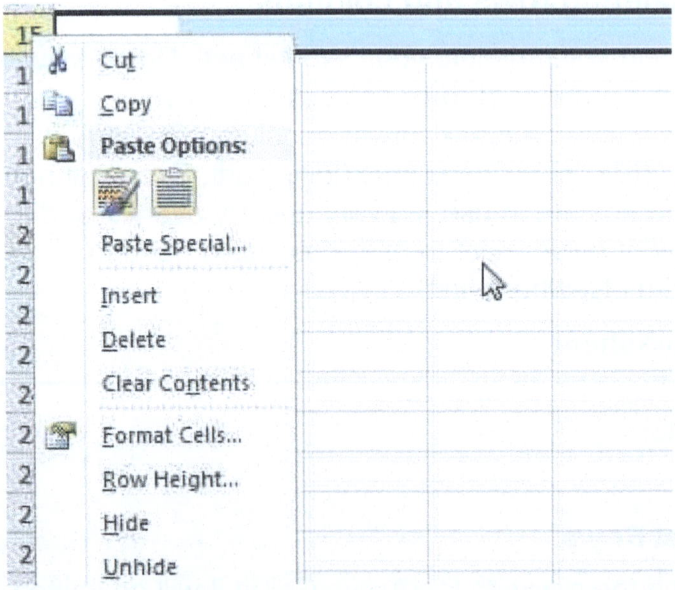

Right clicking on the **'15'** brings up this menu – select Insert to insert a row here.

To delete a row from your worksheet

- Select the **'Home'** tab
- Select **'Delete'**
- Select **'Delete Sheet Rows'**

The data in the row will be deleted, and the rows underneath shifted **UP**

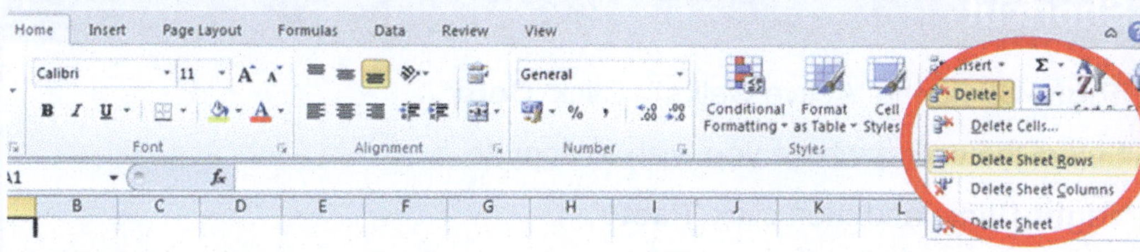

To delete a column from your worksheet

- Select the **'Home'** tab
- Select **'Delete'**
- Select **'Delete Sheet Columns'**

The data in the column will be deleted, and the columns underneath shifted **UP**

Shortcut

'Right-Click' the row number(s) or column letter(s) you wish to delete, then click **'Delete'**

2.6 Copy, Cut, Paste and AutoFill

Copy and paste

Excel allows you to copy data from the 'Active Cell(s)' to other cells.

- Click in the active cell(s)
- Select the **'Home'** tab
- Press the **'Copy'** button
- Select the cell (or cells) where you wish to copy to
- Press the **'Paste'** button

Copy and paste are together on the Ribbon

Shortcut

'**Right-Click**' the 'Active Cell(s)'. Click '**Copy**'.

Select the cell(s) where you wish to copy to.

'**Right-Click**' and then click '**Paste**'.

Shortcut

Highlight the active cells.

Ctrl-c will copy the selected cell(s)

Ctrl-v will paste the copied cell(s) to the location you have selected

Cut and paste

Excel allows you to move data from the 'Active Cell(s)' to other cells.

- Click in the active cell(s)
- Select the **'Home'** tab
- Press the **'Cut'** button 
- Select the cell (or cells) where you wish to move to
- Press the **'Paste'** button 

Cut and paste are together on the Ribbon

Shortcut

'**Right-Click**' the 'Active Cell(s)'. Click '**Cut**'.

Select the cell(s) where you wish to copy to.

'**Right-Click**' and then click '**Paste**'.

Shortcut

Highlight the active cells.

Ctrl-x will copy the selected cell(s)

Ctrl-v will paste the copied cell(s) to the location you have selected

AutoFill

The AutoFill tool is an incredibly useful feature within Excel. In the main it is used to quickly copy data into neighbouring cells, but it has several other uses that can save time and effort.

To copy a cell's contents into adjacent cells, hover the mouse pointer over the **bottom right** of the cell. The mouse pointer should change from a fat cross (✚) to a normal cross:

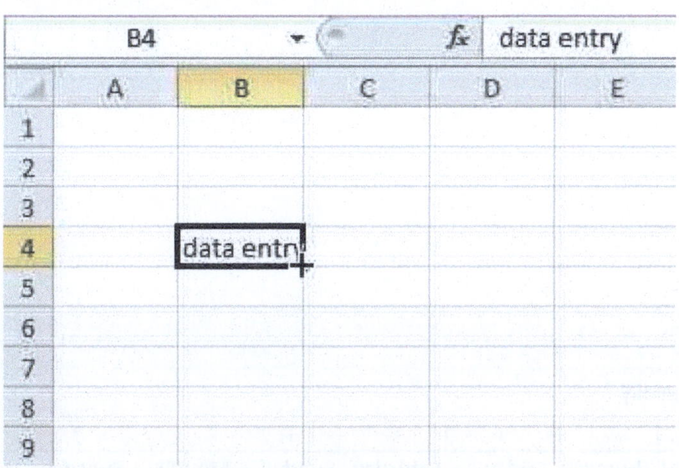

Once the pointer has changed as shown, **left click** and **drag** the mouse in the direction you wish to copy the information.

Release the mouse button to complete the fill.

Autofill becomes especially useful when copying formulas (see later), and can also be used to save time when typing out common lists, such as days of the week, or repetitive sequences.

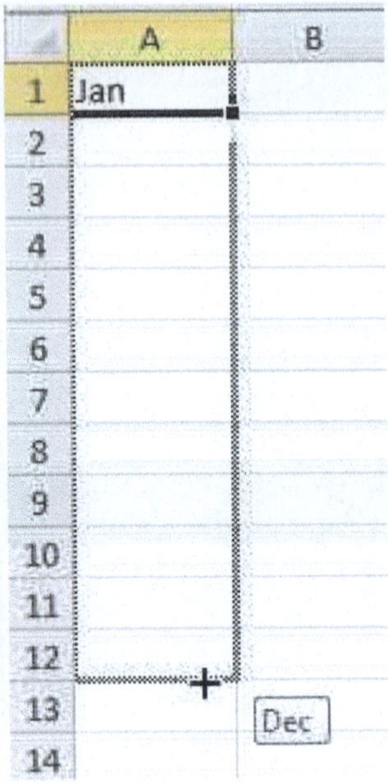

Here, 'Jan' has been typed into cell A1. Autofill has been used to 'drag' the cell down for 12 rows. You can see a pop up over B13 there's a box saying 'Dec' – this is telling us that the Autofill is going to put 'Dec' in cell A12 – the last cell in the fill.

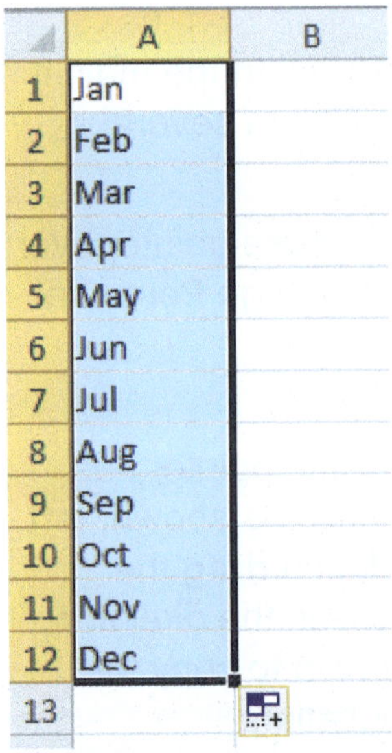

The Autofill is complete. Note that if cell A1 was 'January', the other cells would be populated with the full month name too.

Days of the week are another common autofill.

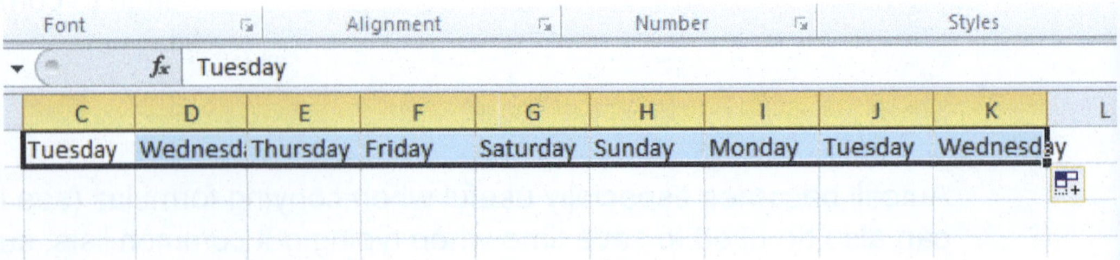

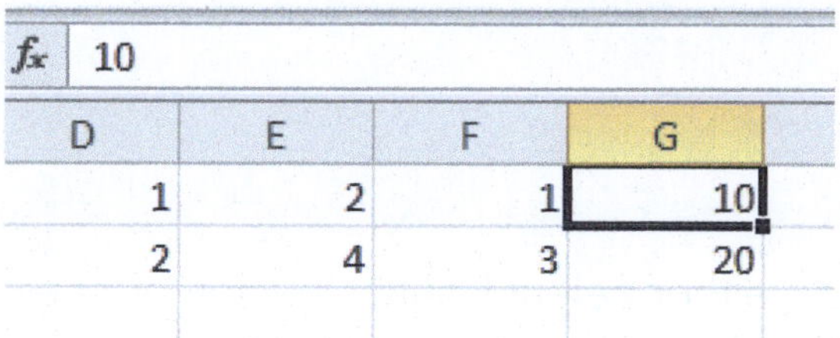

fx 10

D	E	F	G
1	2	1	10
2	4	3	20

You can also autofill sequences of numbers – 4 examples shown here. To do this you need to have at least the first 2 numbers of the sequence. Highlight both cells and then 'drag' the cells down.

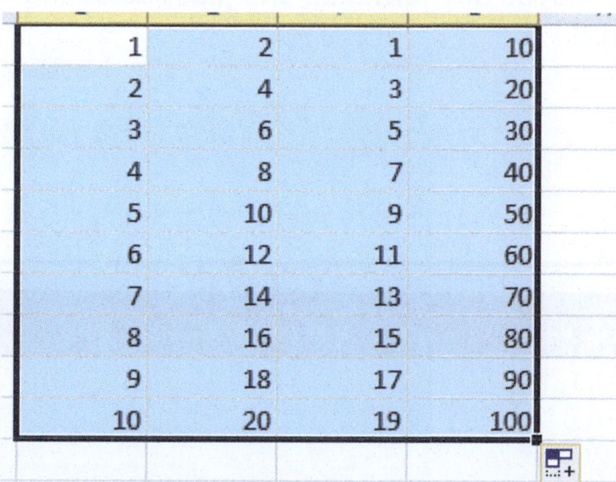

1	2	1	10
2	4	3	20
3	6	5	30
4	8	7	40
5	10	9	50
6	12	11	60
7	14	13	70
8	16	15	80
9	18	17	90
10	20	19	100

AutoFill completes the sequence.

2.7 Paste Special

There is another function 'Paste Special'. This function allows you to paste different aspects of what could be contained in a cell. Certain parts of these will be covered in later sessions. In the main what this function does is self explanatory. However, it is explained briefly below.

- **Copy** the cell(s) you wish to Paste
- **Select** the destination cell(s)
- **Left-click** the down arrow underneath the **Paste** button on the **Home** tab
- Select **Paste Special**

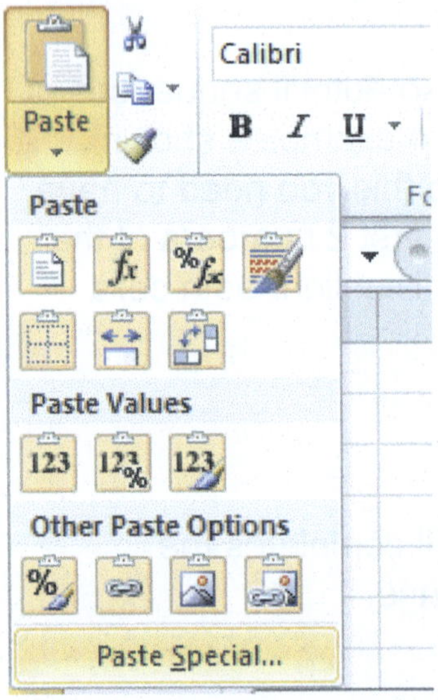

Here you can either select Paste Special, or one of the buttons shown to paste certain features only. Hover over each button to see what they do – a very commonly used one in Paste Values, which removes any formulas and just pastes the cell values.

Shortcut

Ctrl-c to copy the cells

Ctrl-Alt-v to paste special

The Paste Special menu gives all of the options available:

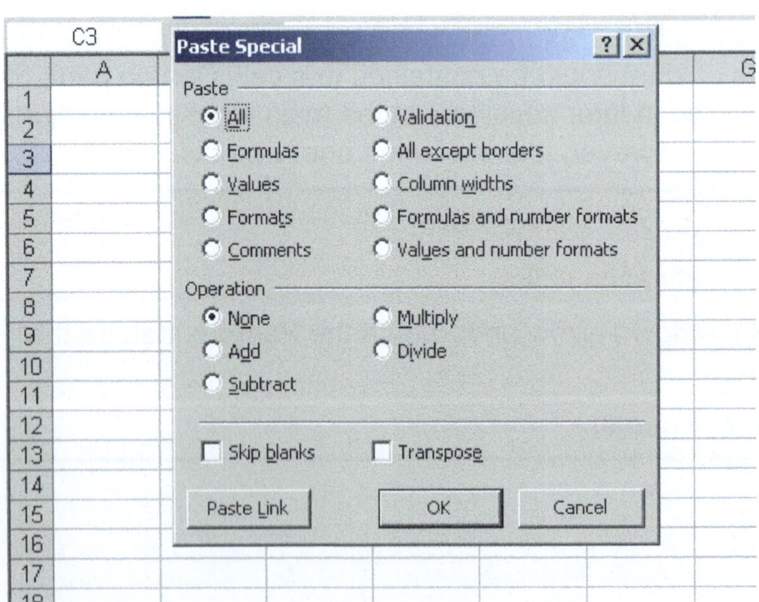

(i) **'All'** pastes content, formula and formatting but it will not alter column width.

(ii) **'Formulas'** pastes the formula from the cell(s) to the new location, without affecting the formatting of the destination cell.

(iii) **'Values'** pastes the value of a cell and not the formula that may have created the value.

(iv) **'Formats'** pastes any formatting that you might have carried out to the new cell(s). This includes cell shading, borders and number formats, but not column width.

(v) **'Comments'** pastes any comments that have been entered into a cell to the new location. '**Comments'** allow you to write a note about a particular cell for you – and others – to see.

Once you have written your comment you will be able to delete and/or hide it by 'Right-Clicking' again in the 'Active Cell'.

(vi) **'Validation'** pastes any data validation rules that you might have created. This will be covered in a later session.

(vii) **'All except borders', 'Column widths', 'Formulas and number formats' and 'Values and number formats'** are derivatives of the above and are self explanatory.

You will also note that part of the 'Paste-Special' dialogue box allows you to carry out operations. For example the **'add'** operation will add the value of the 'Active Cell' to the value of the cell(s) that you are pasting to. It will add formula outcomes to values and it will also add formulas to formulas.

The last part of the 'Paste-Special' dialogue box allows two other actions

(i) **'Skip Blanks'** ignores the content –formatting etc – of a cell with no data in it. However, it does maintain the gaps between non-adjacent cells.

(ii) **'Transpose'** is a useful tool for pasting the content of a column into a row, and vice-versa.

2.8 Activity

The activities in this guide are designed to test your knowledge on the techniques shown in this chapter. They may also use techniques used in previous chapters, to build up your knowledge. Suggested answers are available on MyKaplan, although it is better to refer to the notes and try to understand the methods than look straight at the answers.

Activity 2-1

This activity allows you to practice navigating a workbook, and entering simple data.

(a) Open the file **Simple Report** in the **Activities** folder. The aim is to create a simple report showing just sales and profits for each month. The layout of the report will be:

	Jan	*Feb*	*Mar*
Sales			
Profit			

(b) First, the **Summary Report** worksheet needs a heading. **Copy** the Heading from the **Existing Data** worksheet and **Paste** it into cell A1 on the summary report worksheet.

(c) In cells A3 and A4 on the **Summary Report** worksheet, type 'Sales' and 'Profit' respectively

(d) In cells B2:I2, we need the months of the year. You can either type these manually, or (quicker) use Autofill. Type January in B2, and AutoFill to the right to create the months.

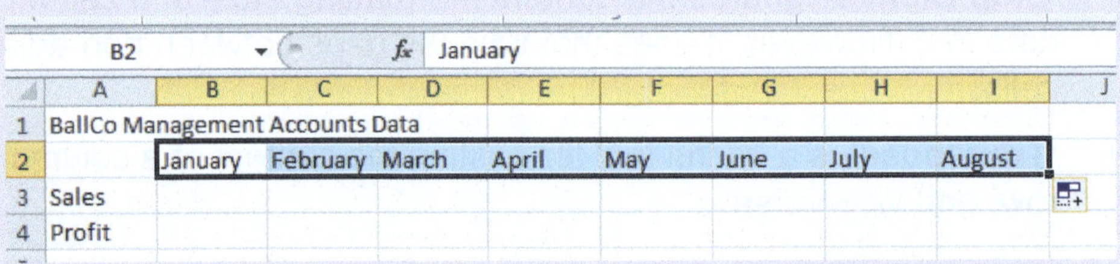

(e) It has now been pointed out that the August sales figure in the **Existing Data** is incorrect, and should be 7223. Edit the August sales to reflect this. The profit will update automatically.

(f) We now need to put the sales and profit data in the report. We could just type it in, but it's much quicker to **copy** the information. Unfortunately, a straight copy/paste won't work – the existing data has months as rows, the summary has months as columns.

Use **Paste Special** to copy the data. **Select** cells B3:B10 and **copy** them.

(g) 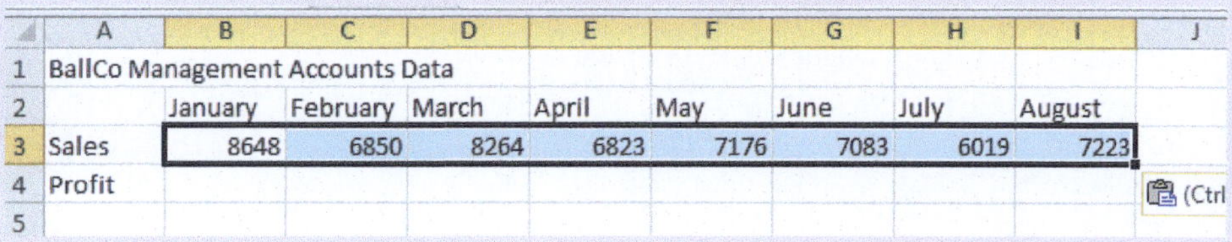

On the **Summary report** worksheet, use **Paste special** in cell B3, and select **Transpose**.

(h) Repeat for profits. However, the profits are worked out by using a **formula**. We only want the values of the profits, as the formulas won't work. Using **Paste Special**, select **transpose** and **values.**

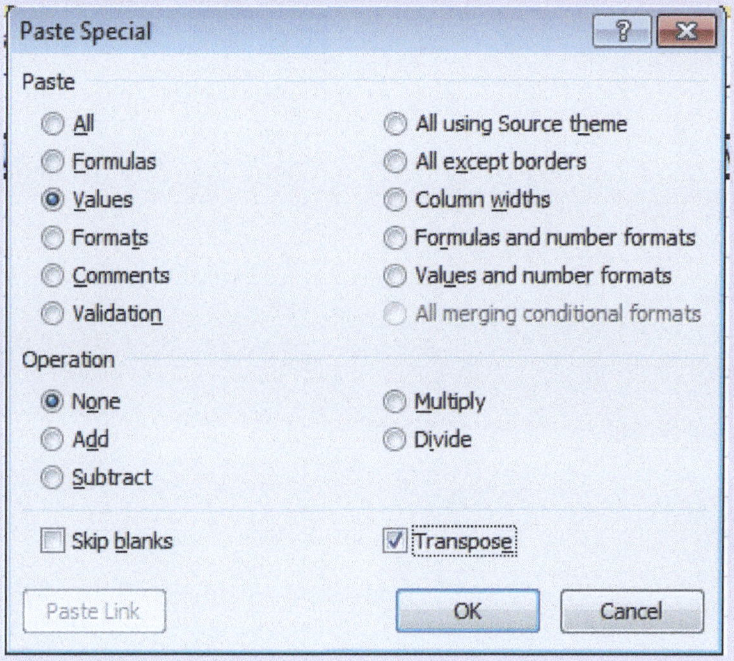

(i) The September figures have been received. On the **Summary report** worksheet, add the following data for September in column;

Sales – 7579

Profit – 3444

(j) It has now been decided to enter a half-year total after June's figures. **Insert** a column between June and July, and in row 2, type 'Half Year'.

The half year values are:

Sales – 44844

Profit – 23739

(k) Save the file as **Activity 2-1** in the **Solutions** folder. Close the file.

Formatting your worksheet

3

3.1 Introduction

In this chapter you will learn how to change the visual appearance of a spreadsheet so that relevant data is shown. You will also learn how to use the correct formatting.

KNOWLEDGE

1.1 Identify what numerical and other information is needed in the spreadsheet and how it should be recorded.

3.1 Explain how to present and format spreadsheet information effectively to meet needs.

3.2 Select and use appropriate tools and techniques to format cells, rows, columns and worksheets effectively.

Formatting is a process whereby you change the visual aspects of your worksheet. Your assessment will involve you formatting worksheets to meet specific demands. You will in all likelihood be told what formatting is required and you will be assessed on whether or not you have complied with the instructions in the case-study.

The types of formatting you are required to be able to do are:

1 Adjust row height and column width.

2 Add borders and shading to cells and cell ranges.

3 Formatting text and numbers.

4 Hide columns and rows.

3.2 The format cells menu

Most formatting options can be found within the Format Cells menu, and if you are unsure this should be the first place to look. To view the Format Cells menu:

- Select the cell(s) you wish to format
- In the **Home** menu, select **Format Cells**

OR

- **Right-Click** on the cell(s) to format
- Select Format Cells

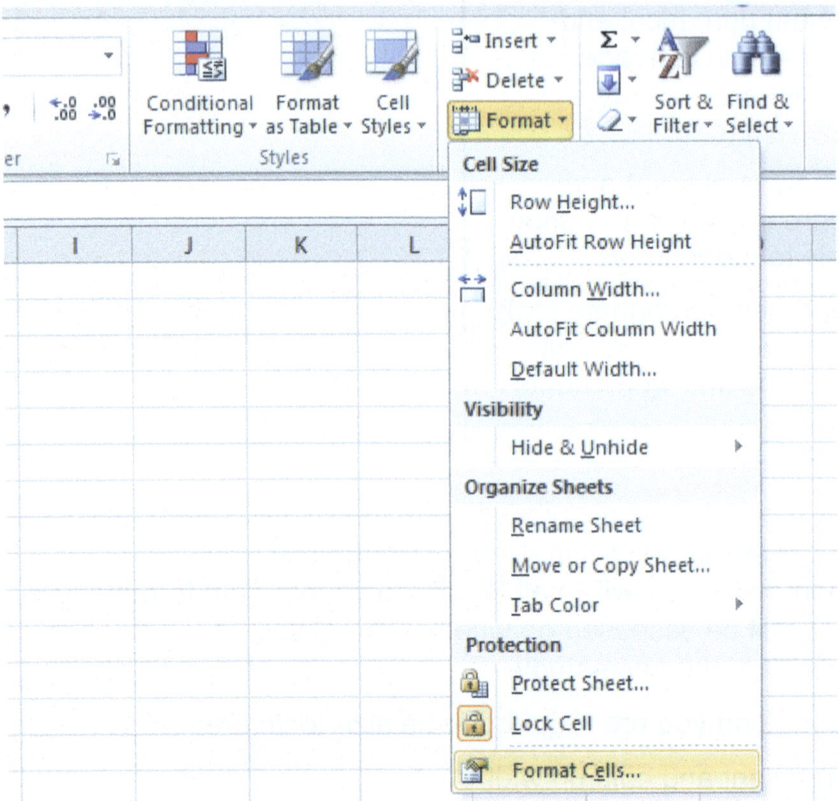

Shortcut

Press **Ctrl-1** to bring up the format cells menu.

The **Format Cells** menu has several options, as summarised below:

Number Changes number formats, for example the number of decimal places, currency type or percentages.

Alignment Allows adjustment of where data is shown within a cell for example left or right alignment, and merging cells together.

Font Appearance and size of text, along with special features like bold and underline.

Border Affects the cell itself, rather than the data within – place lines of varying size and colours around the cell.

Fill Colour the cell in various shades and patterns.

Protection Affects whether a cell can be edited (dealt with later).

To Exit the menu, click OK to accept any changes, or Cancel to reject them.

The above options will be discussed in turn.

3.3 Number formats

Although the name implies that this affects numbers, this option will change the way information within all selected cells will be displayed. Its primary use is to display numeric information in a user-friendly fashion.

General

The default format is 'General', where no special formatting will apply.

	50
	15.6
	1005
	-516
	text
	text and 2432

This sample data shows how Excel displays numbers and text by default – with no special formatting.

Number

This format gives more options on how to display numbers. The options are number of decimal places, whether to separate thousands with a comma, and how to display negative numbers:

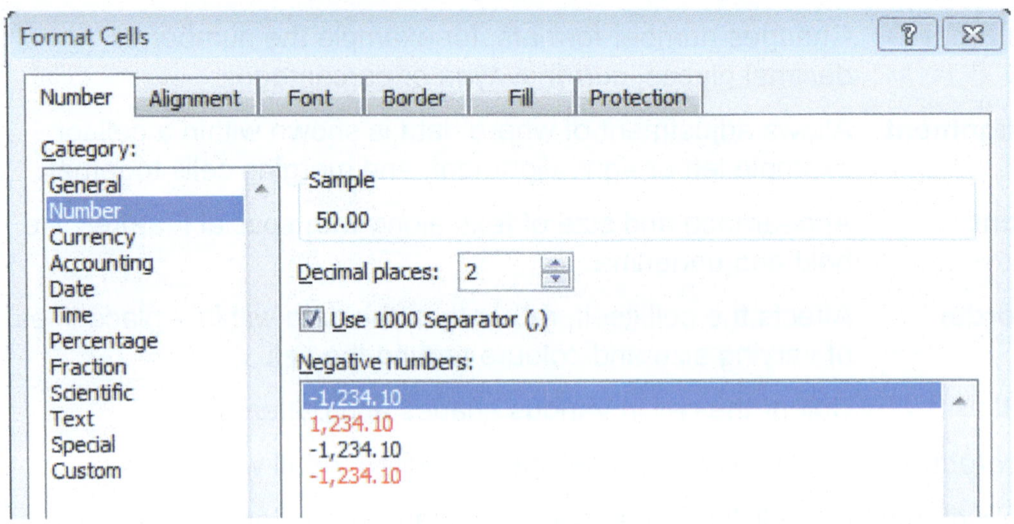

The Sample window shows what the cell will look like with the current options selected. The 1000 separator is an excellent way of making numeric data easier to read. The negative number option can be used to display negative numbers as red, with or without a minus sign.

50.00
15.60
1,005.00
-516.00
text
text and 2432

The same information now formatted as a Number. Note that the text information in the bottom two cells is unchanged – even though there is a number in the final cell, Excel recognises it as text only, and will not format the number separately (this can be done, but is beyond the scope of the syllabus).

Currency

This is very similar to **Number**, with the added option of putting a currency symbol at the front of the number:

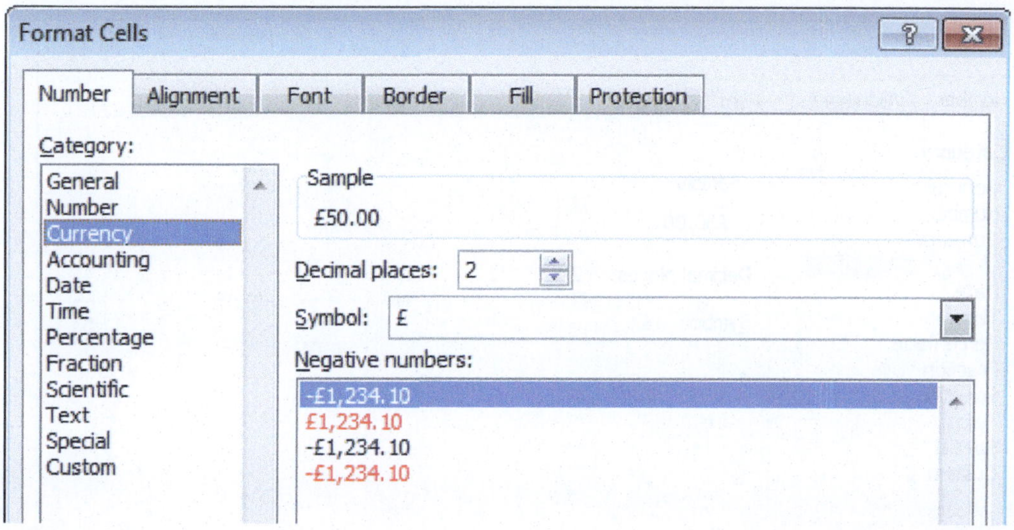

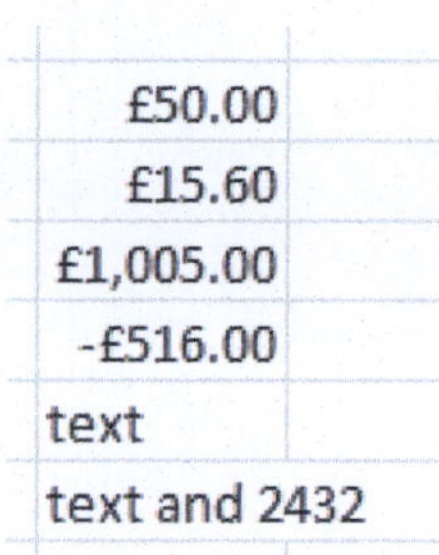

The only difference is the "£" sign at the front of the numbers.

Accounting

This is very similar to **Currency**, but decimal points and currency symbols will be lined up in a column, potentially making it easier to interpret data:

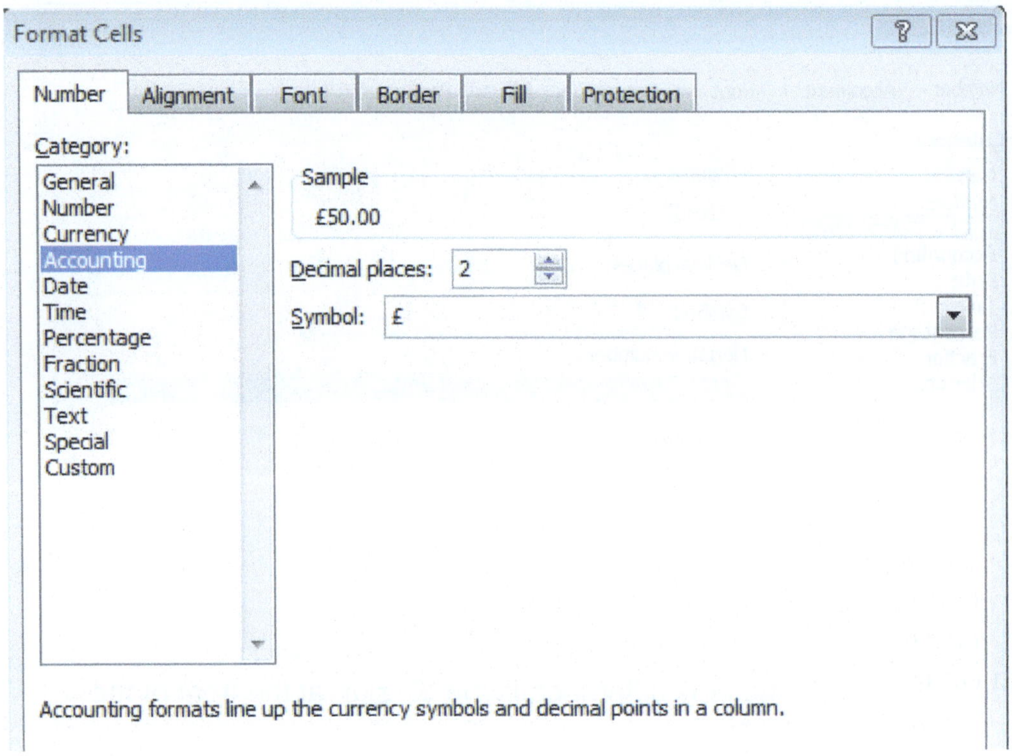

£ 50.00
£ 15.60
£1,005.00
-£ 516.00
text
text and 2432

It's a matter of personal choice as to which you prefer.

Percentage

This enables numbers to be displayed with a '**%**' symbol at the end, and also multiplies the value in the cell by 100 – this will be covered in more detail later.

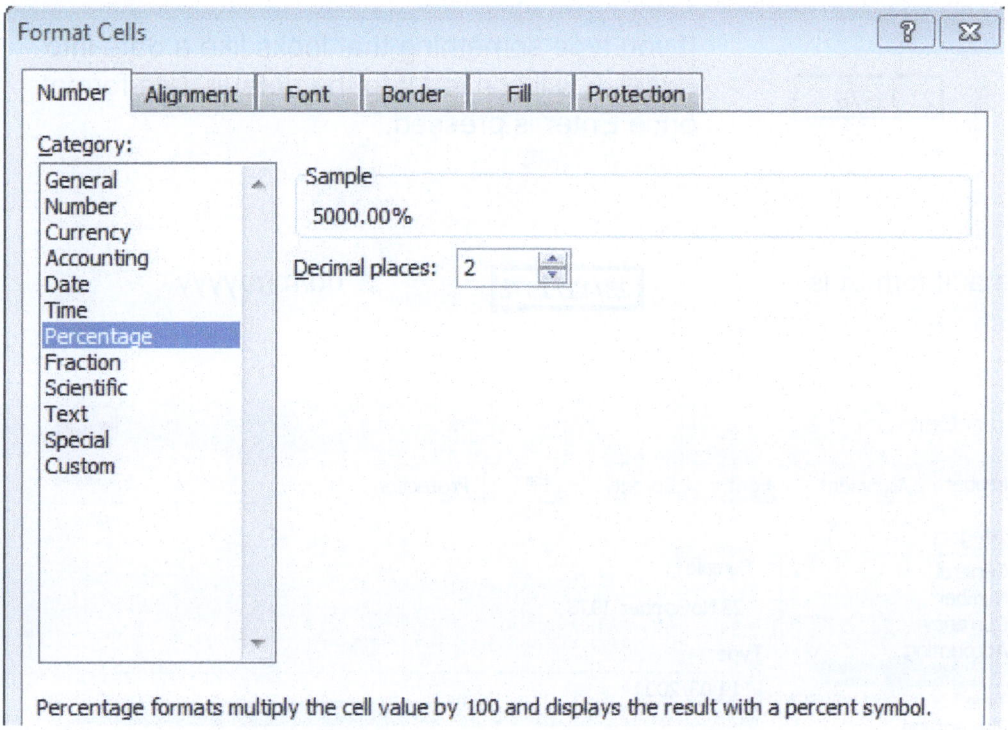

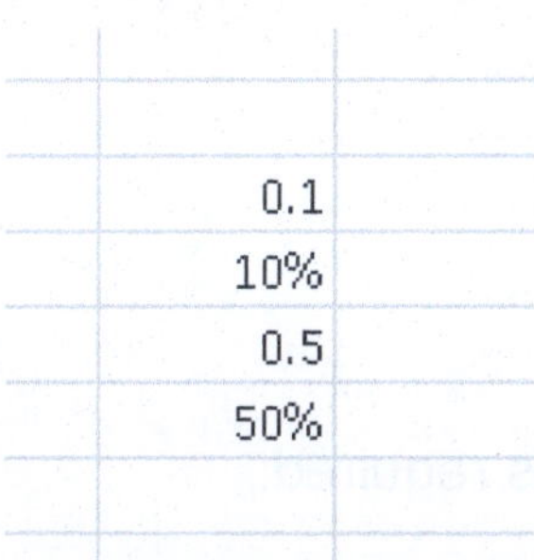

If 0.1 is typed in a cell and percentage formatting is applied then this will be changed to 10%. 0.5 will be changed to 50%. The % format will come in very useful later on.

Date

The **Date** format is used to display dates in various different ways. The best thing to do is type the date in you wish to use, and then select the different options until you find the one you want:

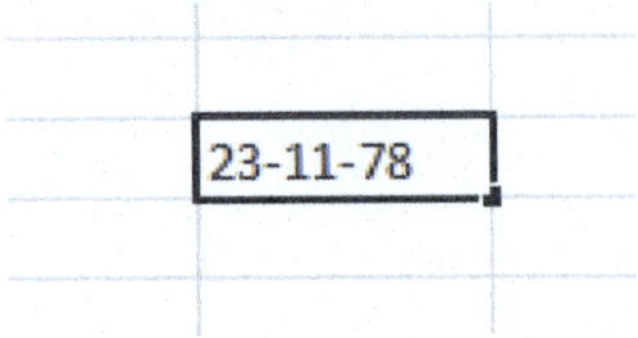

If you type something that looks like a date into Excel, it will convert it to the default date format once Enter is pressed.

Default format is

dd/mm/yyyy

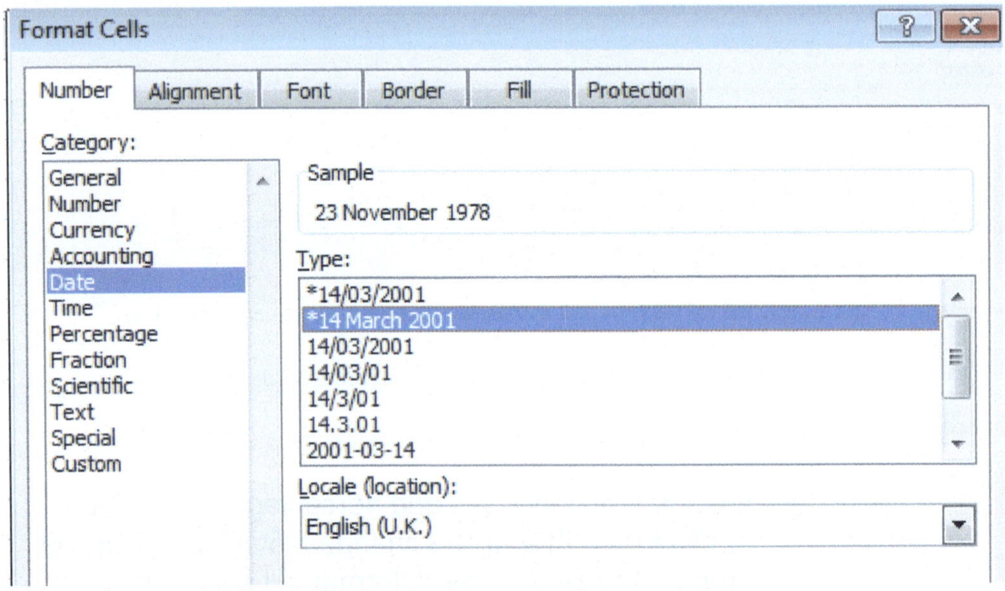

Choosing the appropriate option will display the date as required.

Custom

In the **custom** number list there are a number of formats that can be adapted to create the formatting required.

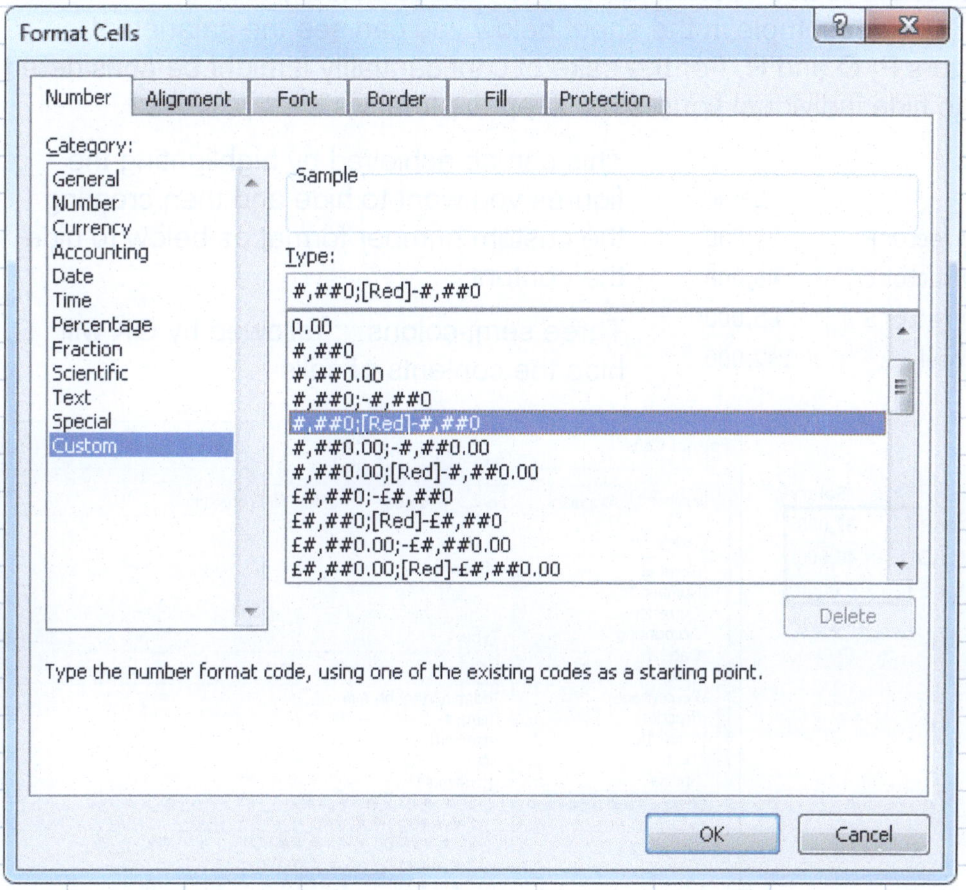

If chose the option highlighted in blue above -2345.68 would become:

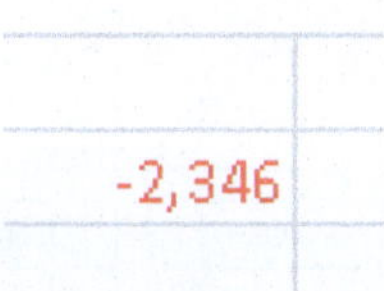

#,##0;[Red]-#,##0, formats numbers to have no decimal places and negative numbers shown in red with a minus sign in front.

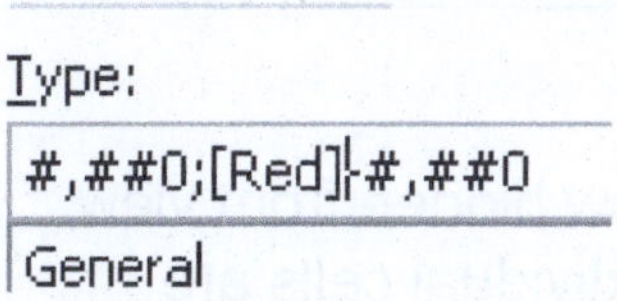

You can change this to use brackets instead of the minus sign:

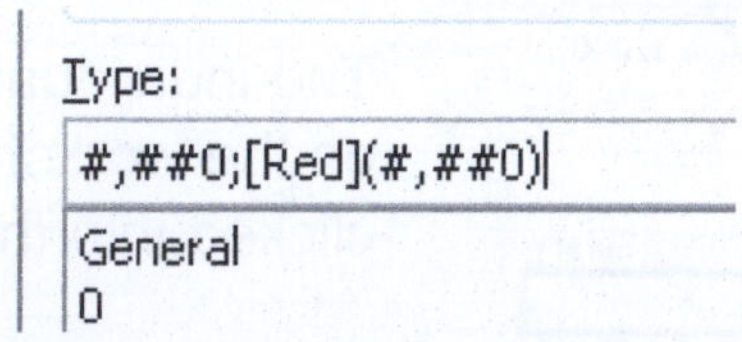

The value now looks like:

You can also change the colour if required to Black, Green, White, Blue, Magenta, Yellow, or Cyan or keep it as Red, by changing the word in square brackets [ ].

It is possible to use custom number formats to actually hide the content of a cell[s]. For example in the sheet below you can see the salaries of Directors P, Q and R. For the sake of confidentiality it might be considered best to hide individual figures but keep the total visible.

	Salary
Director P	32,000
Director Q	45,000
Director S	65,000
Total	142,000

This can be achieved by highlighting the figures you want to hide and then creating the custom number format as below to hide the content.

Three semi-colons ;;; followed by OK will hide the contents of cells

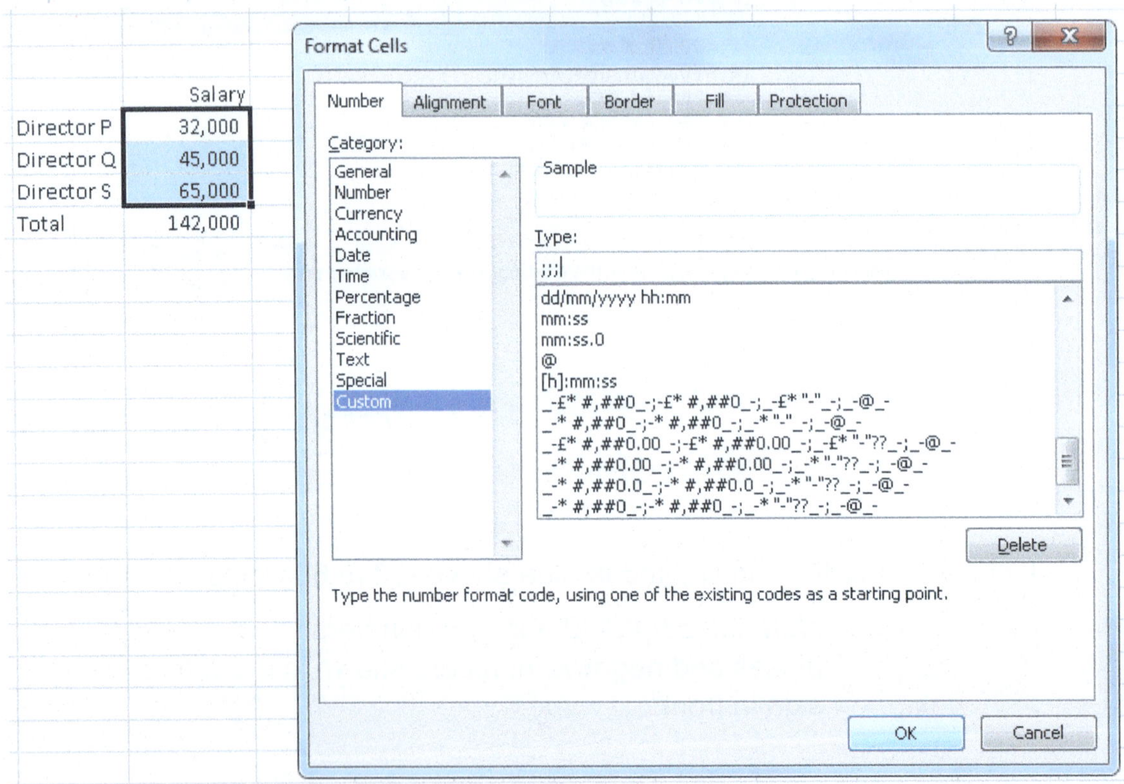

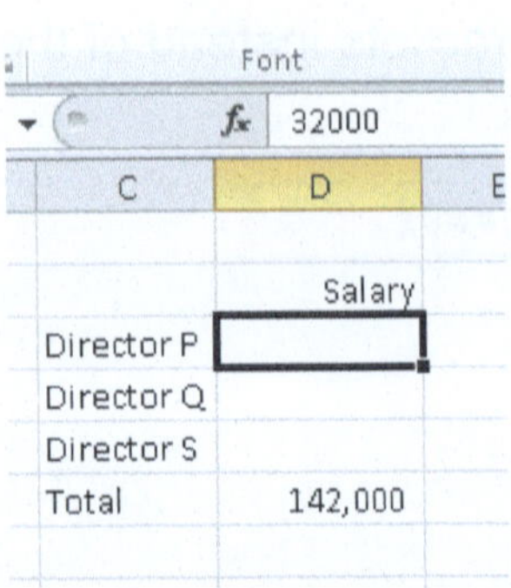

The individual salaries are now hidden from view on the worksheet but if the individual cells are clicked into the values still show in the formula bar.

Other formats

The other formats are not usually required, but can be experimented with – if something goes wrong, just Undo what you did, or select a different number format.

IMPORTANT NOTE ON FORMATTING!

It is worth noting that changing the number format of a cell HAS NO EFFECT on the actual number within the cell. For example, if the cell contains the value 15.6, and you change the format to zero decimal places, the value of the cell used in calculations will still be 15.6, even though 16 will be displayed.

This is dealt with in more detail when discussing the ROUND function.

Shortcuts

There are several shortcuts available to change the Number Format on the **Home menu**.

Number formats can be chosen directly, or percentage symbols, 1000 separators and number of decimal points changed.

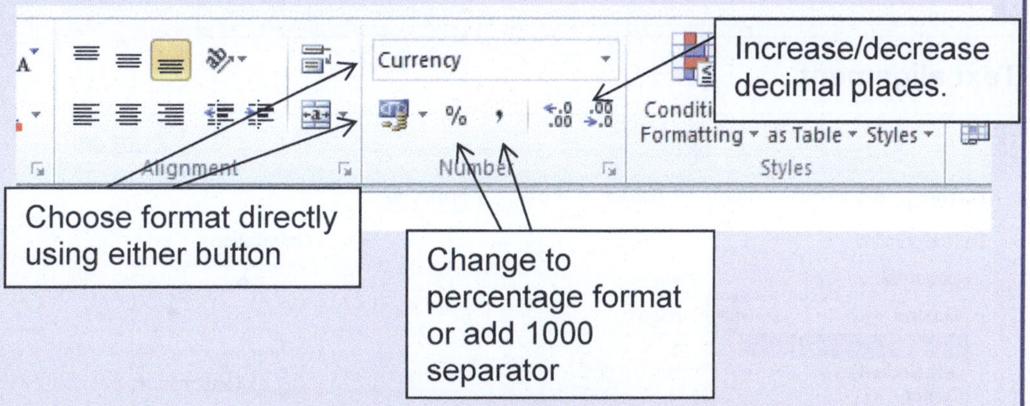

3.4 Alignment

The **Alignment** tab allows you to choose where in a cell text will be displayed, as well as the options to wrap text, merge cells, shrink text to fit in cells and also adjust orientation of the text in a cell:

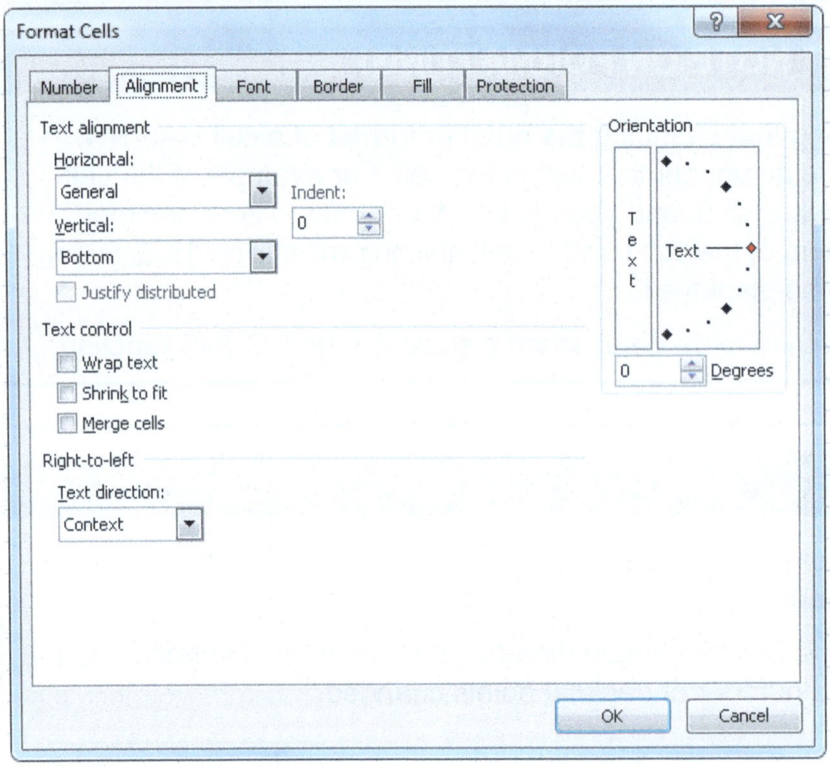

Text alignment

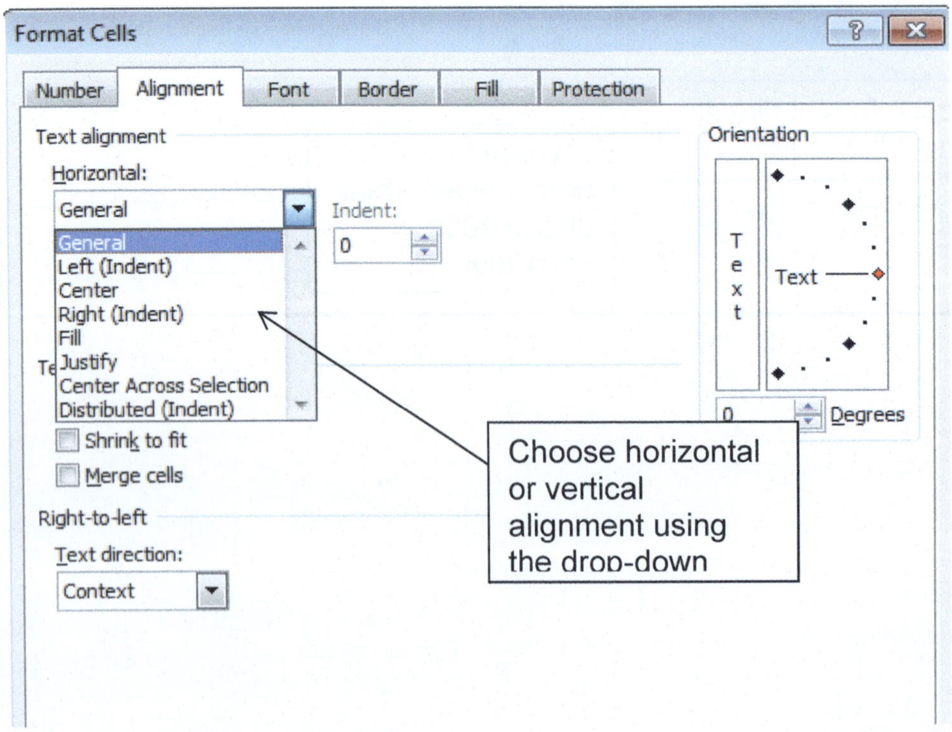

Wrap text

This allows all contents of a cell to be displayed on multiple lines within the one cell.

Select the cells that need to the text to be wrapped in and then in the **Alignment** menu, tick the **Wrap text** tickbox, and click **OK**.

The contents of the cell will now appear over 2 or more rows within the single cell.

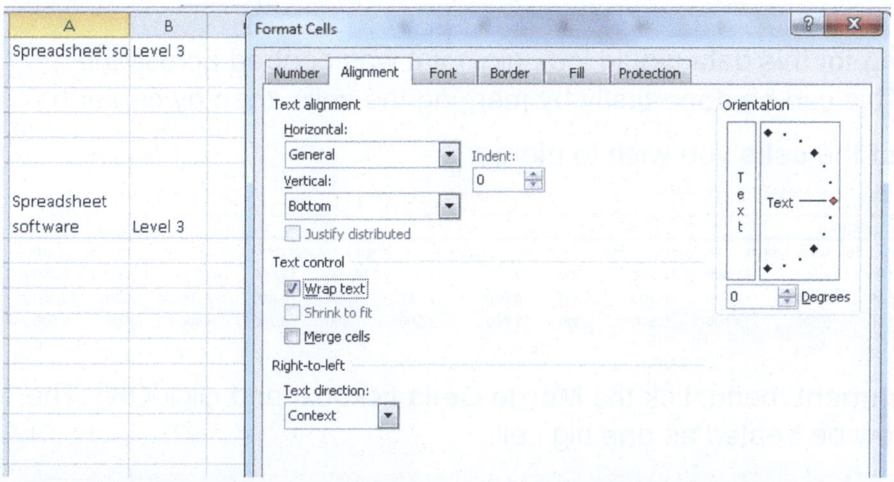

Shrink to fit

An alternative to wrapping the text is to decrease the size of the text to fit in the cell. Again select the cell that needs adjusting and click in the **Shrink to fit** tickbox and click **OK**.

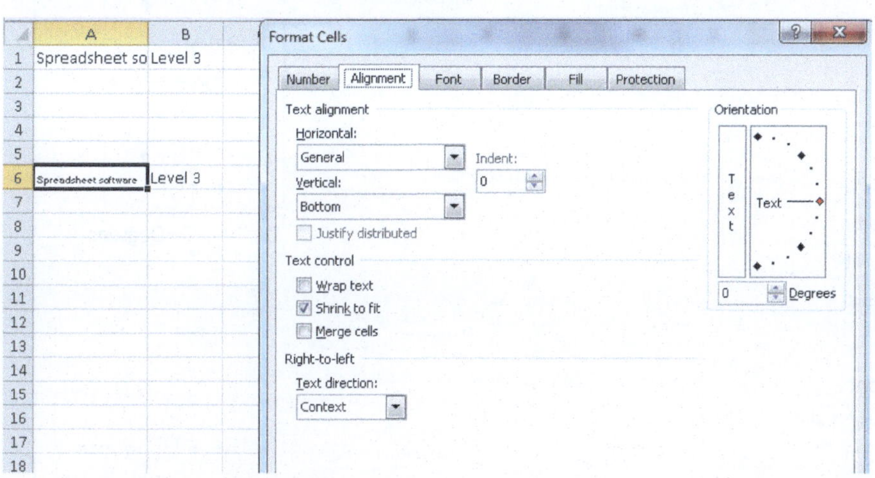

Merge cells

Merging cells joins them together so Excel treats them as one cell. This can be useful for headings that run over more than one column, for example, or if you wish to create a heading across a whole page.

	A	B	C	D	E	F	G	H	I	J	K	L	M	N
1	Monthly Profit Calculations													
2		January	February	March	April	May	June	July	August	Septembe	October	Novembe	December	
3	Sales	10,000	12,500	11,000	12,200	12,500	13,000	11,000	16,000	15,000	15,500	12,000	10,200	
4	Costs	6,500	7,000	7,000	6,700	7,200	8,000	7,500	8,200	6,800	7,100	5,500	5,200	
5	Profit	3,500	5,500	4,000	5,500	5,300	5,000	3,500	7,800	8,200	8,400	6,500	5,000	
6														

The heading for this data would look nicer if it was centred across the columns. This can be done firstly by merging the cells, then by centering.

First, **select** the **cells** you wish to merge:

	A	B	C	D	E	F	G	H	I	J	K	L	M
1	Monthly Profit Calculations												
2		January	February	March	April	May	June	July	August	Septembe	October	Novembe	December
3	Sales	10,000	12,500	11,000	12,200	12,500	13,000	11,000	16,000	15,000	15,500	12,000	10,200
4	Costs	6,500	7,000	7,000	6,700	7,200	8,000	7,500	8,200	6,800	7,100	5,500	5,200
5	Profit	3,500	5,500	4,000	5,500	5,300	5,000	3,500	7,800	8,200	8,400	6,500	5,000

In the **Alignment** menu, tick the **Merge Cells** tickbox, and click **OK**. The cells will now be treated as one big cell.

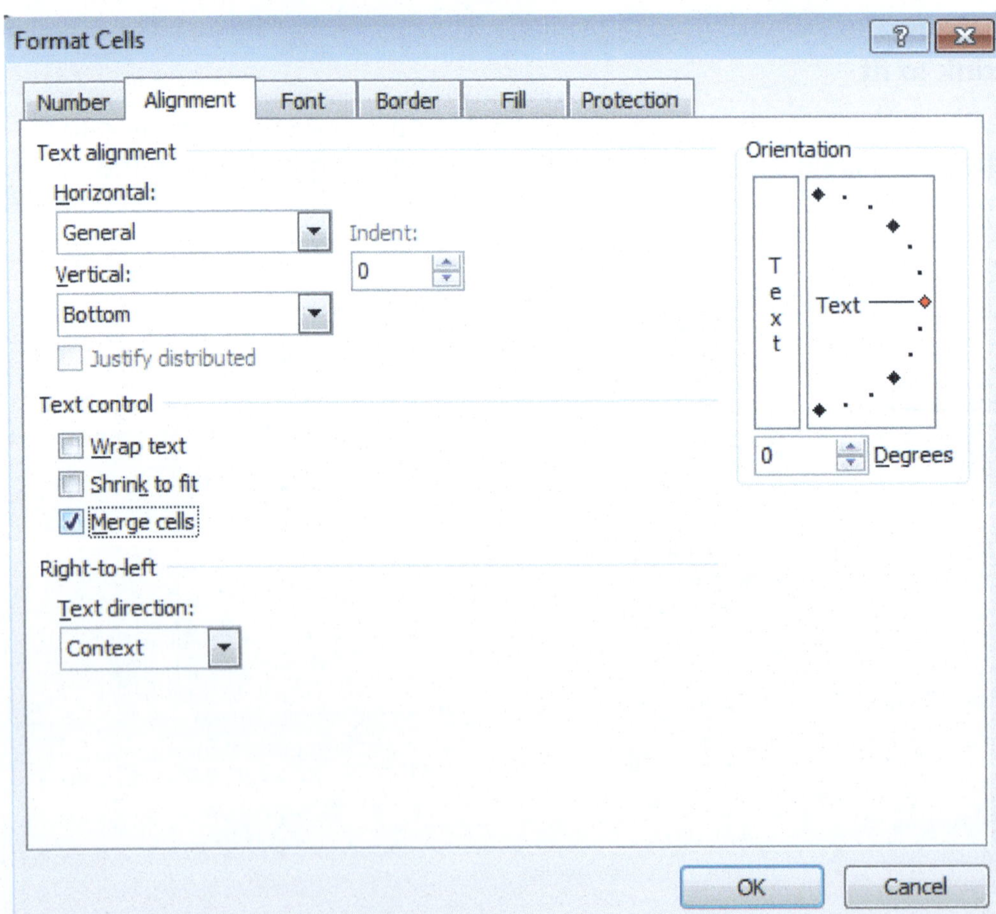

	A	B	C	D	E	F	G	H	I	J	K	L	M
1	Monthly Profit Calculations												
2		January	February	March	April	May	June	July	August	Septembe	October	Novembe	December
3	Sales	10,000	12,500	11,000	12,200	12,500	13,000	11,000	16,000	15,000	15,500	12,000	10,200
4	Costs	6,500	7,000	7,000	6,700	7,200	8,000	7,500	8,200	6,800	7,100	5,500	5,200
5	Profit	3,500	5,500	4,000	5,500	5,300	5,000	3,500	7,800	8,200	8,400	6,500	5,000
6													

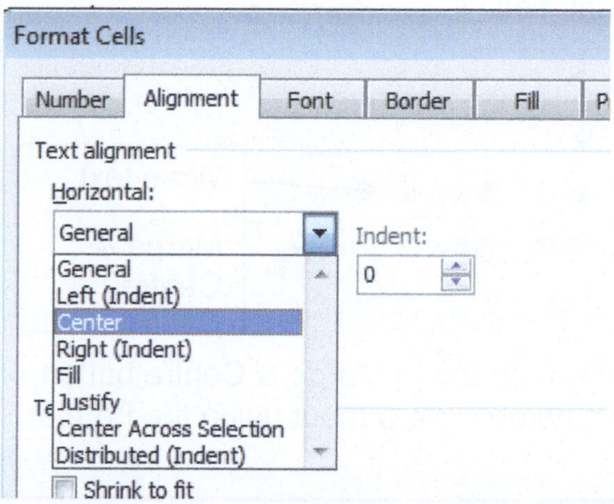

In the Alignment menu then select **Horizontal Alignment** as **Center** to show your heading in the centre of the data.

A	B	C	D	E	F	G	H	I	J	K	L	M
						Monthly Profit Calculations						
	January	February	March	April	May	June	July	August	Septembe	October	Novembe	December
Sales	10,000	12,500	11,000	12,200	12,500	13,000	11,000	16,000	15,000	15,500	12,000	10,200
Costs	6,500	7,000	7,000	6,700	7,200	8,000	7,500	8,200	6,800	7,100	5,500	5,200
Profit	3,500	5,500	4,000	5,500	5,300	5,000	3,500	7,800	8,200	8,400	6,500	5,000

Orientation

Using orientation allow you to rotate the text in a cell to a diagonal angle or vertical orientation. This is often useful for labelling columns that are narrow.

As with the other alignment formatting, highlight the text that needs the orientation changed and choose the degree of angle you require:

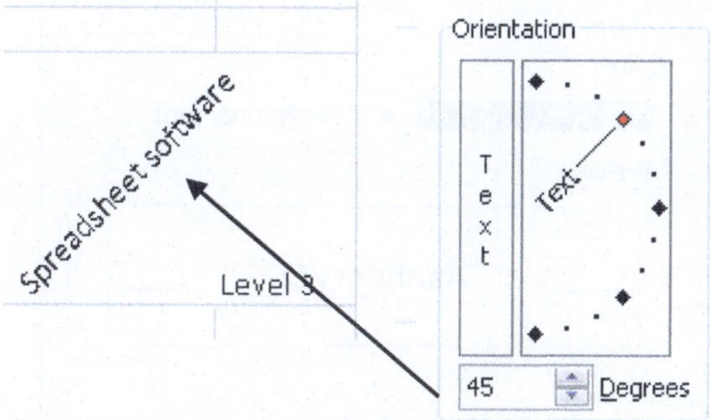

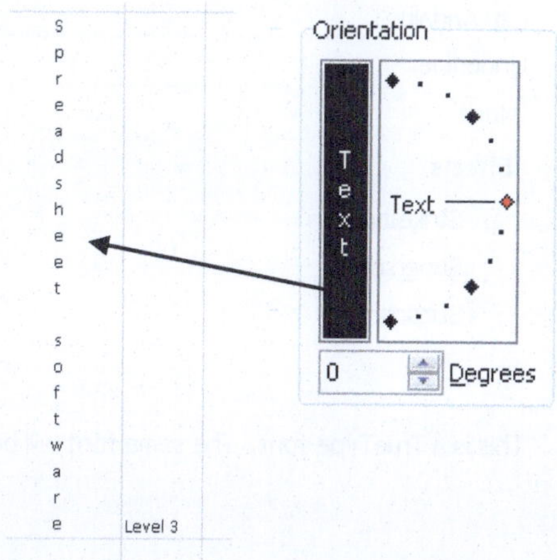

Shortcuts

Home tab, alignment section:

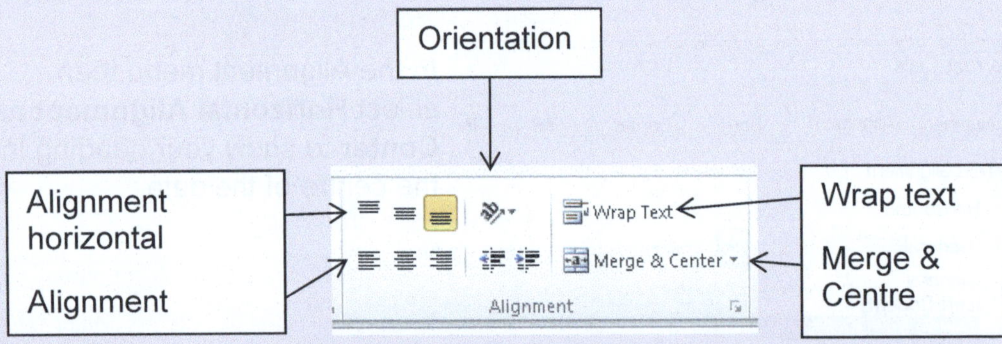

Note that clicking on the small arrow next to the Merge & Centre button also gives you options to merge/unmerge cells without using the Format Cells menu.

3.5 Font

This is used to change the font type, size, and colour and to add effects to the text – the options are fairly self-explanatory:

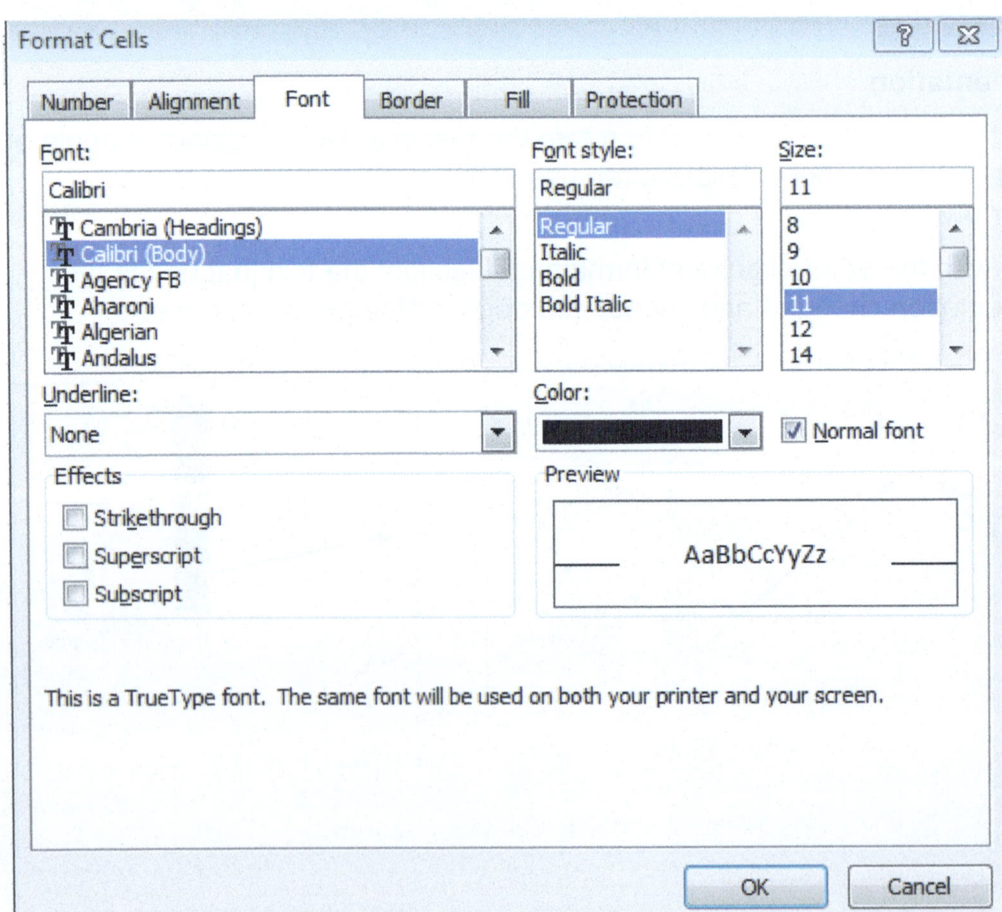

The **Underline** option allows you to use the **Double Accounting**

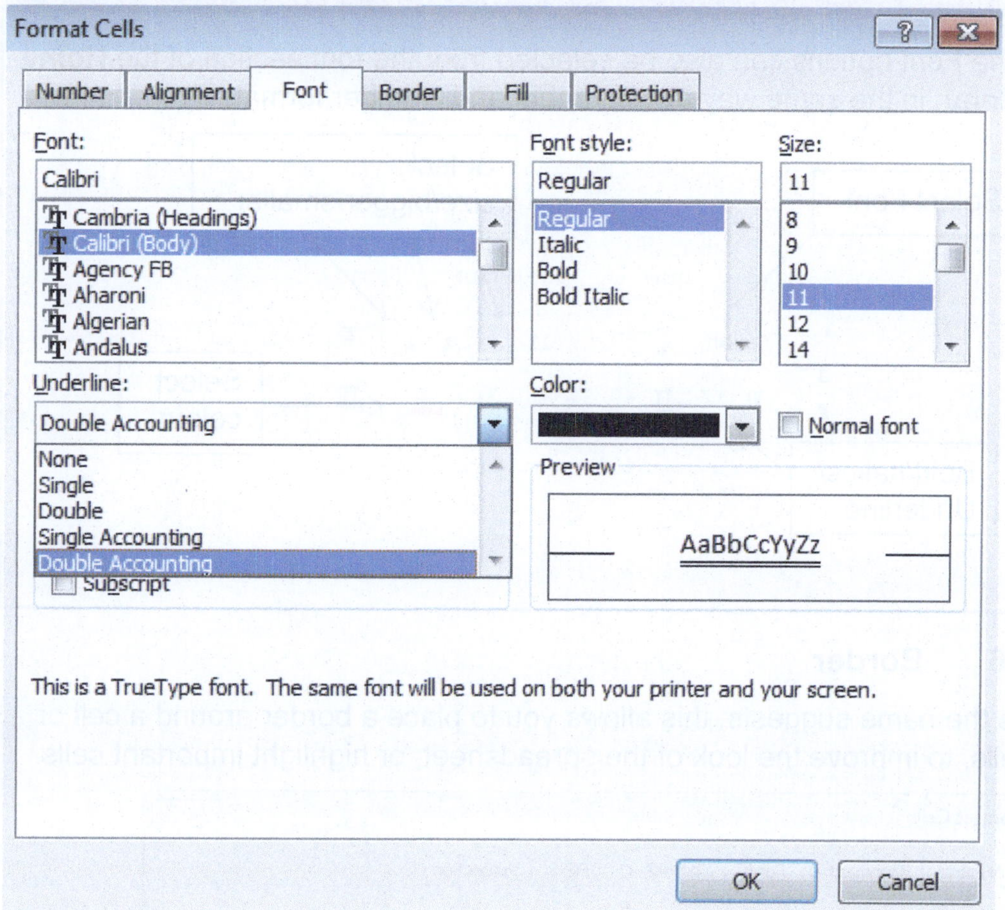

Underline.

	A	B	C	D	E	F	G	H	I	J	K	L	M
1						Monthly Profit Calculations							
2		January	February	March	April	May	June	July	August	Septembe	October	Novembe	December
3	Sales	10,000	12,500	11,000	12,200	12,500	13,000	11,000	16,000	15,000	15,500	12,000	10,200
4	Costs	6,500	7,000	7,000	6,700	7,200	8,000	7,500	8,200	6,800	7,100	5,500	5,200
5	Profit	3,500	5,500	4,000	5,500	5,300	5,000	3,500	7,800	8,200	8,400	6,500	5,000

Double Accounting Underline shown under the Profit calculations.

The title of this information could also be made bold, by selecting the bold option in Font Style:

					Monthly Profit Calculations							
	January	February	March	April	May	June	July	August	Septembe	October	Novembe	December
Sales	10,000	12,500	11,000	12,200	12,500	13,000	11,000	16,000	15,000	15,500	12,000	10,200
Costs	6,500	7,000	7,000	6,700	7,200	8,000	7,500	8,200	6,800	7,100	5,500	5,200
Profit	3,500	5,500	4,000	5,500	5,300	5,000	3,500	7,800	8,200	8,400	6,500	5,000

Shortcuts

The Font options can also be selected from the font section of the **Home Menu**, in the same way as alignment and Number formats.

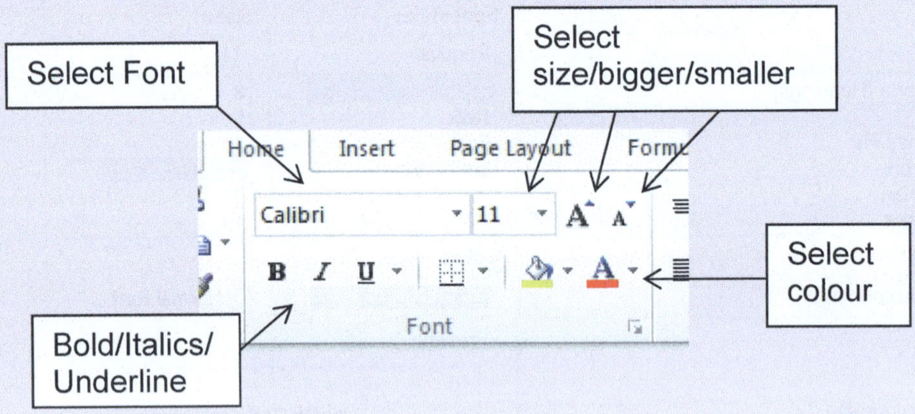

3.6 Border

As the name suggests, this allows you to place a border around a cell or cells, to improve the look of the spreadsheet, or highlight important cells.

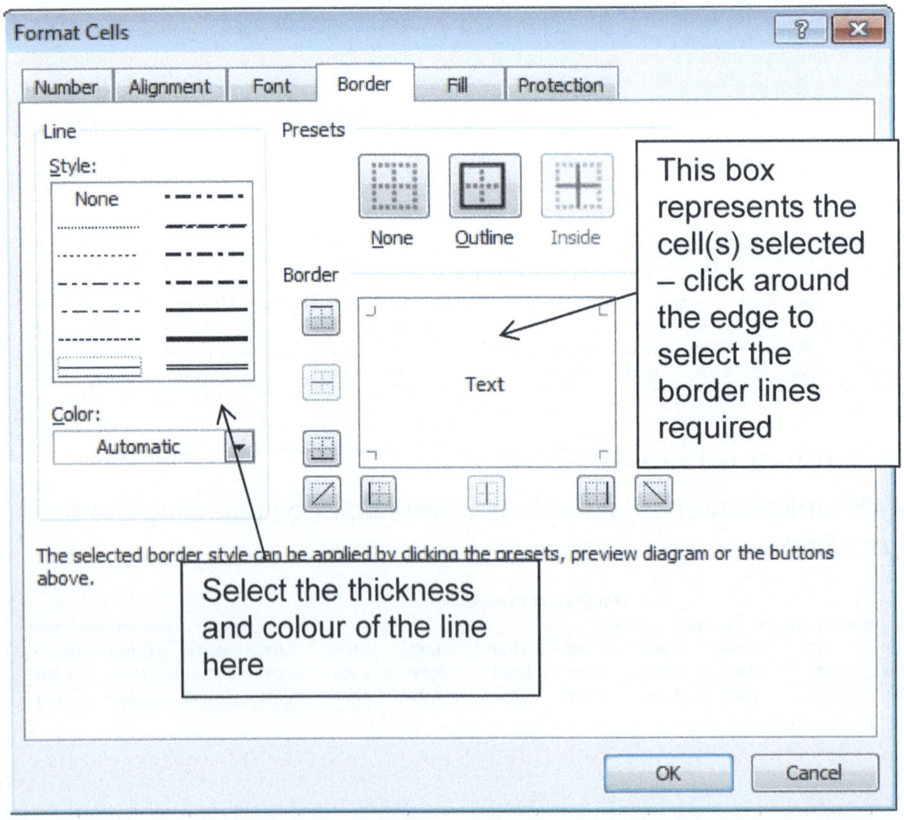

For example, a thick red border can be applied.

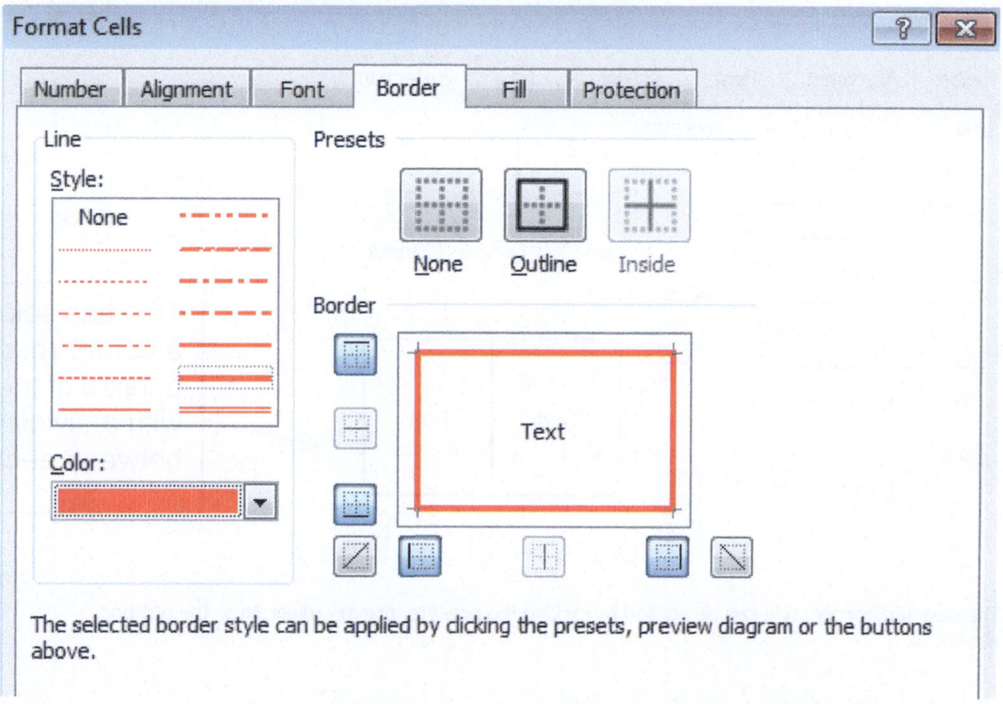

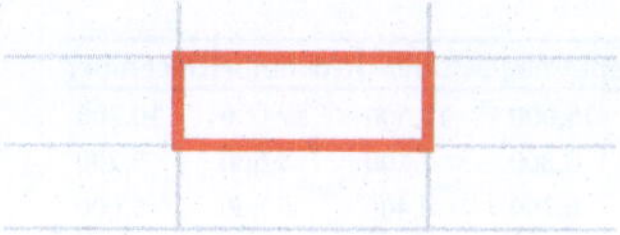

The border around the cell will be changed accordingly. To delete a border, follow the same steps but select **none** for the border.

If several cells are selected, the same borders will be applied to each:

A	B	C	D	E	F	G	H	I	J	K	L	M
						Monthly Profit Calculations						
	January	February	March	April	May	June	July	August	Septembe	October	Novembe	Decembe
Sales	10,000	12,500	11,000	12,200	12,500	13,000	11,000	16,000	15,000	15,500	12,000	10,200
Costs	6,500	7,000	7,000	6,700	7,200	8,000	7,500	8,200	6,800	7,100	5,500	5,200
Profit	3,500	5,500	4,000	5,500	5,300	5,000	3,500	7,800	8,200	8,400	6,500	5,000

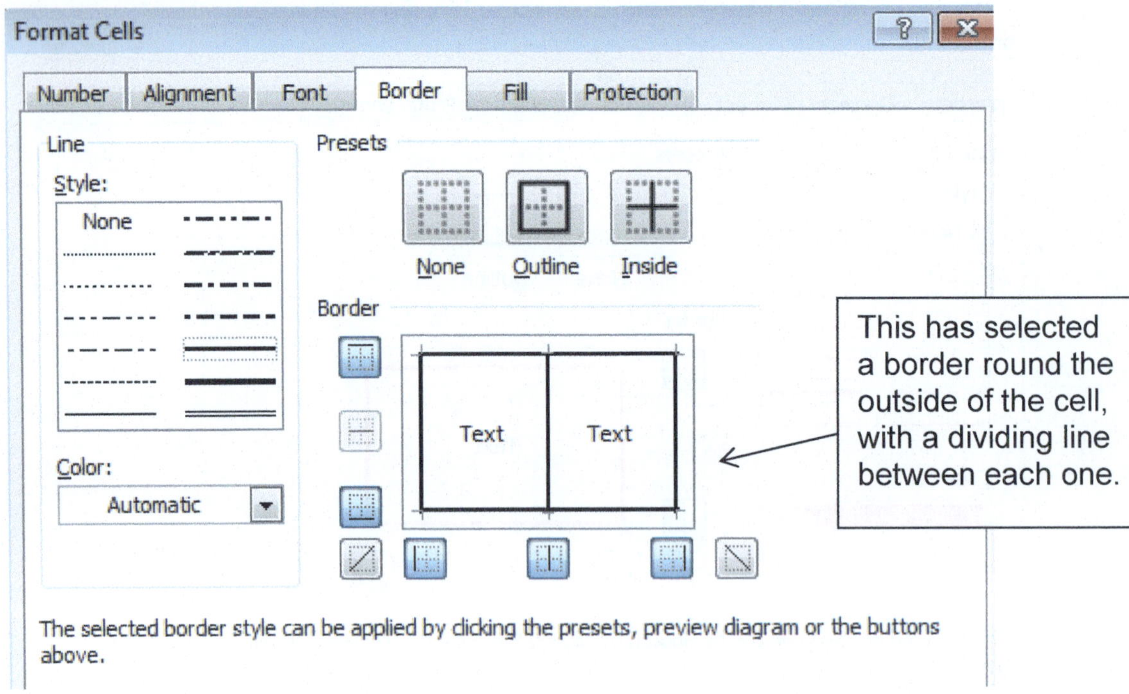

	A	B	C	D	E	F	G	H	I	J	K	L	M
1							Monthly Profit Calculations						
2		January	February	March	April	May	June	July	August	Septembe	October	Novembe	December
3	Sales	10,000	12,500	11,000	12,200	12,500	13,000	11,000	16,000	15,000	15,500	12,000	10,200
4	Costs	6,500	7,000	7,000	6,700	7,200	8,000	7,500	8,200	6,800	7,100	5,500	5,200
5	Profit	3,500	5,500	4,000	5,500	5,300	5,000	3,500	7,800	8,200	8,400	6,500	5,000

Shortcut

Borders can be applied directly using the **borders** button in the **Home Menu**

The appropriate border can be selected directly from here.

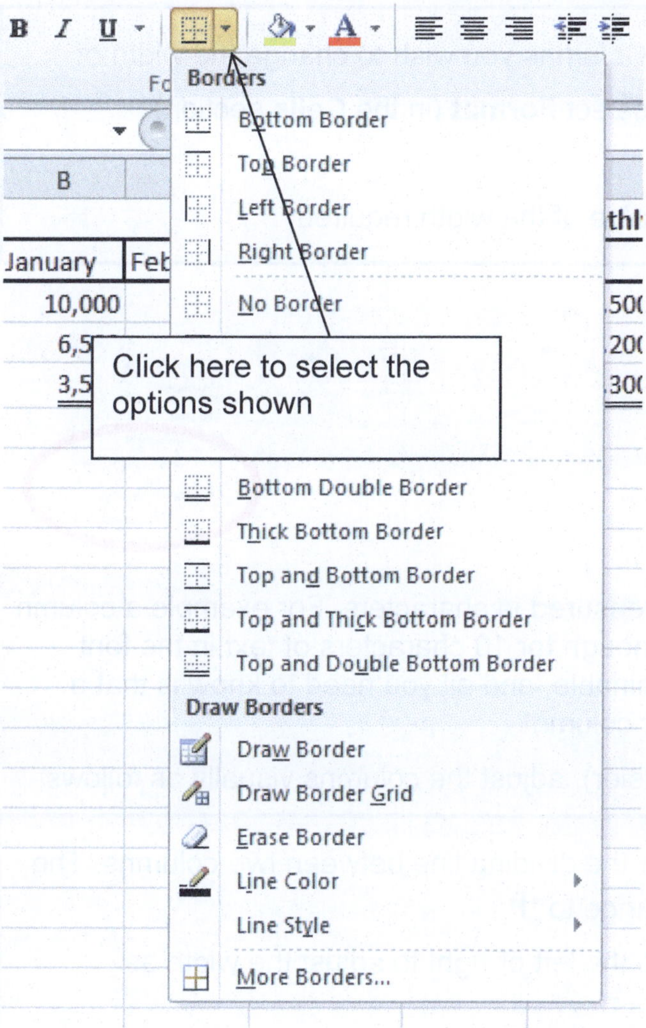

3.7 Adjusting row and column widths

Adjusting column width

You may need to adjust column widths so that all of your data is shown. For example in the screenshot below, columns J, L and M are not wide enough to display the month properly.

	A	B	C	D	E	F	G	H	I	J	K	L	M
1						Monthly Profit Calculations							
2		January	February	March	April	May	June	July	August	Septembe	October	Novembe	December
3	Sales	10,000	12,500	11,000	12,200	12,500	13,000	11,000	16,000	15,000	15,500	12,000	10,200
4	Costs	6,500	7,000	7,000	6,700	7,200	8,000	7,500	8,200	6,800	7,100	5,500	5,200
5	Profit	3,500	5,500	4,000	5,500	5,300	5,000	3,500	7,800	8,200	8,400	6,500	5,000
6													

There are several ways to adjust the column width.

- Select the Column or Columns you wish to change the width of
- In the **'Home Menu'**, select **Format** (in the **Cells** section)
- Select Column Width
- Type in the numeric value of the width required.

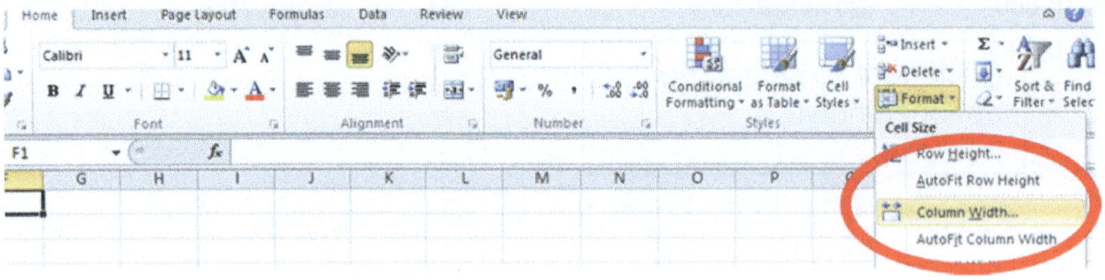

Note – column widths are measured in characters. For example a column width of 10 would be wide enough for 10 characters of text in the font being used. This is not examinable, and all you need to know is that a bigger number gives a wider column!

Alternatively (and usually easier), adjust the columns visually as follows:

- Hover the mouse over the dividing line between two columns. The mouse pointer will change to 
- **Left click** and **drag** to the left or right to adjust the width as required
- Release the mouse button to accept the new width.

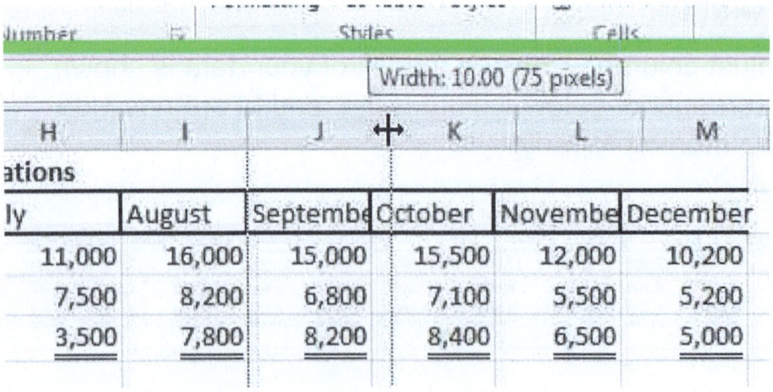

Drag the mouse to the left or right to adjust the column width.

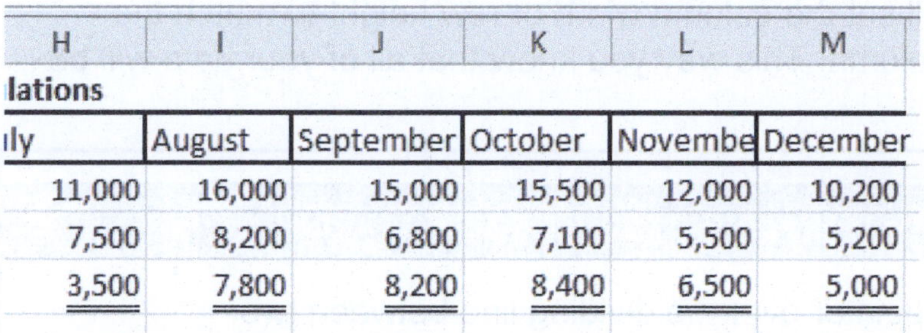

Once the mouse button is released, the column will be the correct width.

Adjusting row height

This works in exactly the same way as adjusting column widths.

- Select the Row or Rows you wish to change the height of
- In the **'Home Menu'**, select **Format** (in the **Cells** section)
- Select Row Height
- Type in the numeric value of the width required.

Or

- Hover the mouse over the dividing line between two rows. The mouse pointer will change to ✛
- **Left click** and **drag** up or down to adjust the height as required
- Release the mouse button to accept the new height.

3.8 Autofit

A very useful feature for setting column widths/row heights is **Autofit**. You may have seen this option when selecting a column width:

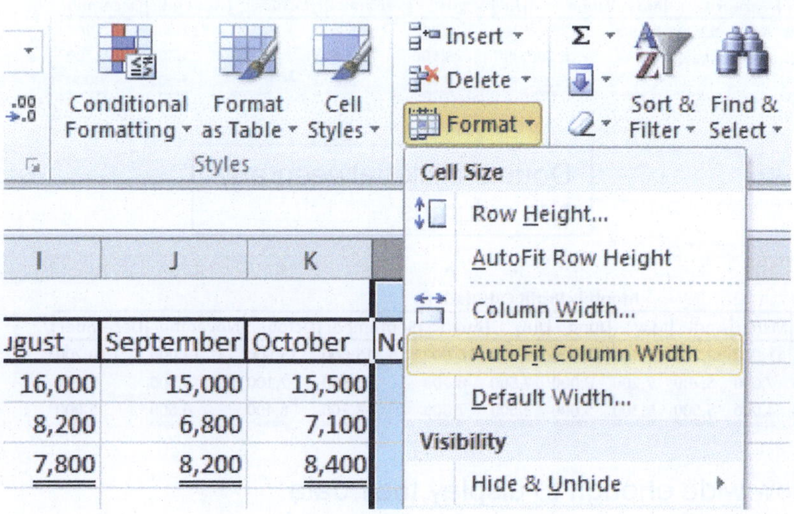

Selecting Autofit will set the column width or row height to match the largest cell in the column. This way you know that all of your data will be visible.

Shortcut

Hover the mouse pointer over the dividing line between two columns/rows and **DOUBLE CLICK** to autofit.

Autofit all rows/columns

After your work is finished, it is sensible to Autofit all rows/columns to ensure that everything is visible. This is quickly and easily achieved as follows:

- Click the **Select All Cells** button in the top left of the spreadsheet
- Autofit **ANY** column
- Autofit **Any** row

All columns and rows will be correctly adjusted.

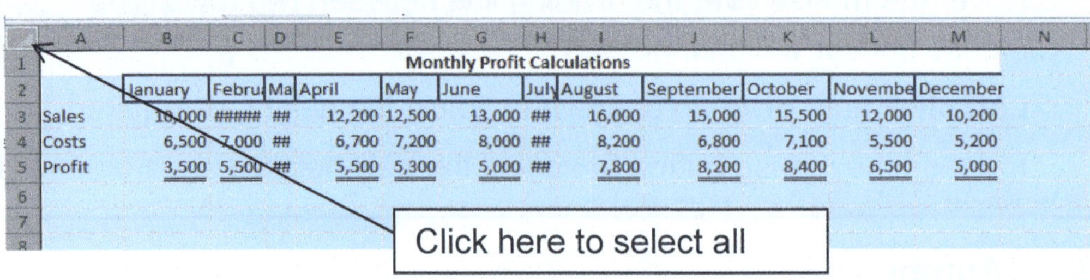

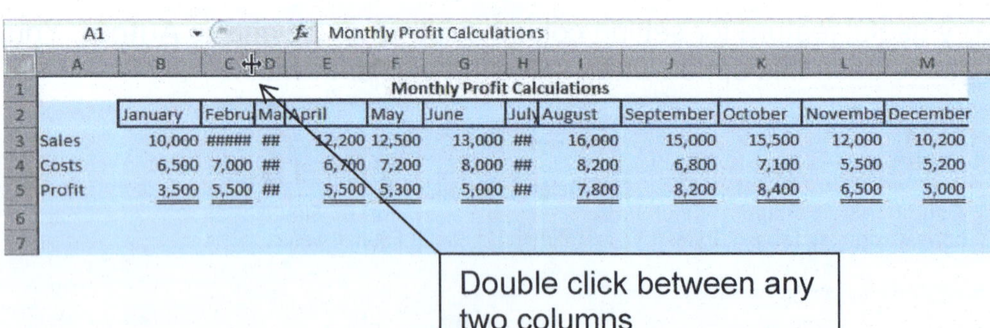

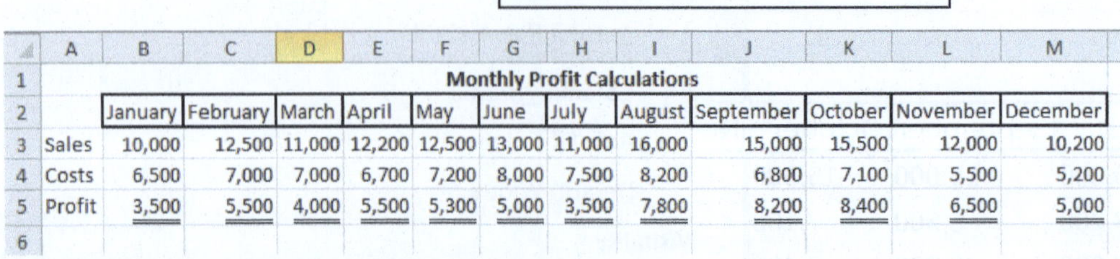

	A	B	C	D	E	F	G	H	I	J	K	L	M
1							Monthly Profit Calculations						
2		January	February	March	April	May	June	July	August	September	October	November	December
3	Sales	10,000	12,500	11,000	12,200	12,500	13,000	11,000	16,000	15,000	15,500	12,000	10,200
4	Costs	6,500	7,000	7,000	6,700	7,200	8,000	7,500	8,200	6,800	7,100	5,500	5,200
5	Profit	3,500	5,500	4,000	5,500	5,300	5,000	3,500	7,800	8,200	8,400	6,500	5,000
6													

All columns are now wide enough to display their data.

3.9 Hide and unhide columns and rows

It is possible to hide columns or rows on a worksheet. Select the column(s) or row(s) that need to be hidden and on the **Home** tab in the **Cells** section you will find **Format**. Click on the down arrow and choose **Hide & unhide** and select the option you want.

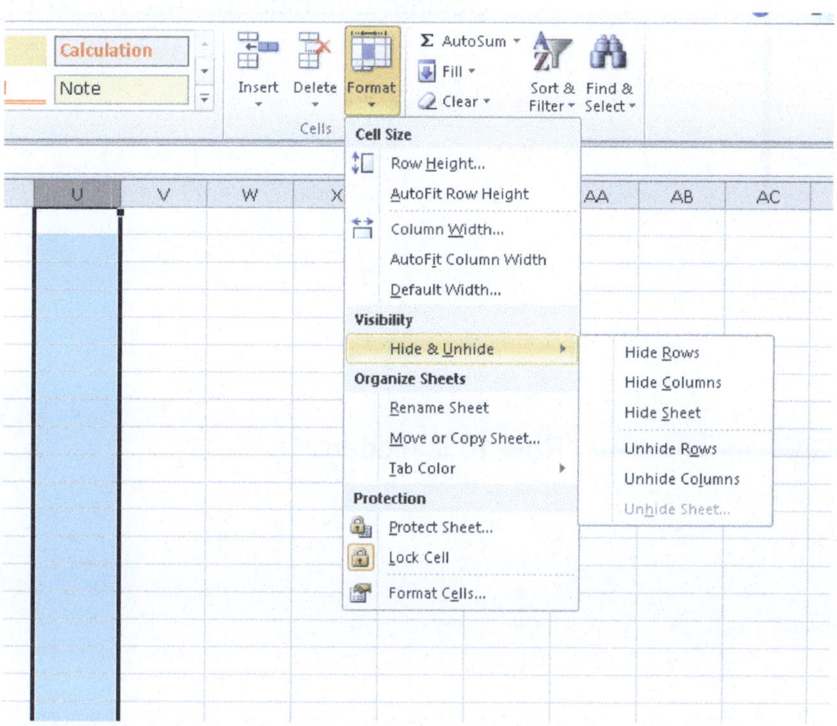

This can also be done by right clicking on the mouse:

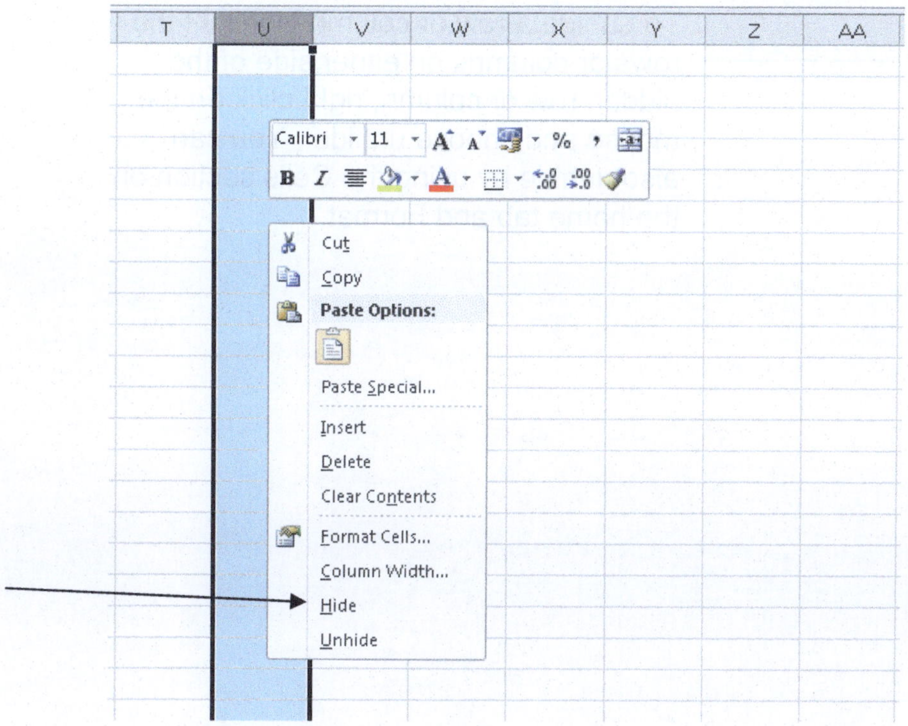

You can see if a column or row is hidden as the letter or number representing the column or row is missing.

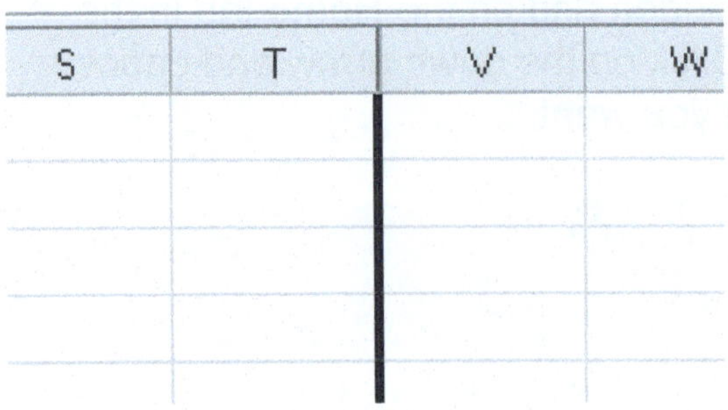

Column U is hidden:

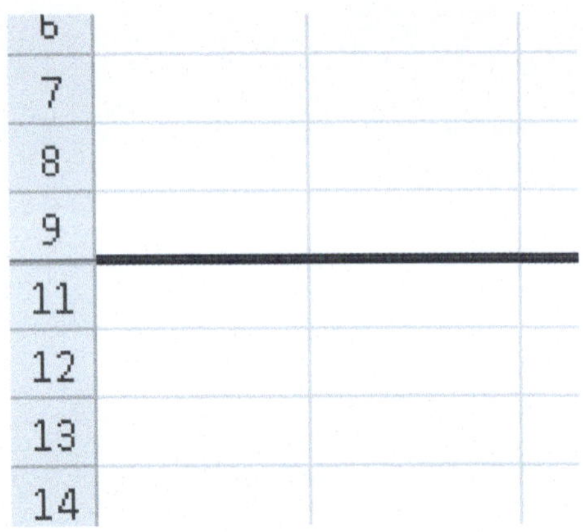

Row 10 is hidden:

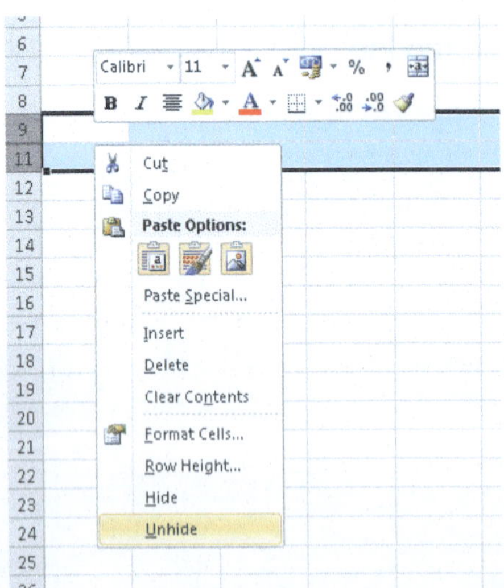

To unhide a row or column highlight the rows or columns on either side of the hidden row or column, right click on the mouse and choose unhide. You can also unhide by using the Cells section on the home tab and Format.

3.10 Activity

The activities in this guide are designed to test your knowledge on the techniques shown in this chapter. They may also use techniques used in previous chapters, to build up your knowledge. Suggested answers are available on MyKaplan, although it is better to refer to the notes and try to understand the methods than look straight at the answers.

Activity 3-1

This activity allows you to practice essential formatting techniques which are required as part of the SDST syllabus.

(a) Open the **Unformatted Report** file from the **Activities** folder.

(b) **Merge** and **Center** the title on the **Summary report** sheet across the data. **Bold** and **Underline** the title, and change the **font size** to **16**.

(c) Change the **number format** of the numbers to **Number**, with **0 decimal places** and **1000 separator**.

(d) Apply a **double accounting underline** to the profit figures.

(e) **Fill** the Half year information in cells H2:H4 using **yellow**. Place a single line **border** around the edge of cells H2:H4 and **remove** the **double underline** from cell H4.

(f) **Insert** a row between the title and Months

(g) **Autofit** all column widths.

(h) **Save** the file in the **Solutions** folder as **Activity 3-1**.

Simple calculations and data analysis

4

4.1 Introduction

This chapter will explain to you how to create simple functions and to understand how Excel performs calculations.

KNOWLEDGE
2.2 Select and use a wide range of appropriate functions and formulas to meet calculation requirements.

In this session you will be introduced to the following:

1. Simple Calculations using + - * and /
2. Using cell references
3. Copying formulas
4. Auto-sum
5. Calculation of percentages
6. Sort and Filter

4.2 Simple calculations

We have already seen how to enter numeric and text information into cells in Excel. However, Excel's primary purpose is to manipulate the raw data through calculations and formulas. One of the main things you will use Excel for is simple calculations. The most basic (and most common) calculations are the mathematical functions addition +, subtraction -, multiplication * and divide /.

To use these, you need to tell Excel that you are using a **FUNCTION**. To do this, enter an equals sign, '=', before the calculation you require.

So, to find the answer to 3+5, type in any cell

=3+5 and press **Enter**.

As you type, the formula is displayed above, in the formula bar, as well as on the spreadsheet itself.

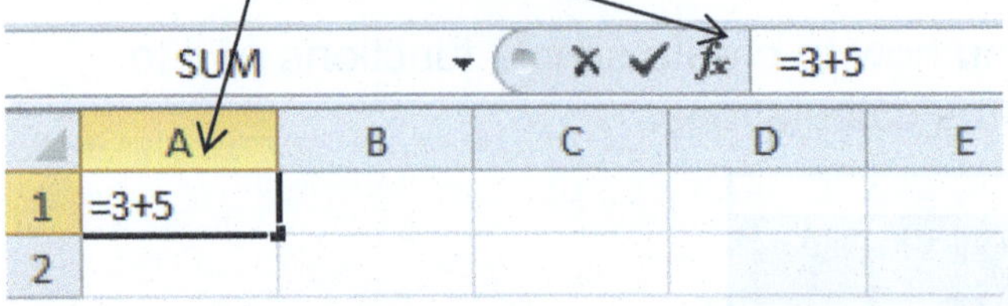

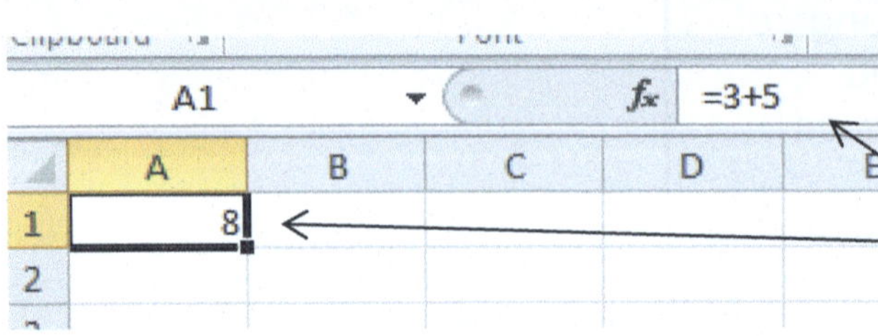

Once enter is pressed, the result of the calculation is shown on the spreadsheet, but the calculation itself is still shown in the formula bar.

Excel can be used in this way as a simple calculator by entering the calculation required, using +, -, * or /.

4.3 Calculations using existing values

The real power of Excel comes to the fore when using the values in other cells as part of your calculations. Take the following example:

	A	B	C	D
1	Name	Hourly Rate	Hours Worked	Pay
2	Srnicek	£8.60	30	
3	Watson	£8.60	20	
4	Peacock	£9.00	20	
5	Albert	£11.50	25	
6	Beresford	£10.50	30	
7	Batty	£12.00	40	
8	Lee	£13.00	42	
9	Beardsley	£14.00	35	
10	Ginola	£16.00	15	
11	Shearer	£18.00	35	
12	Ferdinand	£16.00	32	
13				

We need to find each person's pay – as the hourly rate * hours worked. You could simply type each one in, for example **'=8.60*30'** for Srnicek. This is time consuming and not much better than using pen and paper.
We can instead tell Excel to 'take the value in cell B2 and multiply by the value in cell C2'

	A	B	C	D	E
1	Name	Hourly Rate	Hours Worked	Pay	
2	Srnicek	£8.60	30	=b2	
3	Watson	£8.60	20		
4	Peacock	£9.00	20		
5	Albert	£11.50	25		
6	Beresford	£10.50	30		
7	Batty	£12.00	40		
8	Lee	£13.00	42		
9	Beardsley	£14.00	35		
10	Ginola	£16.00	15		
11	Shearer	£18.00	35		
12	Ferdinand	£16.00	32		
13					

Each cell is referred to by its column and row reference. To perform the calculation, start with the '=' sign to show that you want to perform a calculation. Then type the cell reference of the cell you wish to use. A box will appear around the cell.

	A	B	C	D	E
1	Name	Hourly Rate	Hours Worked	Pay	
2	Srnicek	£8.60	30	=b2*c2	
3	Watson	£8.60	20		
4	Peacock	£9.00	20		
5	Albert	£11.50	25		
6	Beresford	£10.50	30		
7	Batty	£12.00	40		
8	Lee	£13.00	42		
9	Beardsley	£14.00	35		
10	Ginola	£16.00	15		
11	Shearer	£18.00	35		
12	Ferdinand	£16.00	32		
13					

Finish off the calculation as required – the cell references are just saying "use whatever number is in this cell".

Note that although the column letters are always displayed in capitals, if you enter them in lower case it does n0t matter.

D2 | f_x | =B2*C2

	A	B	C	D
1	Name	Hourly Rate	Hours Worked	Pay
2	Srnicek	£8.60	30	£258.00
3	Watson	£8.60	20	
4	Peacock	£9.00	20	
5	Albert	£11.50	25	
6	Beresford	£10.50	30	
7	Batty	£12.00	40	
8	Lee	£13.00	42	
9	Beardsley	£14.00	35	
10	Ginola	£16.00	15	
11	Shearer	£18.00	35	
12	Ferdinand	£16.00	32	
13				

The result of the calculation is shown – note that the actual calculation being performed is shown in the formula bar above.

Any calculation can be performed using existing information in cells – this allows complex analysis to be undertaken relatively easily.

One huge benefit of this is that if the numbers in the data cells change, then the calculation will be updated to reflect this.

D2 | f_x | =B2*C2

	A	B	C	D
1	Name	Hourly Rate	Hours Worked	Pay
2	Srnicek	£8.60	25	£215.00
3	Watson	£8.60	20	
4	Peacock	£9.00	20	
5	Albert	£11.50	25	
6	Beresford	£10.50	30	
7	Batty	£12.00	40	
8	Lee	£13.00	42	
9	Beardsley	£14.00	35	
10	Ginola	£16.00	15	
11	Shearer	£18.00	35	
12	Ferdinand	£16.00	32	

Changing the hours worked to 25 has given an updated value in the pay column.

You can use any cell within your formulas, in the same way.

	A	B	C	D	E	F
1	Name	Hourly Rate	Hours Worked	Pay	10% Bonus	
2	Srnicek	£8.60	25	£215.00	=D2*10%	
3	Watson	£8.60	20			
4	Peacock	£9.00	20			
5	Albert	£11.50	25			

Will give

	A	B	C	D	E	F
1	Name	Hourly Rate	Hours Worked	Pay	10% Bonus	
2	Srnicek	£8.60	25	£215.00	£21.50	
3	Watson	£8.60	20			
4	Peacock	£9.00	20			
5	Albert	£11.50	25			

IMPORTANT NOTE – when entering cell references into a formula, rather than typing the reference **'B2'**, you can **LEFT-CLICK** on the cell you wish to use. This way you are less likely to type the wrong cell reference.

4.4 Copying formulas

In the previous example, a formula has been entered into cells D2 and E2. We need to perform the same calculation for the other 10 staff. It would be incredibly time consuming to have to manually enter the calculation into each cell – sometimes spreadsheets can have several thousand rows!

Fortunately Excel deals with this problem very easily. Using the same copy and paste feature seen in chapter 2, we can duplicate formulas used to speed up calculations.

fx =B2*C2

C	D	E	F
Hours Worked	Pay	10% Bonus	
25	£215.00	£21.50	
20			

Ctrl-C to copy the formula (or whichever method you prefer)

fx =B3*C3

C	D	E
Hours Worked	Pay	10% Bonus
25	£215.00	£21.50
20	£172.00	

Ctrl-V can be used to paste the formula. Notice how the formula has been updated to use **Row 3** rather than Row 2. This is due to 'relative' referencing (covered in chapter 7)

You can paste the formula to more than one cell, as required:

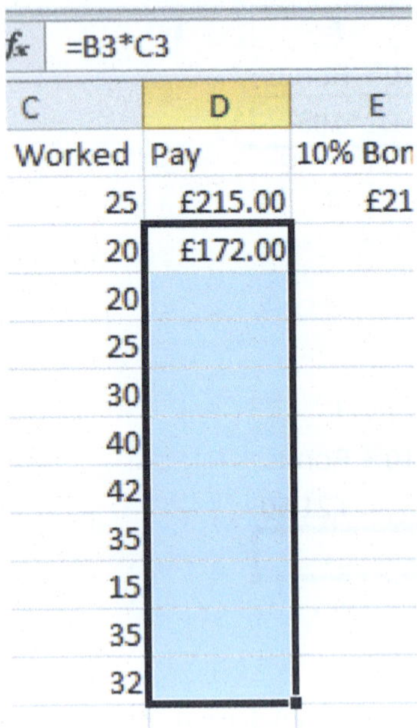

Select all the cells the formula is required in, before pasting.

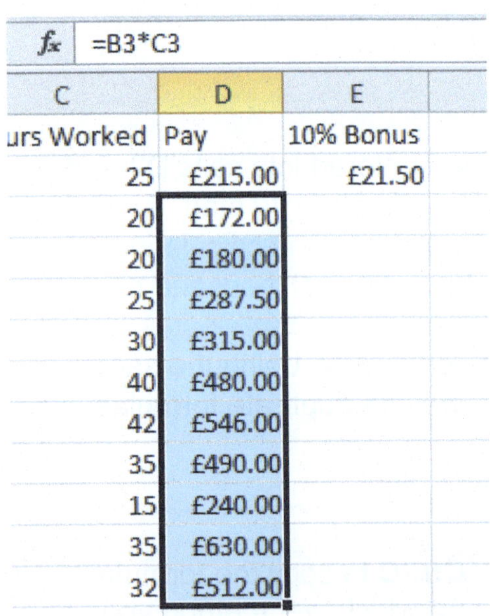

The formula has been successfully copied.

If you find that the values do not change then your spreadsheet may not be set up to perform calculations automatically. Go to the Formula tab and check **Calculation Options** – click **Automatic**.

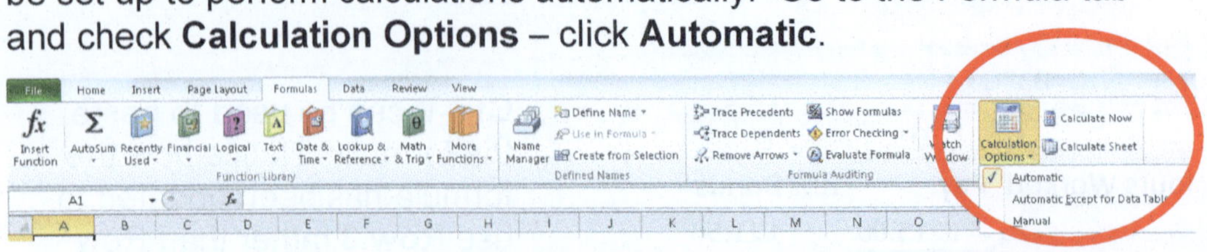

Using Autofill

Another quick way to copy formulas is to use the Autofill function explained in chapter 2. Formulas can be "dragged" up, down, left or right to copy them:

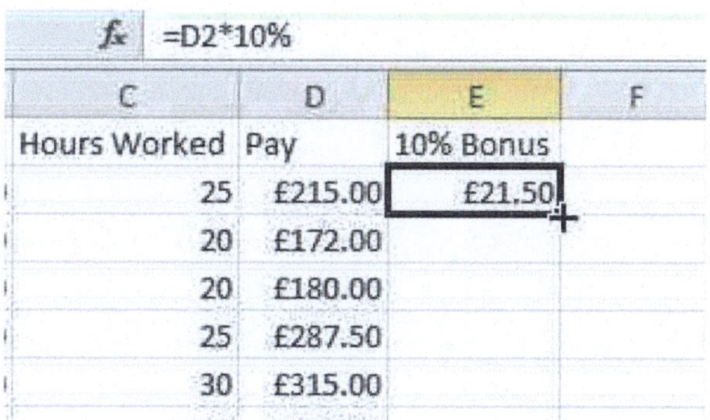

Hover the mouse over the bottom-right corner of the cell until the cursor changes.

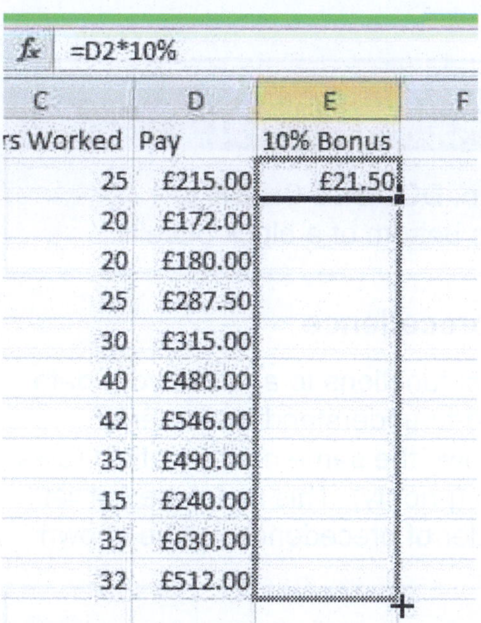

Drag the mouse in the direction you want the formulas copied, and let go of the mouse button.

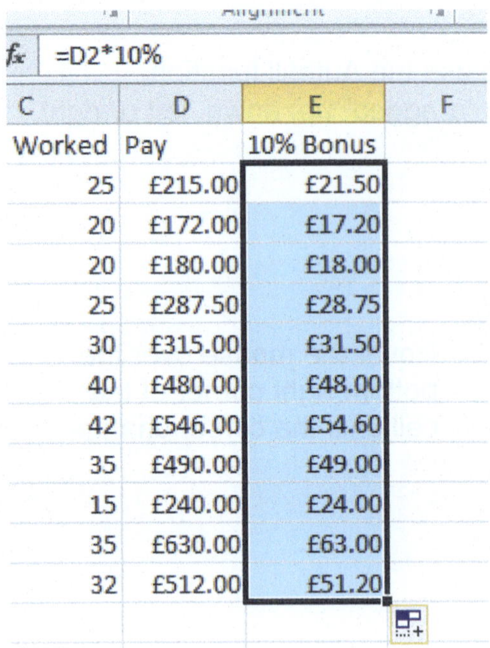

=D2*10%

C	D	E	F
Worked	Pay	10% Bonus	
25	£215.00	£21.50	
20	£172.00	£17.20	
20	£180.00	£18.00	
25	£287.50	£28.75	
30	£315.00	£31.50	
40	£480.00	£48.00	
42	£546.00	£54.60	
35	£490.00	£49.00	
15	£240.00	£24.00	
35	£630.00	£63.00	
32	£512.00	£51.20	

Shortcut

Instead of dragging the Autofill box down, **DOUBLE CLICK** to automatically copy formulas down to the bottom of a block of cells.

4.5 Operators and the order of precedence

You are going to use simple mathematical functions to analyse your data but in order that you can do this you need to understand the order of priority given to each function. Excel follows the same mathematical rules. Below is a list of the order of precedence (priority). This is not the full list and later on during the course the full order of precedence will be shown.

Operator	Symbol	Order of Precedence
Brackets	()	1
Multiplication	*	2
Division	/	2
Addition	+	3
Subtraction	-	3

The order of precedence determines which operators Excel will use first in its calculations. It can be seen above that Excel will calculate a formula that contains multiplication or division before it calculates and addition or subtraction. By inserting brackets around part of a formula it forces Excel to calculate the content of the brackets first, followed by the remainder of the formula. You can have multiple sets of brackets in a formula as you will see in later chapters when you deal with more complex calculations.

Important

You may have come across the phrase BODMAS during a maths class. This stands for Brackets Off, Divide, Multiply, Add, Subtract – the order of precedence.

Continuing with the same example, we can demonstrate the order of precedence. We need to calculate the tax each person will pay, as 20% of their total pay.

To calculate this using one formula we need to add up two cells, and then multiply the total by 20%. However, due to the order of operations, care must be taken.

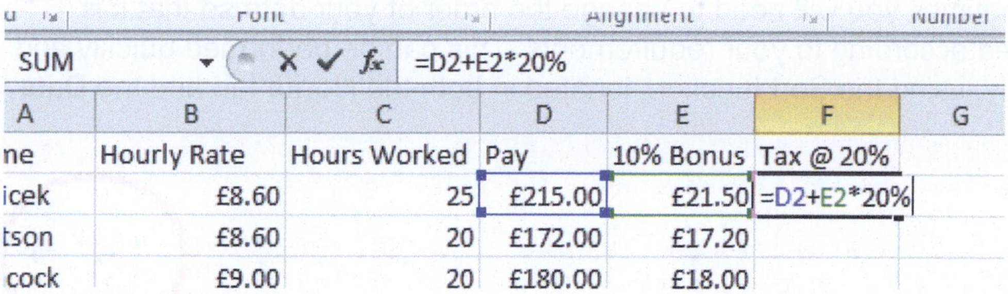

It would be tempting to type the above, as this is what we're trying to do – add up the two cells then multiply by 20%. However, Excel reads this as:

Multiply E2 by 20%, and then add on D2.

So the answer comes out as £219.30

To get round this problem, you must use brackets – put the calculation you want to happen first in brackets, to force the order as required. So:

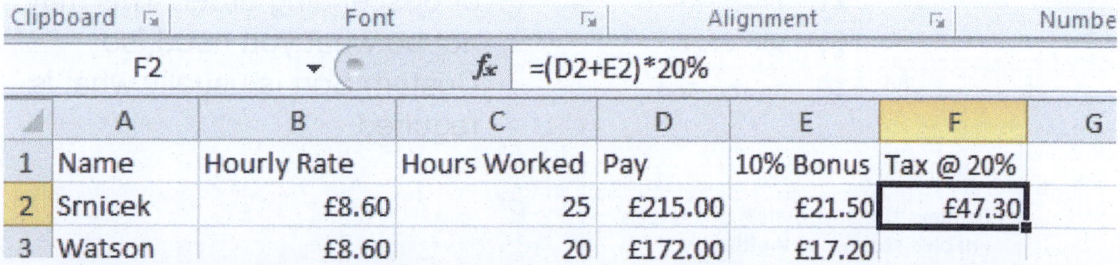

It's often worth sense checking the result of a calculation – a simple typo can give unpredictable results!

4.6 Calculation of percentage

To calculate percentages you can use:

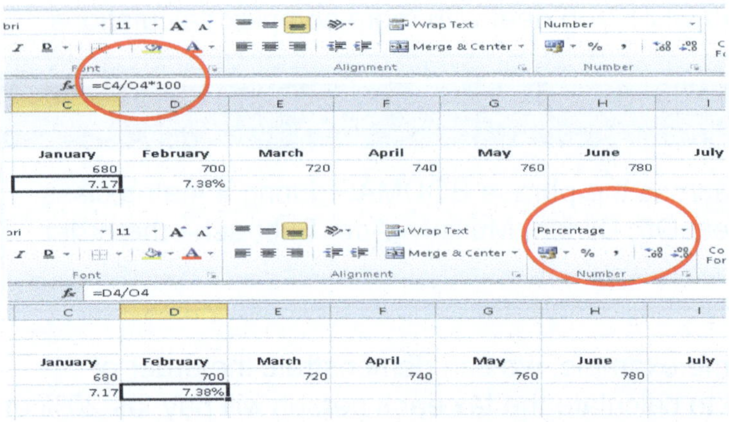

Simple mathematical formula (note formula bar) or format the cells as percentages. The percentage format can be found on the numbers tab of 'Format Cells'.

Alternatively it can be found on the format toolbar as a **%** icon.

4.7 Sorting data

Sometimes you will need to change the order of your data so that it is sorted according to your requirements. This can be performed quickly and easily, using the Sort function, located in both the **Home** tab and the **Data** tab.

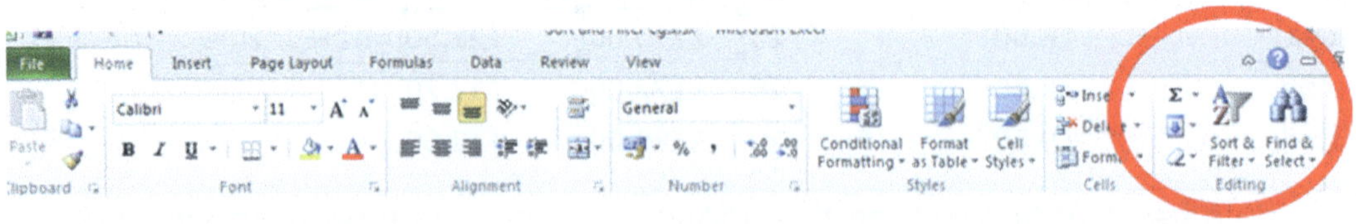

To sort, select the data you wish to sort, and click on the **Sort** button.

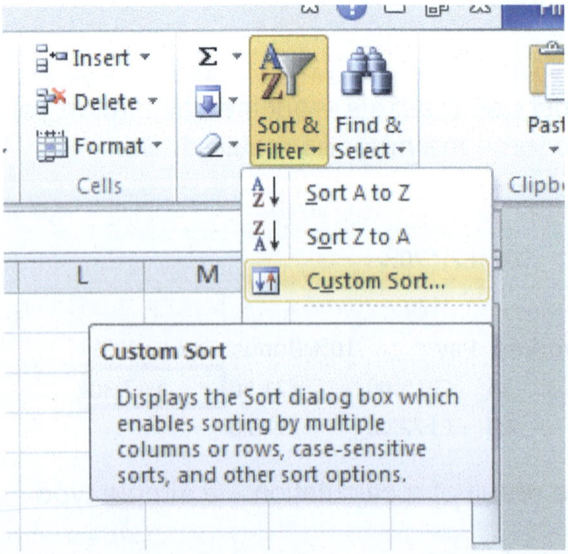

Sort A to Z and Z to A will sort data into either ascending order or descending order. This may not be what you need, so Custom Sort is usually what is required.

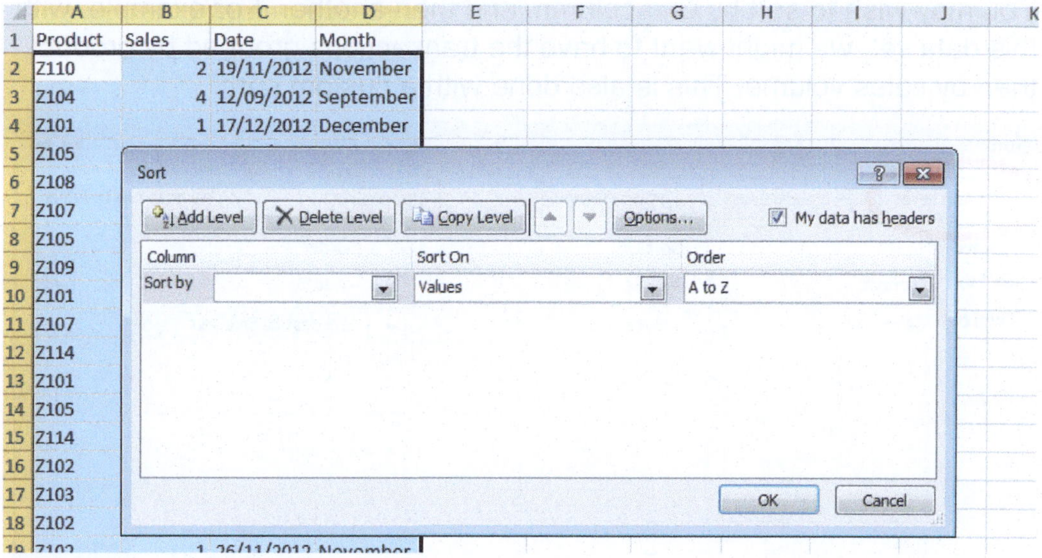

The Sort menu is displayed. Your data should have headers (titles), but if it doesn't, uncheck the check box.

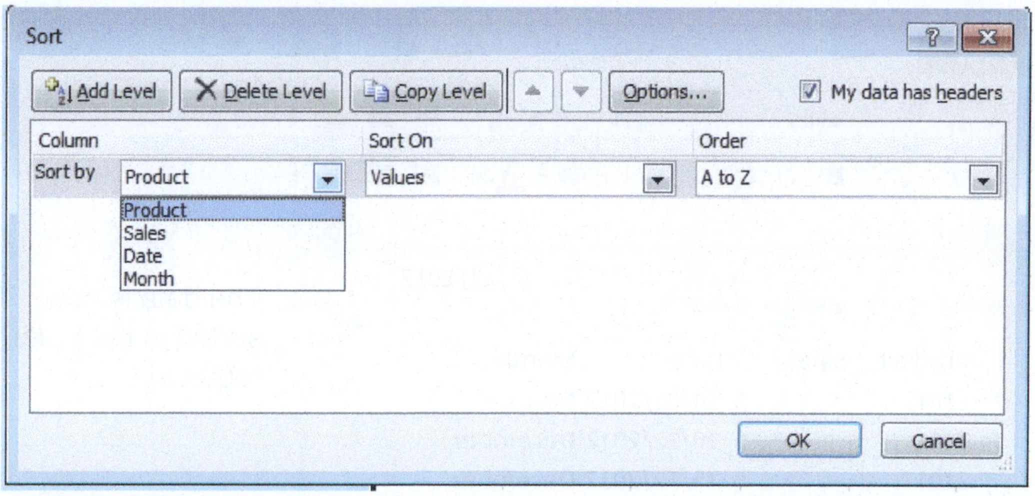

Select the column you wish to sort by, and click OK. The data will be sorted.

You may wish to sort by one column, and then another. For example, with this data set, we might want to have the transactions grouped by product, then by sales volume. This is also done with a custom sort:

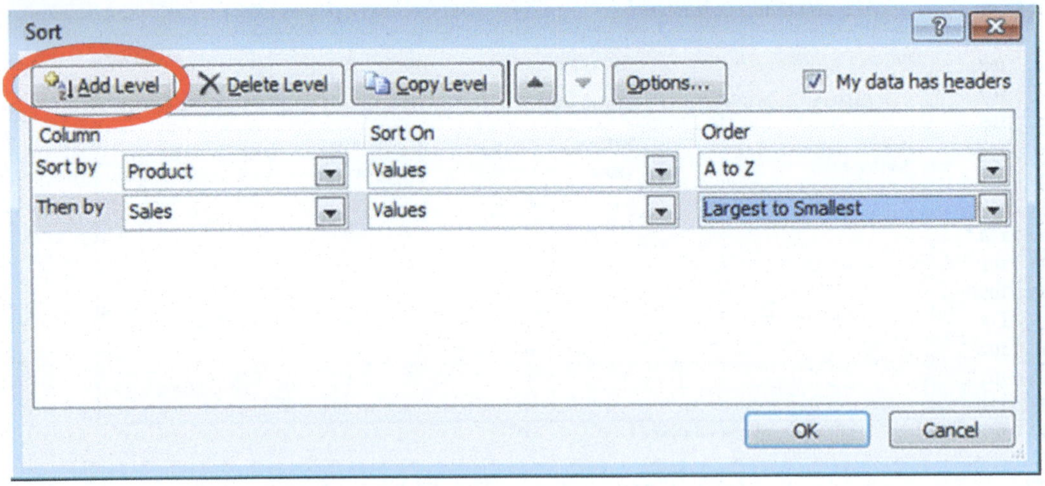

Clicking on **Add Level** will allow you to add more sort criteria. Delete Level will remove any unwanted levels.

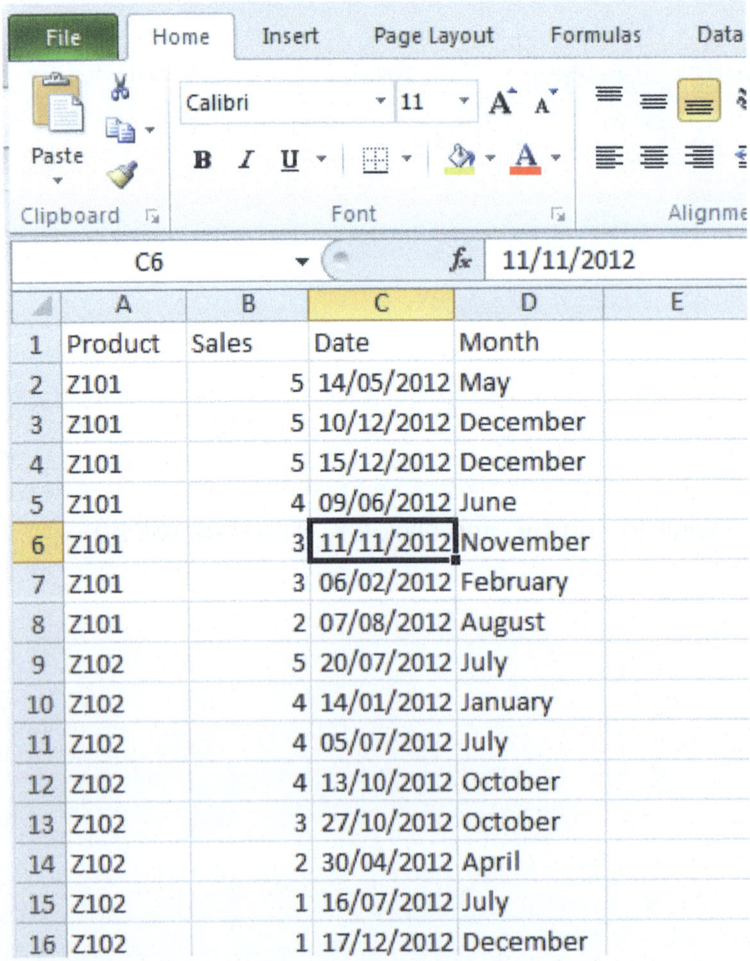

The data is now sorted in the order required.

Sorting by date

It is very common to want to sort by day/date. This could cause trouble – if we sort on a column containing months, for example, these will be sorted in alphabetical order – obviously months don't happen in alphabetical order. As mentioned previously when using **Autofill**, the order of days of the week and months of the year are recognised by Excel:

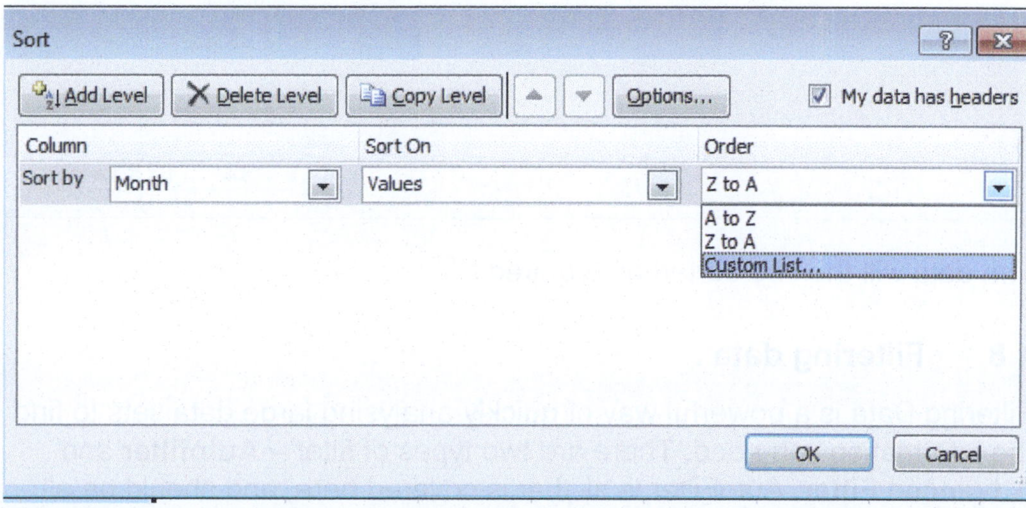

Choose custom list when sorting by month or days, and select the relevant list required.

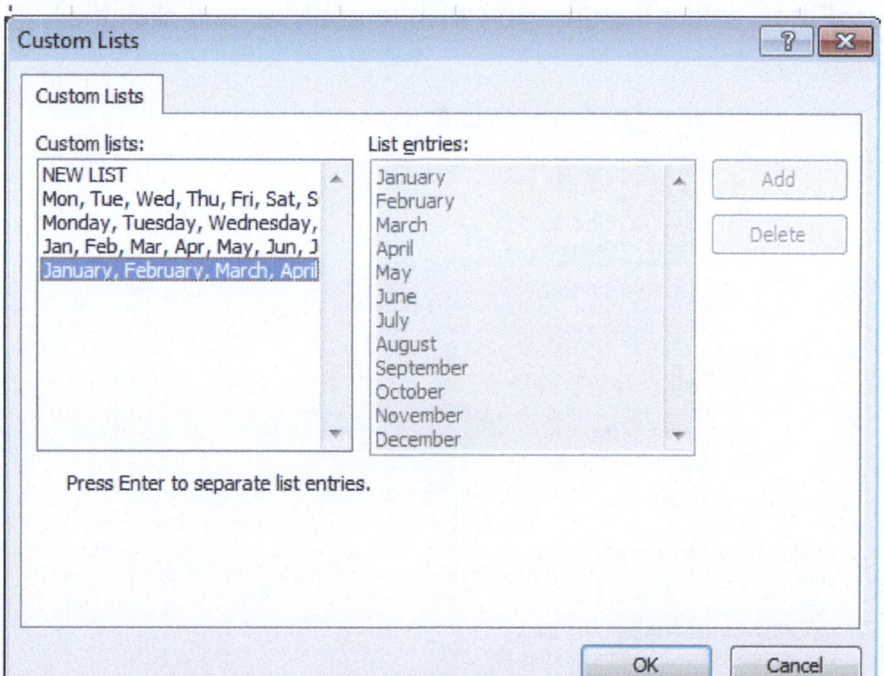

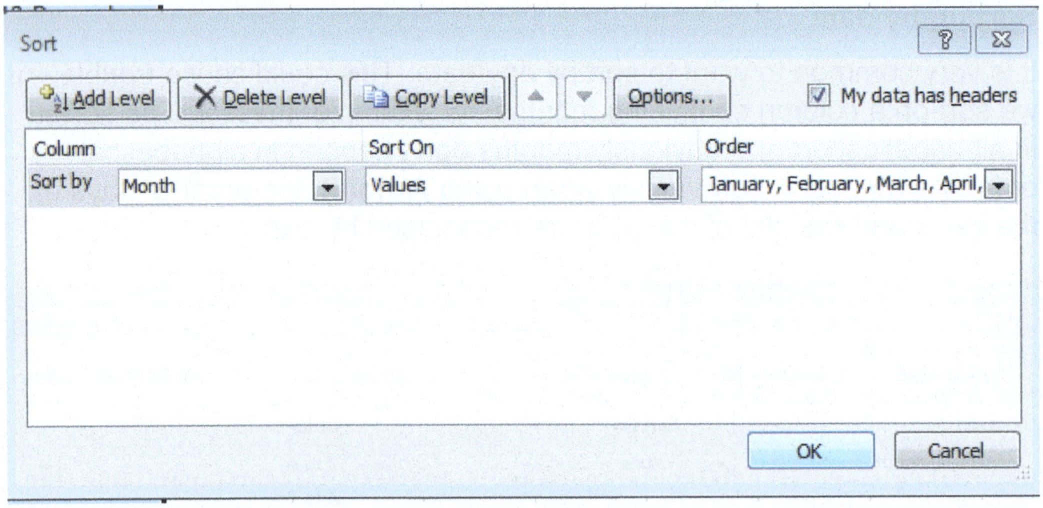

The data will then be sorted as required.

4.8 Filtering data

Filtering Data is a powerful way of quickly analysing large data sets to find the information you need. There are two types of filter – **Autofilter** and **Advanced Filter**. AutoFilter is all that is covered here, and should be all that is required – Advanced Filter is only required very rarely and not as part of the SDST syllabus.

To apply **AutoFilter**, select the data you wish to analyse, and click the Filter button.

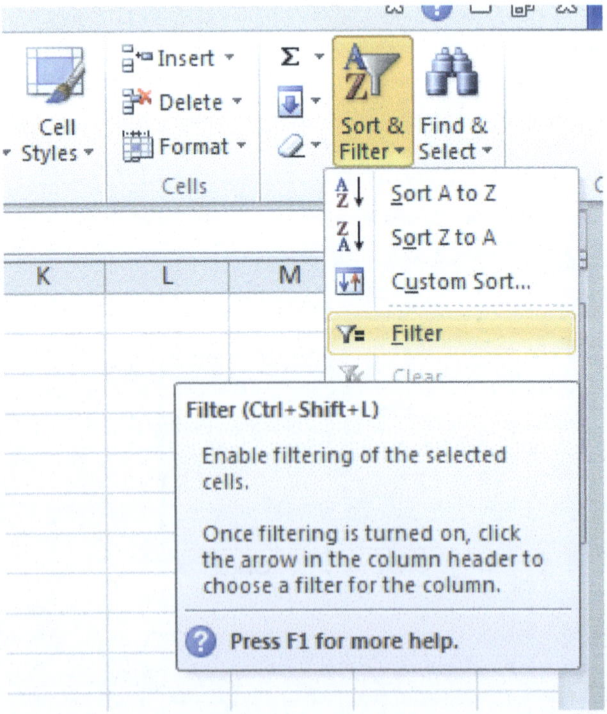

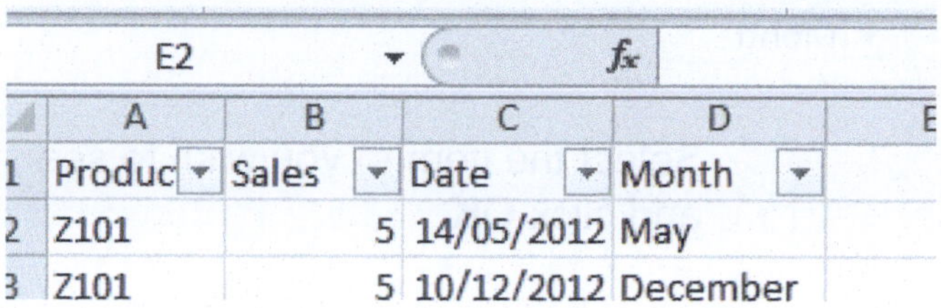

The arrows at the top of each column are the Filters – click on one to apply a Filter. Once the filter is in place, rows which do not meet the criteria applied will be hidden.

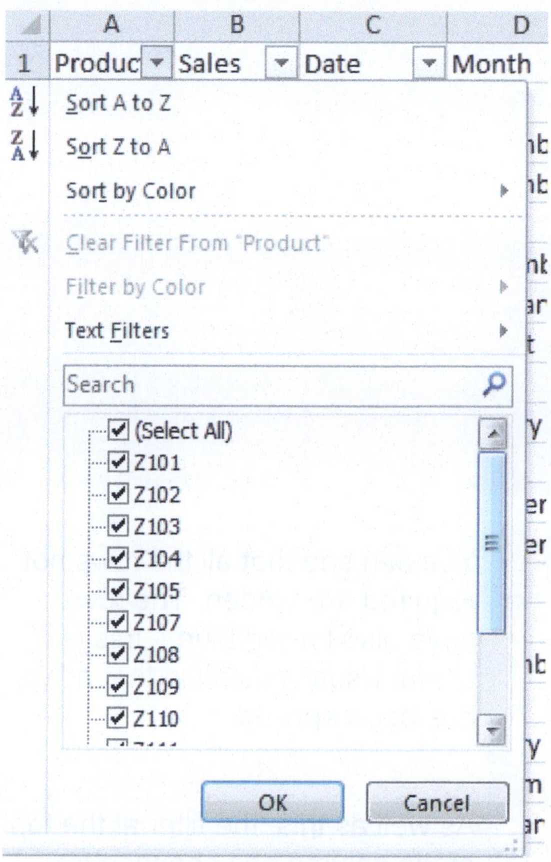

Clicking on the Filter at the top of column A also gives the option to Sort your data.

You can simply check/uncheck the items you wish to see/not see. Clicking the (Select All) box will also deselect all items if they are all selected.

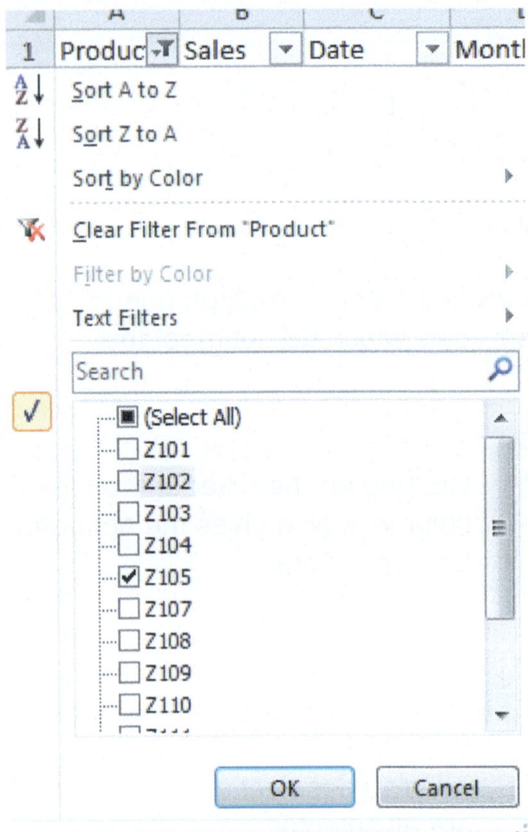

Select the item(s) you wish to see and click **OK**.

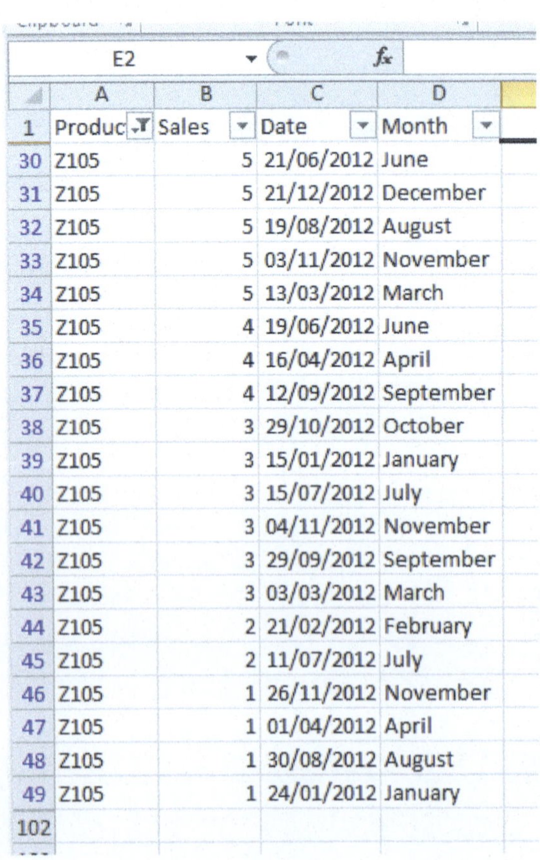

	A	B	C	D
1	Produc	Sales	Date	Month
30	Z105	5	21/06/2012	June
31	Z105	5	21/12/2012	December
32	Z105	5	19/08/2012	August
33	Z105	5	03/11/2012	November
34	Z105	5	13/03/2012	March
35	Z105	4	19/06/2012	June
36	Z105	4	16/04/2012	April
37	Z105	4	12/09/2012	September
38	Z105	3	29/10/2012	October
39	Z105	3	15/01/2012	January
40	Z105	3	15/07/2012	July
41	Z105	3	04/11/2012	November
42	Z105	3	29/09/2012	September
43	Z105	3	03/03/2012	March
44	Z105	2	21/02/2012	February
45	Z105	2	11/07/2012	July
46	Z105	1	26/11/2012	November
47	Z105	1	01/04/2012	April
48	Z105	1	30/08/2012	August
49	Z105	1	24/01/2012	January
102				

You can see that all the rows not required are hidden. The rows have also turned blue – this is a useful visual indication that a filter has been applied.

As well as this, the filter at the top of the column has changed to show that a filter is in place.

You can continue to apply filters to other columns as required.

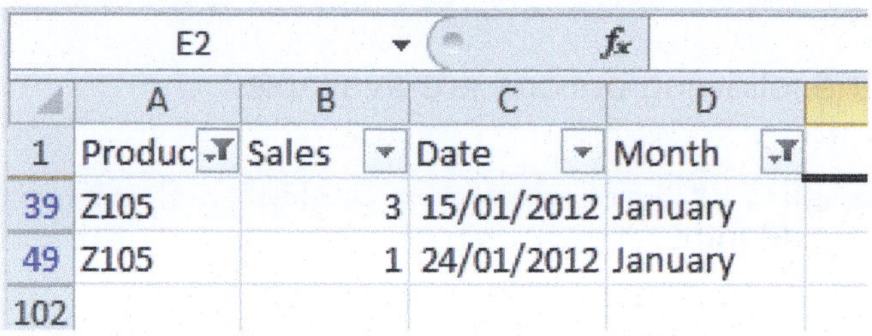

For example - Z105 sales in January filtered by product and month.

Removing Filters

Either click back in the filter and **Select All**, or within the **Sort & Filter** button, click the **Clear** option.

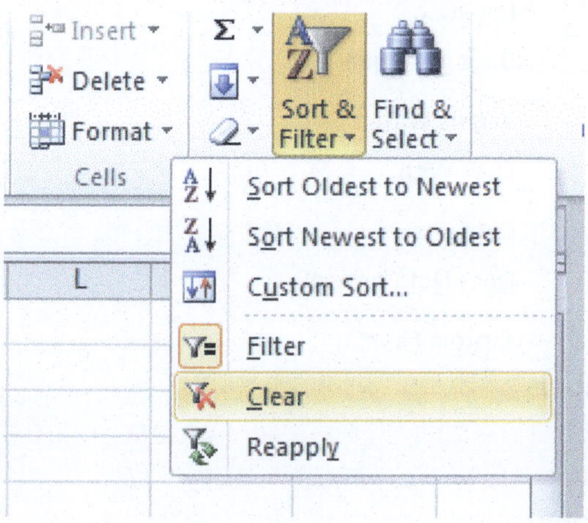

This will clear all current Filters.

Other Filtering options

Depending on the data in the row you are applying the filter to, different options will be available.

Text Filters

If the column contains text, the following options are available.

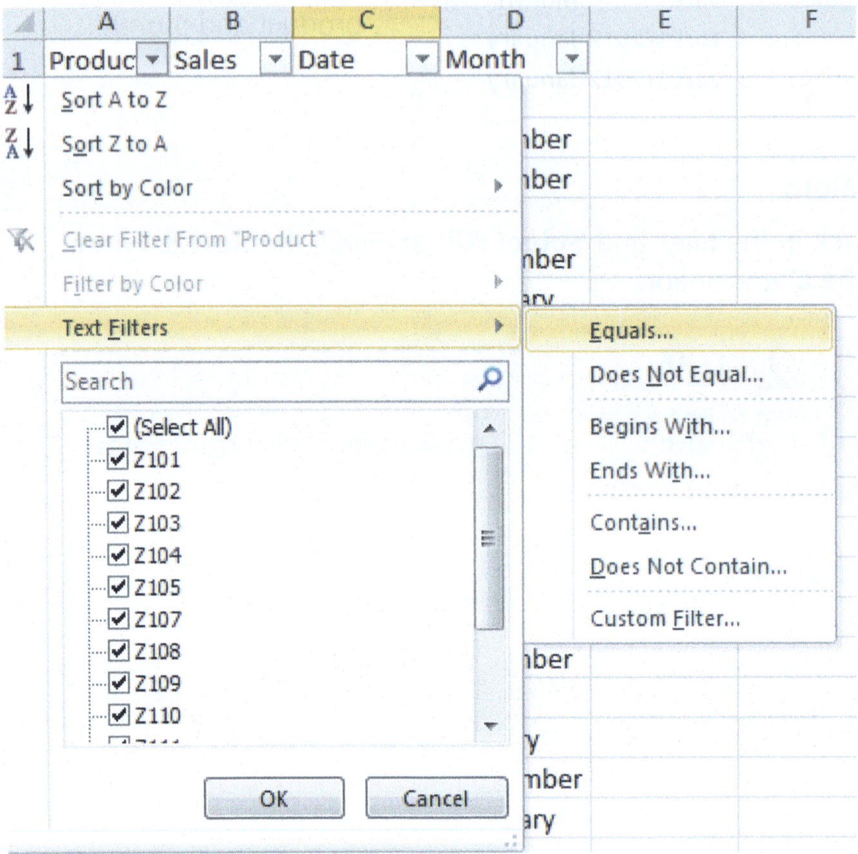

These should be self-explanatory. Custom Filter allows you to apply two constraints in your filter.

Numeric Filters

For purely numeric data, the following options are available:

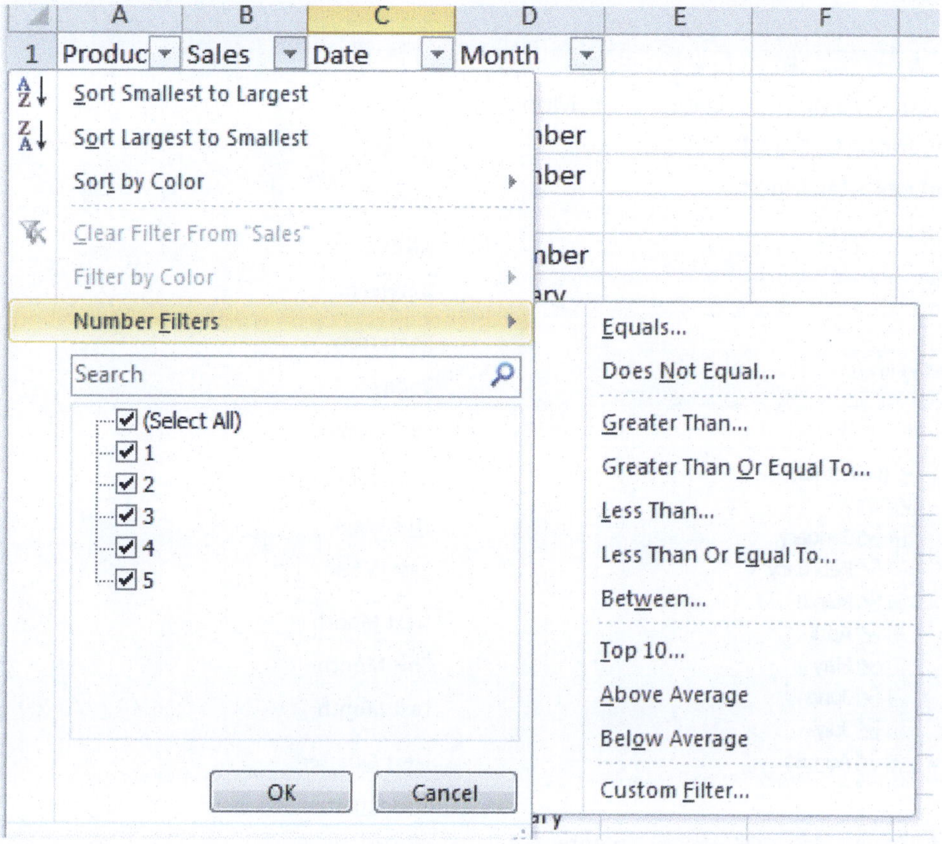

Date Filters

If the column contains dates only, there are many options available for your filter.

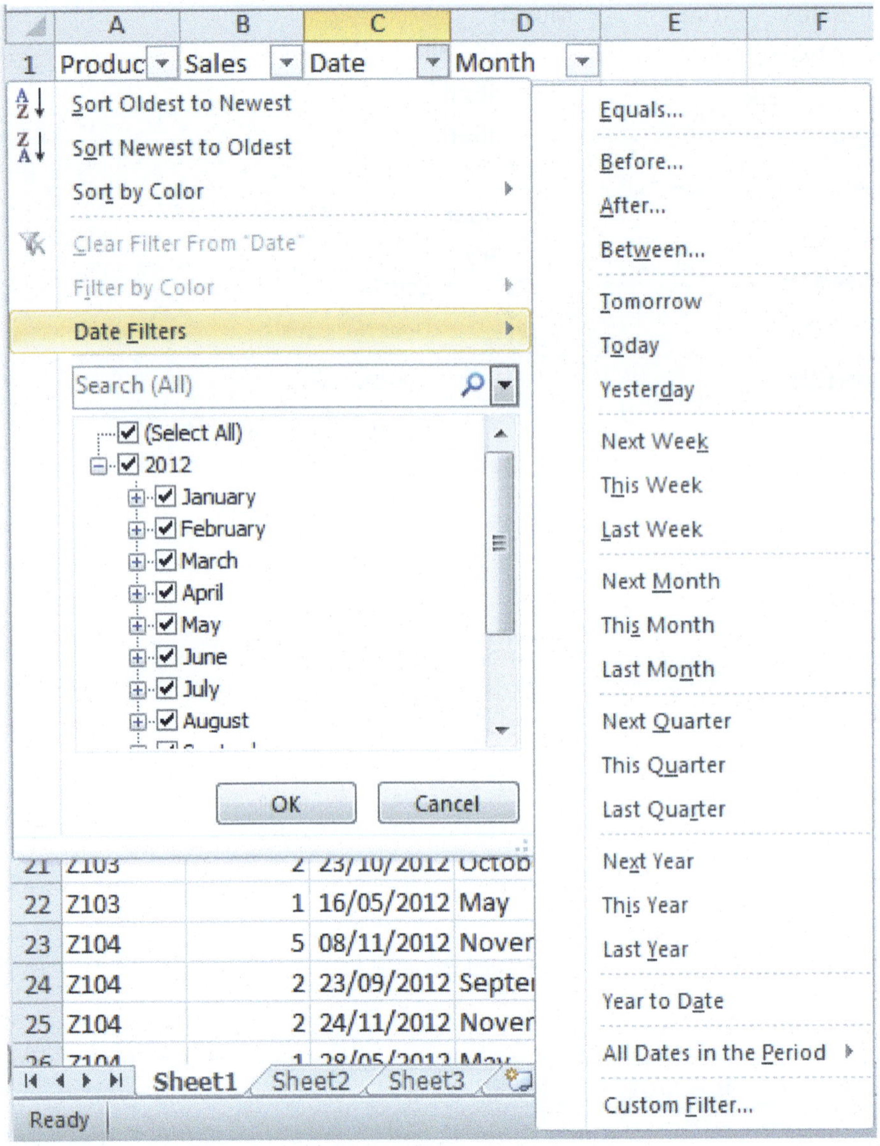

4.9 Concatenate

The **CONCATENATE** function can be used to join items such as text, numbers, cell references, or a combination of those items.

For example, if your worksheet contains a person's first name in cell A1 and the person's last name in cell B1, you can combine the two values in another cell by using the following formula:

=CONCATENATE(A1," ",B1)

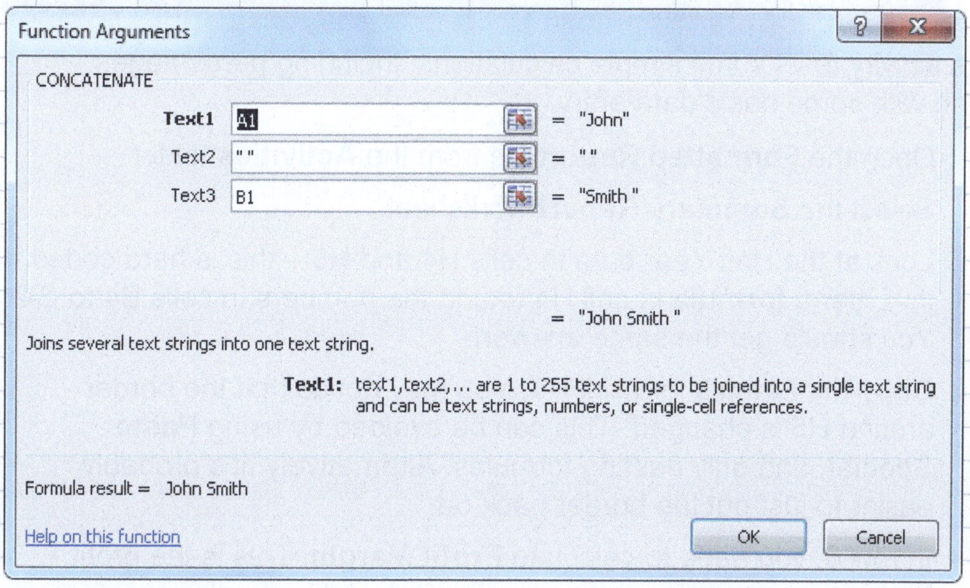

The second argument in this example (**" "**) is a space character. You must specify any spaces or punctuation that you want to appear in the results as an argument that is enclosed in quotation marks.

4.10 Activities

The activities in this guide are designed to test your knowledge on the techniques shown in this chapter. They may also use techniques used in previous chapters, to build up your knowledge. Suggested answers are available on MyKaplan, although it is better to refer to the notes and try to understand the methods than look straight at the answers.

Activity 4-1

This activity tests some simple calculations, including percentages, along with some basic data entry.

(a) Open the **Formatted Report** file from the **Activities** folder.

(b) Select the **Summary Report** worksheet.

(c) Look at the Half Year data in cells H4 and H5 – this is hard coded in. Enter a **formula** in cell H4 to add the numbers in cells B4 to G4. You should get the same answer!

(d) **Copy** the formula into cell H5. You may notice that the border around H5 is changed. This can be avoided by using **Paste Special**, and only pasting formulas. Alternatively, it's probably easier to just put the border back on.

(e) In row 6, you need to calculate **Profit Margin**. This is the profit figure as a percentage of sales. The calculation for this is:

Profit/Sales*100%

However, using the percentage format, the *100 is not required.

Enter 'Profit Margin' in A6, and add a formula to divide profit by sales in columns B-K.

	A	B	C	D	E	F	G	H	I	J	K
1		**BallCo Management Accounts Data**									
2											
3		January	February	March	April	May	June	Half year	July	August	September
4	Sales	8,648	6,850	8,264	6,823	7,176	7,083	44,844	6,019	7,223	7,579
5	Profit	4,701	3,496	5,202	3,641	3,967	2,732	23,739	2,081	4,219	3,444
6	Profit	0.54359	0.510365	0.629	0.53	0.55	0.39	0.529368	0.35	0.5841	0.45441351
7											

(f) Now change the format of these numbers to **percentage**, 1 decimal place

(g) The final quarter's results are:

Oct – Sales 8243, Profit 4343

Nov – Sales 8496, Profit 4611

Dec – Sales 7199, Profit 3290

Add this information to the report, along with the Profit Margin calculations.

(h) Add a total in column O for the second half of the year. Either enter this manually, or (better), copy and paste the Half year formulas and formatting – they will add up the previous 6 months' data.

O3 | fx | 2nd Half

	A	B	C	D	E	F	G	H	I	J	K	L	M	N	O
1			BallCo Management Accounts Data												
2															
3		January	February	March	April	May	June	Half year	July	August	September	October	Novembe	Decembe	2nd Half
4	Sales	8,648	6,850	8,264	6,823	7,176	7,083	44,844	6,019	7,223	7,579	8,243	8,496	7,199	44,759
5	Profit	4,701	3,496	5,202	3,641	3,967	2,732	23,739	2,081	4,219	3,444	4,343	4,611	3,290	21,988
6	Profit	54.4%	51.0%	62.9%	53.4%	55.3%	38.6%	52.9%	34.6%	58.4%	45.4%	52.7%	54.3%	45.7%	49.1%
7															

Change the column title to 2nd Half.

(i) **Autofit** Columns, and **Save** the file as **Activity 4-1** in the **Solutions** folder.

Activity 4-2

This activity allows you to practice Sorting and Filtering Data. It is important that after each step you check that the data is in the correct order.

(a) Open the **Eastern Region** file in the **Activities** folder.

(b) Autofit the Column Widths so the data can be viewed.

(c) **Sort** the data by Salesperson (A to Z) (remove sort).

(d) **Sort** the data by Month – January-December (remove sort).

(e) **Sort** the data by Month (January – December), then by Product code (add level).

(f) Add an **AutoFilter** to the data.

(g) Apply a filter to column A to only show sales from June and July.

(h) Apply a filter to column F to only show James Beardsley's data.

(i) Apply a filter to column C to only show amounts greater than or equal to 100.

(j) Save the file as **Activity 4-2** in the **Solutions** folder.

Page setup, presentation and printing 5

5.1 Introduction

This chapter will ensure that you are able to provide a document that is ready to publish and print showing only the necessary information that needs printing.

KNOWLEDGE
3.4 Select and use appropriate page layout to present, print and publish spreadsheet information.

At some point it is extremely likely that you will need to publish or print your spreadsheets. In this session you will be introduced to the following:

1 Headers and Footers.

2 Page Margins, Page Breaks and Orientation.

3 Set print area.

4 Print Preview and Print.

5.2 Headers and Footers

Headers and Footers are used to provide information in a document such as document titles, data owner, version numbers, page numbers, dates etc. **These are essential** as you may be asked to add headers or footers to your work for your SDST assessment.

To add them, use the **Insert** tab, then **Header & Footer**.

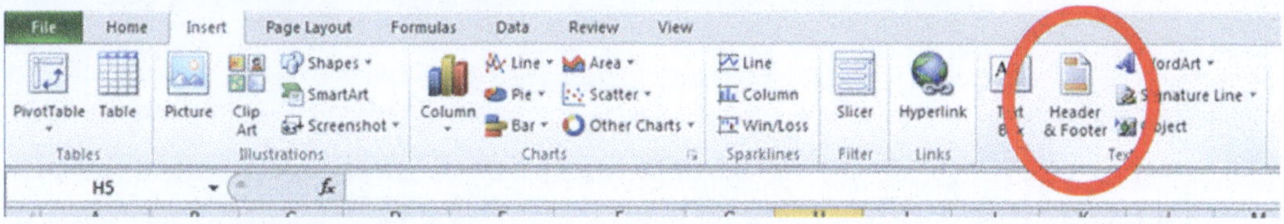

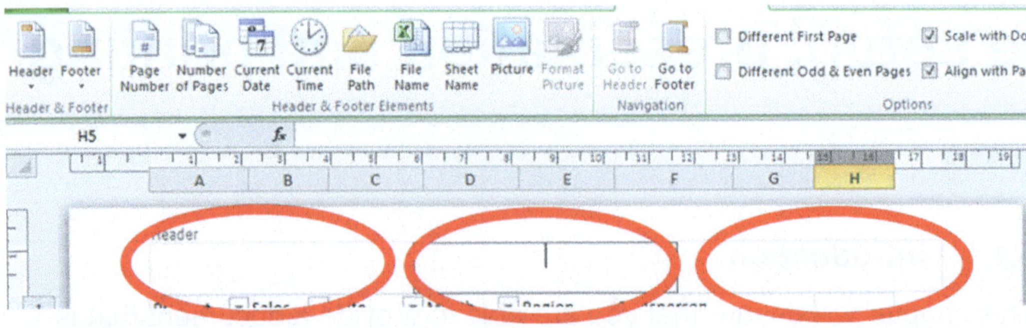

You will be taken to the Header – the page is split into three sections, where you can type in the header required. You can also select from the **Header & Footer Elements** in the Ribbon. These are fairly self-explanatory, but nothing too complicated is required for your assessment.

To edit the **Footer**, either navigate to the bottom of the page and click in the footer, or click the **Go to Footer** button.

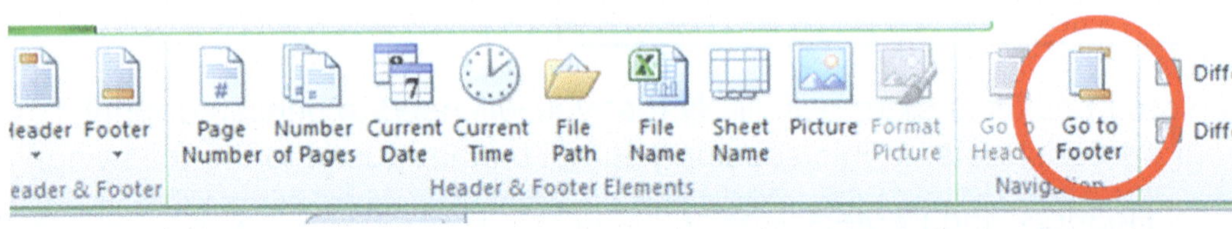

5.3 Page Margins, Page Breaks and Orientation

All three of these options can be adjusted from the **Page Layout** tab.

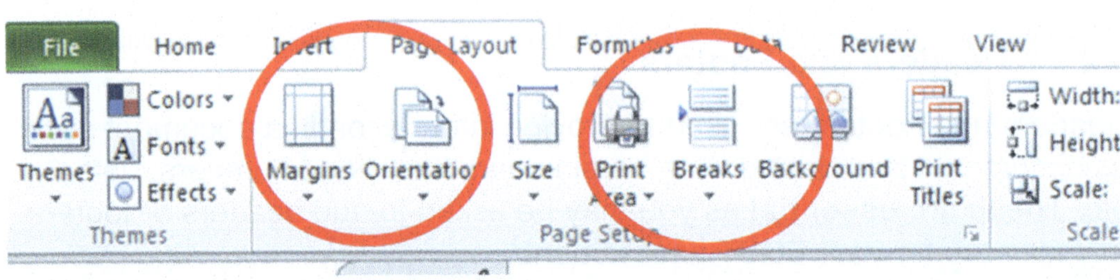

Margins

To prepare documents so that they are visually pleasing – especially for printing – you need to set the page margins. Select the **Margins** button.

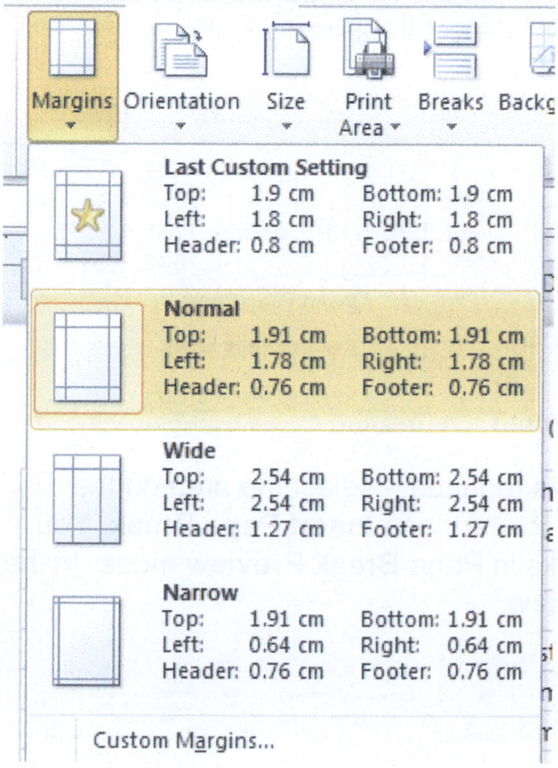

A few standard options are shown.

For more flexibility select the **Custom Margins** option.

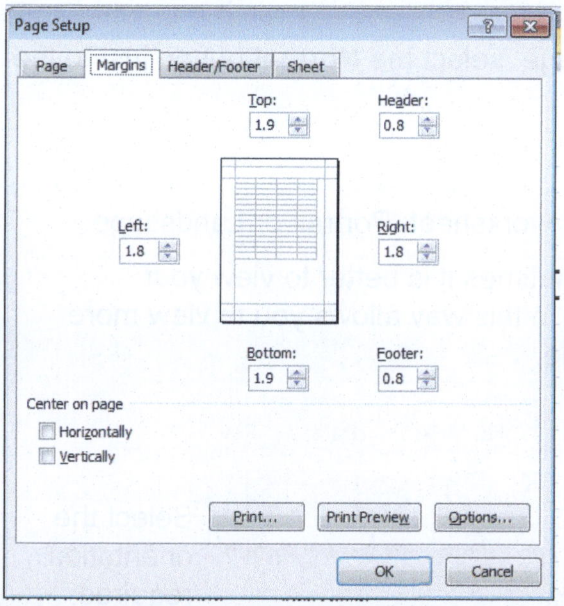

Each individual margin can be adjusted as required.

Once you have selected your margins these will be indicated on your worksheet by broken dashed lines.

Page Breaks

With your margins set, Excel will automatically insert a break in the data so that the right amount of data is displayed on a page. However, you will find that sometimes a natural break in the data is apparent and that you want to insert your own 'Page Break'. Select the **Breaks** button.

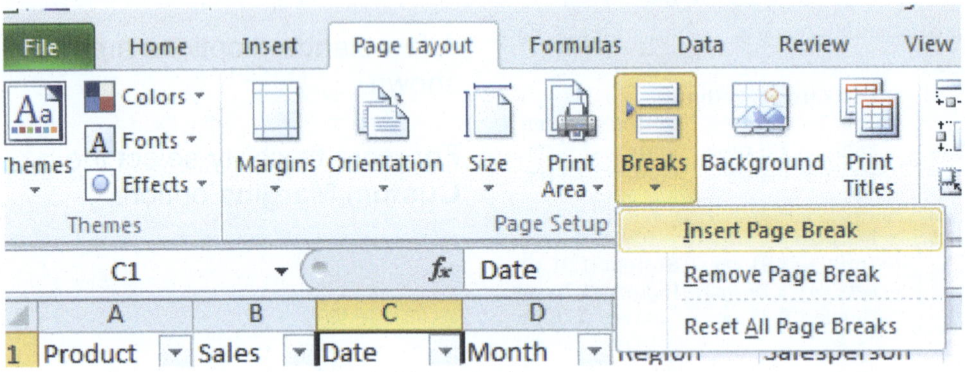

Use this to add or remove breaks as required – select the area on the sheet you would like the new page to start, and **Insert Page Break**. You can also view (and edit) page breaks in **Page Break Preview** mode. In the **View** tab, select **Page Break Preview**.

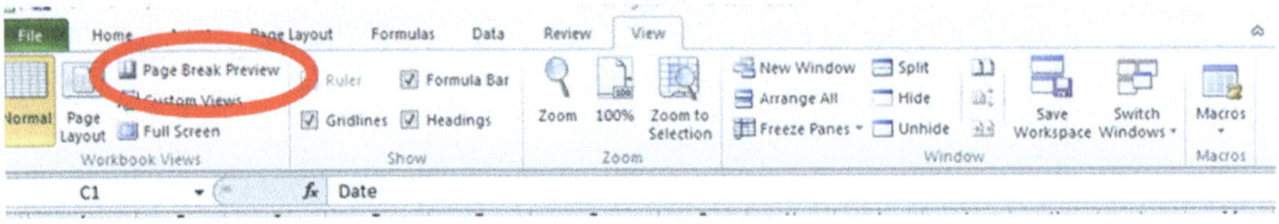

To return to normal view at any stage, select the **Normal** button just to the left of Page Break Preview.

Orientation

There are 2 ways to orientate your worksheet: Portrait or Landscape.

Excel defaults to 'Portrait', but sometimes it is better to view your document in 'Landscape'. Viewing in this way allows you to view more columns [but fewer rows] on a page.

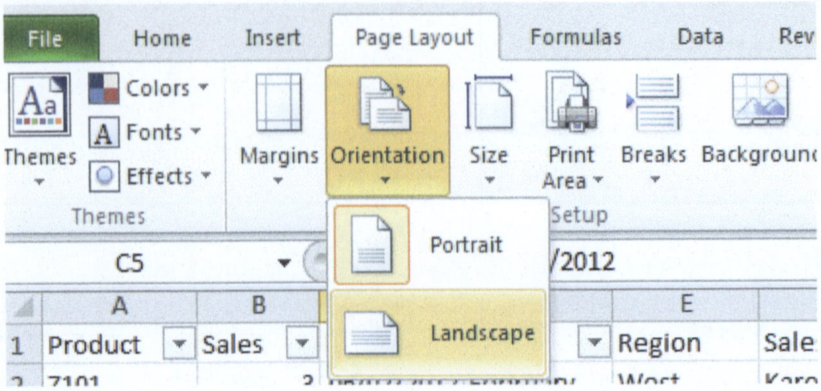

Select the orientation required.

5.4 Set Print Area

Sometimes you may want to print only part of a document. This is quite easy to do. Simply highlight the cells you wish to print, and click the **Set Print Area** button on the Page Layout tab.

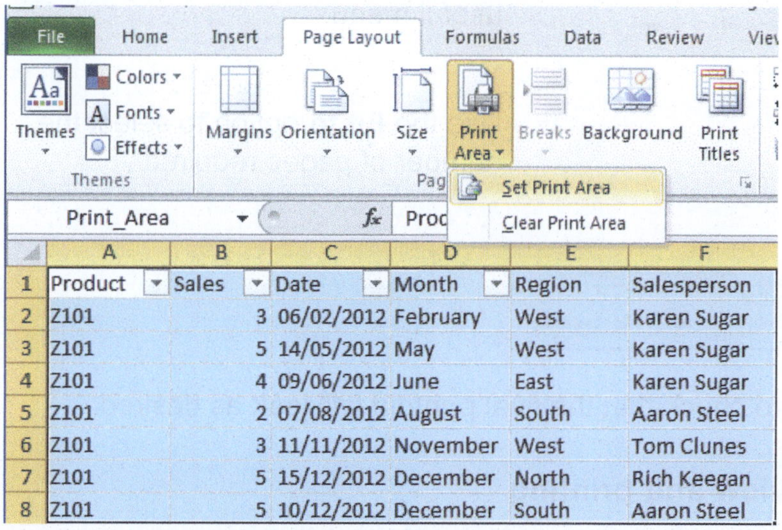

Choose **Clear Print Area** to remove this setting.

5.5 Fitting the data onto one or more sheets

One of the most useful features regarding printing is the ability to specify how many pages you want your data to appear on. Excel will then change the size of the font accordingly. Obviously this has practical limits – if you try and squeeze 1,000 lines of data onto one page, it will be impossible to read! However, it is invaluable for making your work look professional and user-friendly.

One way to do this is using the **Page Setup** menu. This is accessed by clicking on the arrow in the bottom corner of the Page Setup section of the **Page Layout** menu.

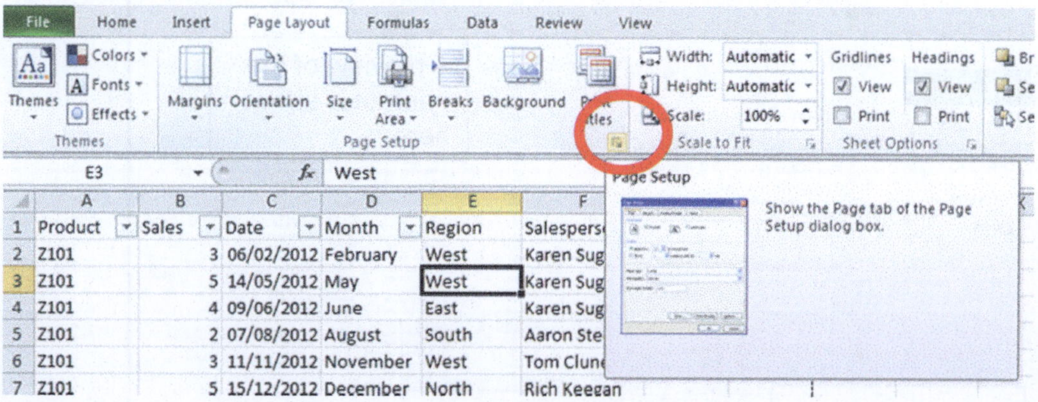

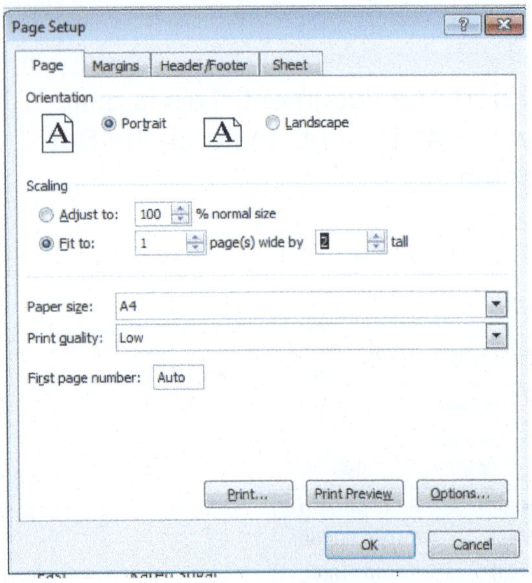

Several of the options already discussed can also be edited in this useful menu.

Use the **Fit to** option to select the number of pages required.

Use Print Preview to check that the final printout will look as desired.

5.6 Print preview and printing

Print preview has changed since Excel 2007. Rather than being a separate window view, Print Preview is found within the **File** tab, by clicking **Print**.

Having made all the adjustments to the data, format etc you will be in a position to print your document. Before you do this you should review it one more time – just to make sure. This is 'Print Preview'. When you are happy that your document is in the condition that you want it to be then you are in a position to 'Print'.

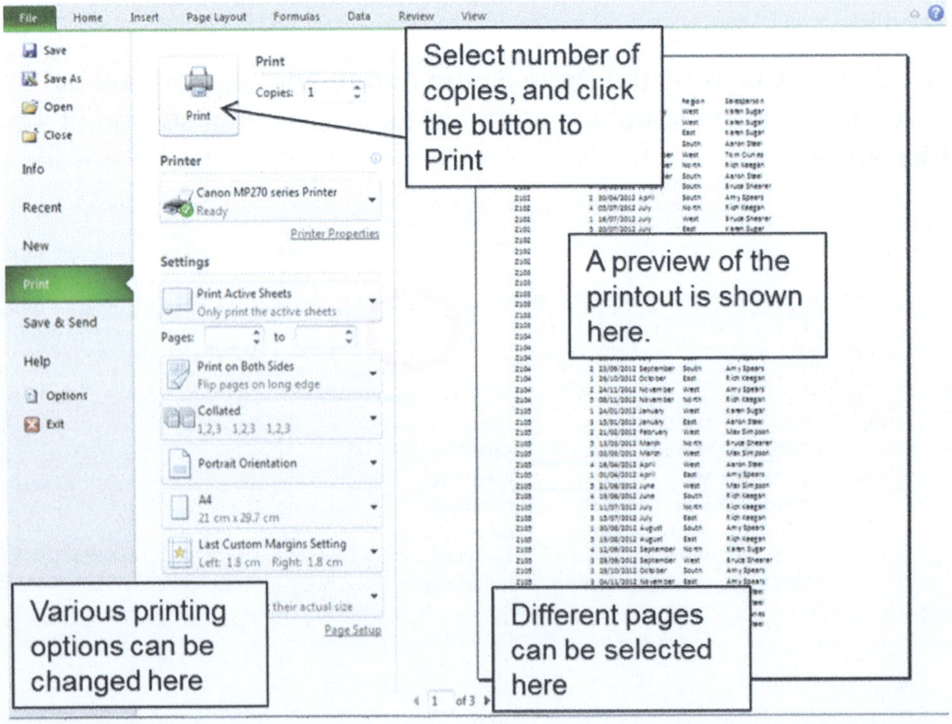

5.7 Activities

It is essential that before you submit any document you check that the print setup has been performed correctly – these techniques can be applied to any document. The following activities give you the chance to practice some of the more important ones specifically, but try the other techniques yourself on any document.

Activity 5-1

This activity requires you to setup a document ready for printing.

(a) Open the **Report for Printing** file in the **Activities** folder.

(b) Add a Footer to the document – with your name in the left section, and today's date in the right.

Note you can use the **Design** tab to insert the date, or just type it in.

(c) Return to Normal view (use the **View** tab).

(d) Change the **Orientation** to **Landscape**. Notice how the page breaks move.

(e) Go to **Print Preview.** Notice that the report requires two pages.

(f) Use **Page Setup** to fit the report to 1 page wide by 1 page tall.

(g) Note that the Print Preview shows the whole report.

(h) Save the file as **Activity 5-1** in the **Solutions** folder.

Activity 5-2

This activity is again centred on Printing a document, but also highlighting the use of Filters to find the information you need.

(a) Open the **Eastern Region** file in the **Activities** folder.

(b) **AutoFit** Column widths.

(c) Go to **Print Preview** – notice that the data spans 2 pages.

(d) Use **Page Setup** to fit the printout to 1 page wide by 1 page tall.

(e) Note that while this is possible, it will be hard to read. Exit print preview (click the **home** tab).

(f) Apply an **Autofilter** to the data.

(g) Sort the data by month – January-December, then by product, A-Z.

(h) Apply a filter so that only James Beardsley's sales are shown.

(i) Go to **Print Preview** – see that the data is visible!

(j) **Save** the file as **Activity 5-2-1** in the **Solutions** folder.

(k) Go back to the data – Filter so that Eva Nasri's sales are visible.

(l) **Save** the file as **Activity 5-2-2** in the **Solutions** folder.

Using Excel Functions

6

6.1 Introduction

This chapter will explain to you how to use functions within Excel.

KNOWLEDGE
2.2 Select and use a wide range of appropriate functions and formulae to meet calculation requirements.

In this session you will be introduced to some of the most commonly used and useful functions within Excel, which you will be required to use throughout your assessment.

6.2 Functions

In the previous chapter, we started to perform simple calculations. This is very useful, but more flexibility and speed comes from **Functions**.

These are specific words which tell Excel to perform much more than just adding up a couple of cell values. They range from the relatively simple functions like **SUM**, which we shall see in a moment, to more complicated tools.

Using a function

As mentioned at the start of the previous chapter, to enter a function into a cell, always start with an **EQUALS SIGN** first.

You then type the **NAME** of the function, followed by an **OPEN BRACKET** '**(**'.

The **ARGUMENTS** of the function are then required. These tell Excel exactly what to do, and depend on the function required. If more than one argument is needed, they must be separated by a **COMMA**.

The function is ended with a **CLOSE BRACKET** '**)**'.

This will become more important as we look at different functions.

6.3 The Insert Function button

A great way of getting used to functions within Excel is the **Insert Function** button *fx* located just above the column names.

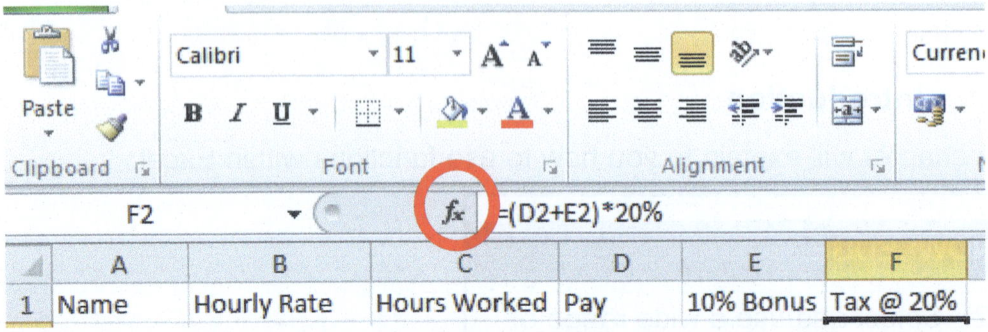

Clicking this button brings up the **Insert Function** menu, which can help work out which function is required.

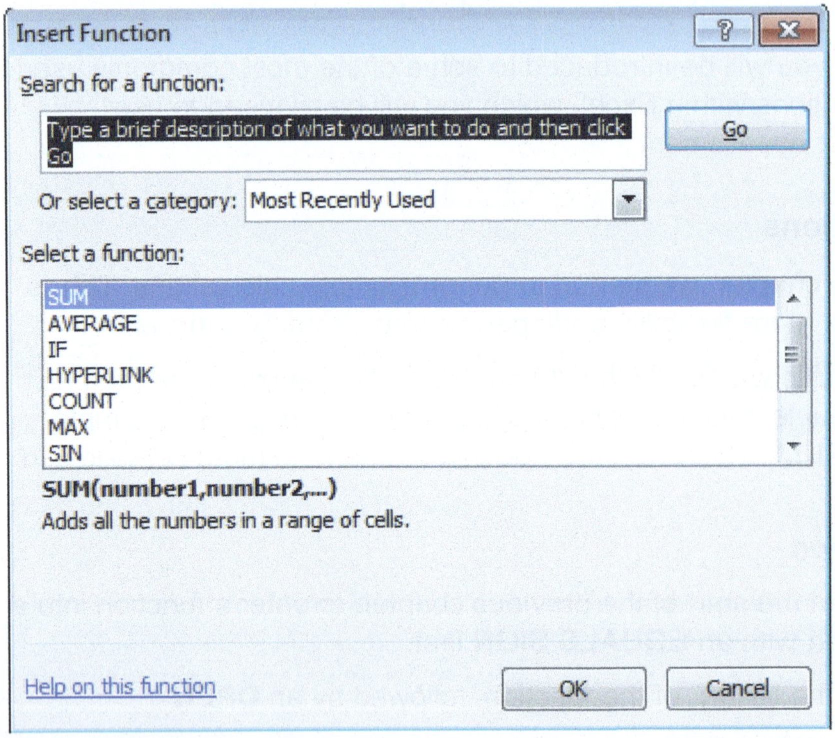

This allows you to type in – in plain English, what you require, and several options will be provided based on your search.

Using **Insert Function** also provides a more user-friendly way of entering the calculation you require, as we shall see.

6.4 SUM

SUM is probably the most commonly used function in Excel. As the name suggests, it is used to add up a selection of numbers. As discussed previously, you could use the **Insert Function** button:

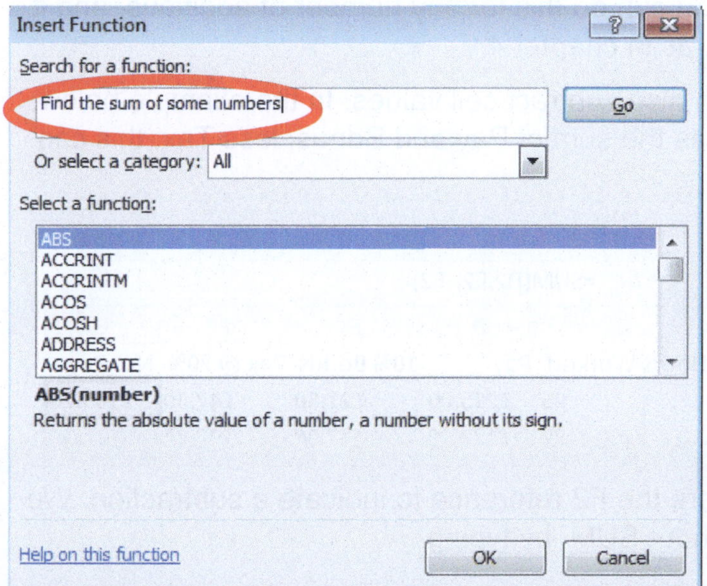

Type in what you require and click the **Go** button.

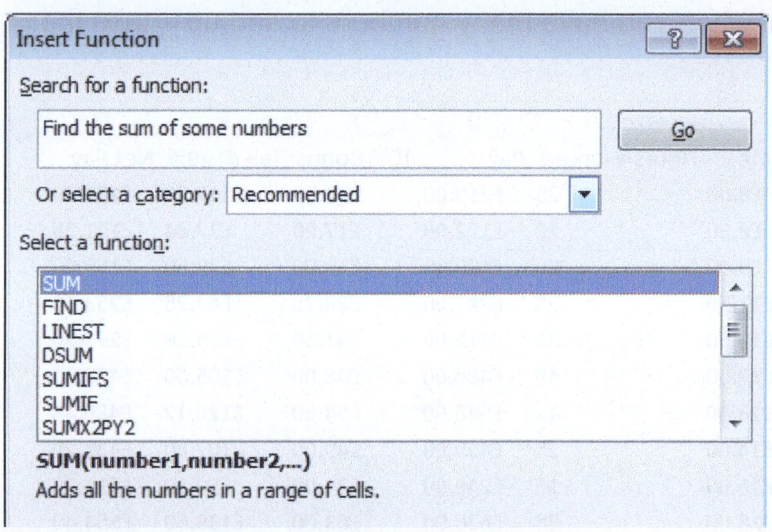

Choose the appropriate formula. Check the description to see if it going to perform the correct function.

To use the **SUM** function is described as:

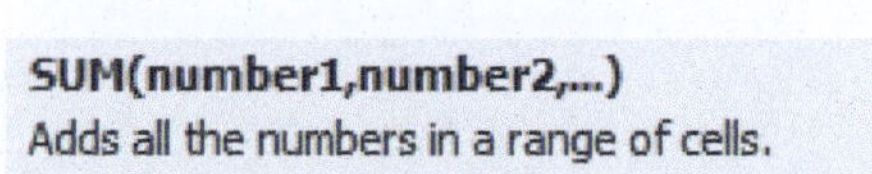

This shows how the function should be typed into a cell. As it is a function, you start with an '**=**' first, even though this is omitted in the description.

Number1,number2,... are the **ARGUMENTS**. In the case of SUM, these are the numbers (or cells) you wish to add. Each number you wish to add should be separated by a **comma**. For example, typing

=SUM(3,5)

will return the value 8. You can do this for any number of additions, and it is no different to using **+**, as in chapter 4.

Just like using **+**, you can also subtract cell values. In the example below, we want to find Net Pay as the sum of Pay and Bonus, less Tax; this can be done using SUM:

Clipboard | Font | Alignment | Number

G2 | f_x =SUM(D2,E2,-F2)

	A	B	C	D	E	F	G
1	Name	Hourly Rate	Hours Worked	Pay	10% Bonus	Tax @ 20%	Net Pay
2	Srnicek	£8.60	25	£215.00	£21.50	£47.30	£189.20

Note the minus sign before the F2 reference to indicate a subtraction. We could have done this without SUM, by typing

=D2+E2-F2

SUM is really useful when you have many numbers to add up – take the following example:

	A	B	C	D	E	F	G
1	Name	Hourly Rate	Hours Worked	Pay	10% Bonus	Tax @ 20%	Net Pay
2	Srnicek	£8.60	25	£215.00	£21.50	£47.30	£189.20
3	Watson	£8.60	20	£172.00	£17.20	£37.84	£151.36
4	Peacock	£9.00	20	£180.00	£18.00	£39.60	£158.40
5	Albert	£11.50	25	£287.50	£28.75	£63.25	£253.00
6	Beresford	£10.50	30	£315.00	£31.50	£69.30	£277.20
7	Batty	£12.00	40	£480.00	£48.00	£105.60	£422.40
8	Lee	£13.00	42	£546.00	£54.60	£120.12	£480.48
9	Beardsley	£14.00	35	£490.00	£49.00	£107.80	£431.20
10	Ginola	£16.00	15	£240.00	£24.00	£52.80	£211.20
11	Shearer	£18.00	35	£630.00	£63.00	£138.60	£554.40
12	Ferdinand	£16.00	32	£512.00	£51.20	£112.64	£450.56
13	**Total**						
14							

We now wish to put Total figures into columns C, D, E, F and G. Using the methods already discussed, we would either type:

=C2+C3+C4….+C12

Or

=SUM(C2,C3,C4,…,C12)

Neither of which is ideal – nor would it be practical if we had a list of hundreds of numbers to add up. Fortunately, Excel has an easy solution – rather than referring to an individual cell, we can refer to a **RANGE** of cells. We want to add the block of cells from C2 to C12, and would write that as **C2:C12** (the **:** indicating a range). Our **SUM** would be:

=SUM(C2:C12)

However, it is worth looking at how to enter this into a cell.

Direct cell entry

If you know the function required (as we do here), you can just type it in to the cell directly, as follows:

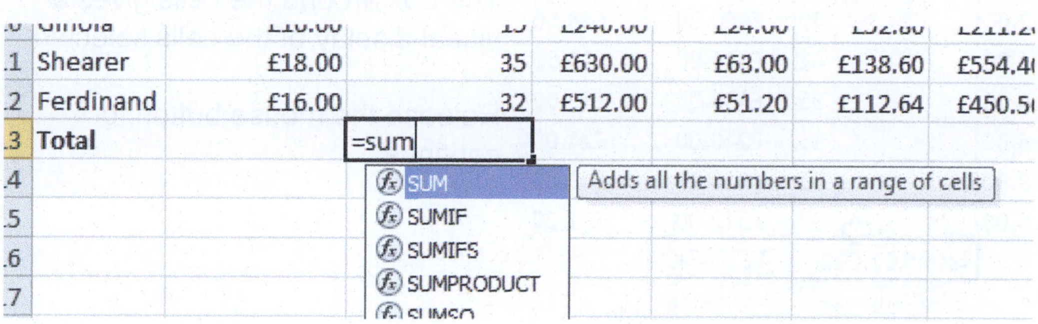

As you type, Excel will suggest possible functions. Note again the equals sign to start the function.

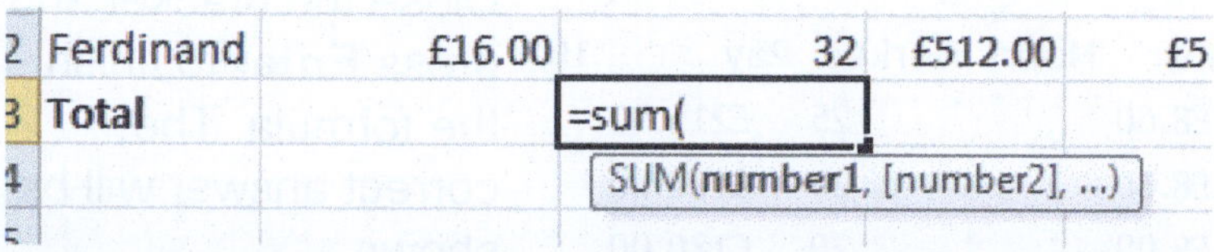

Open a bracket to enter the arguments. Note that the required format for the function is shown – **number1** is highlighted in bold showing that Excel is expecting you to enter the first number here. This becomes especially useful with more complex functions, as it helps you work out which part of the function you are on.

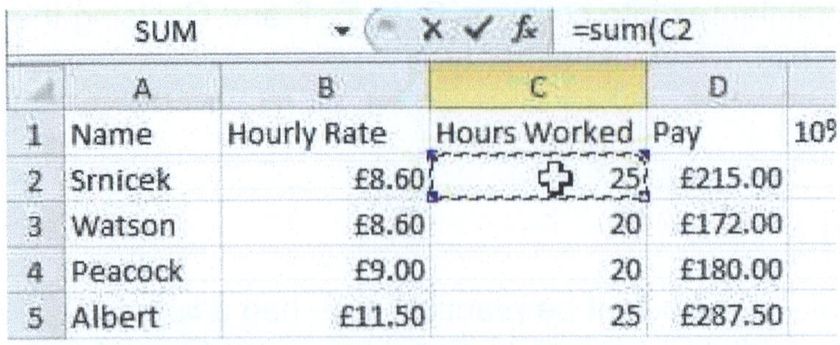

SUM | =sum(C2

	A	B	C	D	
1	Name	Hourly Rate	Hours Worked	Pay	10%
2	Srnicek	£8.60	25	£215.00	
3	Watson	£8.60	20	£172.00	
4	Peacock	£9.00	20	£180.00	
5	Albert	£11.50	25	£287.50	

Left-click (and hold) on the first cell you wish to include. Note the formula is updated.

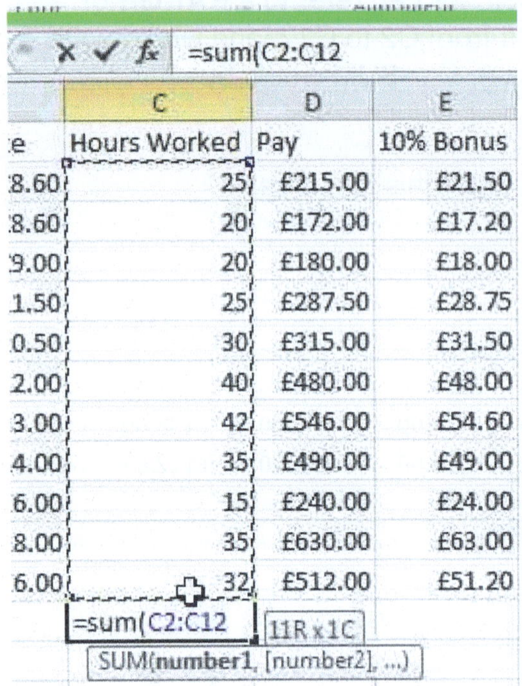

=sum(C2:C12

	C	D	E
e	Hours Worked	Pay	10% Bonus
8.60	25	£215.00	£21.50
8.60	20	£172.00	£17.20
9.00	20	£180.00	£18.00
1.50	25	£287.50	£28.75
0.50	30	£315.00	£31.50
2.00	40	£480.00	£48.00
3.00	42	£546.00	£54.60
4.00	35	£490.00	£49.00
6.00	15	£240.00	£24.00
8.00	35	£630.00	£63.00
6.00	32	£512.00	£51.20
	=sum(C2:C12	11R x 1C	

SUM(**number1**, [number2], ...)

Drag the mouse down to the last cell you wish to include – the formula is automatically updated with the correct syntax. This saves you having to remember how to type the cell reference.

The box around the cells gives a visual display of the cells selected.

Release the mouse button to continue.

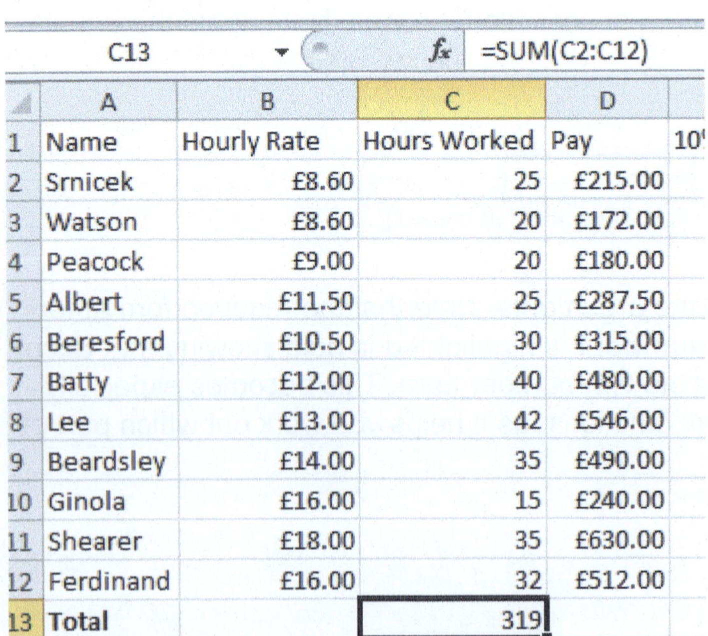

C13 | =SUM(C2:C12)

	A	B	C	D	
1	Name	Hourly Rate	Hours Worked	Pay	10'
2	Srnicek	£8.60	25	£215.00	
3	Watson	£8.60	20	£172.00	
4	Peacock	£9.00	20	£180.00	
5	Albert	£11.50	25	£287.50	
6	Beresford	£10.50	30	£315.00	
7	Batty	£12.00	40	£480.00	
8	Lee	£13.00	42	£546.00	
9	Beardsley	£14.00	35	£490.00	
10	Ginola	£16.00	15	£240.00	
11	Shearer	£18.00	35	£630.00	
12	Ferdinand	£16.00	32	£512.00	
13	**Total**		319		

Close the bracket and press **Enter** to finish the formula. The correct answer will be shown.

Using Insert Function

Although **SUM** is relatively straightforward to use, it's worth seeing how using **Insert Function** gives a different way of entering formulae.

To enter the sum into cell D13, after selecting the **SUM** function from the **Insert Function** menu:

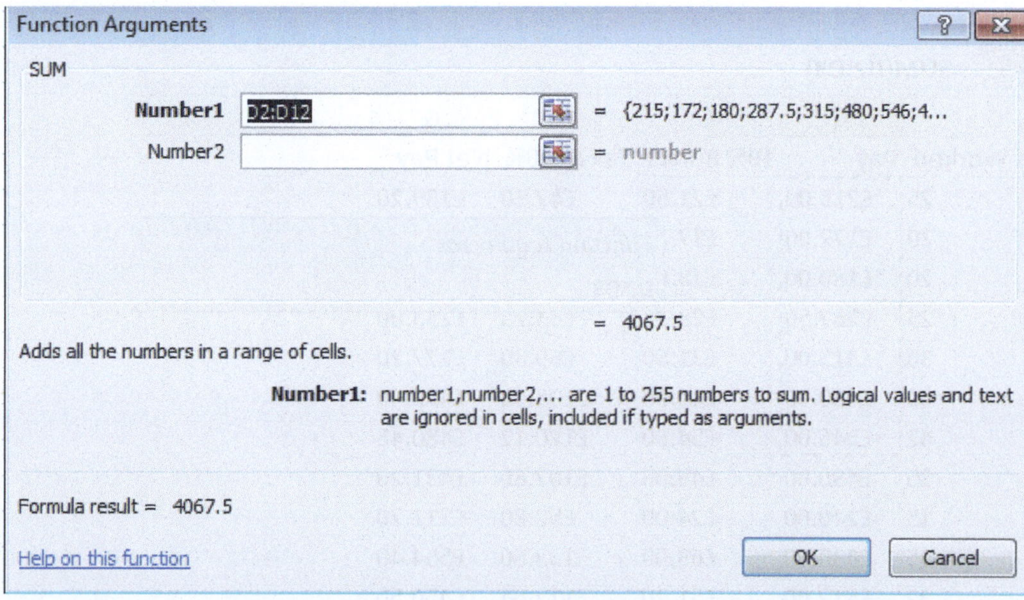

The Function Arguments dialogue box is displayed. This shows the arguments required – note that although only 2 are shown here, if more numbers are required then they will be added automatically.

Number1 has already been populated with the required range – D2:D12. Clicking **OK** would give the required answer. This is because Excel "guesses" which numbers you're likely to be adding up – it's not always correct, but it is here. It's a feature discussed later under the **Autosum** function.

If this wasn't correct, you could simply type in the numbers or range required into the Number1 box. However, you may prefer to use the method just shown, and select the cells visually – this is also possible. The button at the end of the box is a **REFERENCE BUTTON**, which appears throughout Excel. If you click on this, you can then select the cells required as before:

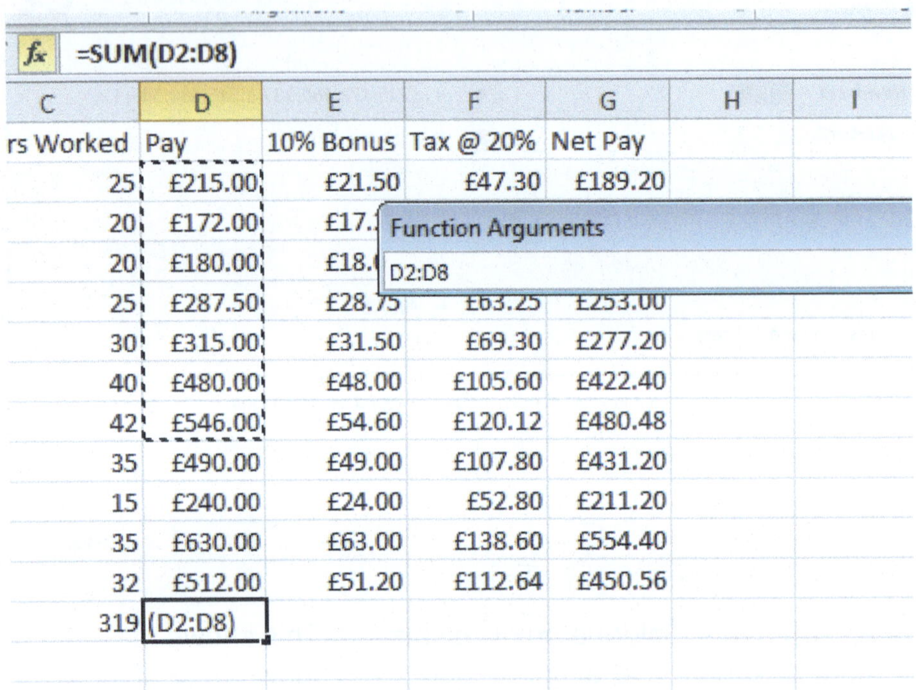

Once the correct cells are selected, press Enter. Click on the **OK** button to continue. The advantage of this method is that Excel automatically deals with the syntax – commas between arguments and open and closed brackets are added automatically (as well as the equals sign at the start).

Reminder

As we need totals for all 5 columns, these can be copied across as discussed in chapter 4.

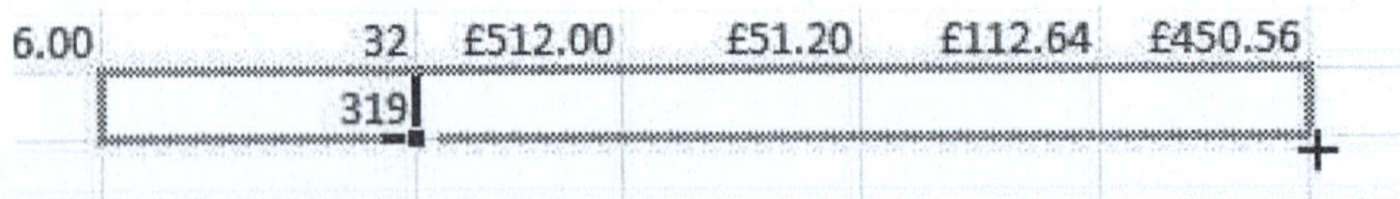

Drag across

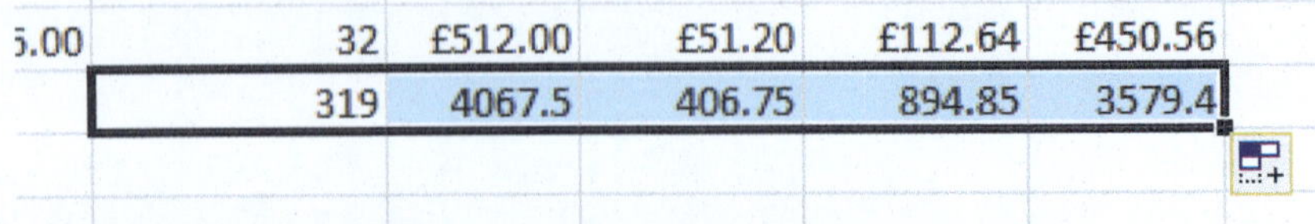

Note that the formatting is not consistent with the numbers above it – this would need to be adjusted.

6.5 AVERAGE

Another commonly used function is **AVERAGE**. This takes the average of a selection of numbers by adding them all up and dividing by how many numbers there are (arithmetic mean). It works in exactly the same way as SUM – the arguments are all the numbers or cells you wish to take the average of.

SUM | f_x =average(C2:C12

	A	B	C	D	E
1	Name	Hourly Rate	Hours Worked	Pay	10% Bonus
2	Srnicek	£8.60	25	£215.00	£21.50
3	Watson	£8.60	20	£172.00	£17.20
4	Peacock	£9.00	20	£180.00	£18.00
5	Albert	£11.50	25	£287.50	£28.75
6	Beresford	£10.50	30	£315.00	£31.50
7	Batty	£12.00	40	£480.00	£48.00
8	Lee	£13.00	42	£546.00	£54.60
9	Beardsley	£14.00	35	£490.00	£49.00
10	Ginola	£16.00	15	£240.00	£24.00
11	Shearer	£18.00	35	£630.00	£63.00
12	Ferdinand	£16.00	32	£512.00	£51.20
13	**Total**		319	£4,067.50	£406.75
14	**Average**		=average(C2:C12		
15			AVERAGE(**number1**, [number2], ...)		

Type =average(into the destination cell.

Select the cells you wish to find the average value of.

Close the brackets.

12	Ferdinand	£16.00	32	£512.00	£51.20	£112.64	£450.56
13	**Total**		319	£4,067.50	£406.75	£894.85	£3,579.40
14	**Average**		29	369.7727	36.977273	81.35	325.4
15							

The formula can then be copied across as before.

Note – the results can be checked – whenever cells are selected, the **Status Bar** at the bottom of the screen gives information, including the average, about those cells.

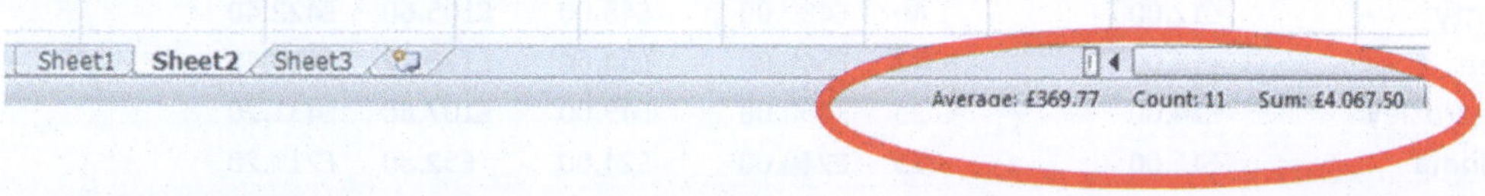

The average and sum are shown. Count is the number of cells with a value in.

6.6 MAX and MIN

You may be asked to find the biggest or smallest number in a list – use the **MAX** and **MIN** functions to do this. The format is again the same as **SUM**, for example:

=MAX(3,2,6,15,12,9)

will return the value 15, as this is the biggest number in the list. It is more useful to find the biggest number in a range of cells:

C15 | *fx* =MAX(C2:C12)

	A	B	C	D	E	F	G
1	Name	Hourly Rate	Hours Worked	Pay	10% Bonus	Tax @ 20%	Net Pay
2	Srnicek	£8.60	25	£215.00	£21.50	£47.30	£189.20
3	Watson	£8.60	20	£172.00	£17.20	£37.84	£151.36
4	Peacock	£9.00	20	£180.00	£18.00	£39.60	£158.40
5	Albert	£11.50	25	£287.50	£28.75	£63.25	£253.00
6	Beresford	£10.50	30	£315.00	£31.50	£69.30	£277.20
7	Batty	£12.00	40	£480.00	£48.00	£105.60	£422.40
8	Lee	£13.00	42	£546.00	£54.60	£120.12	£480.48
9	Beardsley	£14.00	35	£490.00	£49.00	£107.80	£431.20
10	Ginola	£16.00	15	£240.00	£24.00	£52.80	£211.20
11	Shearer	£18.00	35	£630.00	£63.00	£138.60	£554.40
12	Ferdinand	£16.00	32	£512.00	£51.20	£112.64	£450.56
13	**Total**		319	£4,067.50	£406.75	£894.85	£3,579.40
14	**Average**		29	£369.77	£36.98	£81.35	£325.40
15	**Max**		42				

So you can easily see in this case the most hours worked in the period.

Using **MIN** will show the smallest:

C16 | *fx* =MIN(C2:C12)

	A	B	C	D	E	F	G
1	Name	Hourly Rate	Hours Worked	Pay	10% Bonus	Tax @ 20%	Net Pay
2	Srnicek	£8.60	25	£215.00	£21.50	£47.30	£189.20
3	Watson	£8.60	20	£172.00	£17.20	£37.84	£151.36
4	Peacock	£9.00	20	£180.00	£18.00	£39.60	£158.40
5	Albert	£11.50	25	£287.50	£28.75	£63.25	£253.00
6	Beresford	£10.50	30	£315.00	£31.50	£69.30	£277.20
7	Batty	£12.00	40	£480.00	£48.00	£105.60	£422.40
8	Lee	£13.00	42	£546.00	£54.60	£120.12	£480.48
9	Beardsley	£14.00	35	£490.00	£49.00	£107.80	£431.20
10	Ginola	£16.00	15	£240.00	£24.00	£52.80	£211.20
11	Shearer	£18.00	35	£630.00	£63.00	£138.60	£554.40
12	Ferdinand	£16.00	32	£512.00	£51.20	£112.64	£450.56
13	**Total**		319	£4,067.50	£406.75	£894.85	£3,579.40
14	**Average**		29	£369.77	£36.98	£81.35	£325.40
15	**Max**		42				
16	**Min**		15				
17							

6.7 Autosum

Autosum is a useful shortcut to perform any of the above functions (and a few others) quickly and easily. The **Autosum** button can be found in the top right of the **Home** menu.

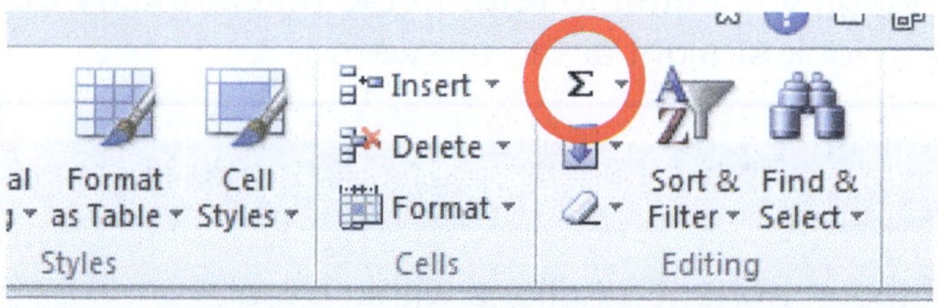

Instead of entering the function in the normal way, click in the destination cell and click the autosum button:

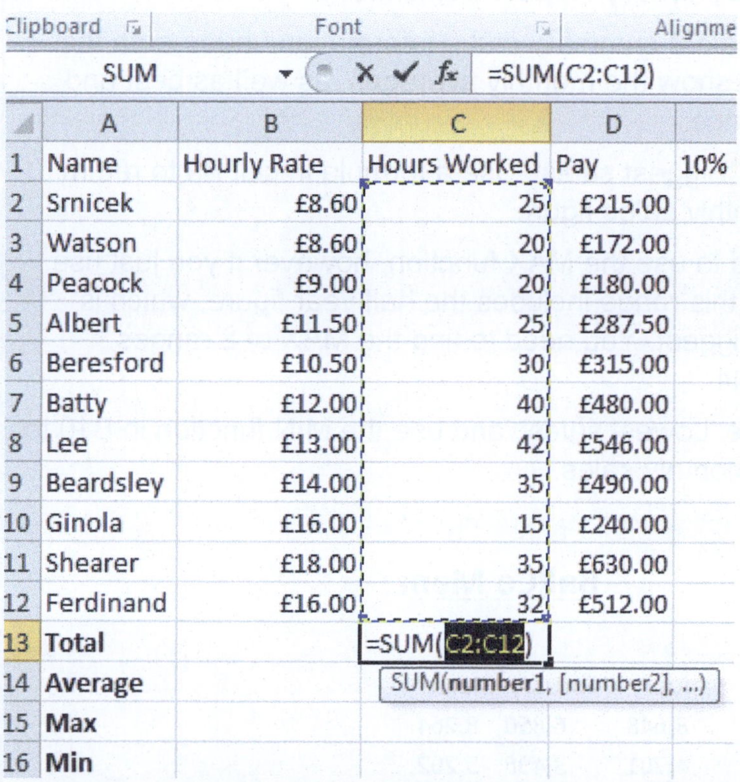

	A	B	C	D	
1	Name	Hourly Rate	Hours Worked	Pay	10%
2	Srnicek	£8.60	25	£215.00	
3	Watson	£8.60	20	£172.00	
4	Peacock	£9.00	20	£180.00	
5	Albert	£11.50	25	£287.50	
6	Beresford	£10.50	30	£315.00	
7	Batty	£12.00	40	£480.00	
8	Lee	£13.00	42	£546.00	
9	Beardsley	£14.00	35	£490.00	
10	Ginola	£16.00	15	£240.00	
11	Shearer	£18.00	35	£630.00	
12	Ferdinand	£16.00	32	£512.00	
13	**Total**		=SUM(C2:C12)		
14	**Average**				
15	**Max**				
16	**Min**				

Excel will put in a SUM function, and guess at the cells required.

If these are incorrect, you can reselect the cells needed in the normal way.

To insert a function other than sum, click on the small triangle to the right of the autosum button, and select the function required:

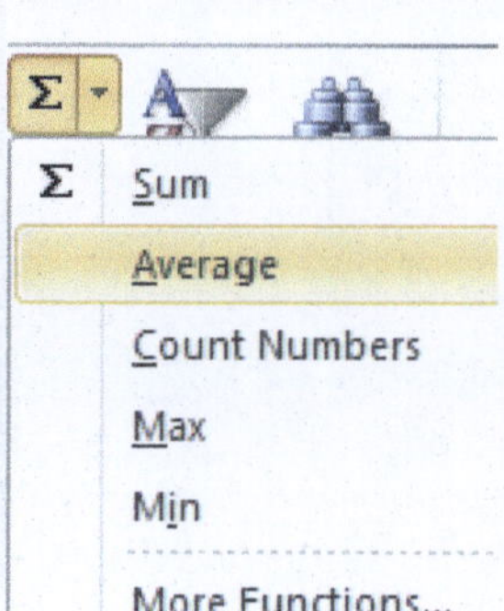

These are the most commonly required functions, although selecting the 'More Functions' option actually allows you to select any function available within Excel.

6.8 Activities

The activities in this guide are designed to test your knowledge on the techniques shown in this chapter. They may also use techniques used in previous chapters, to build up your knowledge. Suggested answers are available on MyKaplan, although it is better to refer to the notes and try to understand the methods than look straight at the answers.

Activity 6-1

This activity uses some of the important functions within excel – AVERAGE, MIN and MAX.

(a) Open the **Report needing summary** file in the **Activities** folder, and select the **Summary Report** worksheet.

(b) We need to create a summary of the information underneath the report. This will show the monthly averages, as well as best and worst performance.

(c) In cell A9, type 'Biggest sales'. Use a formula in cell B9 to return the largest monthly sales figure.

Hint – you need to use the MAX function, however if you just use =MAX(B4:N4), this range includes the half year figure, which is obviously the biggest. You need to find the MAX of 2 ranges – B4:G4 and I4:N4.

(d) In cell A10, type 'Lowest sales', and use the MIN function in B10 to find the worst monthly sales.

	A	B	C	D
1			**BallCo Mana**	
2				
3		January	February	March
4	Sales	8,648	6,850	8,264
5	Profit	4,701	3,496	5,202
6	Profit Margin	54.4%	51.0%	62.9%
7				
8				
9	Biggest Sales	8,648		
10	Lowest sales	6,019		
11				

(e) Change the value in C4 to 1000 – check that the value in B10 alters to reflect this.

(f) **Undo** the last command to restore February's sales.

(g) In A12, type 'Average Profit', and use a formula in B12 to calculate the **average monthly profit figure**.

(h) **Merge** and **Center** the title so that it is centered across all of the information.

(j) **Autofit** Column widths and **save** the file as **Activity 6-1** in the **Solutions** folder.

Activity 6-2

This activity is primarily included to allow more practice with percentage calculations, and use of brackets in a calculation. It also reinforces the functions already introduced.

(a) Open the **Southern Sales data** workbook in the **Activities** folder. This contains sales by month for 5 salespeople. We need to populate the Annual Statistics 2012 table.

(b) The **Sales** row is already populated. Use a similar approach to find the Average, Maximum and Minimum for each salesperson, and the totals on the right hand side.

Annual Statistics 2012

	SALES1	SALES2	SALES5	SALES3	SALES4	Totals
Average	155	130	155	164	187	158
Maximum	210	140	220	180	205	220
Minimum	100	120	100	142	150	100
Sales	1,860	1,560	1,860	1,969	2,245	9,494
Percentage Increase						
Percentage of Total Sales						

(c) We now need the percentage increase. This is the percentage increase in sales from January to December – calculated as

Increase in sales/January sales *100

As in Activity 4-1, we don't need the *100, as the percentage format will do that for us.

(d) If you are struggling to get the percentages to work, remember that you need to put the increase in sales calculation in **brackets** so that is calculated before dividing by January sales.

Annual Statistics 2012

	SALES1	SALES2	SALES3	SALES4	SALES5	Totals
Average	155	130	155	164	187	158
Maximum	210	140	220	180	205	220
Minimum	100	120	100	142	150	100
Sales	1,860	1,560	1,860	1,969	2,245	9,494
Percentage Increase	110.0%	7.7%	120.0%	-6.5%	7.9%	35.4%
Percentage of Total Sales						

(e) Calculate each salesperson's sales as a percentage of the total (K21) to 1 decimal place.

(f) **Save** the file as **Activity 6-2** and close it.

Cell referencing

7.1 Introduction

This chapter will guide you through the importance of referencing cells and how to create various types of cell referencing – including referencing to different workbooks or worksheets. You will also learn how to switch between viewing the results of our formulas and the formulas themselves.

KNOWLEDGE	
1.3	Combine and link data from different sources.
2.2	Select and use a wide range of appropriate functions and formulas to meet calculation requirements.

In chapter 4, simple formulas were introduced into your worksheet. These formulas were based on looking at the content of the individual cells and producing a mathematical answer.

You can create different types of formulas that use cell references to create the solution that you are looking for. This is particularly useful when you are using a particular number in a calculation that is used in different places and is also prone to change – such as tax rates.

There are three types of cell referencing that you have to be able to use for your assessment.

1 Relative cell referencing

2 Absolute cell referencing

3 Mixed cell referencing.

Note – the type of cell referencing used only matters when you COPY the formulas to other cells within the spreadsheet.

You may also need to refer to cells on another workbook or worksheet. This is relatively straightforward, but can create complicated looking formulas.

7.2 Relative cell referencing

This has already been introduced when dealing with functions. We have already seen that if you copy a formula down, the row number is updated. Likewise, if you copy a formula across, the column is updated. This is the type of referencing most people are used to.

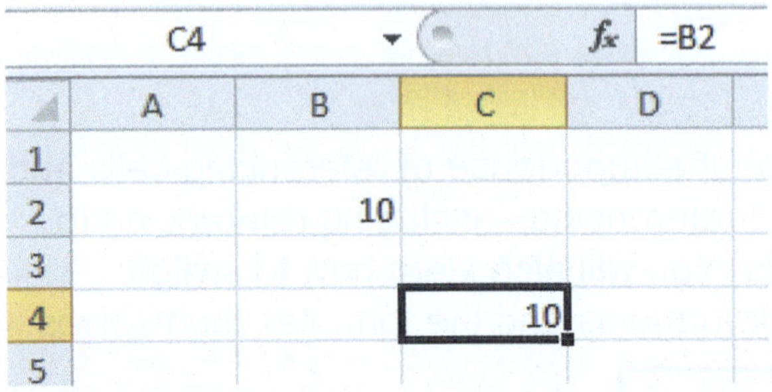

The formula in cell C4 is **=B2**. This means that when the value in cell B2 is changed, C4 will be updated to show this (C4 is **LINKED** to B2).

With relative referencing like this, if you **Copy** and **Paste** the formula in cell C4 into another cell, the reference to B2 will change. The way it works is as follows:

- If you copy the formula **UP**, the row number decreases.
- If you copy the formula **DOWN**, the row number increases.
- If you copy the formula **RIGHT**, the column letter increases.
- If you copy the formula **LEFT**, the column letter decreases.

It is easiest to see this in action. If we copy the formula into cell D3:

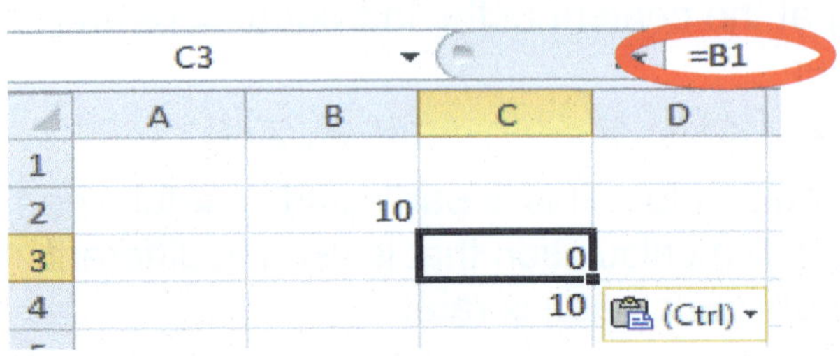

Here you can see the formula has been copied **UP** a row, so the row number in the reference has reduced by one. As there is no entry in cell B1, the result is shown as zero.

Similarly, we can copy the formula down, say three rows:

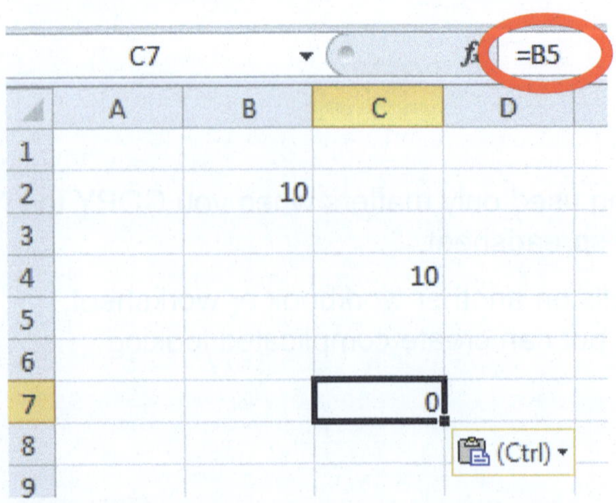

Copying the formula down three rows increases the row number by three.

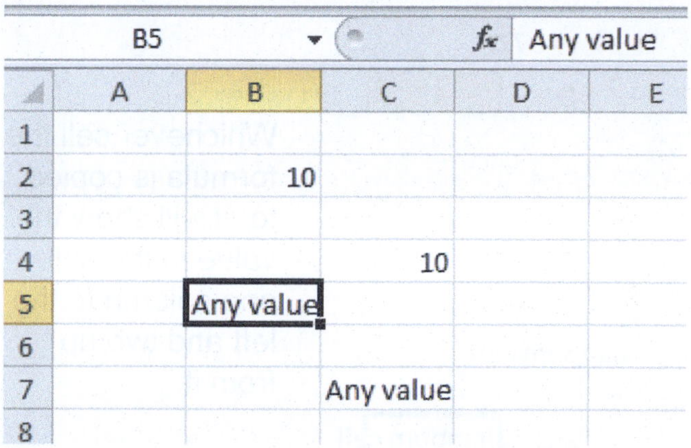

As you can see, typing any value in to B5 means that cell C7 is updated to reflect this.

Copying the formula across works in the same way:

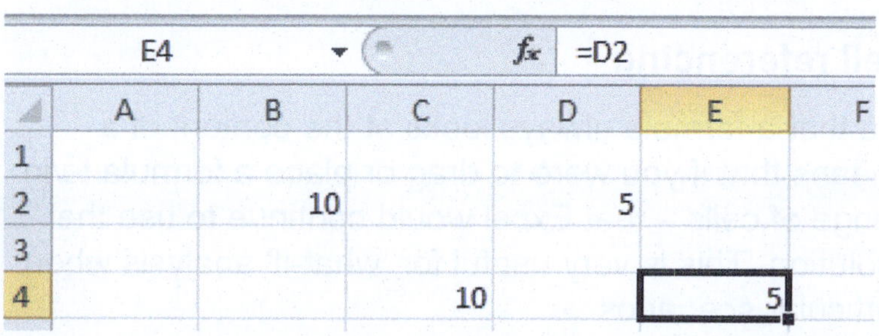

Copying across two columns updates the "B" to a "D" in the formula, as D is two letters after B in the alphabet.

NOTE – this can lead to errors! If you copy the formula two columns to the left, the "B" should be reduced by two, but there is no letter two before B, so an error is shown:

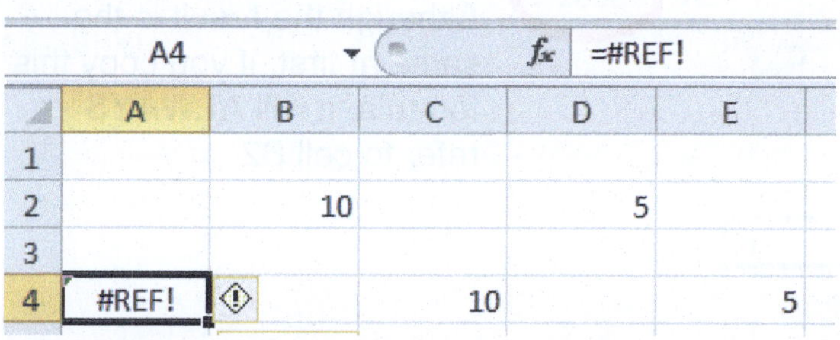

The way relative referencing really works is as the name suggests – the cell reference is relative to the current cell. For example the formula **=B2** shown in cell C4 is really saying "return the value in the cell one column to the left and two rows up from this one".

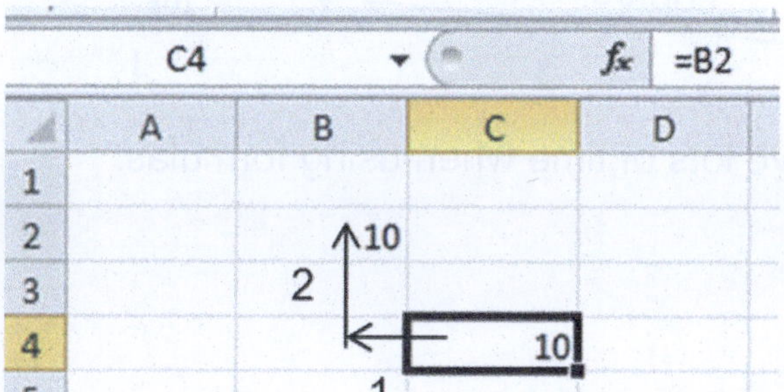

The reference **B2** is relative to the cell the formula is in, C4.

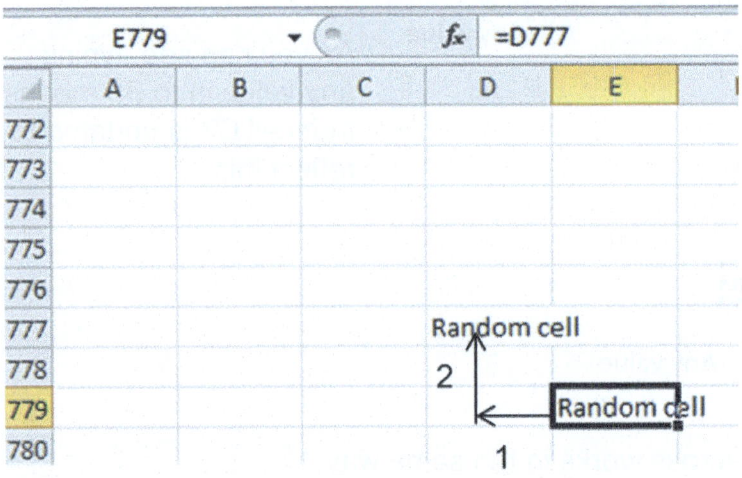

Whichever cell the formula is copied to, it will show the value in the cell one column to the left and two up from it.

7.3 Absolute cell referencing

This is used to ensure that a formula always looks at the content of a particular cell. This means that if you were to drag or place a formula to/in a different cell – or range of cells – that Excel would continue to use that cell to calculate the solution. This is very useful for 'what-if' analysis when you are looking at particular scenarios.

To create an **Absolute** reference we use a **$** sign before the letter and the number in the cell reference:

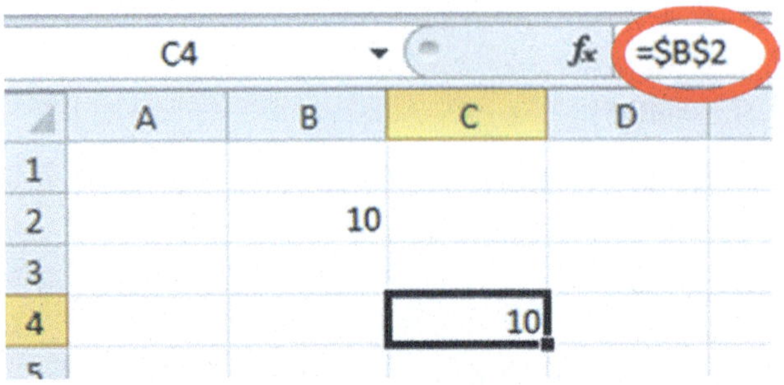

Although the result is the same at first, if you copy this formula, it will **ALWAYS** refer to cell B2.

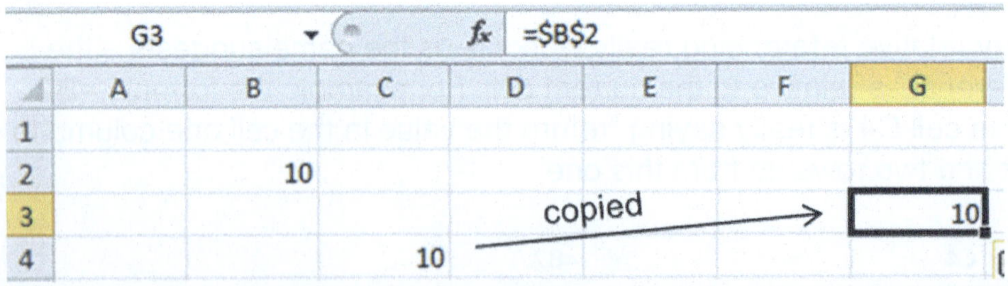

Absolute cell referencing can save lots of time when using formulas.

SUM =B4*8

	A	B	C
1			
2			
3	Staff number	Hours worked	Basic pay
4	F0254	35	=B4*8
5	F0255	32	
6	F0256	34	
7	F0257	35	
8	F0258	30	
9	F0259	40	
10	F0260	38	

Here, we need to work out basic pay for each staff member. If each member of staff is paid £8 per hour, the formula shown would work.

However, every time the labour rate changed, we would have to update all the formulas. Much better would be to enter the labour rate in one cell, and only update that when the rate changes. This also makes the spreadsheet easier to follow:

SUM =B4*B1

	A	B	C
1	Labour rate:	£8.00	
2			
3	Staff number	Hours worked	Basic pay
4	F0254	35	=B4*B1
5	F0255	32	
6	F0256	34	
7	F0257	35	
8	F0258	30	
9	F0259	40	
10	F0260	38	

The formula refers to the labour rate in cell B1 (formatted as currency), and will update with a new labour rate. We would like to copy this formula down to the rows below.

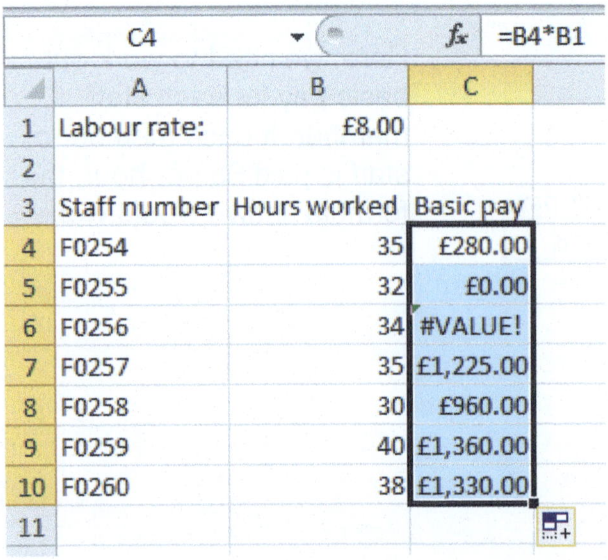

C4 =B4*B1

	A	B	C
1	Labour rate:	£8.00	
2			
3	Staff number	Hours worked	Basic pay
4	F0254	35	£280.00
5	F0255	32	£0.00
6	F0256	34	#VALUE!
7	F0257	35	£1,225.00
8	F0258	30	£960.00
9	F0259	40	£1,360.00
10	F0260	38	£1,330.00
11			

Using **Autofill**, as seen in the last chapter, gives disastrous results!

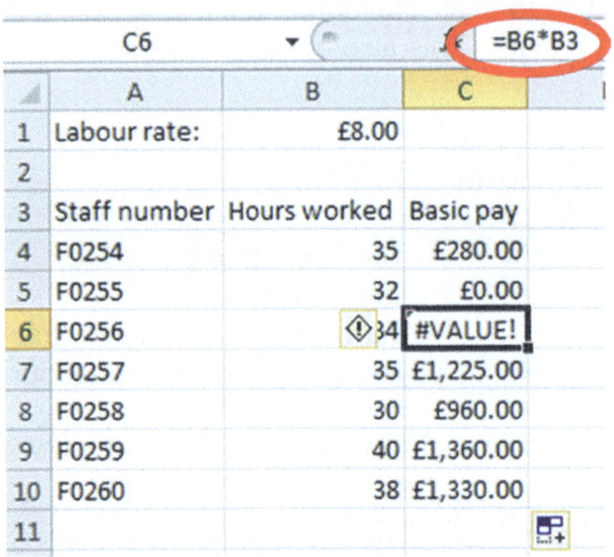

C6 =B6*B3

	A	B	C
1	Labour rate:	£8.00	
2			
3	Staff number	Hours worked	Basic pay
4	F0254	35	£280.00
5	F0255	32	£0.00
6	F0256	34	#VALUE!
7	F0257	35	£1,225.00
8	F0258	30	£960.00
9	F0259	40	£1,360.00
10	F0260	38	£1,330.00
11			

Further investigation reveals the problem, while the correct hours worked are being used (cell B6), instead of multiplying by cell B1 as required, the reference has been updated to B3 – because a **RELATIVE** reference has been used.

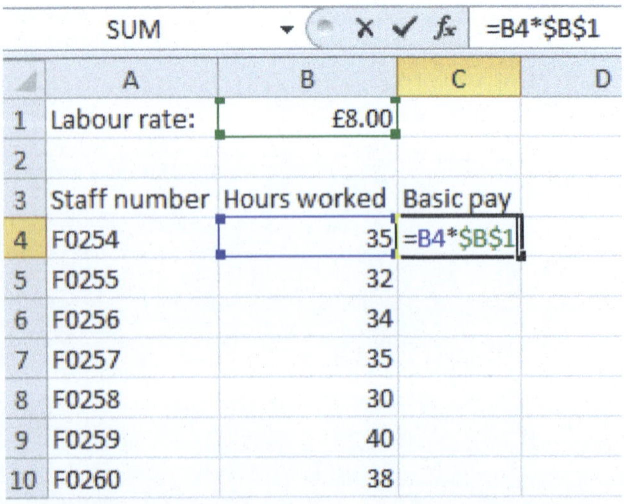

SUM =B4*$B$1

	A	B	C	D
1	Labour rate:	£8.00		
2				
3	Staff number	Hours worked	Basic pay	
4	F0254	35	=B4*$B$1	
5	F0255	32		
6	F0256	34		
7	F0257	35		
8	F0258	30		
9	F0259	40		
10	F0260	38		

The **$** signs in the reference indicate an **ABSOLUTE** reference.

C4 | f_x | =B4*$B$1

	A	B	C	D
1	Labour rate:	£8.00		
2				
3	Staff number	Hours worked	Basic pay	
4	F0254	35	£280.00	
5	F0255	32	£256.00	
6	F0256	34	£272.00	
7	F0257	35	£280.00	
8	F0258	30	£240.00	
9	F0259	40	£320.00	
10	F0260	38	£304.00	

The formulas all now refer to cell **B1**, as required.

7.4 Mixed cell referencing

This is a combination of both **Absolute** and **Relative** referencing. Remember, the type of referencing is only relevant when you copy a formula. You might want the row number to be relative (i.e. change when you copy), but the column to remain fixed.

The **$** sign used in absolute referencing above is key here. When we used the absolute reference **$B$1**, what we really said was "keep the column and the row fixed." It can be broken up as **$B** – keep the column fixed, and **$1**, keep the row fixed.

D2 | f_x

	A	B	C	D
1	Labour rate:	Bonus %		
2	£8.00	10%		
3				
4	Staff number	Hours worked	Basic pay	Bonus
5	F0254	35		
6	F0255	32		
7	F0256	34		
8	F0257	35		
9	F0258	30		
10	F0259	40		
11	F0260	38		

Let's take a similar example:

We need to calculate basic pay in the same way. We can use an absolute reference like before, but a mixed reference is actually better.

C5 | f_x =B5*A$2

	A	B	C	D
1	Labour rate:	Bonus %		
2	£8.00	10%		
3				
4	Staff number	Hours worked	Basic pay	Bonus
5	F0254	35	£280.00	
6	F0255	32		
7	F0256	34		
8	F0257	35		
9	F0258	30		
10	F0259	40		
11	F0260	38		

This formula gives the same result as before. However, when copied down, the **$2** in the reference to cell A2 means that the row will remain fixed as before

C10 | f_x =B10*A$2

	A	B	C	D
1	Labour rate:	Bonus %		
2	£8.00	10%		
3				
4	Staff number	Hours worked	Basic pay	Bonus
5	F0254	35	£280.00	
6	F0255	32	£256.00	
7	F0256	34	£272.00	
8	F0257	35	£280.00	
9	F0258	30	£240.00	
10	F0259	40	£320.00	
11	F0260	38	£304.00	

As the formula has been copied down, the column does not change anyway. The $2 means that cell A2 is still referred to correctly.

D5 | f_x =C5*B$2

	A	B	C	D
1	Labour rate:	Bonus %		
2	£8.00	10%		
3				
4	Staff number	Hours worked	Basic pay	Bonus
5	F0254	35	£280.00	£28.00
6	F0255	32	£256.00	£25.60
7	F0256	34	£272.00	£27.20
8	F0257	35	£280.00	£28.00
9	F0258	30	£240.00	£24.00
10	F0259	40	£320.00	£32.00
11	F0260	38	£304.00	£30.40

You can copy the formula across though, and the bonus is correctly calculated based on cell **B2** – because there is no $ before the A in the original formula, the column is not fixed.

Shortcut

When entering a cell reference in a formula, pressing **F4** repeatedly will cycle through the different types of referencing by adding/removing $ signs as required.

7.5 Viewing formulas

It is very useful, and you will need to show the formulas in the cells rather than the calculation in your assessment. In the **Formulas** tab, select **Show Formulas**.

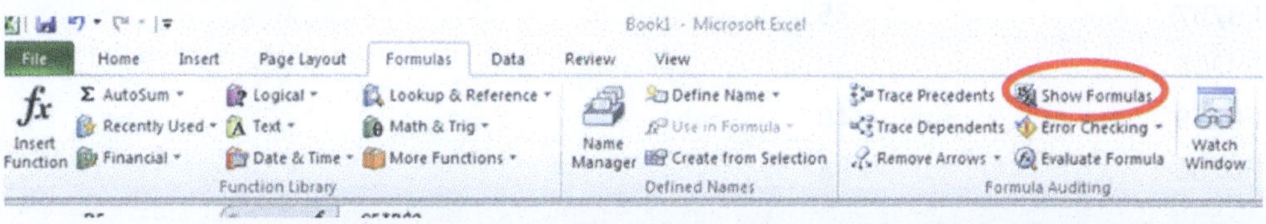

Shortcut

Ctrl + ` [control and grave] will do the same as above. The same routine will also return you to the normal view.

7.6 Referencing other worksheets

We have dealt with cell referencing within a worksheet. It is very common that a calculation will need to refer to a cell on another worksheet within the same workbook. This works in the same way, but now instead of saying "Use the value in cell A1", we need to say "Use the value in Cell A1 on Sheet 2" (for example). The format for this would be:

='Sheet 2'!A1

The 'A1' part of the formula is referring to cell A1 – to specify the sheet name, use the quote marks, followed by an exclamation mark.

This is fairly cumbersome, and prone to typing errors. Fortunately, Excel makes this referencing fairly straightforward to achieve. Remember that when entering a formula, you can click on the cell you wish to use rather than typing its reference. This is true whether the cell is on the current worksheet or not.

NOTE: the use of quote marks is only required if the worksheet name contains two or more items and there are spaces between the items e.g. *worksheet* would not require quote marks but *work sheet* would. The exclamation mark is always required.

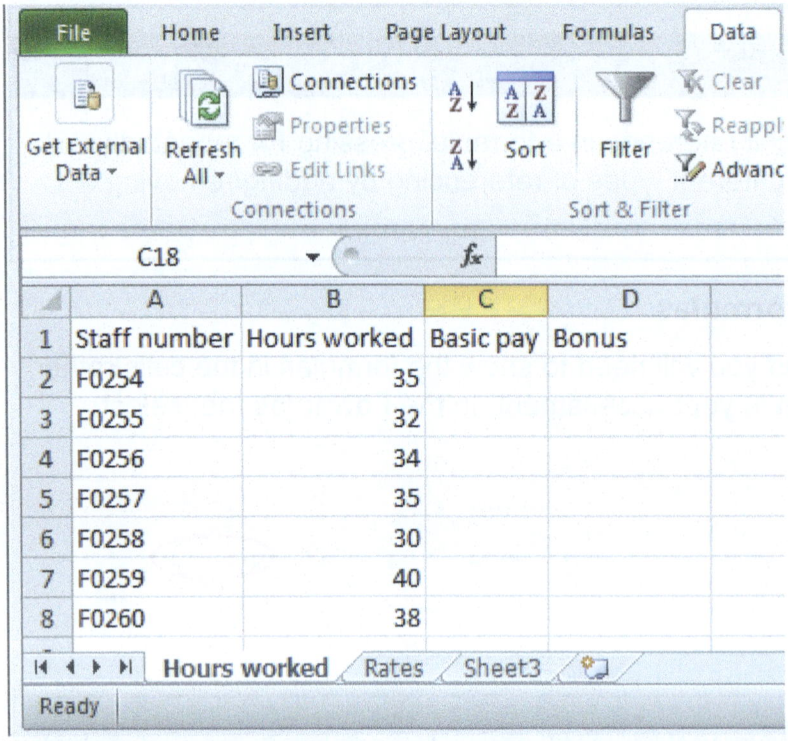

Using the same example, the basic rate of pay and bonus rate are now on the 'Rates' worksheet.

To calculate 'Basic pay', select cell C2 and press '=' to start entering a formula:

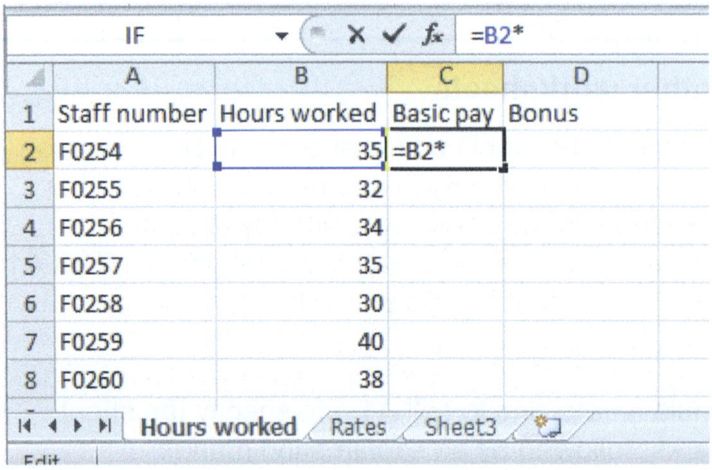

Select the hours worked cell in the usual way (or just type 'B2'). We wish to multiply this by the labour rate, so use '*'. You can now select the labour rate from the Rates worksheet.

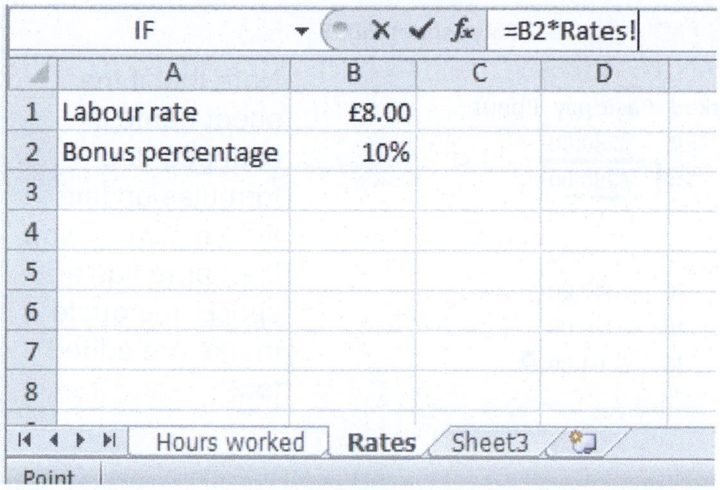

When the Rates sheet is selected, the first part of the reference is automatically filled in. Note that there are no quote marks around the name here as it is one word with no space

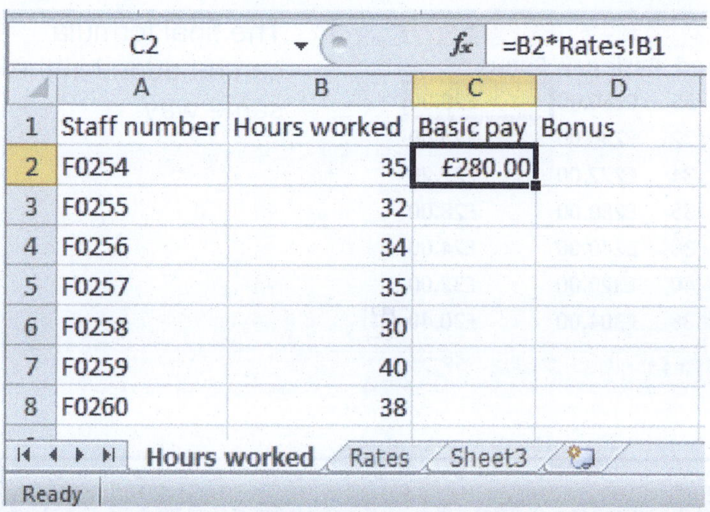

Select the cell, and press **Enter** to complete the formula. This can then be copied in the normal way – the usual referencing rules apply, so we need to use $ signs for an **absolute** reference.

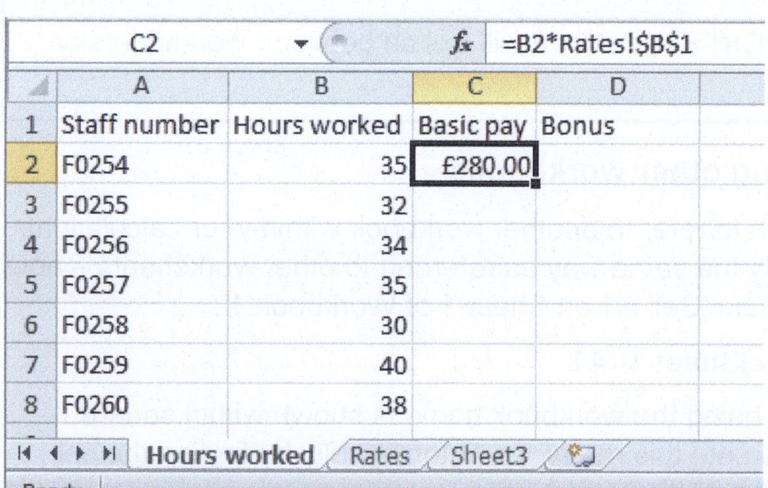

Now the formula can be copied down effectively to achieve the desired result.

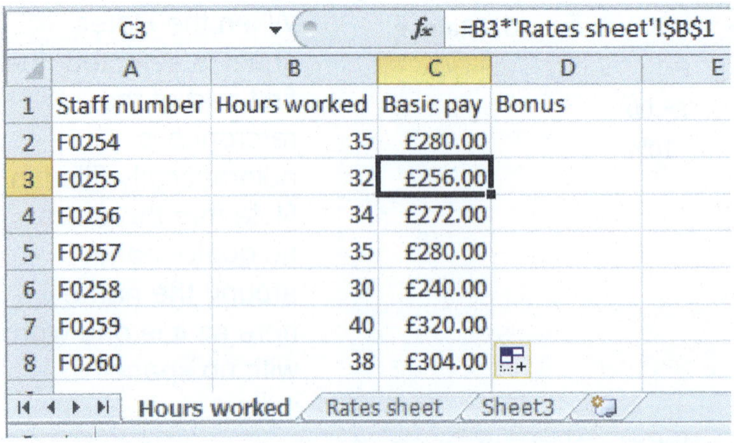

C3 =B3*'Rates sheet'!$B$1

	A	B	C	D	E
1	Staff number	Hours worked	Basic pay	Bonus	
2	F0254	35	£280.00		
3	F0255	32	£256.00		
4	F0256	34	£272.00		
5	F0257	35	£280.00		
6	F0258	30	£240.00		
7	F0259	40	£320.00		
8	F0260	38	£304.00		

Hours worked / Rates sheet / Sheet3

Note that if the sheet name is changed, the formulas update automatically. Now the name has a space, the quote marks are added too.

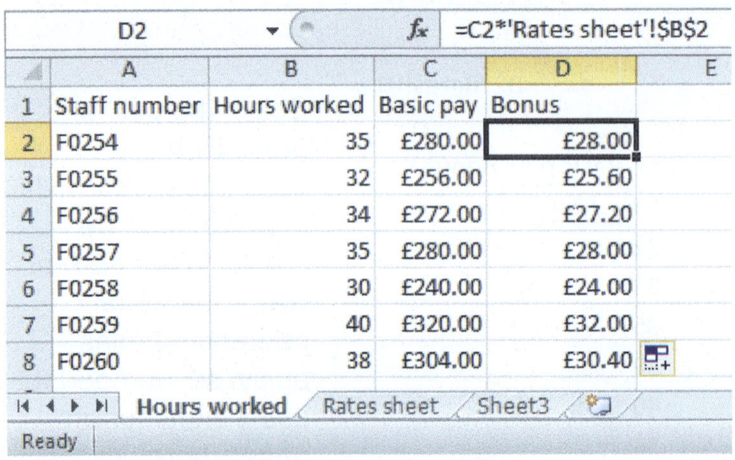

D2 =C2*'Rates sheet'!$B$2

	A	B	C	D	E
1	Staff number	Hours worked	Basic pay	Bonus	
2	F0254	35	£280.00	£28.00	
3	F0255	32	£256.00	£25.60	
4	F0256	34	£272.00	£27.20	
5	F0257	35	£280.00	£28.00	
6	F0258	30	£240.00	£24.00	
7	F0259	40	£320.00	£32.00	
8	F0260	38	£304.00	£30.40	

Hours worked / Rates sheet / Sheet3

Ready

The final formula can be added in the same way.

Shortcut

Ctrl-Page Up and **Ctrl-Page Down** will switch between worksheets on the active workbook.

7.7 Referencing other workbooks

Again, you may wish to refer to another workbook within your calculations. This works in exactly the same way as referring to other worksheets – now our reference would be 'Cell A1 on Sheet 1 of Workbook 1'.

='[Workbook 1.xlsx]Sheet 1'!A1

The only difference being the workbook name is shown within square brackets. You can create this reference automatically by finding the cell you need and clicking on it.

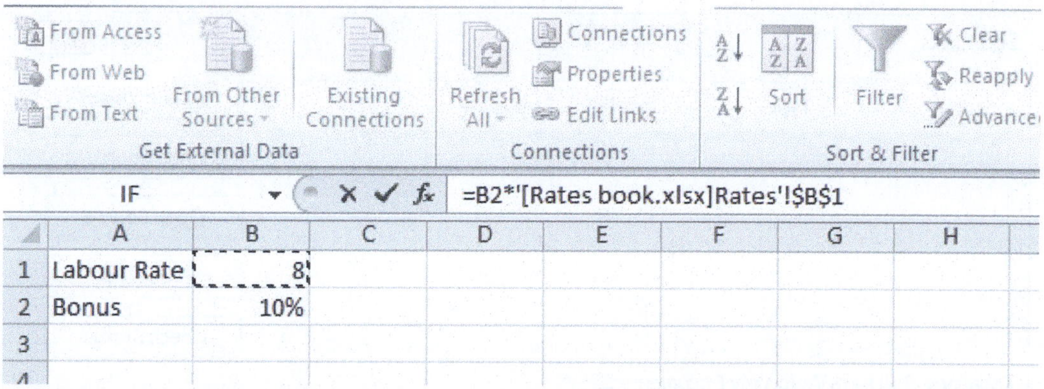

As you select the cell, the formula is populated automatically. Note that by default, **absolute** cell referencing is used – the dollar signs can be removed/added by pressing **F4** as you enter the formula, or manually.

> **Shortcut**
>
> **Ctrl-Tab** and **Ctrl-Shift-Tab** will switch between open workbooks.

7.8 Links

Once a formula is set up referencing another workbook, a **link** has been created. These can be managed using the **Edit links** option in the **Data** tab.

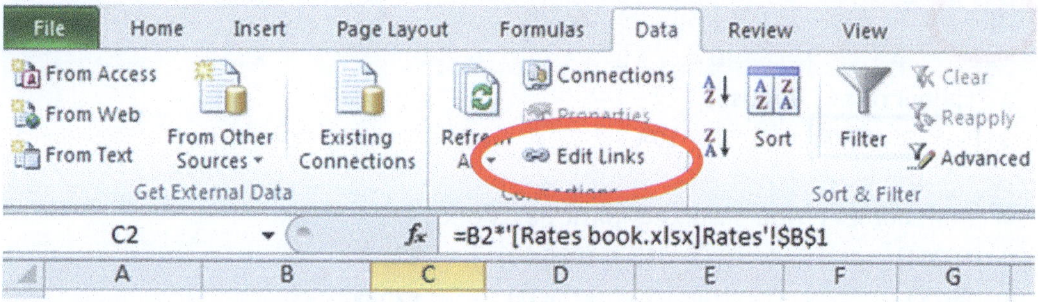

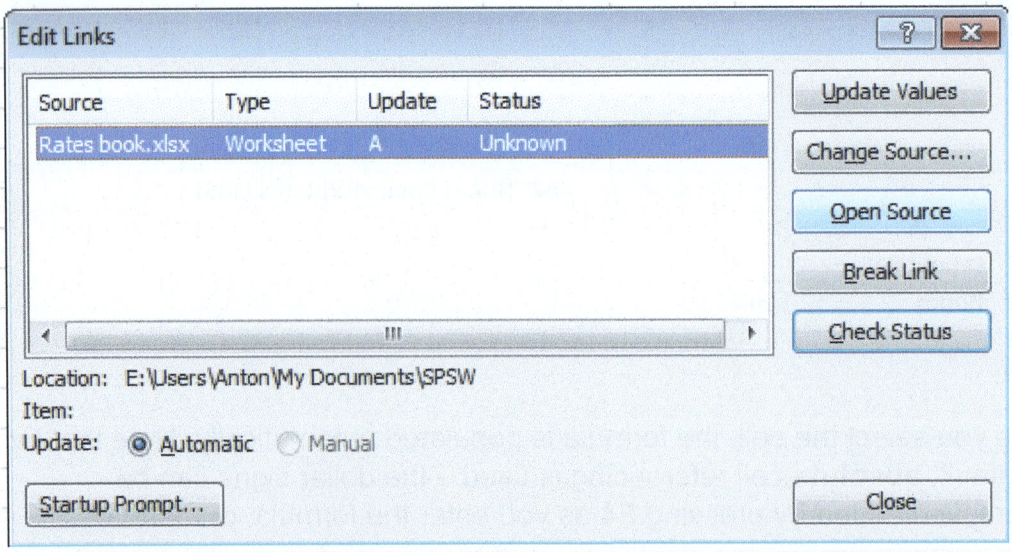

Here, links can be managed if necessary. **Break link** removes the link from the formula – the current value of the formula will be retained.

7.9 Naming cells

Naming cells and ranges of cells can make formulas easier to understand. As we have already seen, each cell has a **reference** made up of its column and row position. Instead of this, it can be given a name. The simplest way to do this is by using the **Name Box**.

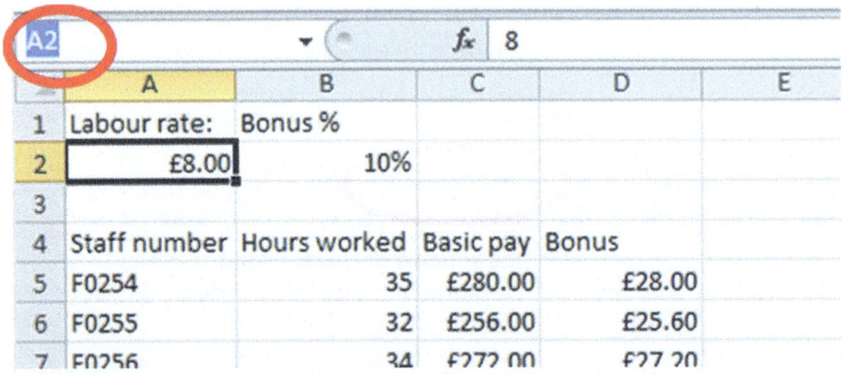

The **Name Box**, showing that Cell **A2** is selected.

To give this cell a **name**, simply type the name in the **Name Box**. There are a few rules for cell names:

- No spaces (underscore is often used instead).
- Your name cannot be a valid cell reference (e.g. AB123).
- The name must be less than 256 characters.
- The name must start with a letter, an underscore or a backslash (\).

- Other valid characters after the first letter are letters, numbers, backslash, full stop and underscore, £ signs should NOT be used.
- Names are not case sensitive.

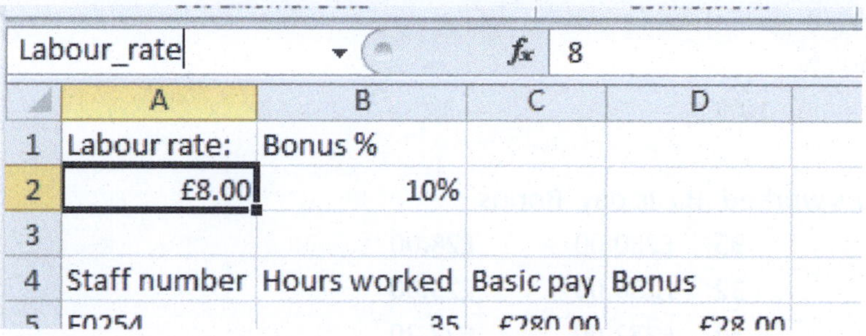

	A	B	C	D
1	Labour rate:	Bonus %		
2	£8.00	10%		
3				
4	Staff number	Hours worked	Basic pay	Bonus
5	F0254	35	£280.00	£28.00

Cell A2 has been named '**Labour_rate**'

This means we can now refer to the cell 'Labour_rate', instead of A2, which can make things easier to understand.

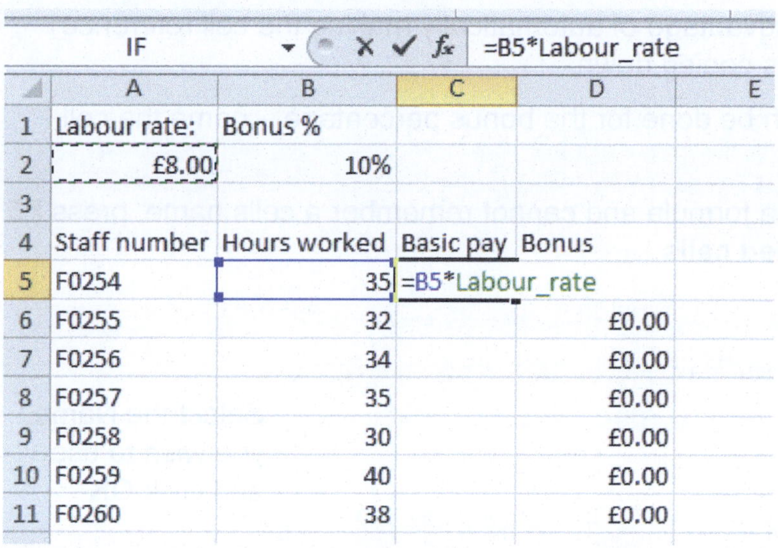

	A	B	C	D	E
1	Labour rate:	Bonus %			
2	£8.00	10%			
3					
4	Staff number	Hours worked	Basic pay	Bonus	
5	F0254	35	=B5*Labour_rate		
6	F0255	32		£0.00	
7	F0256	34		£0.00	
8	F0257	35		£0.00	
9	F0258	30		£0.00	
10	F0259	40		£0.00	
11	F0260	38		£0.00	

When entering the formula, clicking on the cell enters its name rather than its cell reference.

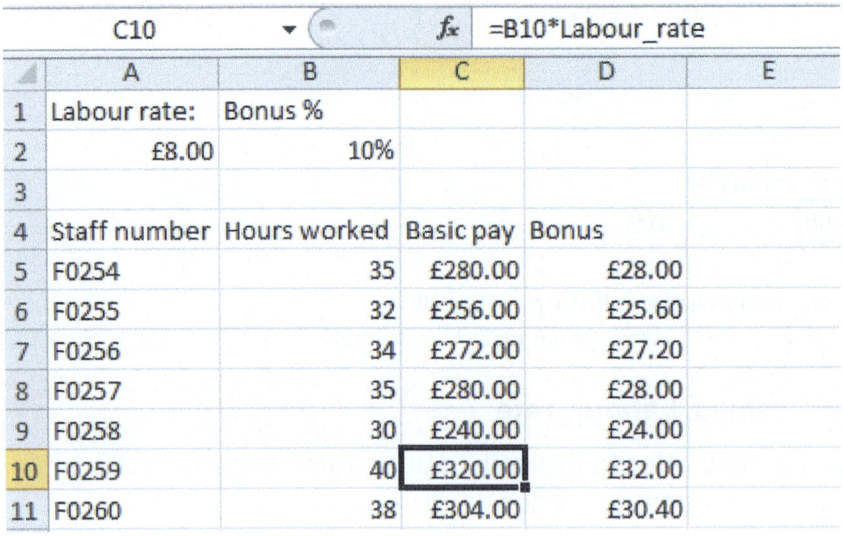
C10 =B10*Labour_rate

	A	B	C	D	E
1	Labour rate:	Bonus %			
2	£8.00	10%			
3					
4	Staff number	Hours worked	Basic pay	Bonus	
5	F0254	35	£280.00	£28.00	
6	F0255	32	£256.00	£25.60	
7	F0256	34	£272.00	£27.20	
8	F0257	35	£280.00	£28.00	
9	F0258	30	£240.00	£24.00	
10	F0259	40	£320.00	£32.00	
11	F0260	38	£304.00	£30.40	

This also has the advantage of automatically making the cell reference **absolute**, when it is copied down.

The same thing can be done for the bonus percentage – name the cell 'Bonus'.

If you are entering a formula and cannot remember a cells name, press **F5** to navigate to **named cells**.

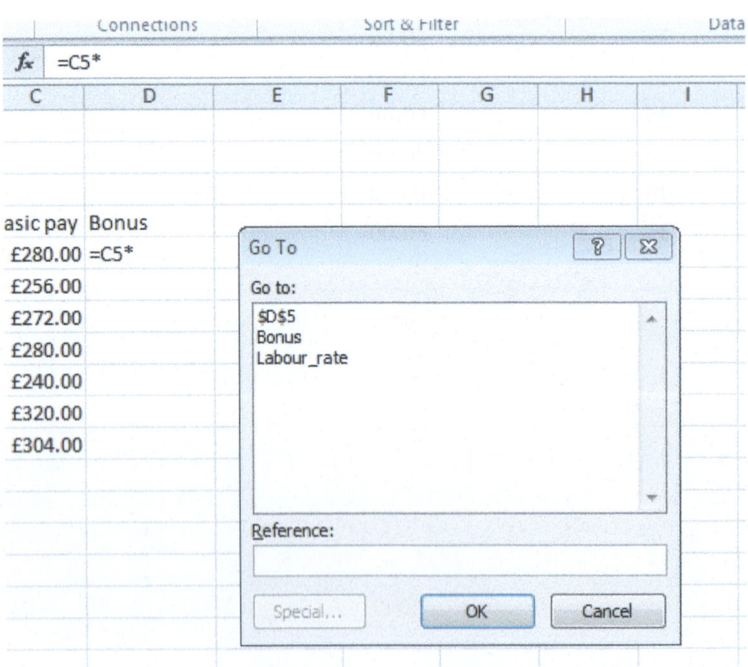

Select the Name you wish to use, and click **OK**.

Other commands to do with Naming Cells can be found in the **Formulas** tab, in the **Defined Names** section.

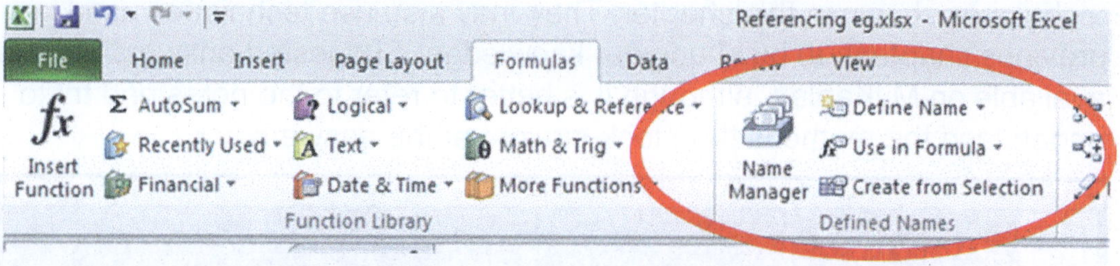

You can use **Define Name** as an alternative way of creating a name. **Use in Formula** is another way of inserting names into a formula, and **Create from Selection** is a way of automatically creating names.

The **Name Manager** is used to Add, Edit and Delete names.

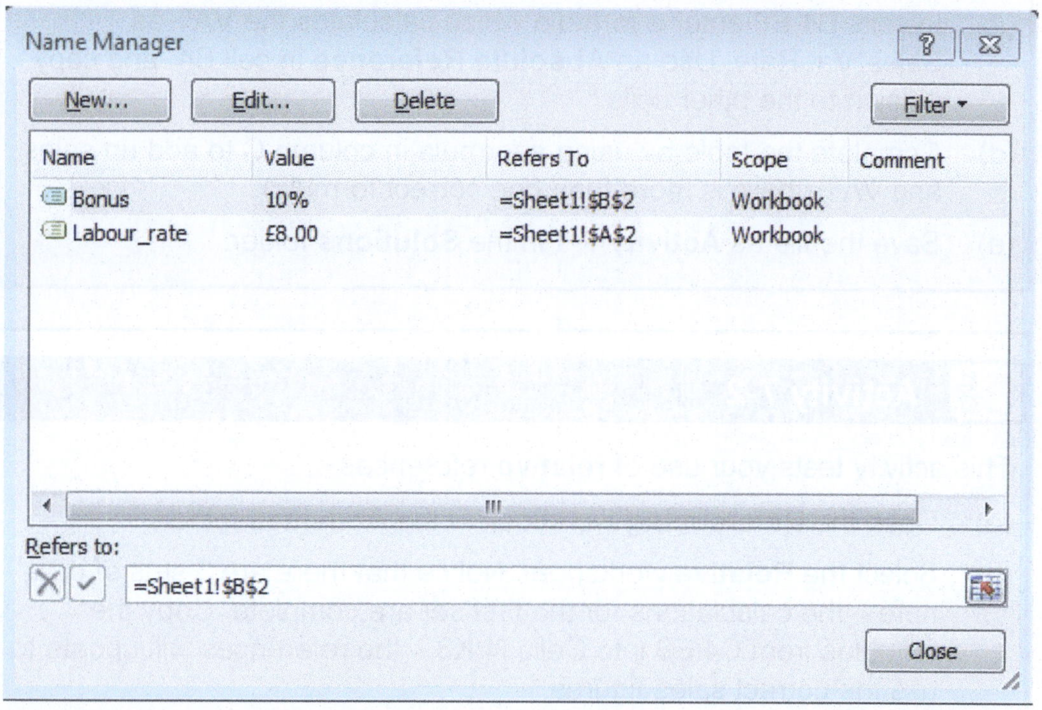

7.10 Activities

The activities in this guide are designed to test your knowledge on the techniques shown in this chapter. They may also use techniques used in previous chapters, to build up your knowledge. Suggested answers are available on MyKaplan, although it is better to refer to the notes and try to understand the methods than look straight at the answers.

Activity 7-1

This activity tests your use of **absolute** references

(a) Open the **Referencing** workbook in the **Activities** folder.

(b) On the **Absolute** worksheet, enter the VAT rate in cell B1 as 20% (this should automatically format as percentage).

(c) In cells B4-B8 enter a formula which calculates the VAT as Sales*Vat Rate. Use an **Absolute Reference** in cell B4, and copy it down to the other cells.

(d) Complete the table by using a formula in column C to add up sales and VAT (there is more than one correct formula).

(e) Save the file as **Activity 7-1** in the **Solutions** folder.

Activity 7-2

This activity tests your use of **relative** references.

(a) Open the **Referencing** workbook in the **Activities** folder.

(b) Select the **Relative** worksheet. Notice that there are 3 sets of data here – the calculations for the first set are complete. Copy the formulas from C4:E8 into Cells I4:K8 – the references will update to use the correct sales figures.

(c) Repeat this to copy the formulas into cells O4:Q4.

(d) **Show Formulas** on this worksheet.

(e) Save the file as **Activity 7-2** in the **Solutions** folder.

Activity 7-3

This activity tests your use of **mixed** referencing.

(a) Open the **Referencing** workbook in the **Activities** folder.

(b) Select the **Mixed Referencing** worksheet. The table will show how our sales will change with varying volume, and with different percentage increases added. Firstly, calculate forecast sales in column B. This will be Volume (col A) * Selling Price (B1). An **absolute** reference should be used on B1.

B14 =A14*$B$1

	A	B	C	D	E	F	G	H
1	Forecast Selling Price	£100	Forecast Sales +	Forecast Sales +	Forecast Sales +	Forecast Sales +	Forecast Sales +	Forecast Sales +
2	Forecast Sales Volume (Units)	Forecast Sales	5%	6%	7%	8%	9%	10%
3	1000	£100,000						
4	1500	£150,000						
5	2000	£200,000						
6	2500	£250,000						
7	3000	£300,000						
8	3500	£350,000						
9	4000	£400,000						
10	4500	£450,000						
11	5000	£500,000						
12	5500	£550,000						
13	6000	£600,000						
14	6500	£650,000						
15								

(c) We now need to calculate the forecast sales plus the percentage increase. This calculation could be:

Forecast sales*(1+percentage increase)

We need to be careful with the referencing. If we start in cell C3, the calculation is **=B3*(1+C2)**. This will give the correct answer of £105,000.

However, when we copy the formula across to the other columns, it will not work. If we copy across into column D, the formula will become **=C3*(1+D2)**. This is not correct, as we need to always refer to column B for the Forecast sales.

So, the formula becomes **=$B3*(1+C2)**. If this is copied across, the top row will be correct.

We also have to consider the reference to C2. If we copy this **down** a row, the formula will become **=$B4*(1+C3)** which is no longer multiplying by the correct percentage. We need to always refer to the row in this part of the formula, which becomes **=$B4*(1+C$2)**

Note: There are different formulas that can be used to calculate the forecast sale plus the percentage increase. The formula could also be =$B3+$B3*C$2

The final result looks like this:

G11 | fx | =$B11*(1+G$2)

	A	B	C	D	E	F	G	H
1	Forecast Selling Price	£100	Forecast Sales +	Forecast Sales +	Forecast Sales +	Forecast Sales +	Forecast Sales +	Forecast Sales +
2	Forecast Sales Volume (Units)	Forecast Sales	5%	6%	7%	8%	9%	10%
3	1000	£100,000	£105,000	£106,000	£107,000	£108,000	£109,000	£110,000
4	1500	£150,000	£157,500	£159,000	£160,500	£162,000	£163,500	£165,000
5	2000	£200,000	£210,000	£212,000	£214,000	£216,000	£218,000	£220,000
6	2500	£250,000	£262,500	£265,000	£267,500	£270,000	£272,500	£275,000
7	3000	£300,000	£315,000	£318,000	£321,000	£324,000	£327,000	£330,000
8	3500	£350,000	£367,500	£371,000	£374,500	£378,000	£381,500	£385,000
9	4000	£400,000	£420,000	£424,000	£428,000	£432,000	£436,000	£440,000
10	4500	£450,000	£472,500	£477,000	£481,500	£486,000	£490,500	£495,000
11	5000	£500,000	£525,000	£530,000	£535,000	£540,000	£545,000	£550,000
12	5500	£550,000	£577,500	£583,000	£588,500	£594,000	£599,500	£605,000
13	6000	£600,000	£630,000	£636,000	£642,000	£648,000	£654,000	£660,000
14	6500	£650,000	£682,500	£689,000	£695,500	£702,000	£708,500	£715,000
15								

(d) Save the file as **Activity 7-3** in the **Solutions** folder.

Activity 7-4

This activity uses a named range to calculate values.

(a) Open the **Referencing** workbook from the **Activities** folder.

(b) Enter the VAT rate in cell A1 of the **Absolute** folder as 20%

(c) **Name** cell B1 vat_rate.

(d) Calculate the VAT in cells B4:B8 using the name vat_rate.

(e) Complete the Total column.

(f) Show Formulas.

(g) Save the file as **Activity 7-4** in the **Activities** folder.

Activity 7-5

This activity tests your use of formulas referencing different worksheets.

(a) Open the **Regional Combined** workbook from the **Activities** folder.

(b) The **Regional Combined Sales** worksheet needs populating with the sum of the values on **District 1** and **District 2** worksheets.

(c) Enter a formula in cell B2 on the totals worksheet which adds cell B2 from District 1 to B2 from District 2.

(d) Copy the formula down and across into the other cells.

(e) Format the numbers in **Number** format, to zero decimal places with a 1000 separator comma.

(f) Save the file as **Activity 7-5** in the **Activities** folder.

Activity 7-6

This activity tests your use of formulas referring to cells in other workbooks, along with some basic formatting and some simple functions.

(a) Open the **District Totals, Northern** and **Southern** workbooks from the **Activities** folder.

(b) The **District Totals** workbook needs populating with the sum of the values on **Northern** and **Southern** workbooks.

(c) Enter a formula in cell B2 on the Totals workbook which adds cell B2 from Northern to Southern.

(d) Copy the formula down and across into the other cells so that all the cells populate with the correct totals (check the referencing in the formula).

(e) Populate the **Total** row with a formula to add the figures.

(f) Place a **Border** around the Total figures – single line on the top of the cell, double line on the bottom.

(g) Calculate the monthly average sales in cell B8.

(h) Format the numbers in **Number** format, to zero decimal places with a 1000 separator comma.

(i) Save the file as **Activity 7-6** in the **Activities** folder.

Conditional formatting

8.1 Introduction

This chapter will guide you on how to apply conditional formatting to cells based upon pre-determined criteria. You will also learn the different ways in which conditional formatting can be applied.

KNOWLEDGE

3.1 Explain how to present and format spreadsheet effectively to meet needs.

3.2 Select and use appropriate tools and techniques to format cells, rows, columns and worksheets effectively.

8.2 What is Conditional Formatting?

Formatting cells has already been discussed in chapter 3 – changing the appearance of cells or the text within them. **Conditional Formatting** is where you can change the format of a cell based on certain conditions.

For example you could want to colour a cell in red if its value is less than a certain number, or make the font bold if its value is equal to a number. In the example below, we might want to highlight any staff member who has worked more than a standard 35 hour week.

	A	B	C	D
1	Labour rate:	Bonus %		
2	£8.00	10%		
3				
4	Staff number	Hours worked	Basic pay	Bonus
5	F0254	35	£280.00	£28.00
6	F0255	32	£256.00	£25.60
7	F0256	34	£272.00	£27.20
8	F0257	35	£280.00	£28.00
9	F0258	30	£240.00	£24.00
10	F0259	40	£320.00	£32.00
11	F0260	38	£304.00	£30.40

8.3 Managing Conditional Formatting Rules

To see any conditional formatting already in place, or to create a conditional format, select the cell(s) you wish to format, and in the **Home**

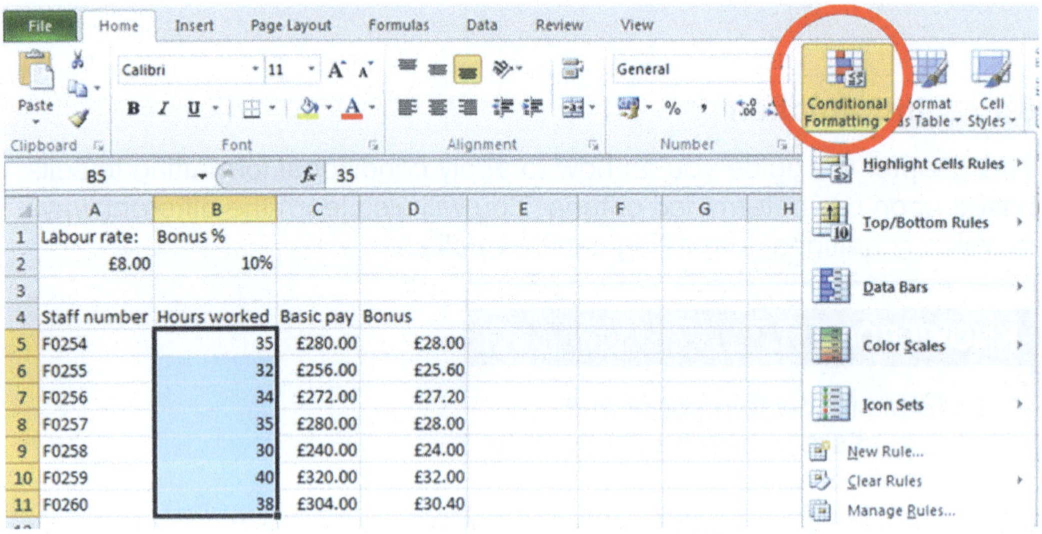

Menu, select **Conditional Formatting**. Several options appear.

Select **Manage Rules** to bring up the Conditional Formatting Rules Manager.

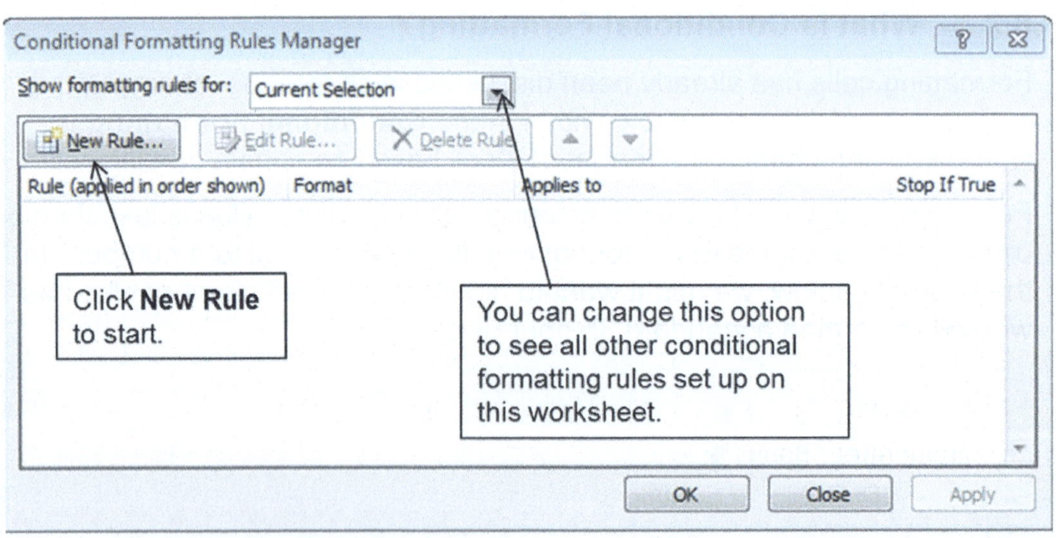

From here you can **Edit** or **Delete** any existing conditional formatting, or create new formatting rules.

8.4 Creating a New Rule

Clicking **New Rule** from the **Rules Manager** menu brings up the following options:

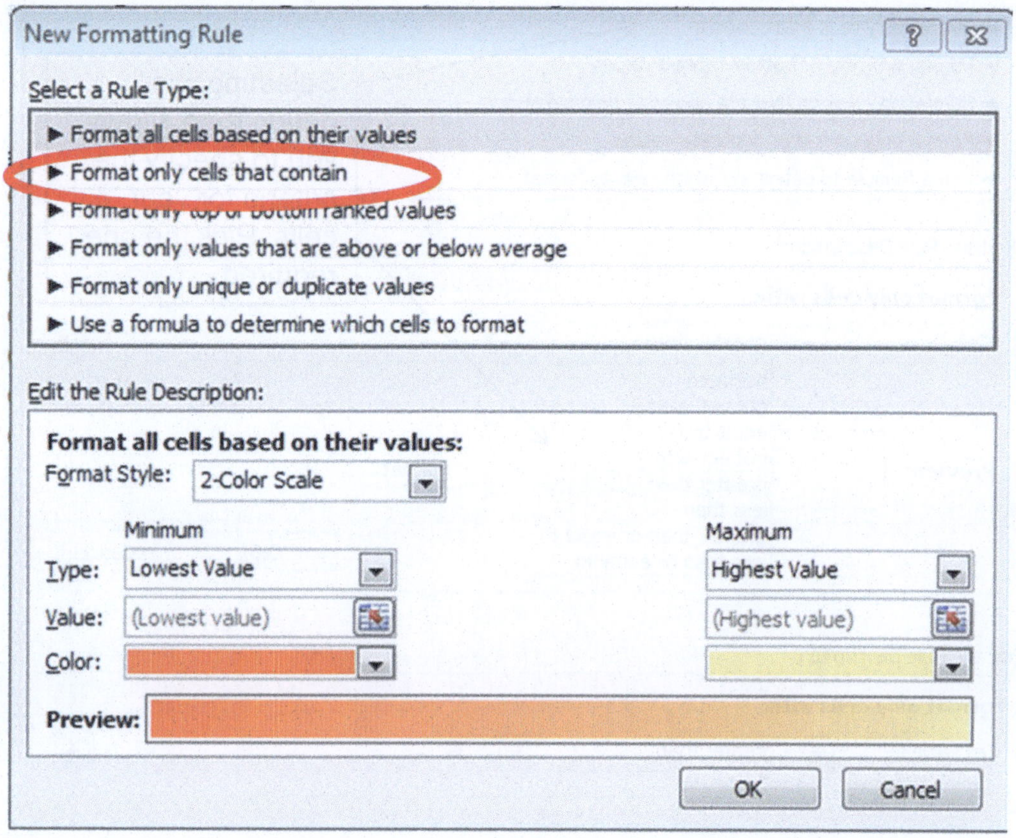

The most frequently used rule is 'Format only cells that contain', circled in red above so we shall focus on how this rule works.

The other rules are useful and reasonably self-explanatory – the trick is to try them, and see what happens. Remember, if it goes wrong, just delete the rule and start again. Only the format of the cells is ever affected, not the content, so you cannot break anything

Selecting '**Format only cells that contain**' gives a menu at the bottom of the page, allowing you to select your criteria.

Cell Value is the most commonly used option, as this can be used to format cells based on numerical values.

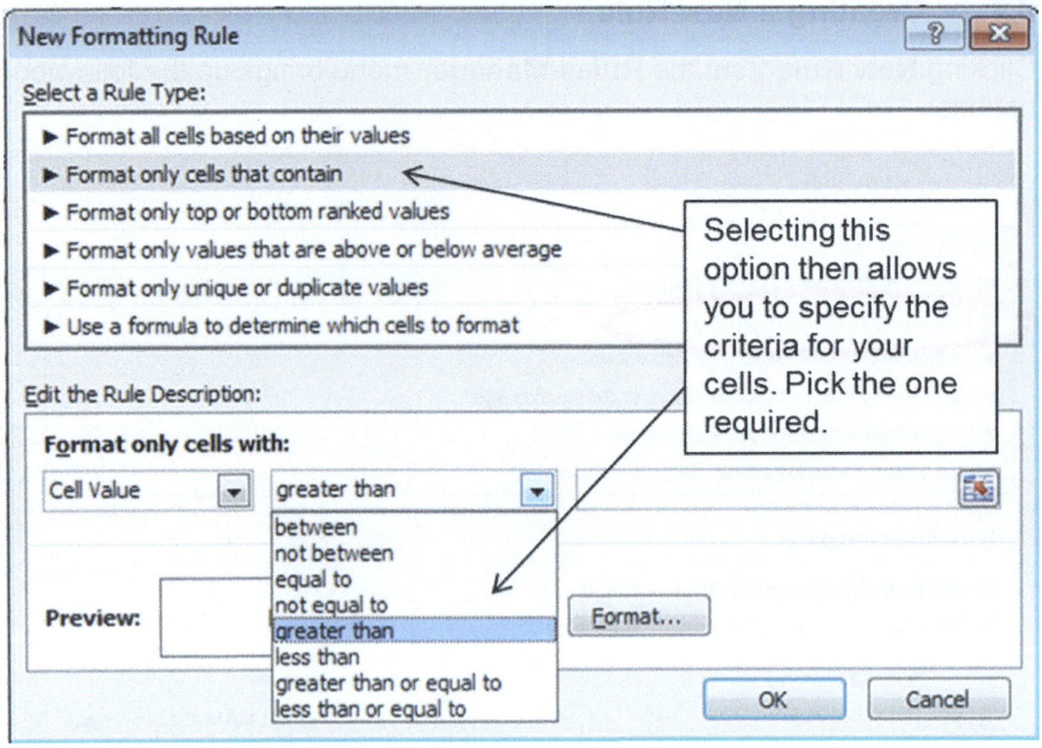

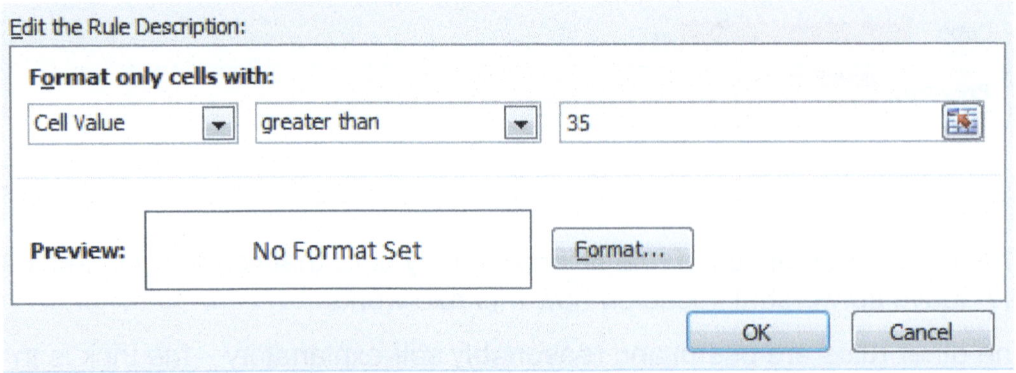

The rule is set up – the formatting will change for any cell (out of the ones selected) whose value is greater than 35. However, no special format has been set. To do this, click the **Format** button.

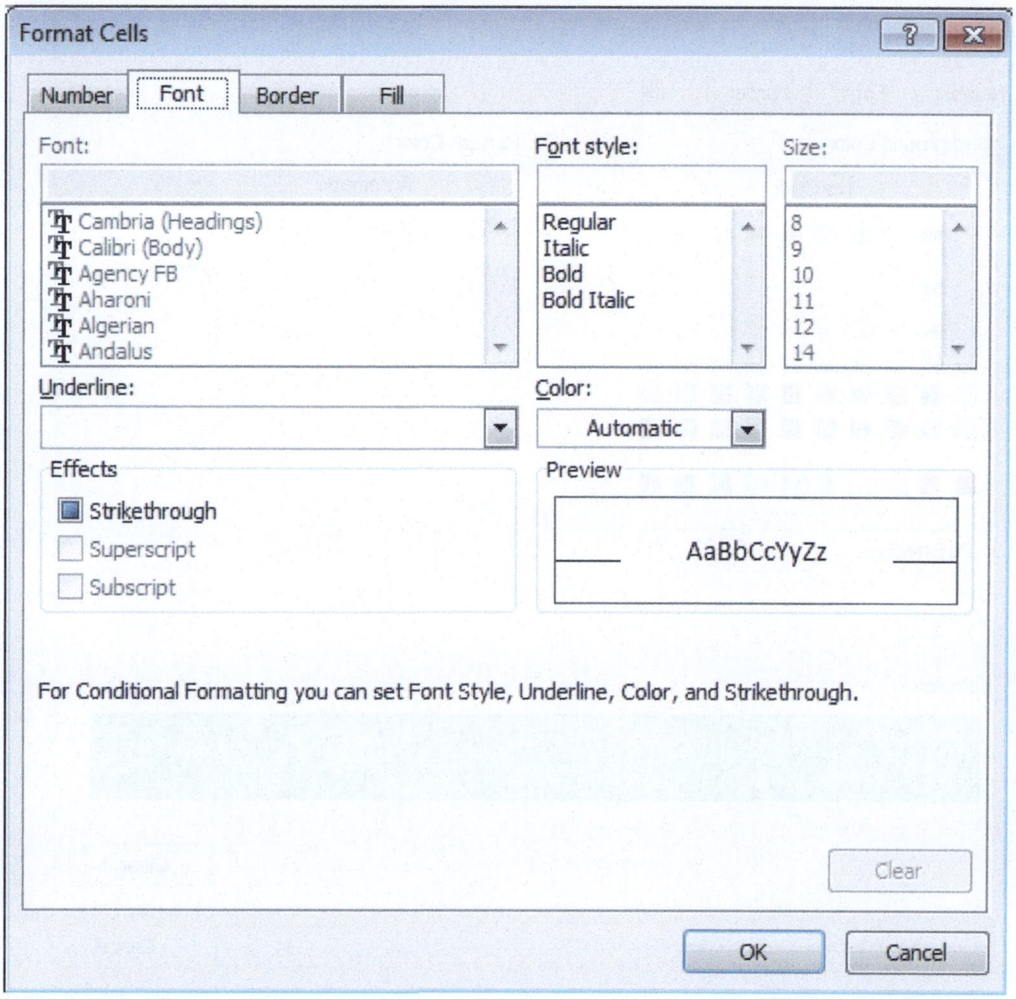

The normal **Format Cells** dialogue box opens – use this to set how you would like the cell to be formatted, if the value is over 35.

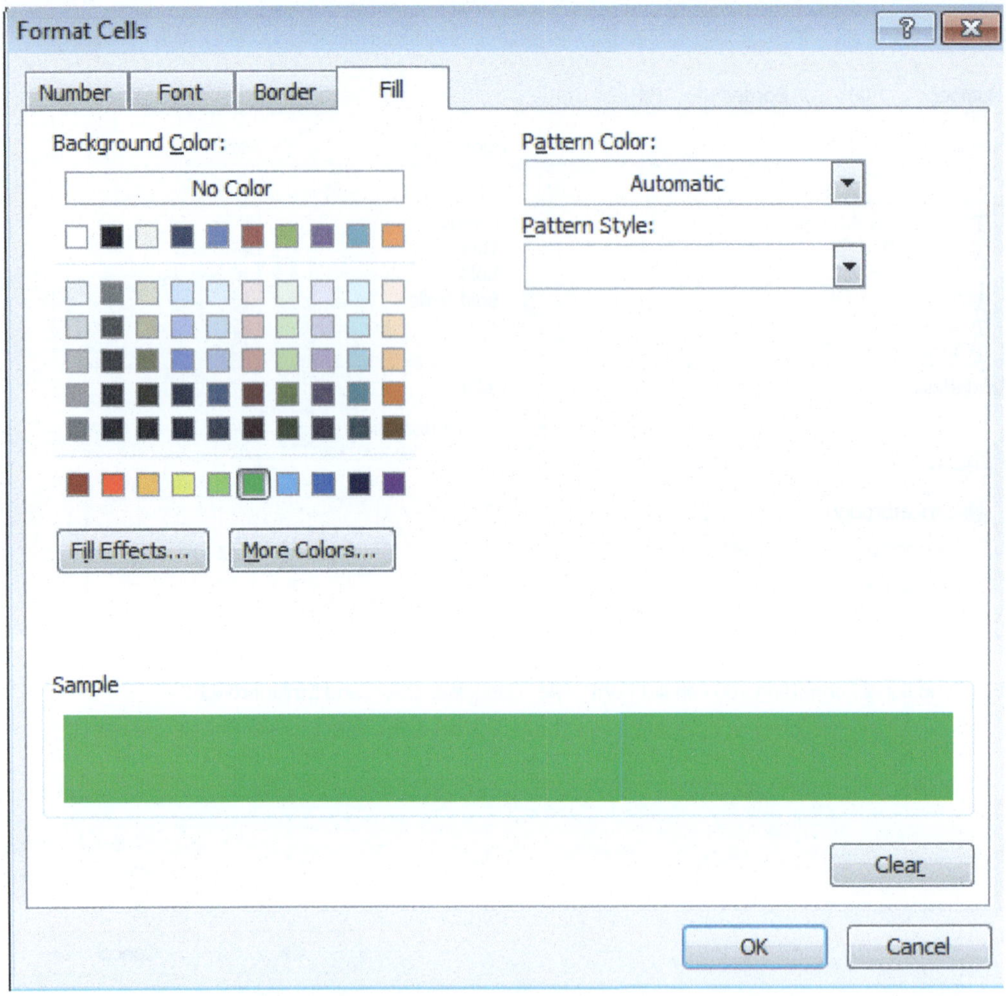

A common use of conditional formatting is to highlight unusual values by colouring the cell – green in this case.

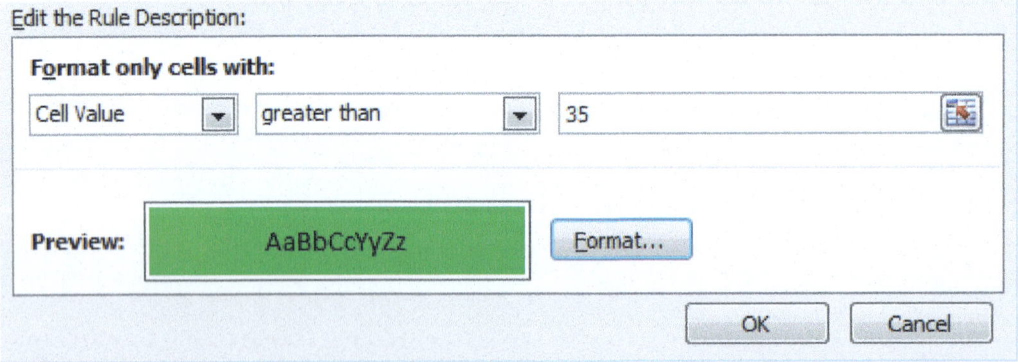

The final rule is shown – any cell with a value greater than 35 will be coloured green.

	A	B	C	D
1	Labour rate:	Bonus %		
2	£8.00	10%		
3				
4	Staff number	Hours worked	Basic pay	Bonus
5	F0254	35	£280.00	£28.00
6	F0255	32	£256.00	£25.60
7	F0256	34	£272.00	£27.20
8	F0257	35	£280.00	£28.00
9	F0258	30	£240.00	£24.00
10	F0259	40	£320.00	£32.00
11	F0260	38	£304.00	£30.40

The final result shows that the two cells with values above 35 are coloured green.

Note that the cell with value 35 is not coloured – the 'greater than or equal to' option would need to be used.

8.5 Multiple Rules

It is possible to have up to 64 conditional formatting rules for any cell.

Extra rules are added in the same way as a new rule – select the cells required and create a new rule. For example a rule to highlight in red any cells with a value below 32 can be used:

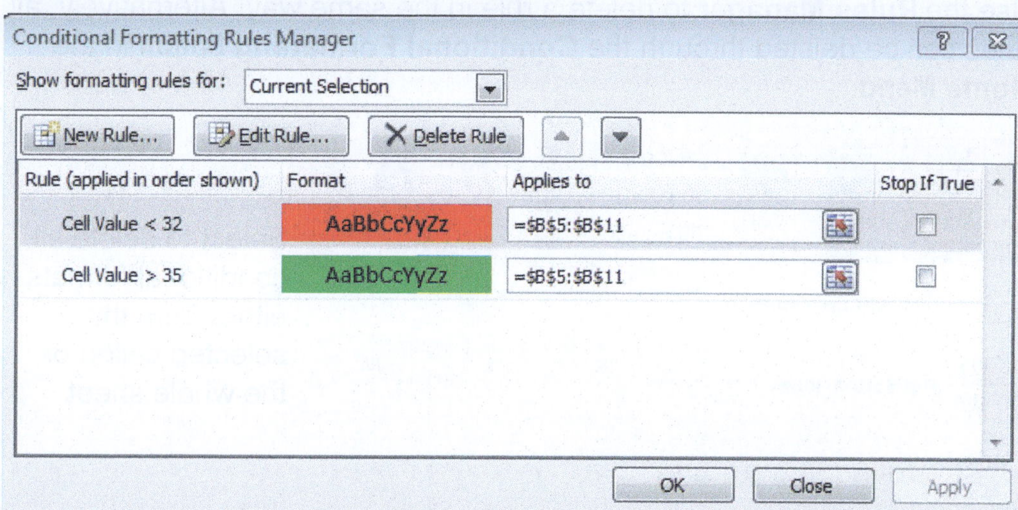

Note that if any of the rules conflict with each other, they will be applied in the order shown. The order of priority can be changed with the arrows next to the Delete Rule box.

8.6 Editing Rules

Edit rules from within the **Rules Manager** box.

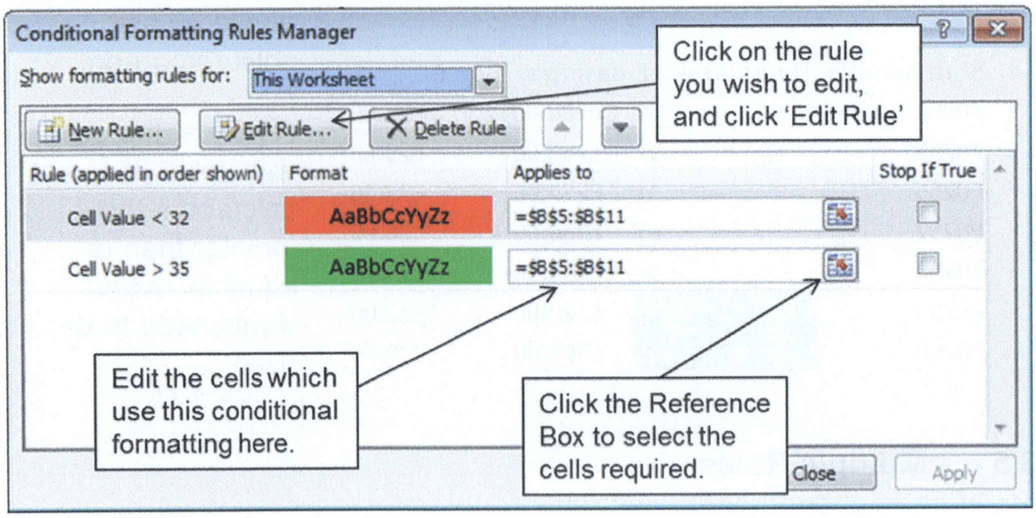

Clicking on **Edit Rule** brings up the same menu as for a New Rule, so make the changes as required.

8.7 Deleting Rules

Use the **Rules Manager** to delete a rule in the same way. Alternatively, all rules can be deleted through the **Conditional Formatting** button in the **Home Menu**.

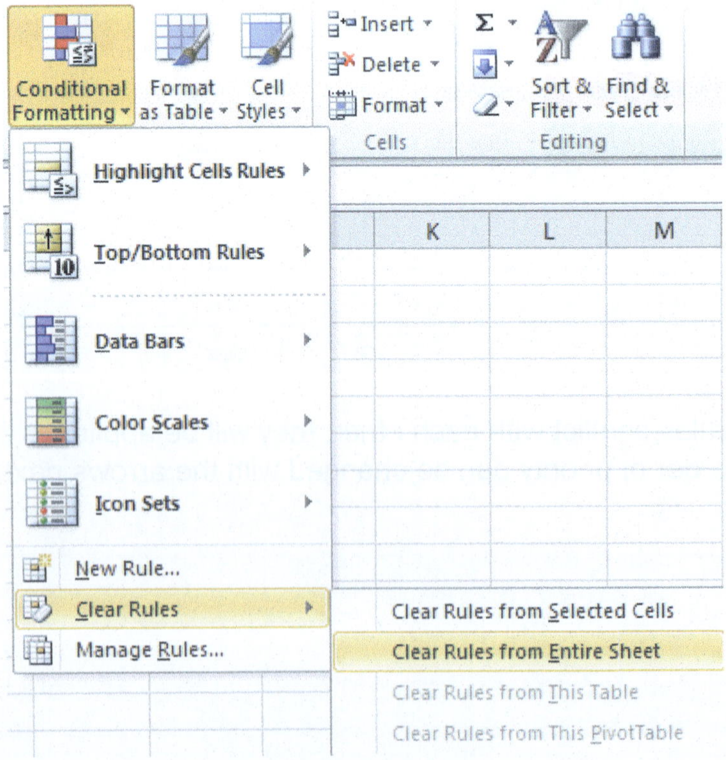

Select to delete all conditional formats either from the selected cell(s) or the whole sheet.

8.8 Rules depending on another cell

Excel is designed to be flexible, and the conditional formatting rules can be designed to refer to the values in other cells. For example, rather than having to change the conditional formatting if the weekly hours changed, we could show them in a separate cell:

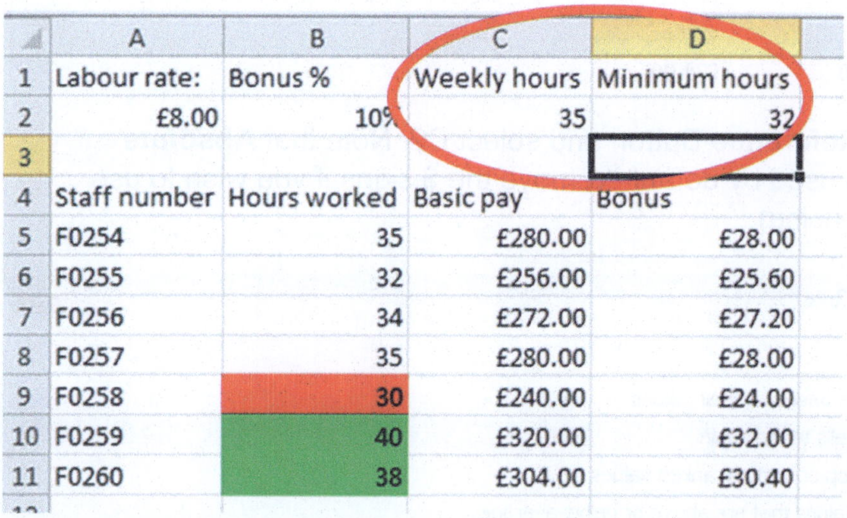

	A	B	C	D
1	Labour rate:	Bonus %	Weekly hours	Minimum hours
2	£8.00	10%	35	32
3				
4	Staff number	Hours worked	Basic pay	Bonus
5	F0254	35	£280.00	£28.00
6	F0255	32	£256.00	£25.60
7	F0256	34	£272.00	£27.20
8	F0257	35	£280.00	£28.00
9	F0258	30	£240.00	£24.00
10	F0259	40	£320.00	£32.00
11	F0260	38	£304.00	£30.40

We would like the conditional formatting to be based on these figures.

Deleting the existing formats and starting again:

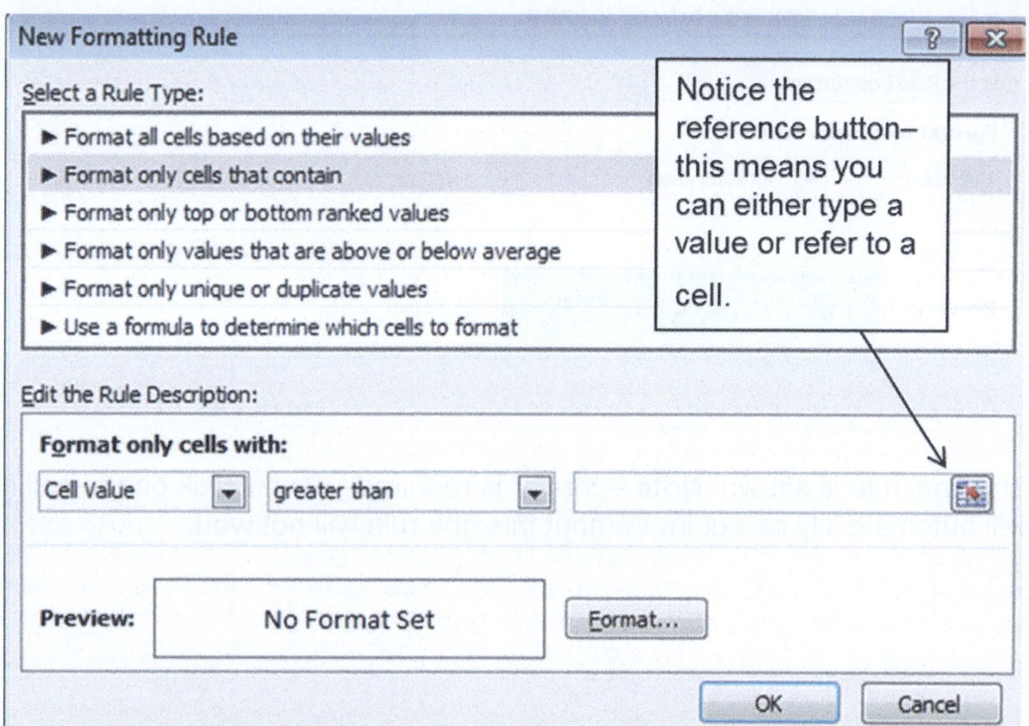

A new rule needs to be set up – formatting all cells with a value greater than that in cell C2.

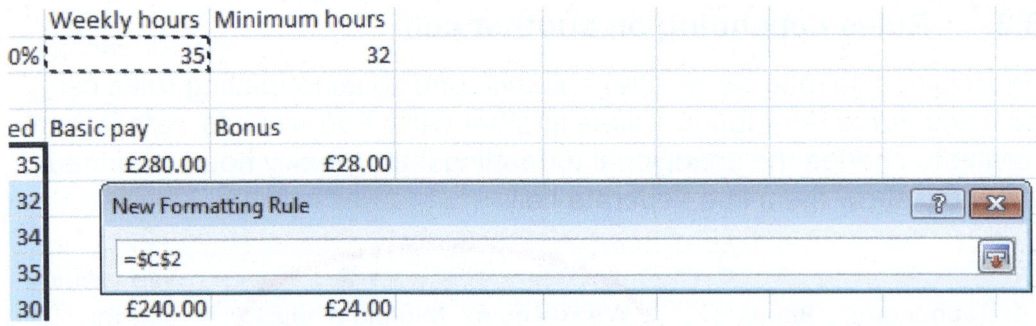

Click on the **Reference** Button and select C2. Note that **Absolute** referencing is used by default (remove the $ signs if you wish to use relative referencing).

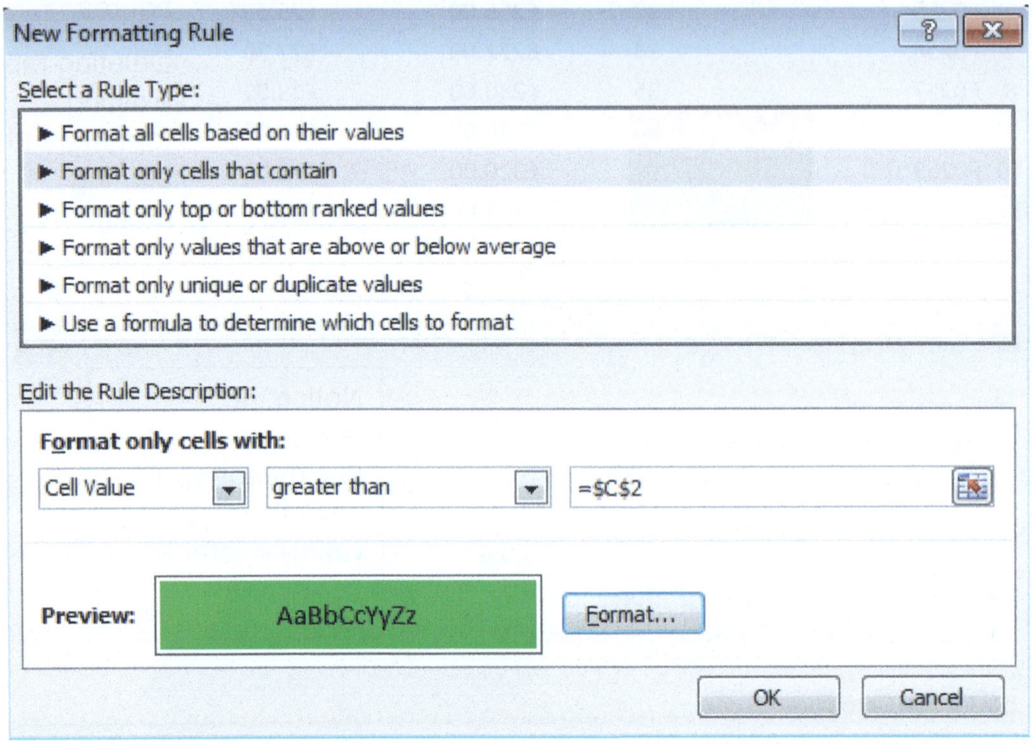

The final rule is shown. **Note** – the **'='** is required – if you click on the cell it will automatically be put in. Without this, the rule will not work.

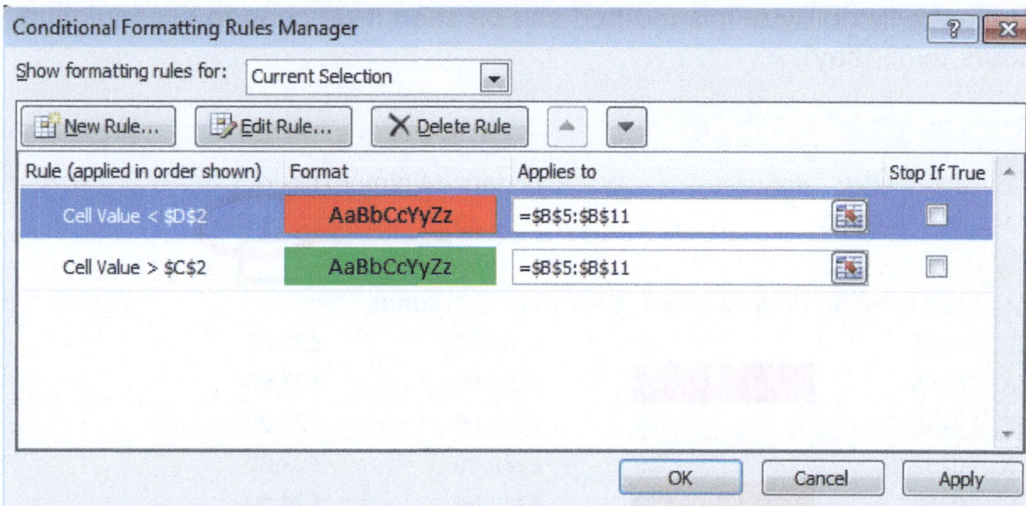

Other rules can be added in the same way. The end result is the same as before:

	A	B	C	D
1	Labour rate:	Bonus %	Weekly hours	Minimum hours
2	£8.00	10%	35	32
3				
4	Staff number	Hours worked	Basic pay	Bonus
5	F0254	35	£280.00	£28.00
6	F0255	32	£256.00	£25.60
7	F0256	34	£272.00	£27.20
8	F0257	35	£280.00	£28.00
9	F0258	30	£240.00	£24.00
10	F0259	40	£320.00	£32.00
11	F0260	38	£304.00	£30.40
12				

The extra flexibility of this method can be seen if we change the minimum hours to 33 (say):

	A	B	C	D
1	Labour rate:	Bonus %	Weekly hours	Minimum hours
2	£8.00	10%	35	33
3				
4	Staff number	Hours worked	Basic pay	Bonus
5	F0254	35	£280.00	£28.00
6	F0255	32	£256.00	£25.60
7	F0256	34	£272.00	£27.20
8	F0257	35	£280.00	£28.00
9	F0258	30	£240.00	£24.00
10	F0259	40	£320.00	£32.00
11	F0260	38	£304.00	£30.40
12				

The extra figure is now highlighted.

NOTE ON CONDITIONAL FORMATTING

Conditional formatting overwrites any existing formatting. If, for example, you try to highlight cells B5:B11 above in yellow, the four already highlighted **WILL NOT CHANGE COLOUR**. This can lead to confusion – if a cell's formatting will not change, check to see if there is conditional formatting in place. This is the most likely reason.

8.10 Activities

The activities in this guide are designed to test your knowledge on the techniques shown in this chapter. They may also use techniques used in previous chapters, to build up your knowledge. Suggested answers are available on MyKaplan, although it is better to refer to the notes and try to understand the methods than look straight at the answers.

Activity 8-1

This activity tests several aspects of **conditional formatting**, along with some simple calculations and referencing.

(a) Open the **Conditional** workbook in the **Activities** folder.

(b) The values in cells B6:G13 need to be populated. Column B is **revenue** – calculated as the sales price (column A) multiplied by the sales volume. The sales volume needs to be used in each row, so the row number in cell G1 must be fixed – you can either use an **absolute** reference, $G$1, or mixed, G$1, it doesn't matter as long as the '1' is held.

(c) The **variable costs** in column C is just the sales volume * variable cost/unit. Again, this will be the same in rows 6-13, so make sure the row numbers in the calculation are fixed.

(d) **Revenue- Variable costs** (contribution) is simply column B minus column C.

(e) **Fixed costs** will be the same whatever the sales price – use an **absolute** reference to refer to the value in G2.

(f) **Total Cost** is column C plus column E.

(g) **Profit** can be calculated a few ways – column D minus column E is one.

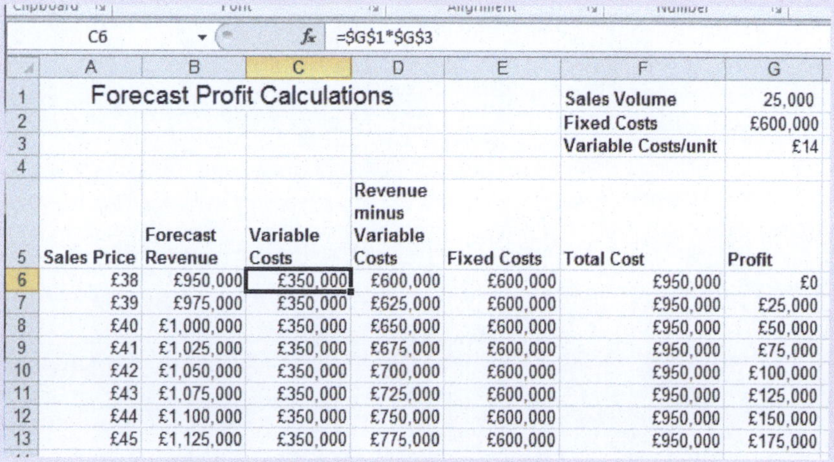

C6 =$G$1*$G$3

	A	B	C	D	E	F	G
1	Forecast Profit Calculations					Sales Volume	25,000
2						Fixed Costs	£600,000
3						Variable Costs/unit	£14
4							
5	Sales Price	Forecast Revenue	Variable Costs	Revenue minus Variable Costs	Fixed Costs	Total Cost	Profit
6	£38	£950,000	£350,000	£600,000	£600,000	£950,000	£0
7	£39	£975,000	£350,000	£625,000	£600,000	£950,000	£25,000
8	£40	£1,000,000	£350,000	£650,000	£600,000	£950,000	£50,000
9	£41	£1,025,000	£350,000	£675,000	£600,000	£950,000	£75,000
10	£42	£1,050,000	£350,000	£700,000	£600,000	£950,000	£100,000
11	£43	£1,075,000	£350,000	£725,000	£600,000	£950,000	£125,000
12	£44	£1,100,000	£350,000	£750,000	£600,000	£950,000	£150,000
13	£45	£1,125,000	£350,000	£775,000	£600,000	£950,000	£175,000

(h) Now the figures are populated, we can add some conditional formats.

Select cell G6, and using the **Manage Rules** menu, apply the following conditional formats:

Cell value<0 – Fill Red

Cell value=0 – Fill Yellow

Cell value>0 – Fill Green

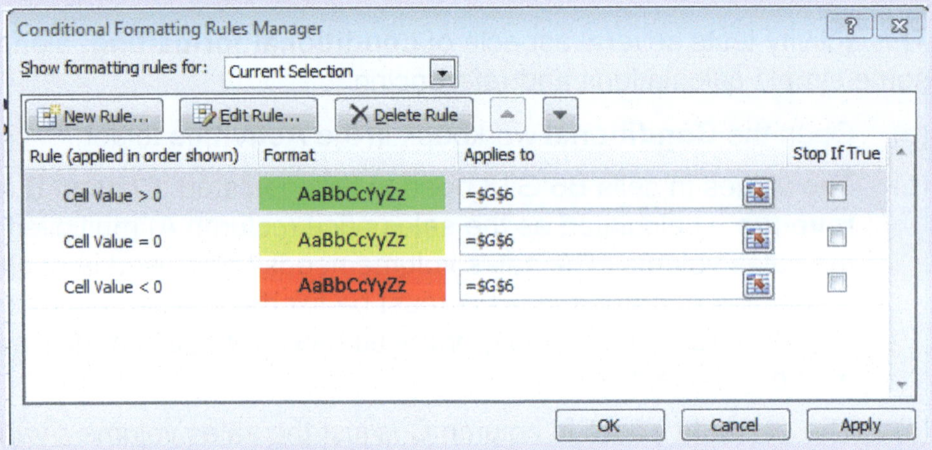

The cell should turn yellow, as profit is zero.

(i) Copy the format down onto cells G7:G13 (use paste special, or just drag). The remaining cells will turn green, as their values are all greater than zero.

(j) Change the **sales volume** in cell **G1** to 20000. Note the change in colour of the formatted cells.

(k) Save the file as **Activity 8-1** in the **solutions** folder.

Activity 8-2

This activity uses slightly more difficult **conditional formatting**, based on the value in another cell.

(a) Open the **CF Report** file in the **Activities** folder.

(b) We want to highlight the largest sales figure in the data – use **conditional formatting** to fill this cell as green. Select cells B4:M4, and set up a new conditional formatting rule. The largest sales figure in cell B9 so we want to format the cell which is equal to this.

	A	B	C	D	E	F	G	H	I	J	K	L	M	N
1						BallCo Management Accounts Data								
2														
3		January	February	March	April	May	June	July	August	September	October	November	December	Total
4	Sales	8,648	6,850	8,264	6,823	7,176	7,083	6,019	7,223	7,579	8,243	8,496	7,199	89,603
5	Profit	4,701	3,496	5,202	3,641	3,967	2,732	2,081	4,219	3,444	4,343	4,611	3,290	45,727
6	Profit Margin	54.4%	51.0%	62.9%	53.4%	55.3%	38.6%	34.6%	58.4%	45.4%	52.7%	54.3%	45.7%	51.0%
7														
8														
9	Biggest Sales	8,648												
10	Lowest sales	6,019												
11														
12	Average Profit	3,811												

(c) Change the value in cell J4 to 10,000. The value in B9 will change, and cell J4 will be coloured green.

(d) Undo the last command to return September sales to 7,579.

(e) Apply a similar conditional format to the sales figures to colour the lowest value red. July will be highlighted.

(f) Apply conditional formatting to cells B5:M5 to **bold** any profits lower than average, and fill the cell blue.

	A	B	C	D	E	F	G	H	I	J	K	L	M	N
1						BallCo Management Accounts Data								
2														
3		January	February	March	April	May	June	July	August	September	October	November	December	Total
4	Sales	8,648	6,850	8,264	6,823	7,176	7,083	6,019	7,223	7,579	8,243	8,496	7,199	89,603
5	Profit	4,701	**3,496**	5,202	**3,641**	3,967	**2,732**	**2,081**	4,219	**3,444**	4,343	4,611	**3,290**	45,727
6	Profit Margin	54.4%	51.0%	62.9%	53.4%	55.3%	38.6%	34.6%	58.4%	45.4%	52.7%	54.3%	45.7%	51.0%
7														
8														
9	Biggest Sales	8,648												
10	Lowest sales	6,019												
11														
12	Average Profit	3,811												

(g) Save the file as **Activity 8-2** in the **Solutions** folder.

Subtotalling

9

9.1 Introduction

This chapter will guide you on how to apply Excel's subtotalling tool to provide a quick and convenient method of data analysis.

KNOWLEDGE

3.2 Select and use appropriate tools and techniques to format cells, rows, columns and worksheets effectively.

Excel has a tool that allows you to do insert subtotals quickly and easily.

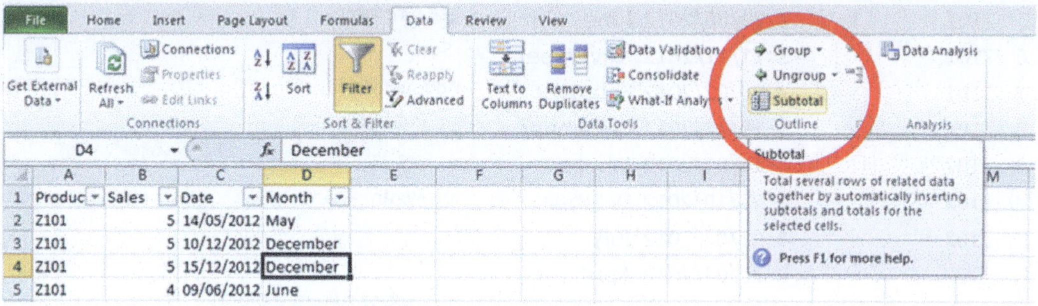

9.2 Creating subtotals

The Subtotal function is found in the **Data** tab, in the **Outline** menu.

Important note – in order for the subtotal to work, the data **MUST** be **sorted** first, in order of the column you wish to subtotal by.

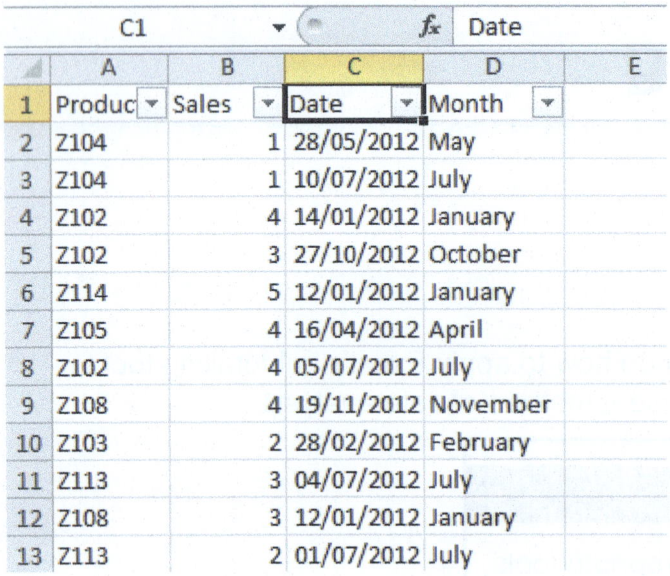

	A	B	C	D
1	Produc	Sales	Date	Month
2	Z104	1	28/05/2012	May
3	Z104	1	10/07/2012	July
4	Z102	4	14/01/2012	January
5	Z102	3	27/10/2012	October
6	Z114	5	12/01/2012	January
7	Z105	4	16/04/2012	April
8	Z102	4	05/07/2012	July
9	Z108	4	19/11/2012	November
10	Z103	2	28/02/2012	February
11	Z113	3	04/07/2012	July
12	Z108	3	12/01/2012	January
13	Z113	2	01/07/2012	July

Here, we may wish to add a subtotal to show the total sales by each product. To do this, we must sort by product first.

See **chapter 4** for more detail on sorting data.

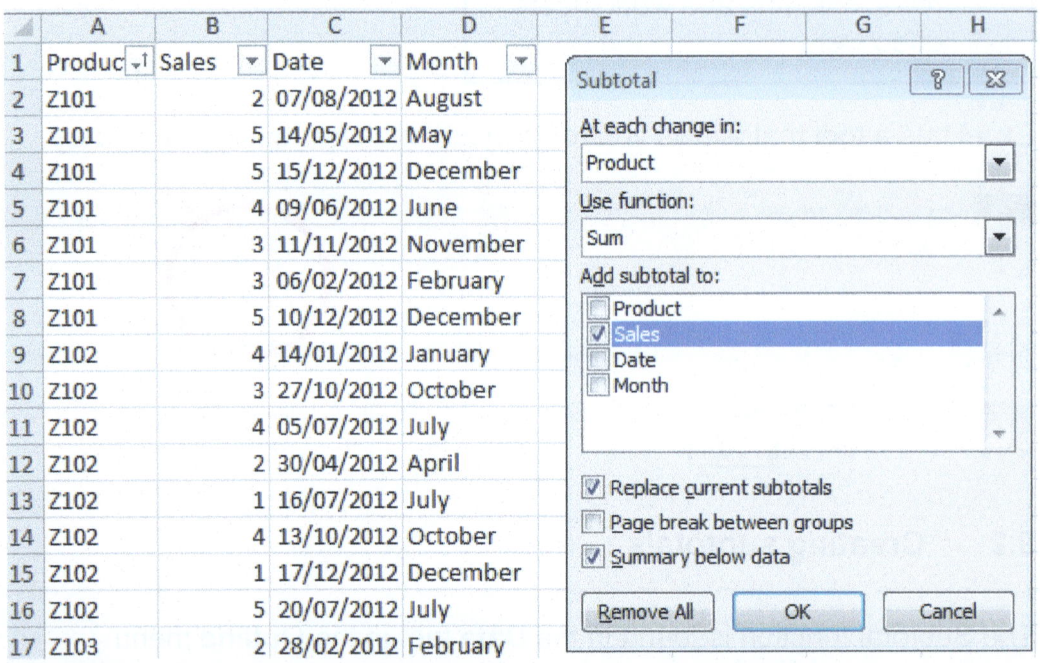

	A	B	C	D
1	Produc	Sales	Date	Month
2	Z101	2	07/08/2012	August
3	Z101	5	14/05/2012	May
4	Z101	5	15/12/2012	December
5	Z101	4	09/06/2012	June
6	Z101	3	11/11/2012	November
7	Z101	3	06/02/2012	February
8	Z101	5	10/12/2012	December
9	Z102	4	14/01/2012	January
10	Z102	3	27/10/2012	October
11	Z102	4	05/07/2012	July
12	Z102	2	30/04/2012	April
13	Z102	1	16/07/2012	July
14	Z102	4	13/10/2012	October
15	Z102	1	17/12/2012	December
16	Z102	5	20/07/2012	July
17	Z103	2	28/02/2012	February

Once the data is sorted, select it, and click the **subtotal** button.

The Subtotal dialogue box will appear. Choose the column you wish to subtotal by – we wish to add a subtotal at each change in product.

The function depends on the information you need. We want a total of the sales, so use **SUM**.

As we want to find the total sales, this is the column we need a subtotal for – note that more than one column can be chosen.

The options at the bottom can be checked or unchecked depending on what you need. Click OK to complete the subtotals.

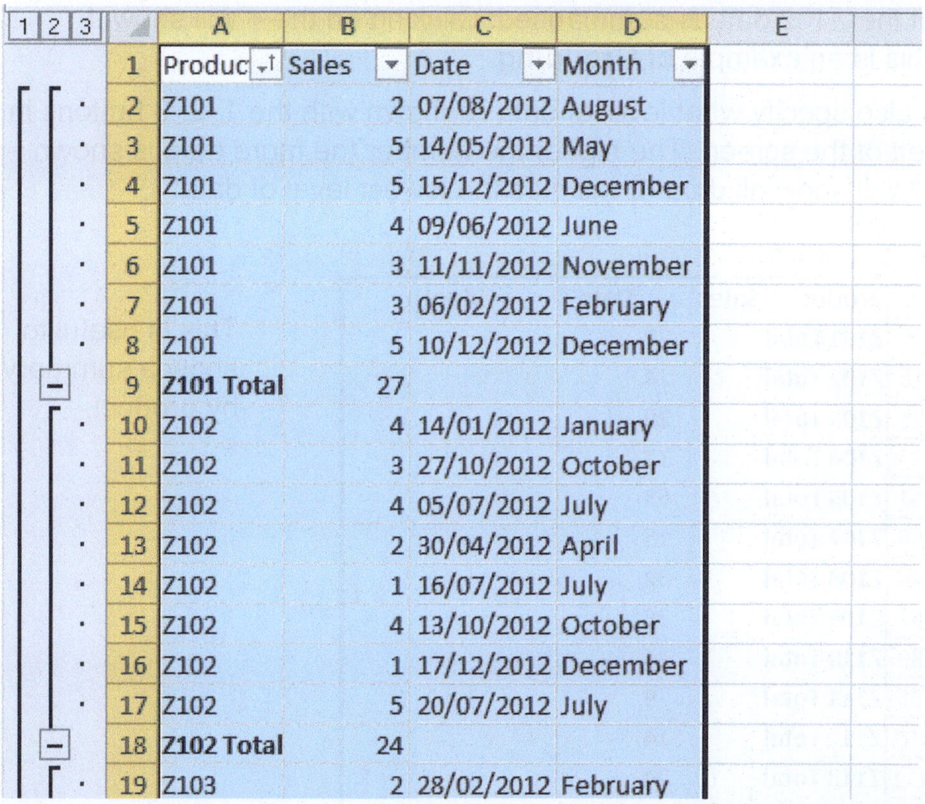

	A	B	C	D
1	Produc	Sales	Date	Month
2	Z101	2	07/08/2012	August
3	Z101	5	14/05/2012	May
4	Z101	5	15/12/2012	December
5	Z101	4	09/06/2012	June
6	Z101	3	11/11/2012	November
7	Z101	3	06/02/2012	February
8	Z101	5	10/12/2012	December
9	**Z101 Total**	27		
10	Z102	4	14/01/2012	January
11	Z102	3	27/10/2012	October
12	Z102	4	05/07/2012	July
13	Z102	2	30/04/2012	April
14	Z102	1	16/07/2012	July
15	Z102	4	13/10/2012	October
16	Z102	1	17/12/2012	December
17	Z102	5	20/07/2012	July
18	**Z102 Total**	24		
19	Z103	2	28/02/2012	February

The subtotals are added below each set of data, as required. Note that some extra buttons have appeared on the left of the sheet too – these allow you to quickly hide and show data. Clicking on the **[–]** boxes will hide the data concerned.

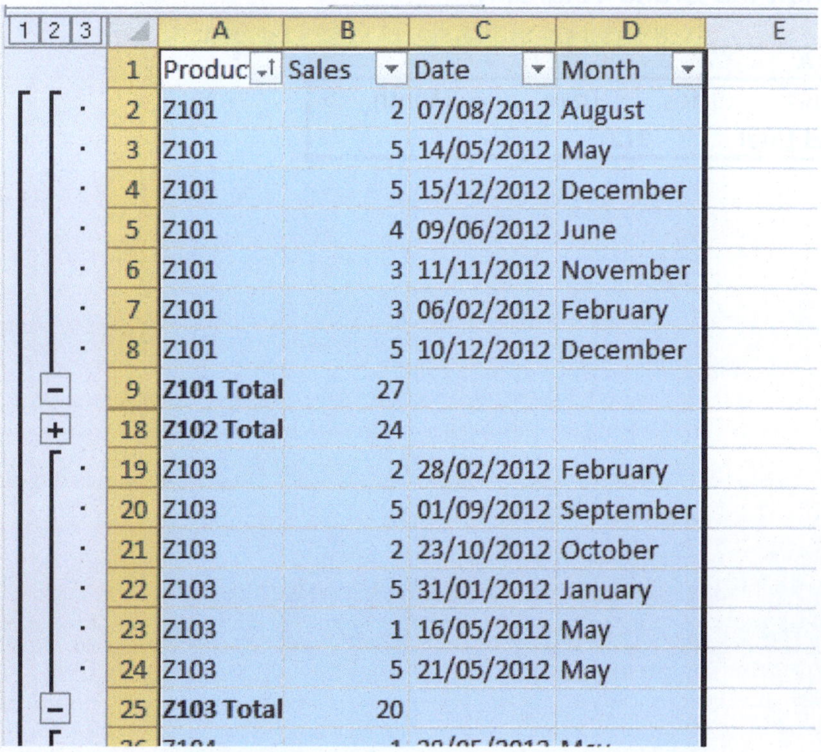

	A	B	C	D
1	Produc	Sales	Date	Month
2	Z101	2	07/08/2012	August
3	Z101	5	14/05/2012	May
4	Z101	5	15/12/2012	December
5	Z101	4	09/06/2012	June
6	Z101	3	11/11/2012	November
7	Z101	3	06/02/2012	February
8	Z101	5	10/12/2012	December
9	**Z101 Total**	27		
18	**Z102 Total**	24		
19	Z103	2	28/02/2012	February
20	Z103	5	01/09/2012	September
21	Z103	2	23/10/2012	October
22	Z103	5	31/01/2012	January
23	Z103	1	16/05/2012	May
24	Z103	5	21/05/2012	May
25	**Z103 Total**	20		

Note that the Z102 data is summarised. Clicking on the + will show it again. This is an example of **Grouping**.

You can also specify what level of data is shown with the 1, 2, 3 buttons in the top left of the screen. The higher the number the more data is shown – clicking **3** will show all data. **2** will hide the lowest level of data:

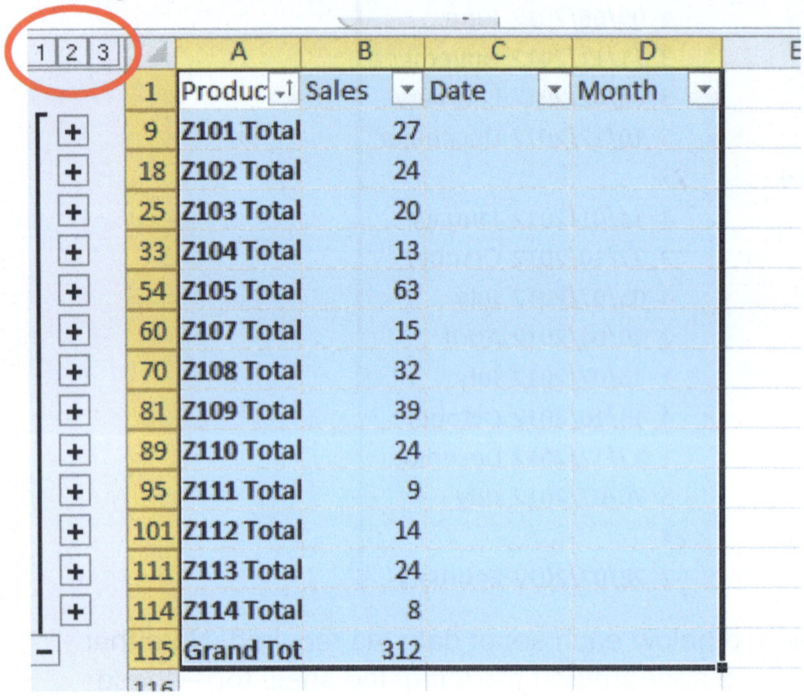

	A	B	C	D
1	Produc	Sales	Date	Month
9	Z101 Total	27		
18	Z102 Total	24		
25	Z103 Total	20		
33	Z104 Total	13		
54	Z105 Total	63		
60	Z107 Total	15		
70	Z108 Total	32		
81	Z109 Total	39		
89	Z110 Total	24		
95	Z111 Total	9		
101	Z112 Total	14		
111	Z113 Total	24		
114	Z114 Total	8		
115	Grand Tot	312		

This is useful to show a summary by product.

Clicking 1 will show the Grand Total only.

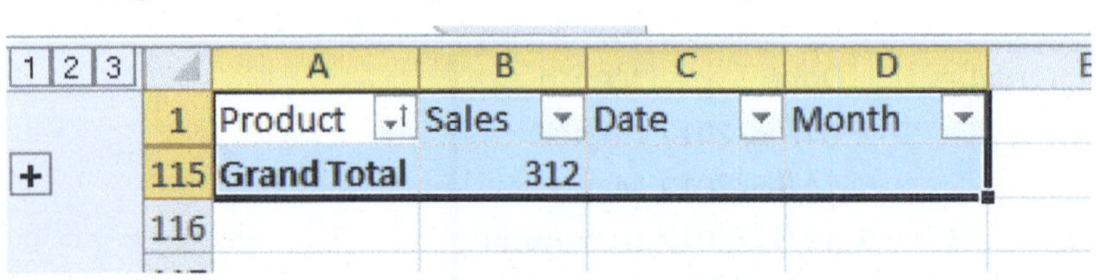

	A	B	C	D
1	Product	Sales	Date	Month
115	Grand Total	312		
116				

9.3 Removing subtotals

Removing subtotals is done in a similar way to adding subtotals – select the data with the subtotals on, and click the **Subtotal** button.

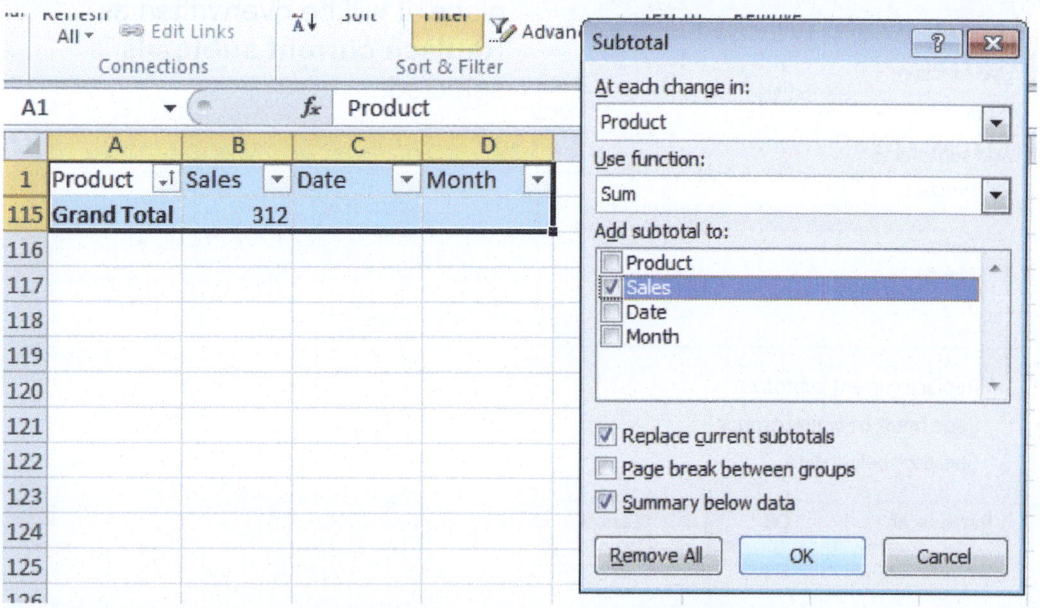

Click the **Remove All** button the remove the subtotals.

9.4 Multiple subtotals

It is possible to have more than one subtotal on a data set. For example we may wish to show sales by product, but then summarised by month within each product.

As with normal subtotalling, the data must be sorted accordingly – if we need to subtotal on 2 bases, we must sort by the column we are subtotalling on first, then by the second subtotal column.

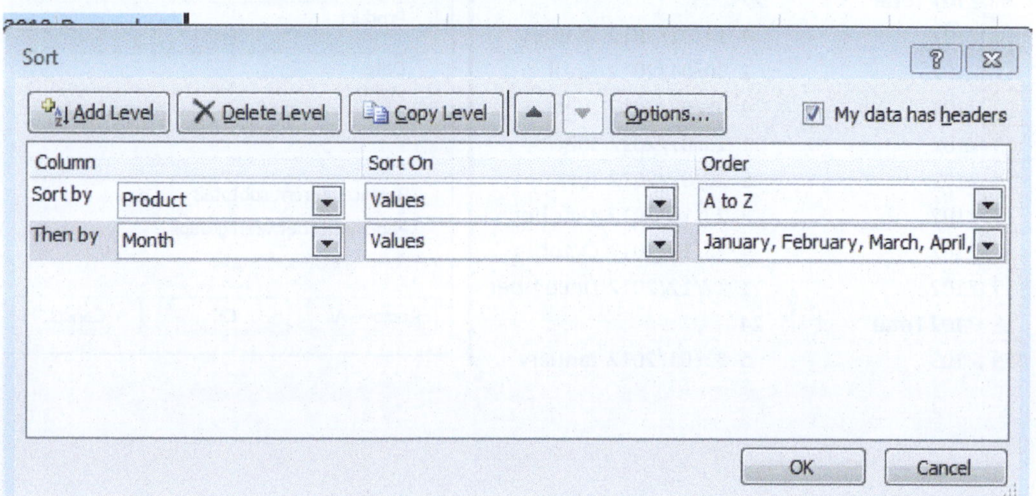

Add the first subtotal in the normal way:

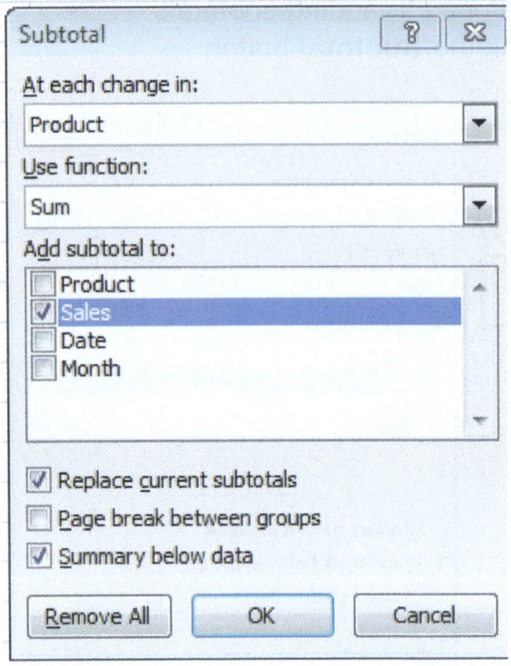

If you already have a subtotal in place, it will be overwritten as **Replace current subtotals** is selected.

To add the second subtotal, simply select the data again (although it should still be selected), and click subtotal again.

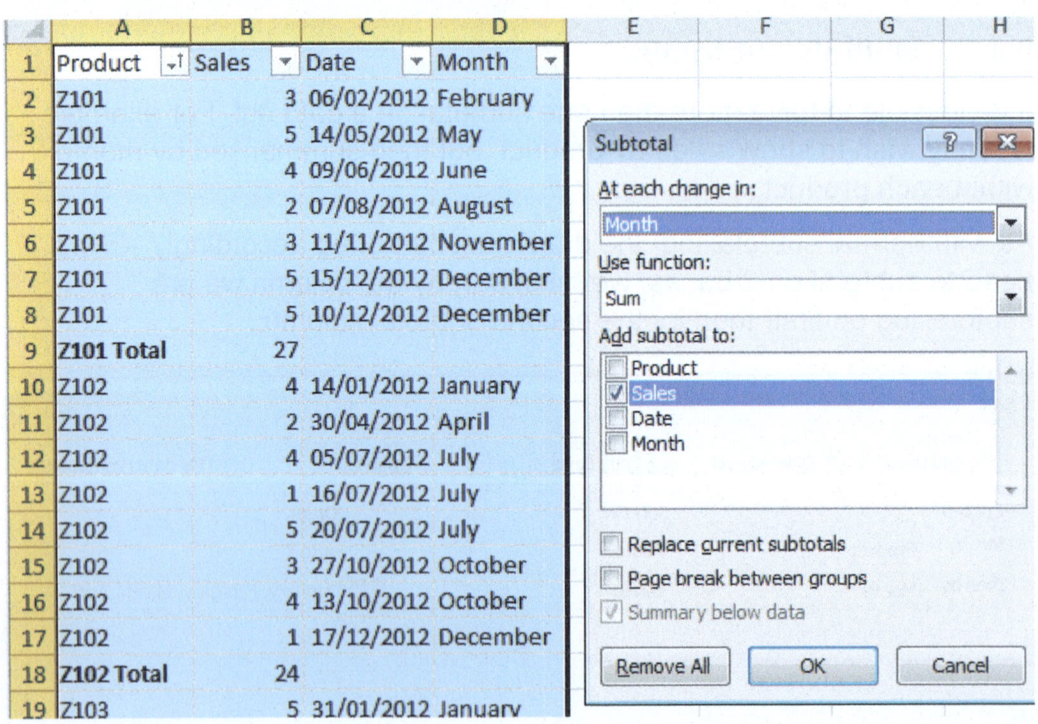

It is essential here that **Replace current subtotals** is unchecked, otherwise the first subtotal will be overwritten.

	A	B	C	D	E
1	Product	Sales	Date	Month	
2	Z101	3	06/02/2012	February	
3		3		**February Total**	
4	Z101	5	14/05/2012	May	
5		5		**May Total**	
6	Z101	4	09/06/2012	June	
7		4		**June Total**	
8	Z101	2	07/08/2012	August	
9		2		**August Total**	
10	Z101	3	11/11/2012	November	
11		3		**November Total**	
12	Z101	5	15/12/2012	December	
13	Z101	5	10/12/2012	December	
14		10		**December Total**	
15	**Z101 Total**	27			

The second subtotals will be inserted. You can see there are now five levels of data to display, and these can be used to quickly show what we need to see.

	A	B	C	D	E	F	G
1	Product	Sales	Date	Month			
3		3		**February Total**			
5		5		**May Total**			
7		4		**June Total**			
9		2		**August Total**			
11		3		**November Total**			
14		10		**December Total**			
15	**Z101 Total**	27					
17		4		**January Total**			
19		2		**April Total**			
23		10		**July Total**			
26		7		**October Total**			
28		1		**December Total**			
29	**Z102 Total**	24					

Level 4 shows the totals for each product and month.

9.5 Activities

The activities in this guide are designed to test your knowledge on the techniques shown in this chapter. They may also use techniques used in previous chapters, to build up your knowledge. Suggested answers are available on MyKaplan, although it is better to refer to the notes and try to understand the methods than look straight at the answers.

Activity 9-1

This activity allows you to practice **adding** and **removing subtotals**. It also acts as a reminder on **Sorting** data, as this is essential for subtotalling.

(a) Open the **Subtotal** file in the **Activities** workbook. This data is already subtotalled by Product.

(b) Remove the subtotals.

(c) Add subtotals for Quantity and Revenue by month (sort by Month).

(d) Select grouping level 2 – to show the monthly totals.

(e) Save the file as **Activity 9-1** in the **Solutions** folder.

Activity 9-2

This activity allows you to practice **adding** and **removing subtotals**. It also acts as a reminder on **Sorting** data, as this is essential for subtotalling.

(a) Open the **Subtotal** file in the **Activities** workbook. This data is already subtotalled by Product.

(b) Remove the subtotals.

(c) Sort the data by Month and by Product Code.

(d) Add a subtotal of Sales Quantity and Revenue by month.

(d) Add another subtotal by Product Code (keeping the other subtotals)

(e) Select grouping level 3 – to show the monthly and product subtotals.

(f) Save the file as **Activity 9-2** in the **Solutions** folder.

Panes, windows and split

10

10.1 Introduction

This chapter will explain to you how to freeze panes and show you how to view two or more worksheets side by side.

KNOWLEDGE

2.1 Explain what methods can be used to summarise, analyse and interpret spreadsheet data and when to use them.

The options required are found on the **View** tab, in the **Window** menu.

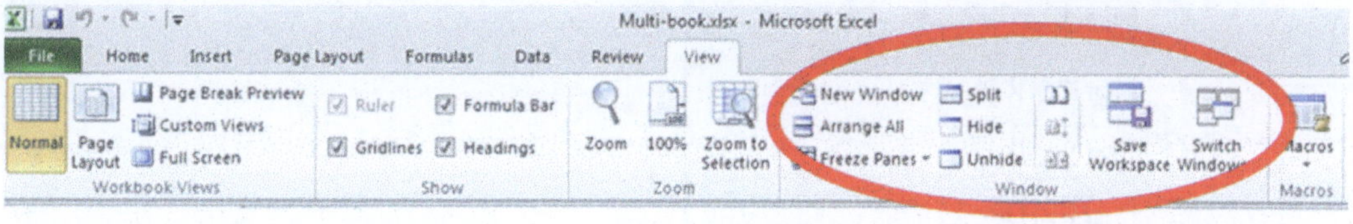

10.2 Freeze panes

When you have a lot of data in a spreadsheet and you want to scroll down or across, it is very handy to be able to 'Freeze Panes'. When you do this Excel will 'freeze' in position all rows above the 'Active Cell' and all columns to the left of the 'Active Cell'.

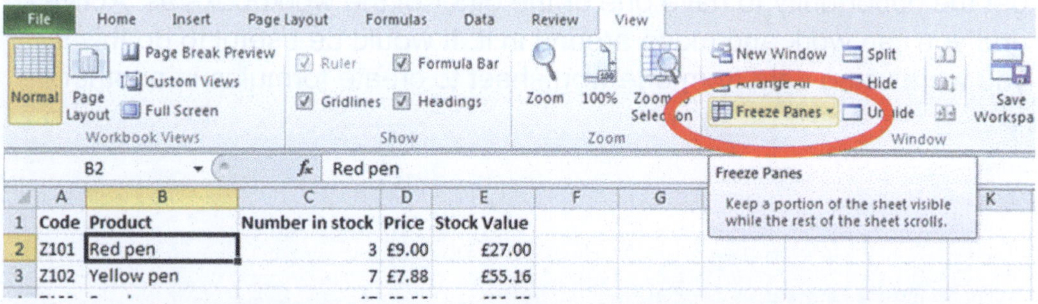

Click on the **Freeze Panes** button within the **View** tab to turn freeze on or off.

This is very useful for large spreadsheets where you want the header row(s) to stay visible, and possibly the first column(s).

10.3 Windows

It is possible to view 2 or more workbooks at the same time. You need to open the workbooks that you want to view first, then select the **Arrange All** button.

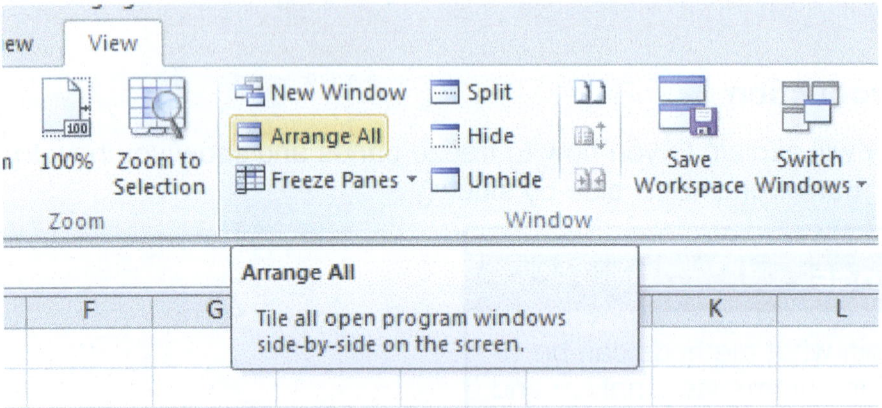

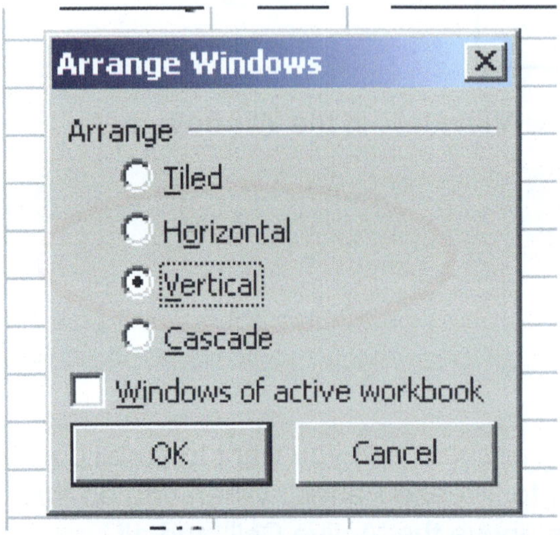

Horizontal and Vertical are often the best options. Using this method you get the opportunity to have one or the other of the workbooks as 'Active', and you can work and move around in it. It would be useful to do this if you were using data from one worksheet to create formulas in another..

10.4 View side-by-side

This is an extension of the Arrange option. You can compare two workbooks side by side. Using this option you can enable **synchronous scrolling** – in effect both workbooks are 'active', so if you scroll down in one, the other scrolls down too.

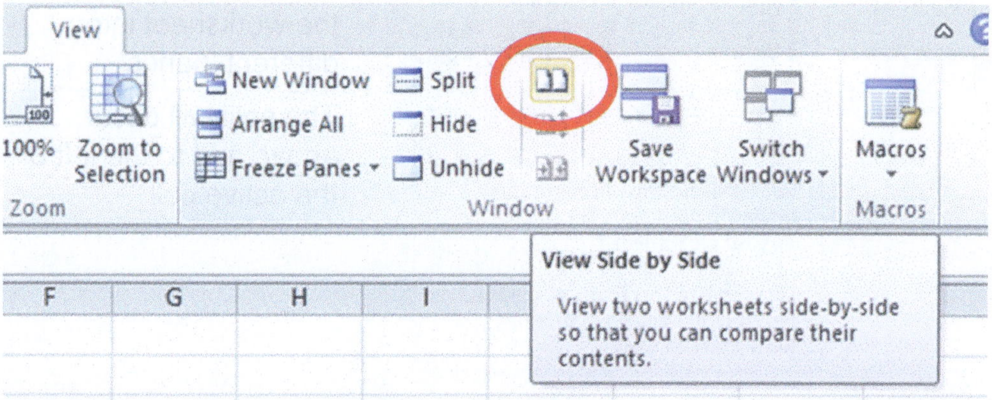

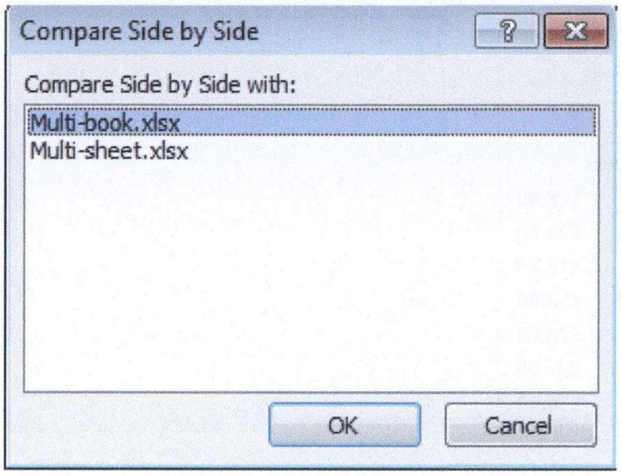

If you have more than two workbooks open, you will be asked which one you wish to compare with the active book.

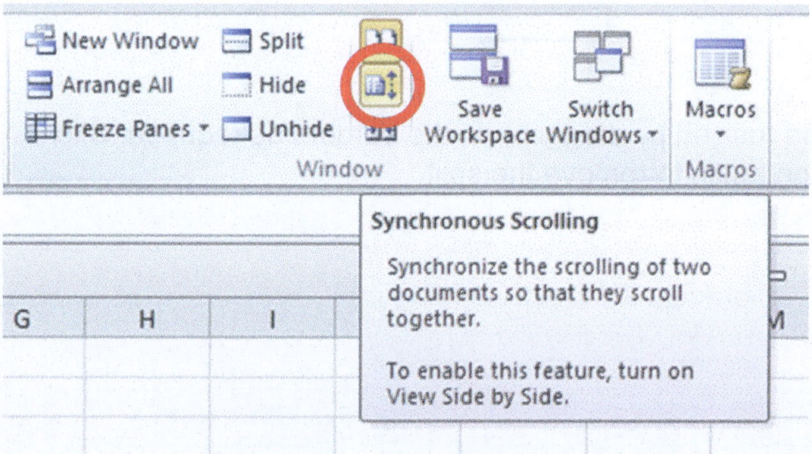

Use this button to turn synchronous scrolling on or off when in this view.

10.5 Splitting a worksheet

This tool is used when you have a great deal of similar data in a worksheet and you wish to make a comparison to 2 different parts.

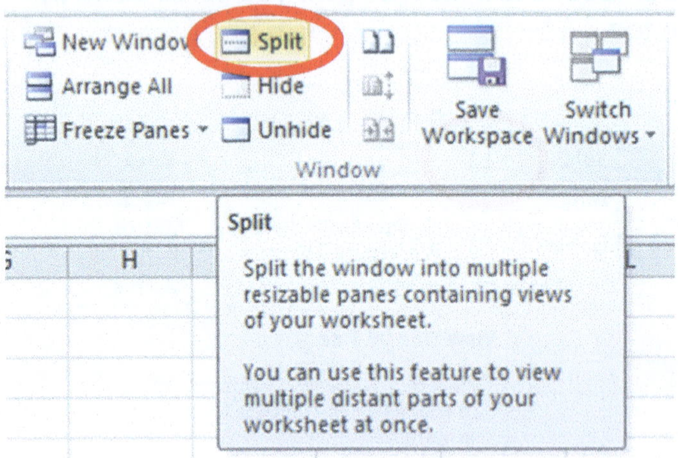

Select this option to split the worksheet into different 'panes'.

The split will occur above and to the left of the active cell.

D19

	A	B	C	D	G	H	I	J	K
1	Labour rate:	Bonus %							
2	£8.00	10%							
3									
4	Staff number	Hours worked	Basic pay	Bonus					
5	F0254	35	£280.00	£28.00					
6	F0255	32	£256.00	£25.60					
7	F0256	34	£272.00	£27.20					
8	F0257	35	£280.00	£28.00					
9	F0258	30	£240.00	£24.00					
10	F0259	40	£320.00	£32.00					
11	F0260	38	£304.00	£30.40					
16									
17									
18									
19									
20									

The panes can be resized by dragging on the borders as required. Click on the **Split** button again to remove the split.

10.6 Hide/Unhide

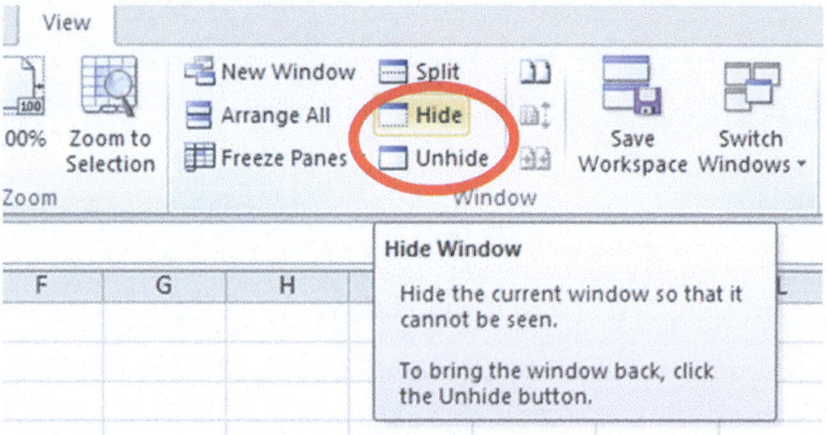

The Hide option can be used to keep a spreadsheet open, but hidden from view. Unhide allows you to show hidden workbooks.

10.7 Activities

These techniques can be used with any spreadsheet – try them out. Have another go at populating the District Totals workbook in Activity 7-6 with the workbooks arranged vertically.

These techniques relate to the appearance of the workbook on the screen, the underlying data will not be affected anyway, so there is no need to worry about accidentally deleting anything important!

Sharing data

11

11.1 Introduction

This chapter will explain how to import data into different formats, how to link data to other applications, and how to embed data.

KNOWLEDGE
1.3 Combine and link data from different sources.

11.2 Types of data formats

Sometimes we are given data that is not in spreadsheet format and will therefore not open up in Excel within the rows and columns that are provided. This data can be in a number of different formats. In this session we are going to look at data that comes in a **delimited format**. Common types of format could be **Text** [.txt] or **CSV** [.csv] files. These are often 'data dumps' from other systems within an organisation, so this technique is very useful in many practical circumstances.

Delimited data comes with characters such as commas or tabs separating each field. Excel will open these data formats but we need to do some work on them first before they are easily viewed.

11.3 CSV files

CSV are probably the most commonly used type of import file. The name means **Comma Separated Values** – each data item is separated by a comma. They can be viewed using programmes such as Microsoft Word or Notepad, and would look something like this.

Stock download.csv - Notepad

File Edit Format View Help

```
Code,Product,Number in stock,Price
Z101,Red pen,3,£9.00
Z102,Yellow pen,7,£7.88
Z103,Purple pen,17,£5.86
Z104,Green pen,13,£1.19
Z105,Red crayon,20,£9.56
Z105,Yellow crayon,4,£7.27
Z107,Purple crayon,9,£1.86
Z108,Green crayon,17,£0.86
Z109,Red ruler,17,£4.55
Z110,Yellow ruler,20,£0.56
Z111,Green ruler,12,£5.35
Z112,Purple ruler,4,£4.88
Z113,Blue calculator,12,£3.53
Z114,Orange calculator,6,£7.16
```

Notice how the rows appear as we would expect to see them, but there are no columns within Notepad, so each data item is separated by a comma. If we copy this into Excel then all the commas would make data manipulation difficult.

While CSV is the most common, any character can be used to separate data items, such as **space**, **semi-colon**, or **tab**.

11.4 Importing CSV or other text files

This is performed using the **Get External Data** menu on the **Data** tab.

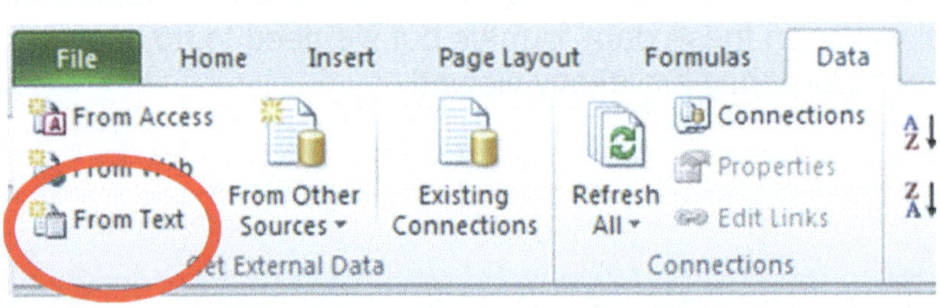

There are a few options here, but the most commonly required is the **From Text** option circled. This allows you to import any type of text file.

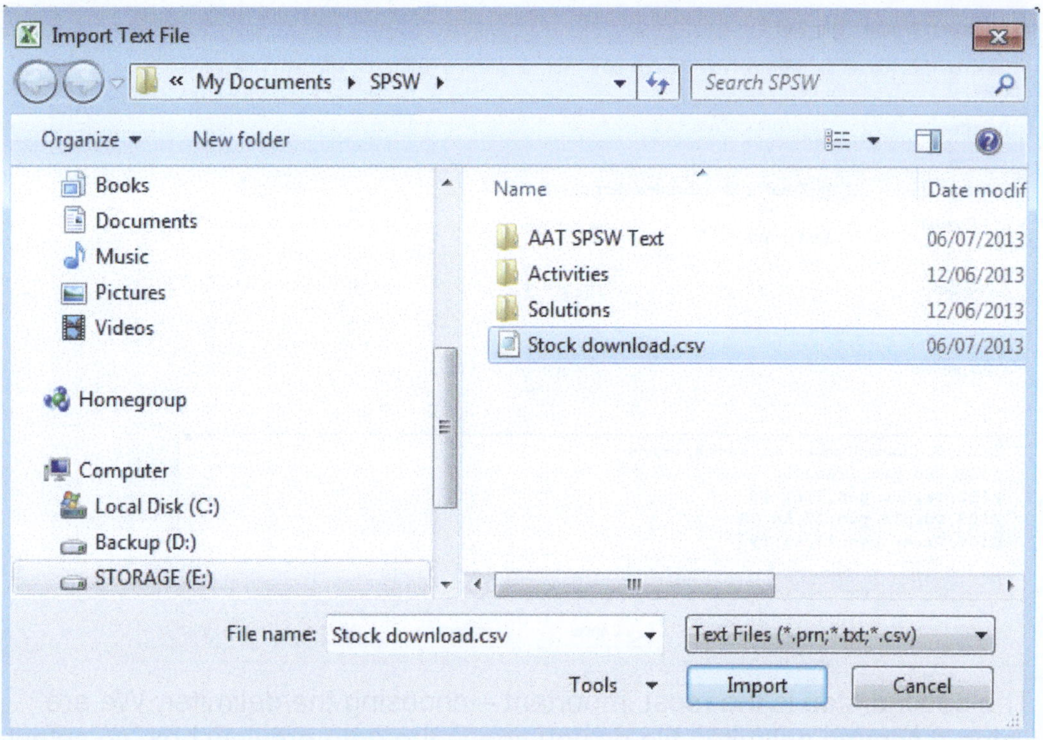

After clicking the **From Text** button, find the file required in the same way as you would when opening a normal Excel file.

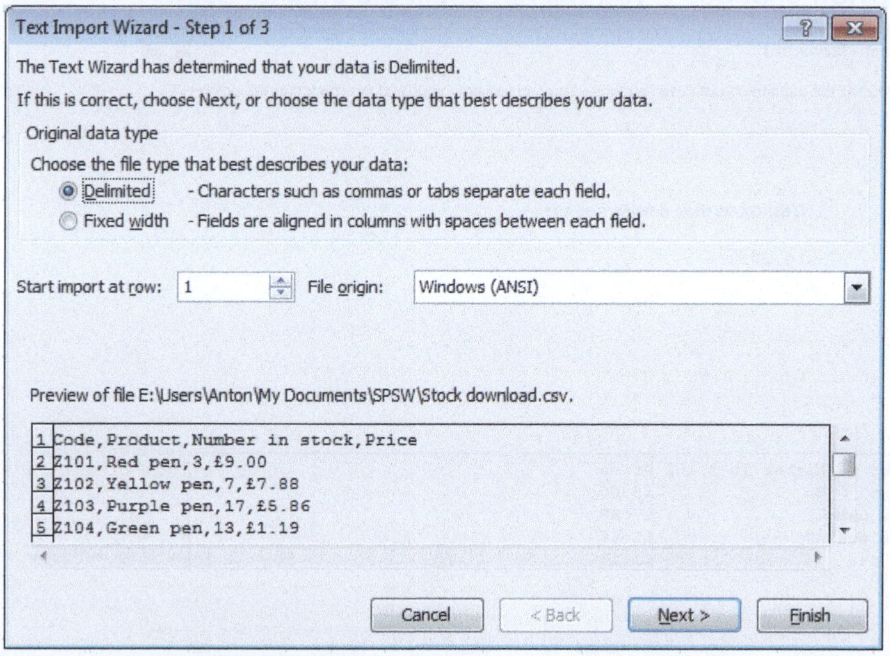

The **Text Import Wizard** will then open. This looks complicated, but there is very little to change – we are dealing with 'Delimited' files, which will be selected by default, so click **Next**.

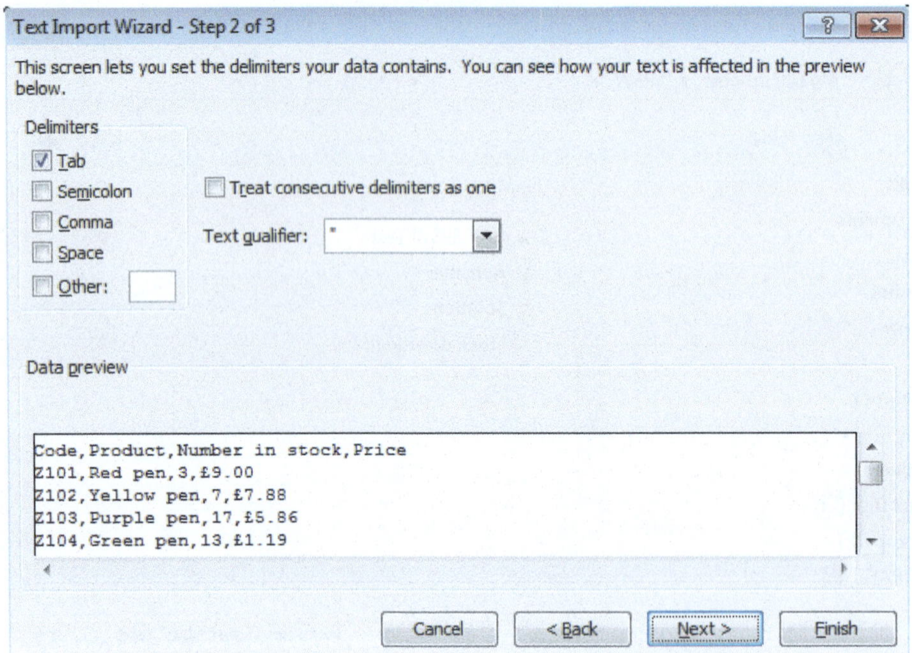

The second step is the most important – choosing the delimiter. We are using a comma delimited file as you see in the data preview box, so select that and unselect tab. It should be fairly clear which character is being used, but if you are not sure try clicking on the different options and see how the preview changes – you will not affect the original data.

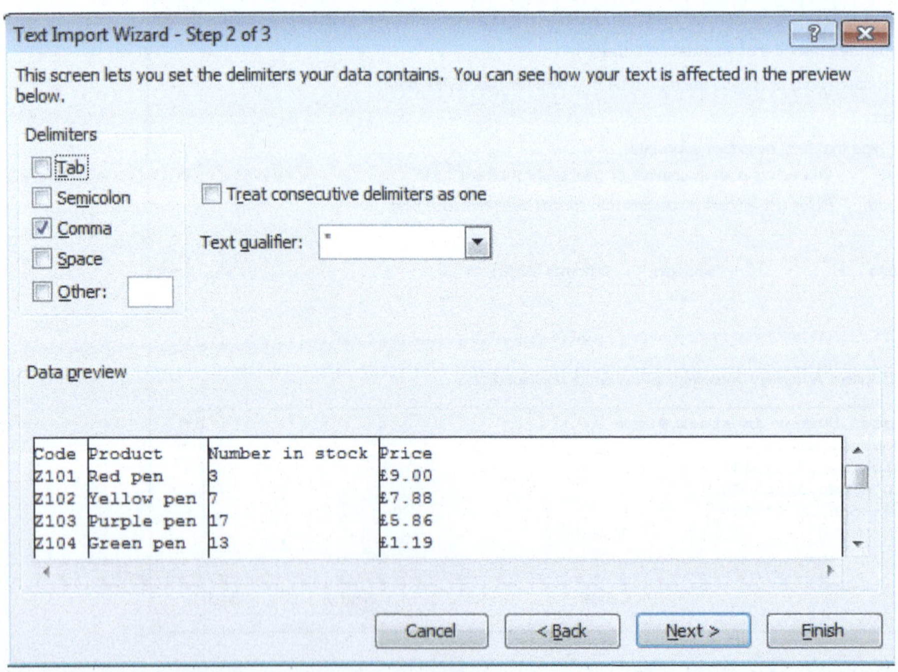

You can see once the correct delimiter is chosen, the commas in the preview are removed and replaced with column breaks, which is exactly what is required. The next step allows each column of data to be formatted or ignored in the import but as we can do that within Excel we could click on **Finish** now. For reference let us look at the final step.

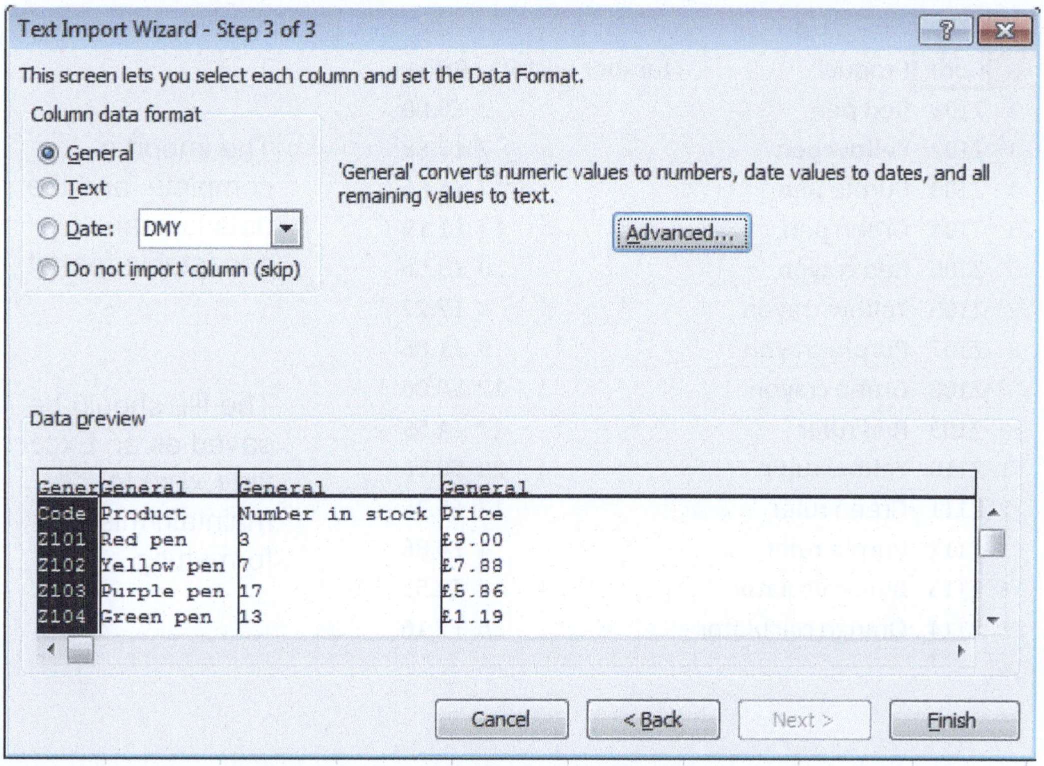

This allows you to set the format of each column (select the column by left-clicking on the column in the Data preview), or to choose not to import a particular column.

Clicking **Finish** completes the import.

Once we have asked Excel to '**Import Data**' we are presented with a dialogue box so that we can choose the data file that we want to import. Once the file is selected we are presented with the following screen.

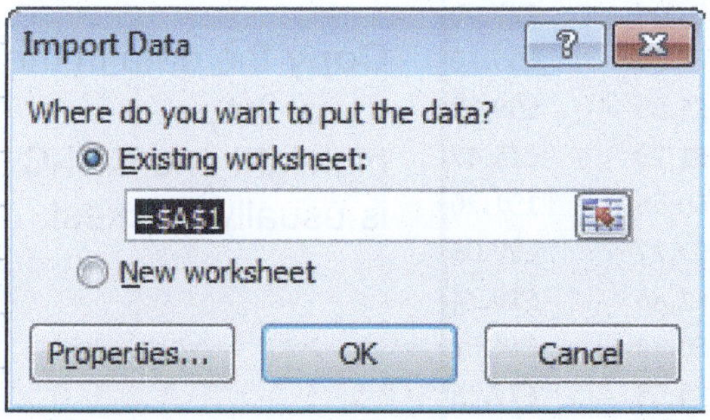

You can then select where you would like the data to be placed. The default is usually acceptable. Click **OK** to proceed.

	A	B	C	D	E
1	Code	Product	Number in stock	Price	
2	Z101	Red pen	3	£9.00	
3	Z102	Yellow pen	7	£7.88	
4	Z103	Purple pen	17	£5.86	
5	Z104	Green pen	13	£1.19	
6	Z105	Red crayon	20	£9.56	
7	Z105	Yellow crayon	4	£7.27	
8	Z107	Purple crayon	9	£1.86	
9	Z108	Green crayon	17	£0.86	
10	Z109	Red ruler	17	£4.55	
11	Z110	Yellow ruler	20	£0.56	
12	Z111	Green ruler	12	£5.35	
13	Z112	Purple ruler	4	£4.88	
14	Z113	Blue calculator	12	£3.53	
15	Z114	Orange calculator	6	£7.16	
16					
17					

The import is complete, and the data is in an acceptable format.

The file should be saved as an Excel file (.xlsx) to maintain this formatting.

11.5 Copying Excel data into other applications

Embedding data

Embedding data is effectively a copy and paste from Excel to another Microsoft Office application such as Word.

To **embed** the data:

	A	B	C	D	E
1	Code	Product	Number in stock	Price	Stock Value
2	Z101	Red pen	3	£9.00	£27.00
3	Z102	Yellow pen	7	£7.88	£55.16
4	Z103	Purple pen	17	£5.86	£99.62
5	Z104	Green pen	13	£1.19	£15.47
6	Z105	Red crayon	20	£9.56	£191.20
7	Z105	Yellow crayon	4	£7.27	£29.08
8	Z107	Purple crayon	9	£1.86	£16.74
9	Z108	Green crayon	17	£0.86	£14.62
10	Z109	Red ruler	17	£4.55	£77.35
11	Z110	Yellow ruler	20	£0.56	£11.20
12	Z111	Green ruler	12	£5.35	£64.20
13	Z112	Purple ruler	4	£4.88	£19.52
14	Z113	Blue calculator	12	£3.53	£42.36
15	Z114	Orange calculator	6	£7.16	£42.96

Copy the data in the usual way – highlight and **Ctrl-C** is usually quickest.

In Word, or whichever application you wish to paste the data into, select Paste Special and choose Paste.

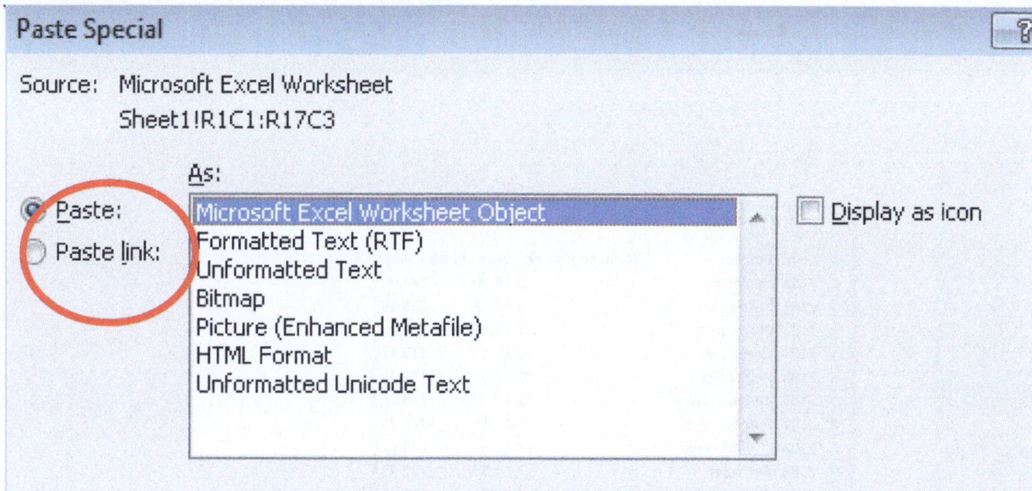

The data is embedded in Word. It can be edited by double-clicking within the data.

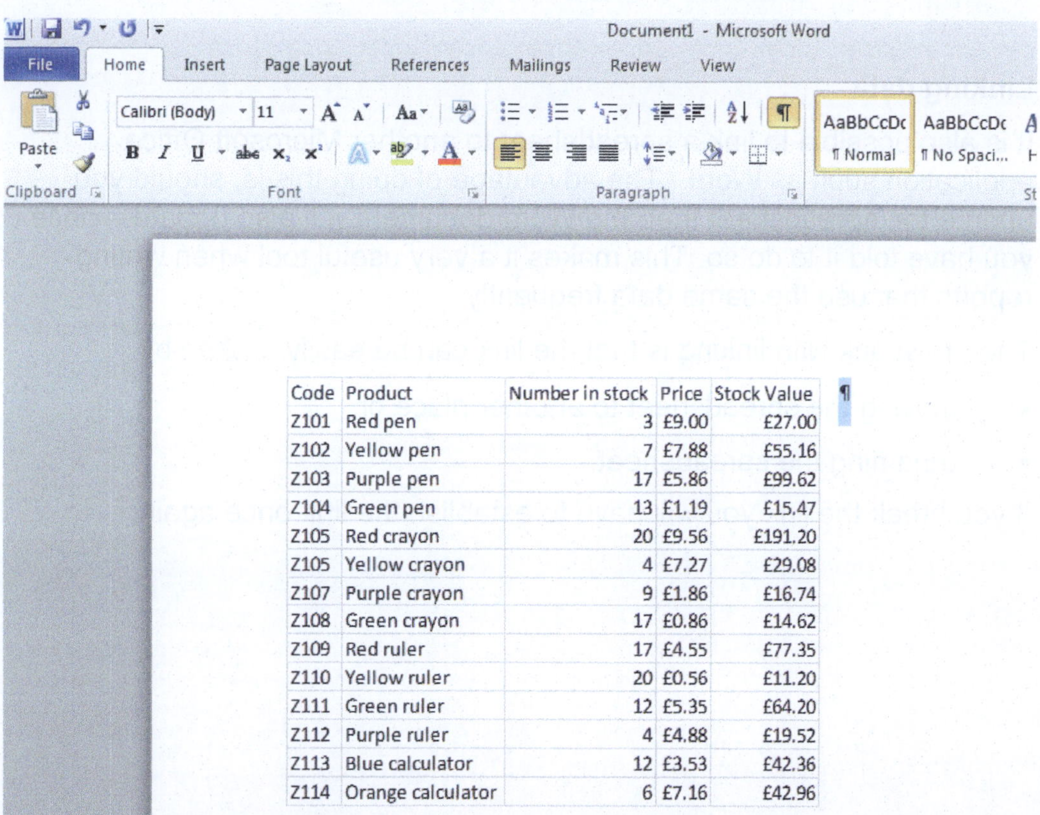

Code	Product	Number in stock	Price	Stock Value
Z101	Red pen	3	£9.00	£27.00
Z102	Yellow pen	7	£7.88	£55.16
Z103	Purple pen	17	£5.86	£99.62
Z104	Green pen	13	£1.19	£15.47
Z105	Red crayon	20	£9.56	£191.20
Z105	Yellow crayon	4	£7.27	£29.08
Z107	Purple crayon	9	£1.86	£16.74
Z108	Green crayon	17	£0.86	£14.62
Z109	Red ruler	17	£4.55	£77.35
Z110	Yellow ruler	20	£0.56	£11.20
Z111	Green ruler	12	£5.35	£64.20
Z112	Purple ruler	4	£4.88	£19.52
Z113	Blue calculator	12	£3.53	£42.36
Z114	Orange calculator	6	£7.16	£42.96

This will effectively open Excel within Word, and allow you to edit as required.

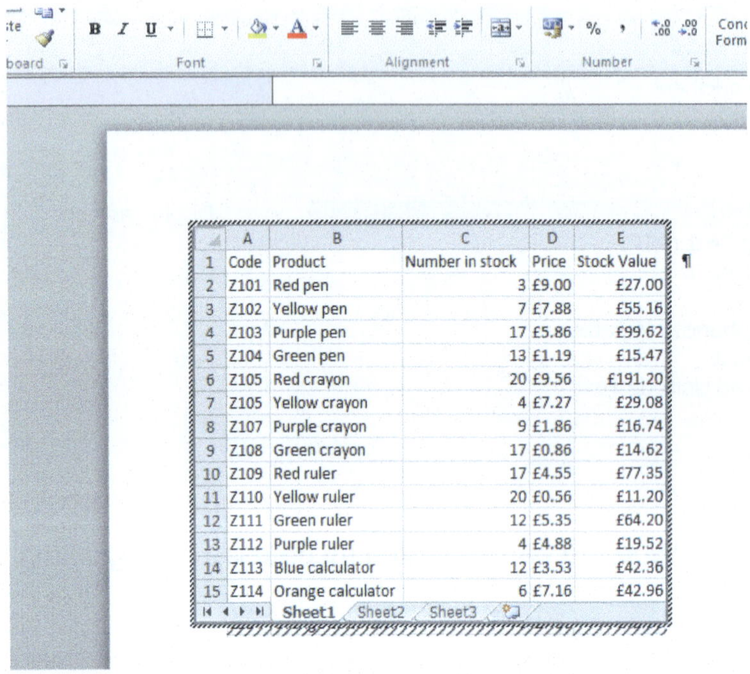

	A	B	C	D	E
1	Code	Product	Number in stock	Price	Stock Value
2	Z101	Red pen	3	£9.00	£27.00
3	Z102	Yellow pen	7	£7.88	£55.16
4	Z103	Purple pen	17	£5.86	£99.62
5	Z104	Green pen	13	£1.19	£15.47
6	Z105	Red crayon	20	£9.56	£191.20
7	Z105	Yellow crayon	4	£7.27	£29.08
8	Z107	Purple crayon	9	£1.86	£16.74
9	Z108	Green crayon	17	£0.86	£14.62
10	Z109	Red ruler	17	£4.55	£77.35
11	Z110	Yellow ruler	20	£0.56	£11.20
12	Z111	Green ruler	12	£5.35	£64.20
13	Z112	Purple ruler	4	£4.88	£19.52
14	Z113	Blue calculator	12	£3.53	£42.36
15	Z114	Orange calculator	6	£7.16	£42.96

Linking data

It is also possible to link a spreadsheet to another Microsoft Office application such as Word. The advantage of doing this is, should you update the spreadsheet then the Word document will also update – once you have told it to do so. This makes it a very useful tool when writing reports that use the same data frequently.

The drawback with linking is that the link can be easily broken by:

- moving the spreadsheet to another place or
- renaming the spreadsheet.

If you break the link you will have to establish the link once again.

To **link** the data to the original Excel file, select Paste Special and then **Paste Link**.

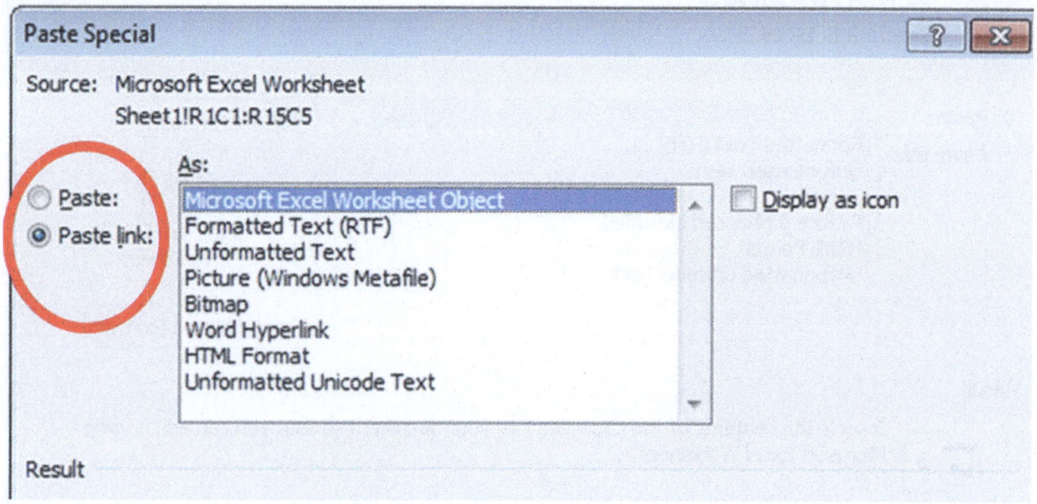

The data will appear in the same way in Word. If data is updated in the Excel file the Word document will also update once you have told word to do so by right-clicking in the word document and clicking **Update link**.

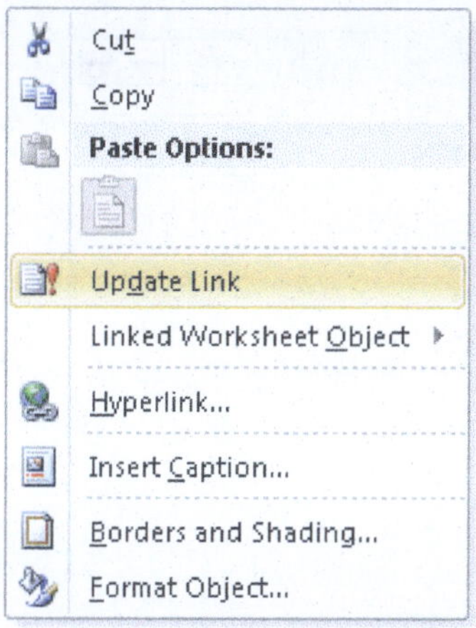

If you double-click on the data in Word to edit it you will be taken to the original workbook within Excel, rather than editing within Word.

Display as Icon

Another option you may need is the **Display as Icon** checkbox. Rather than showing the data itself, an icon (picture) of your choice will be shown. This can prevent your document being cluttered with lots of data, and allow users to click on the icon to see the data as required.

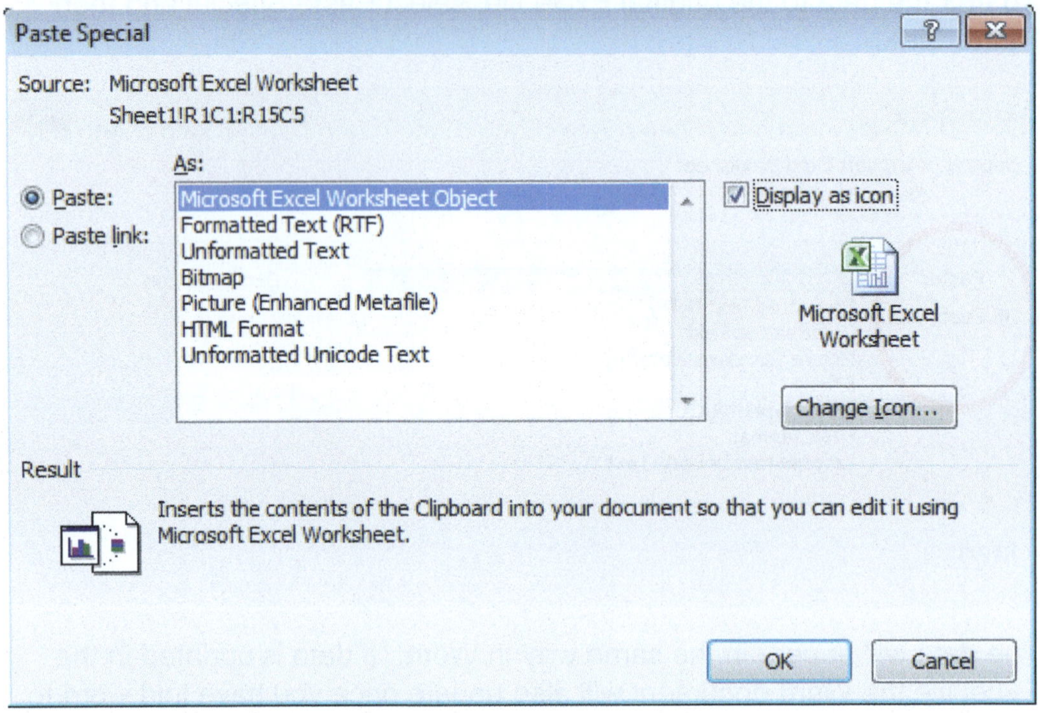

The default icon and caption can be changed by clicking on **Change Icon**.

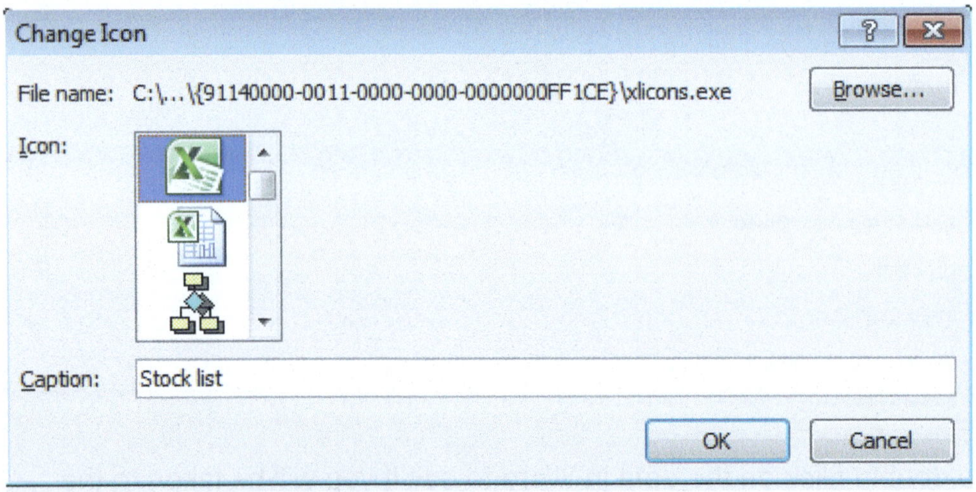

The icon will be shown within the report. This method is the same for both linked and embedded data.

11.6 Embedding objects into Excel

It is possible to paste objects such as pictures and word documents into Excel. This is useful if you want to put a logo or picture into a spreadsheet. If you embed a Word document into a spreadsheet you have the facility to use the Word formatting tools. You can either import a blank word document or one that has been previously saved.

This works in the same way as exporting data from Excel – copy the data, and use the **Paste Special** option to embed or link the data.

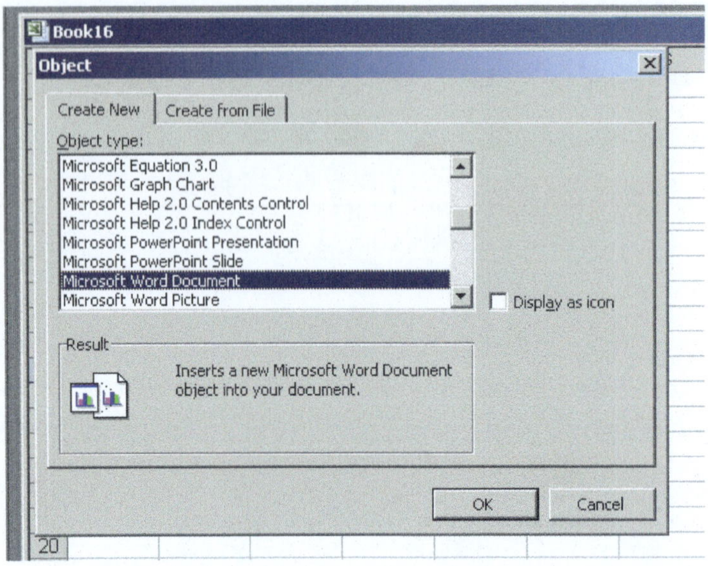

Select the required options to **paste** the information into Excel.

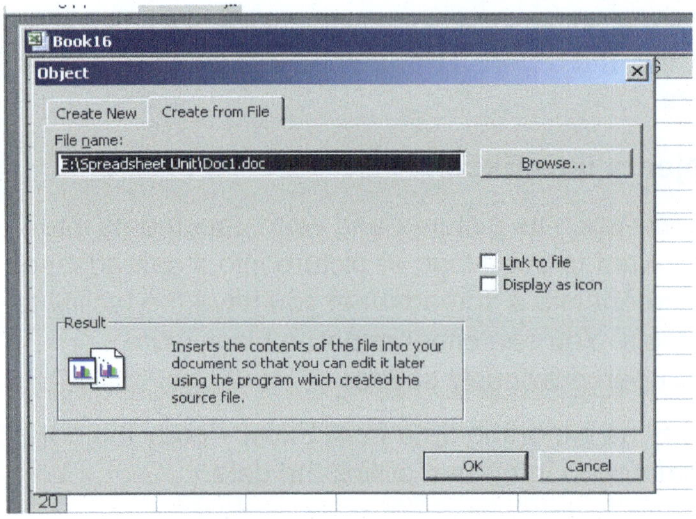

11.7 Activities

The activities in this guide are designed to test your knowledge on the techniques shown in this chapter. They may also use techniques used in previous chapters, to build up your knowledge. Suggested answers are available on MyKaplan, although it is better to refer to the notes and try to understand the methods than look straight at the answers.

Activity 11-1

This activity allows you to practise importing a text file into Excel.

(a) Open a **New** Excel workbook.

(b) In the **Activities** folder, there is a text file called **examresults**. (you may need to save the text file to be able to access it to import it)

(c) Use the **Get External Data** tool in the **Data** tab to import the text file.

(d) When importing, note that the file is **comma delimited**.

(e) Once the file is imported, save the Excel file as **Activity 11-1** in the **Solutions** folder.

Activity 11-2

This activity allows you to practise exporting data from Excel into Microsoft Word.

(a) Open a **New Word document** (in the same way you would open a New Excel Document, but from within Word).

(b) In Excel, open the **Eastern Region3** workbook in the **Activities** folder.

(c) Copy all of the data from the Excel Spreadsheet.

(d) Use **Paste Special** within word to **Embed** the Excel information into Word (no link)

(e) Save the Word Document as **Activity 11-2** in the **Solutions** folder, and close it.

Activity 11-3

This activity allows you to practise exporting data from Excel into Microsoft Word.

(a) Open a **New Word document** (in the same way you would open a New Excel Document, but from within Word).

(b) In Excel, open the **Eastern Region3** workbook in the **Activities** folder.

(c) Copy all of the data from the Excel Spreadsheet.

(d) Use **Paste Special** within word to **Link** the Excel information into Word.

(e) Change the value in cell C2 of the Excel worksheet to 9999. In the word document right click and update the link. Check that the value in the Word document is also changed.

(f) Save the Word Document as **Activity 11-3** in the **Solutions** folder, and close it.

(g) Close the Excel file without saving.

Formulas and functions

12

12.1 Introduction

This chapter will look at the various formulas and functions that are used in Excel and you will learn how to evaluate and write complex formulas.

KNOWLEDGE
2.2 Select and use a wide range of appropriate functions and formulas to meet calculation requirements.

In this session you will learn when and where to use Functions, and how to insert them into formulas so that you get the results you desire.

The Functions that you need to know are:

- Round
- Vlookup and Hlookup
- If, And & Or
- Date
  - Today
  - Now
  - Day, Weekday, Month & Year

It is common for these functions to be used together to get formulas to work effectively and you will be doing this as the chapter progresses.

In an earlier chapter you were introduced to the order of precedence. The table below shows the full order of precedence.

Operator	Symbol	Order of Precedence
Brackets	()	1
Indices (Powers)	^	2
Division	*	3
Multiplication	/	3
Addition	+	4
Subtraction	-	4
Concatenation	&	5
Equal to	=	6
Less than	<	6
Greater than	>	6

It is important to remember this order when putting formulas together (some people use **BIDMAS** (or BODMAS) to remember the first six).

12.2 ROUND

Previously, we have seen how to change the format of cells so that different numbers of decimal places are shown. One important feature of formatting that is often overlooked is that changing the format does not affect the number used.

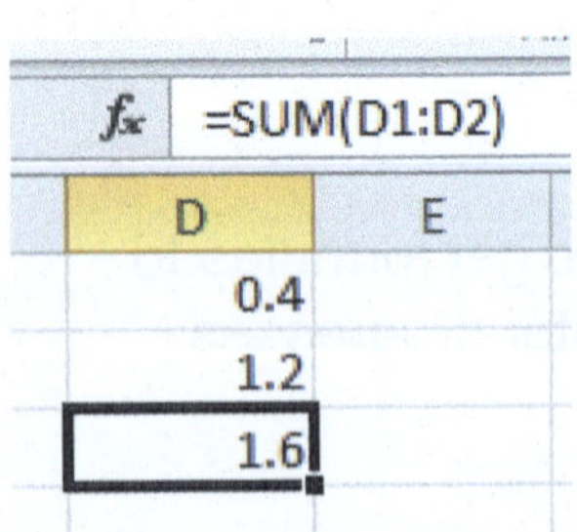

Taking a simple example, 0.4+1.2=1.6

If we change the formatting to show these numbers to 0 decimal places, the result looks odd:

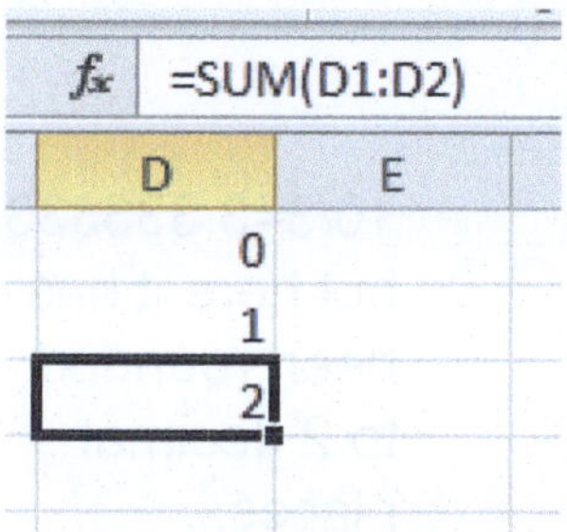

According to this, 0+1=2!

This is because Excel uses the value in the cell, not the displayed format to perform the calculation – it is still calculating 0.4+1.2, then rounding to 0 decimal places.

Instead of changing the format, you may wish to force Excel to round the numbers to a certain number of decimal places – this is often useful when dealing with currency – round to 2 decimal places. To do this, use the **ROUND** function. Like all functions in Excel, it has a set format:

=ROUND(number,num_digits)

'number' and 'num_digits' are the ARGUMENTS, as previously discussed.

number is the number or cell reference which needs rounding

num_digits is the number of decimal places you wish to round to.

For example, if you type =ROUND(4.5682,3), the value shown will be 4.568 – rounded to 3 decimal places:

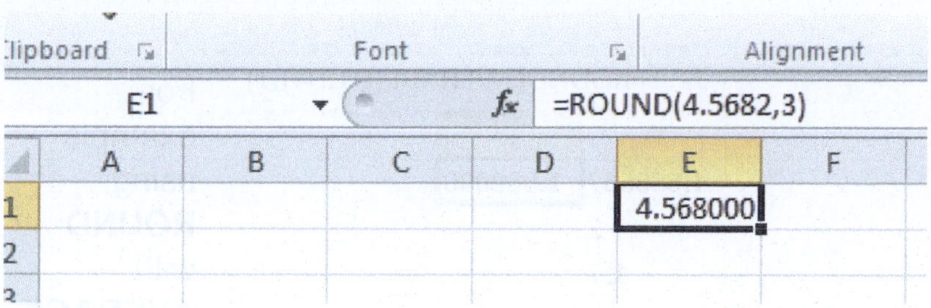

The formatting is shown to 6 decimal places, but the number has been rounded to 3.

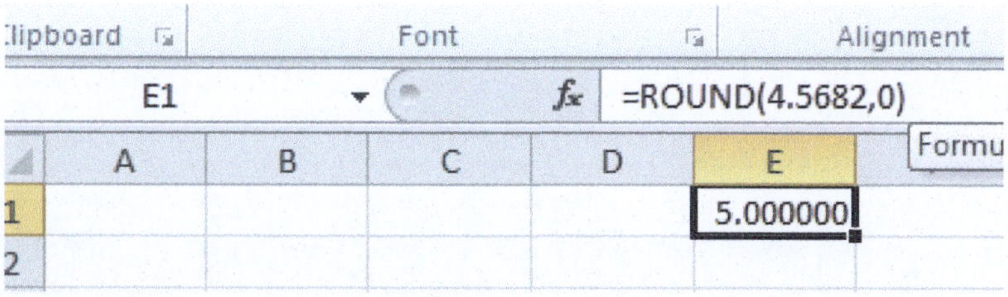

To round to the nearest number, use 0 for **num_digits**.

You can also use round to round calculations:

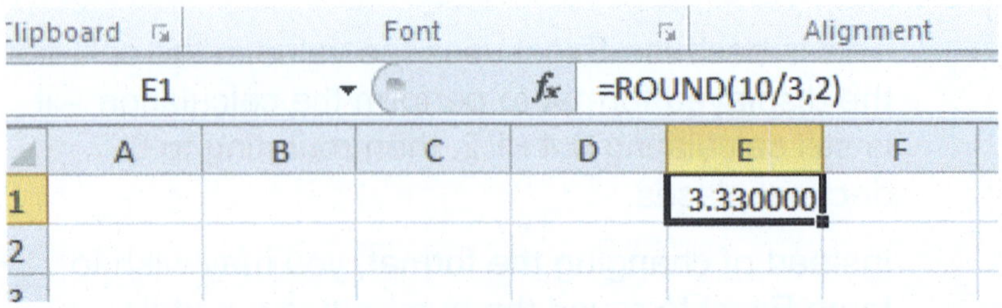

10/3=3.333333 but here it has been rounded to 2 decimal places.

Most usefully though, ROUND can be used to round cell values, by referring to them in the usual way:

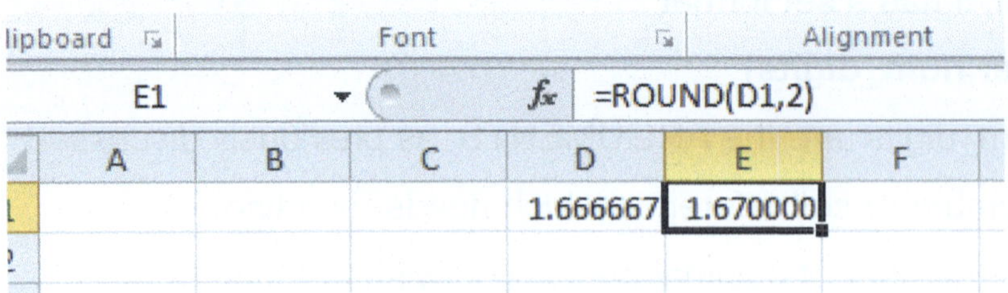

You can combine cell references, calculations and functions when using ROUND.

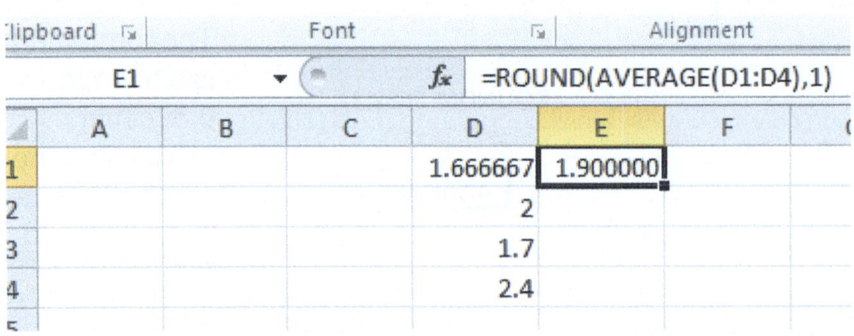

For example using **ROUND** with **AVERAGE**.

12.3 ROUNDUP and ROUNDDOWN

The ROUND function follows normal mathematical rounding rules – 0-4 are rounded down and 5-9 are rounded up. Sometimes you will want to force a number to be rounded up or down, and ROUNDUP or ROUNDDOWN will do this (remember, if you cannot remember the function's name, type what you want to do into the Insert Function menu.

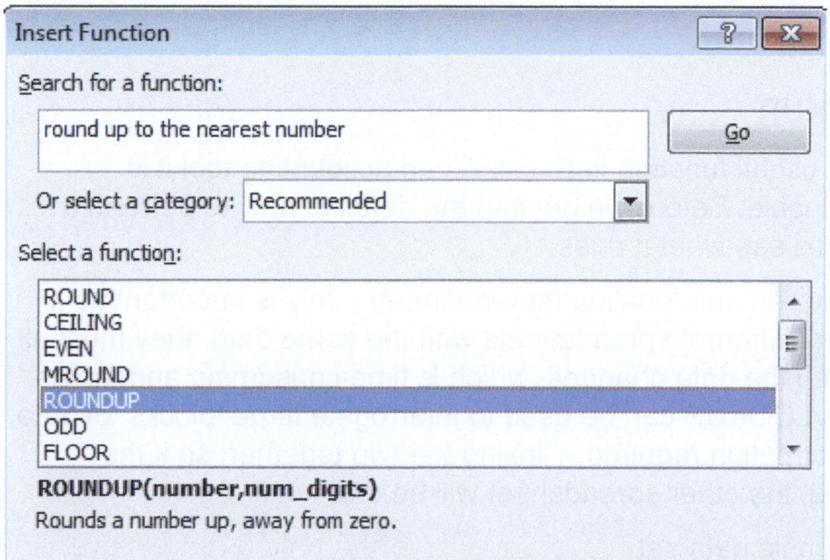

Find the function you need, and click OK.

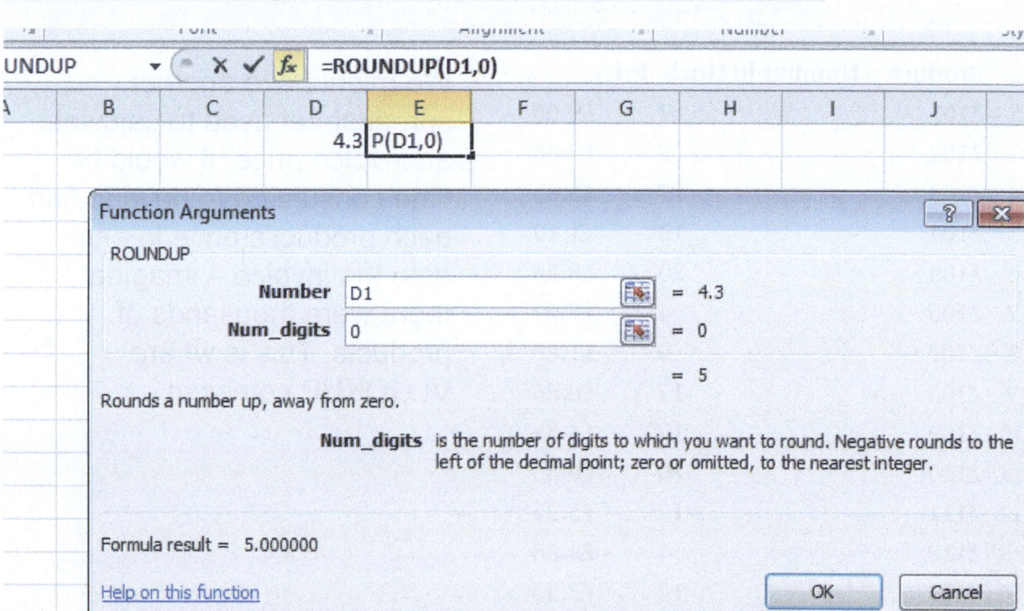

ROUNDUP has exactly the same arguments as ROUND – using the Insert Function option here allows you to enter them in a more user-friendly way – when you click in the argument box help is displayed explaining what is required. The result is also shown before you click OK.

ROUNDDOWN works in exactly the same way:

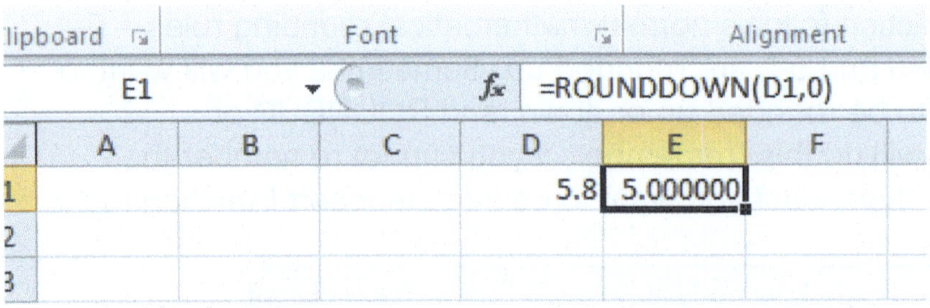

12.4 VLOOKUP

VLOOKUP is a useful function in Excel. As an accounting tool it is absolutely invaluable. Before we get into the detail of how to perform a VLOOKUP, let us see what it does.

Often, data is held in one location (spreadsheet) – this is important as if there are several different spreadsheets with the same data, they must all be updated when the data changes, which is time consuming and may lead to errors. VLOOKUP can be used to interrogate large 'blocks' of data, and find the information required – linking the two together, so if the original is edited, the other spreadsheet will be too.

Let us take a simple data set:

	A	B	C
1	**Product**	**Number in stock**	**Price**
2	Z101	3	£9.00
3	Z102	7	£7.88
4	Z103	17	£5.86
5	Z104	13	£1.19
6	Z105	20	£9.56
7	Z106	4	£7.27
8	Z107	9	£1.86
9	Z108	17	£0.86
10	Z109	17	£4.55
11	Z110	20	£0.56
12	Z111	12	£5.35
13	Z112	4	£4.88
14	Z113	12	£3.53
15	Z114	6	£7.16

We might have another spreadsheet used to calculate an invoice price. It would be time consuming to have to find each product's price to enter it onto the invoice – imagine if there were thousands of products. This is where VLOOKUP comes in.

If we set up the Invoice on the same sheet, for simplicity:

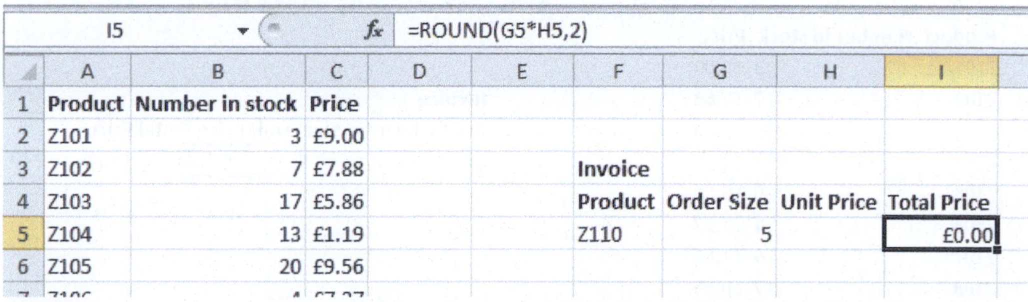

	A	B	C	D	E	F	G	H	I
1	Product	Number in stock	Price						
2	Z101	3	£9.00						
3	Z102	7	£7.88			Invoice			
4	Z103	17	£5.86			Product	Order Size	Unit Price	Total Price
5	Z104	13	£1.19			Z110	5		£0.00
6	Z105	20	£9.56						

We need the unit price of Z110 to calculate the price. In this small data set we can just see that it is £0.56, but VLOOKUP can be used to automatically 'find' the price. VLOOKUP looks more complicated than the other functions we have looked at so far, as it has four arguments, so using Insert Function is a good way to deal with this. The arguments are as follows:

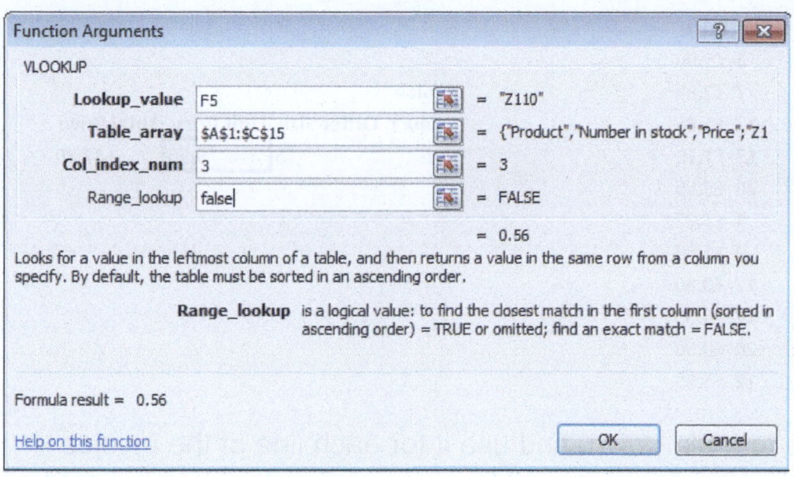

lookup_value – this is the data item you are looking for – in our case the product number.

table_array – this is the range the data is in – i.e. where you are looking.

The first column should contain the item being looked up and absolute referencing needs to be added to ensure that Excel continues to look at the correct data if the vlookup is being used in more than one cell.

col_index_number – this is the column number we want to use from the table_array. We need the price of the product – this is the third column in the table.

[range lookup] – this should either be TRUE or FALSE. The square brackets indicate that this is an optional argument. If you leave it out then Excel will assume its value is TRUE.

- FALSE means that an exact match to the lookup_value must be found – useful for looking up specific items in a list.
- TRUE means the nearest value to the lookup_value will be found – useful if there is a range of values that the lookup_value lies between.

H5 | =VLOOKUP(F5,$A$1:$C$15,3,FALSE)

	A	B	C	D	E	F	G	H	I	J
1	**Product**	**Number in stock**	**Price**							
2	Z101	3	£9.00							
3	Z102	7	£7.88			**Invoice**				
4	Z103	17	£5.86			**Product**	**Order Size**	**Unit Price**	**Total Price**	
5	Z104	13	£1.19			Z110	5	0.56	£2.80	
6	Z105	20	£9.56							
7	Z106	4	£7.27							
8	Z107	9	£1.86							
9	Z108	17	£0.86							
10	Z109	17	£4.55							
11	Z110	20	£0.56							
12	Z111	12	£5.35							

The correct price is shown, and the total price calculated. If the Product Number in F5 is changed, the price changes accordingly:

H5 | =VLOOKUP(F5,$A$1:$C$15,3,FALSE)

	A	B	C	D	E	F	G	H	I	J
1	**Product**	**Number in stock**	**Price**							
2	Z101	3	£9.00							
3	Z102	7	£7.88			**Invoice**				
4	Z103	17	£5.86			**Product**	**Order Size**	**Unit Price**	**Total Price**	
5	Z104	13	£1.19			Z105	5	9.56	£47.80	
6	Z105	20	£9.56							
7	Z106	4	£7.27							
8	Z107	9	£1.86							
9	Z108	17	£0.86							
10	Z109	17	£4.55							
11	Z110	20	£0.56							
12	Z111	12	£5.35							

You can copy this formula down, and use it for each line of the Invoice – using an absolute reference on the table_array means that this will not be changed:

H6 | =VLOOKUP(F6,$A$1:$C$15,3,FALSE)

	A	B	C	D	E	F	G	H	I	J
1	**Product**	**Number in stock**	**Price**							
2	Z101	3	£9.00							
3	Z102	7	£7.88			**Invoice**				
4	Z103	17	£5.86			**Product**	**Order Size**	**Unit Price**	**Total Price**	
5	Z104	13	£1.19			Z105	5	9.56	£47.80	
6	Z105	20	£9.56			Z107	2	1.86	£3.72	
7	Z106	4	£7.27			Z110	1	0.56	£0.56	
8	Z107	9	£1.86			Z113	8	3.53	£28.24	
9	Z108	17	£0.86					**Total**	£80.32	
10	Z109	17	£4.55							
11	Z110	20	£0.56							
12	Z111	12	£5.35							
13	Z112	4	£4.88							
14	Z113	12	£3.53							
15	Z114	6	£7.16							

How does it work?

It is easier to use VLOOKUP if you understand what it is doing. If we use the above example, we are looking for the value of the product in cell **F6**, in the cells from A1-C15, and want the value in the 3rd column.

Value in cell F6

Z107

	A	B	C	D
1	**Product**	**Number in stock**	**Price**	
2	Z101	3	£9.00	
3	Z102	7	£7.88	
4	Z103	17	£5.86	
5	Z104	13	£1.19	
6	Z105	20	£9.56	
7	Z106	4	£7.27	
8	Z107	9	£1.86	
9	Z108	17	£0.86	
10	Z109	17	£4.55	
11	Z110	20	£0.56	
12	Z111	12	£5.35	
13	Z112	4	£4.88	
14	Z113	12	£3.53	
15	Z114	6	£7.16	
16				

3rd col across

Excel 'looks' down the 1st column until it finds a match, then returns the value in the 3rd column of the table.

The value 1.86 will be returned.

Note that only the **FIRST COLUMN IN THE TABLE** is used to search. If the value is not there, an error will be given.

Errors

As mentioned above, if the **lookup_value** cannot be found in the first column of the table, an error will be shown. The cell value will show **#N/A** to indicate the value could not be found.

Invoice			
Product	**Order Size**	**Unit Price**	**Total Price**
Y105	5	#N/A	#N/A
Z107	2	1.86	£3.72
Z110	1	0.56	£0.56
Z113	8	3.53	£28.24
		Total	#N/A

Incorrect product code gives this error – all formulas following on will also show an error. This will be dealt with later.

The other common error with VLOOKUP is **#REF!**. This is a referencing error and will occur if the **col_index_number** is too big. For example, our table is 3 columns wide – if you use **col_index_number** greater than 3, the error will show:

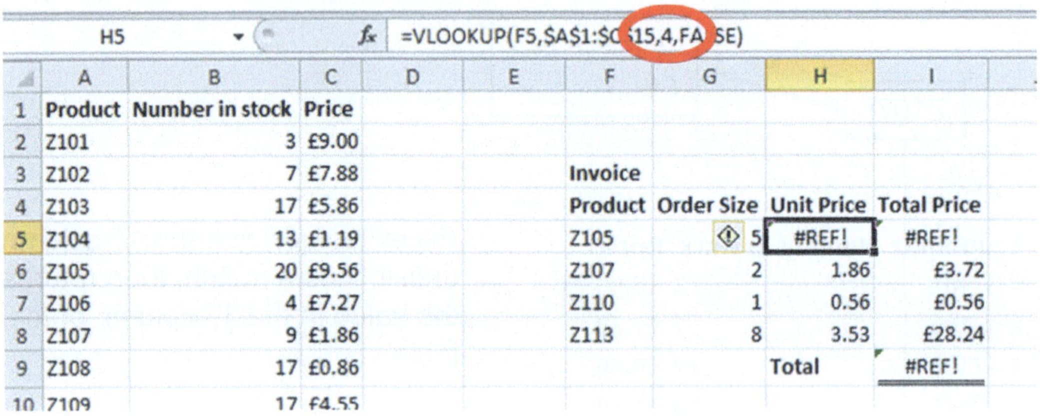

Limitations of VLOOKUP

Duplicates

One big limitation of **VLOOKUP** is that it is not suitable for searching data with duplicate items. The reason for this is that as explained above, Excel looks down each row of the first column until it finds a match – any matches below this will be ignored.

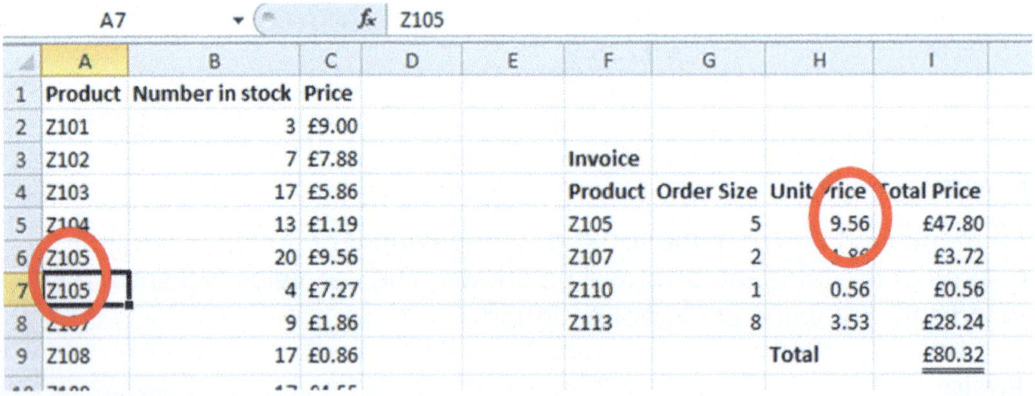

To demonstrate, if there were two product Z105, only the price for the first one will be shown.

First column only

As already mentioned, only the first column of the table is 'searched' for the **lookup_value**, if we extend the example:

	A	B	C	D	E	F	G	H	I	J
1	Product	Code	Number in stock	Price						
2	Red pen	Z101	3	£9.00						
3	Yellow pen	Z102	7	£7.88			Invoice			
4	Purple pen	Z103	17	£5.86			Code	Order Size	Unit Price	Total Price
5	Green pen	Z104	13	£1.19			Z105	5		£0.00
6	Red crayon	Z105	20	£9.56			Z107	2		£0.00
7	Yellow crayon	Z105	4	£7.27			Z110	1		£0.00
8	Purple crayon	Z107	9	£1.86			Z113	8		£0.00
9	Green crayon	Z108	17	£0.86					Total	£0.00
10	Red ruler	Z109	17	£4.55						
11	Yellow ruler	Z110	20	£0.56						
12	Green ruler	Z111	12	£5.35						
13	Purple ruler	Z112	4	£4.88						
14	Blue calculator	Z113	12	£3.53						
15	Orange calculator	Z114	6	£7.16						

The idea is the same – we need to know the price of each one. If you use the following arguments:

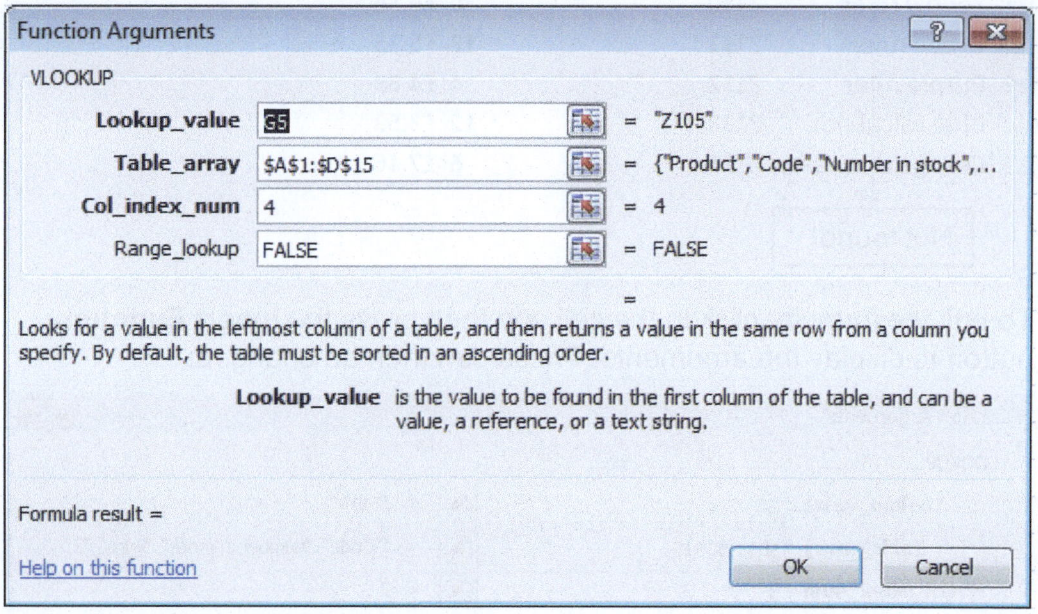

A #N/A error is given. The Col_index_num of 4 is correct, as the price is the 4th column in our table. The problem is that "Z105" cannot be found in the first column:

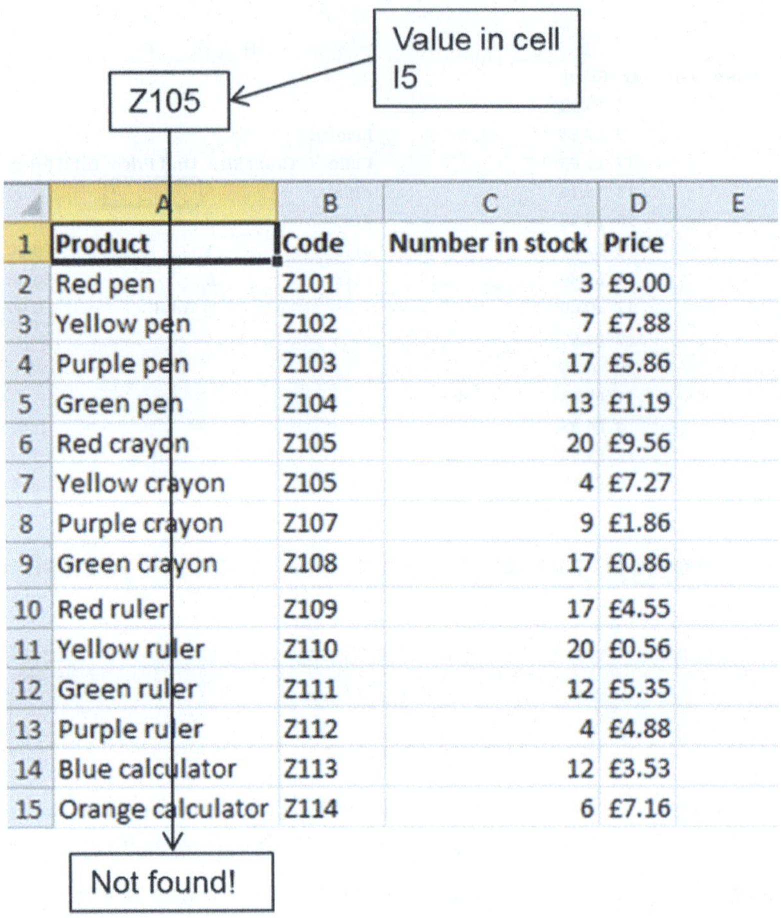

	A	B	C	D	E
1	**Product**	**Code**	**Number in stock**	**Price**	
2	Red pen	Z101	3	£9.00	
3	Yellow pen	Z102	7	£7.88	
4	Purple pen	Z103	17	£5.86	
5	Green pen	Z104	13	£1.19	
6	Red crayon	Z105	20	£9.56	
7	Yellow crayon	Z105	4	£7.27	
8	Purple crayon	Z107	9	£1.86	
9	Green crayon	Z108	17	£0.86	
10	Red ruler	Z109	17	£4.55	
11	Yellow ruler	Z110	20	£0.56	
12	Green ruler	Z111	12	£5.35	
13	Purple ruler	Z112	4	£4.88	
14	Blue calculator	Z113	12	£3.53	
15	Orange calculator	Z114	6	£7.16	

The table MUST start in column B, where the product codes are.

To edit the formula, click in the cell and then press the **Insert Function** button to display the arguments. These can then be changed:

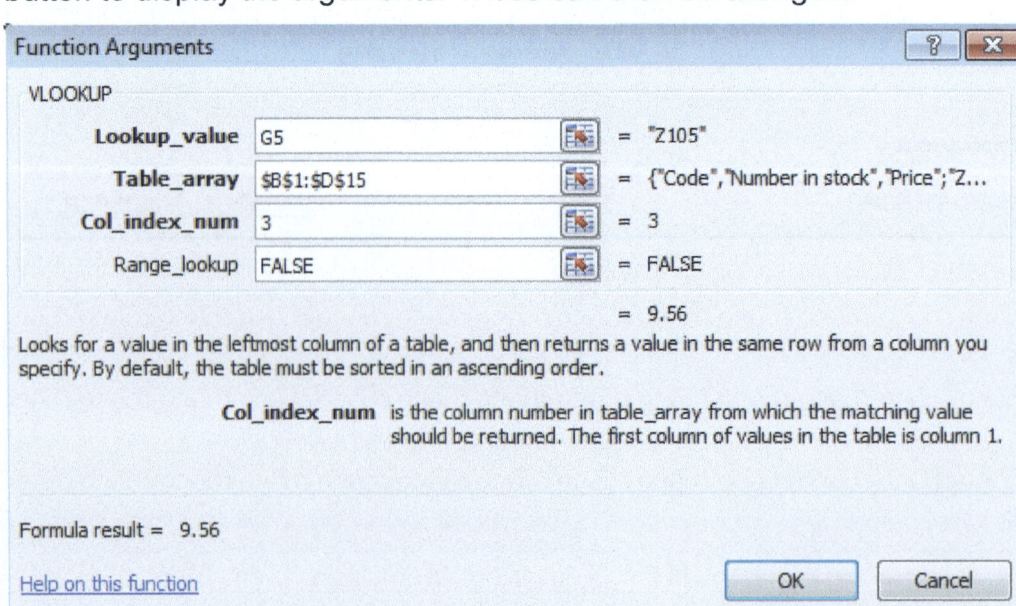

Note that **Table_array** has been altered to start with column B. **Col_index_num** has also been changed – this is because our table starts with column B – the Price column is the third column in our table.

I5 =VLOOKUP(G5,$B$1:$D$15,3,FALSE)

	A	B (Col 1)	C (Col 2)	D (Col 3)
1	**Product**	**Code**	**Number in stock**	**Price**
2	Red pen	Z101	3	£9.00
3	Yellow pen	Z102	7	£7.88
4	Purple pen	Z103	17	£5.86
5	Green pen	Z104	13	£1.19
6	Red crayon	Z105	20	£9.56
7	Yellow crayon	Z105	4	£7.27
8	Purple crayon	Z107	9	£1.86
9	Green crayon	Z108	17	£0.86
10	Red ruler	Z109	17	£4.55
11	Yellow ruler	Z110	20	£0.56
12	Green ruler	Z111	12	£5.35
13	Purple ruler	Z112	4	£4.88
14	Blue calculator	Z113	12	£3.53
15	Orange calculato	Z114	6	£7.16

	G	H	I	J
3	**Invoice**			
4	**Code**	**Order Size**	**Unit Price**	**Total Price**
5	Z105	5	9.56	£47.80
6	Z107	2		£0.00
7	Z110	1		£0.00
8	Z113	8		£0.00
9			Total	£47.80

Cannot Look 'Backwards'

As seen, **VLOOKUP** 'finds' a value in the first column of a table, then returns the value from the appropriate column to the right. What if we wanted to return the value to the left of our column?

	Invoice			
Code	**Product**	**Order Size**	**Unit Price**	**Total Price**
Z105		5	9.56	£47.80
Z107		2	1.86	£3.72
Z110		1	0.56	£0.56
Z113		8	3.53	£28.24
			Total	£80.32

We want to find the product name based on the product code.

	A	B	C	D
1	**Product**	**Code**	**Number in stock**	**Price**
2	Red pen	Z101	3	£9.00
3	Yellow pen	Z102	7	£7.88
4	Purple pen	Z103	17	£5.86
5	Green pen	Z104	13	£1.19
6	Red crayon	Z105	20	£9.56
7	Yellow crayon	Z105	4	£7.27
8	Purple crayon	Z107	9	£1.86
9	Green crayon	Z108	17	£0.86
10	Red ruler	Z109	17	£4.55
11	Yellow ruler	Z110	20	£0.56
12	Green ruler	Z111	12	£5.35
13	Purple ruler	Z112	4	£4.88
14	Blue calculator	Z113	12	£3.53
15	Orange calculator	Z114	6	£7.16

This is not possible here using VLOOKUP, as the Product Code is to the right of the Product column.

One way round this problem is to swap the columns over in the original data, as shown below.

G5 =VLOOKUP(F5,$A$1:$D$15,2,FALSE)

	A	B	C	D	E	F	G	H	I	J
1	**Code**	**Product**	**Number in stock**	**Price**						
2	Z101	Red pen	3	£9.00						
3	Z102	Yellow pen	7	£7.88			**Invoice**			
4	Z103	Purple pen	17	£5.86		**Code**	**Product**	**Order Size**	**Unit Price**	**Total Price**
5	Z104	Green pen	13	£1.19		Z105	Red crayon	5	9.56	£47.80
6	Z105	Red crayon	20	£9.56		Z107	Purple crayon	2	1.86	£3.72
7	Z105	Yellow crayon	4	£7.27		Z110	Yellow ruler	1	0.56	£0.56
8	Z107	Purple crayon	9	£1.86		Z113	Blue calculator	8	3.53	£28.24
9	Z108	Green crayon	17	£0.86					**Total**	£80.32
10	Z109	Red ruler	17	£4.55						

12.5 HLOOKUP

HLOOKUP works in a very similar way to **VLOOKUP**. In **VLOOKUP**, we searched **DOWN** a column to find the value we needed. The 'V' in **VLOOKUP** stands for '**Vertical**' to show this.

Likewise, **HLOOKUP** is a Horizontal Lookup. We will search **ALONG** a row to find the value we need, and then return the value in the nth row of the table:

	A	B	C	D	E	F	G	H	I	J	K	L	M
1		Jan	Feb	Mar	Apr	May	Jun	Jul	Aug	Sep	Oct	Nov	Dec
2	Sales	10,810	10,418	12,530	11,479	14,062	13,303	13,887	14,356	14,604	13,432	13,777	11,300
3	Costs	6,376	7,183	6,017	5,455	5,542	6,218	6,232	7,151	5,776	6,807	6,328	5,557
4	Profit	4,434	3,235	6,513	6,024	8,520	7,085	7,655	7,205	8,828	6,625	7,449	5,743
5													
6													
7													
8	Month	Apr											
9	Profit												

If we wanted to automatically return the correct profit figure depending on the month input into B8, use **HLOOKUP**.

Lookup_value – B8, the month we choose.

Table_array – the table of data – note that only the **FIRST ROW** will be searched, so that must contain the data we are looking for.

Row_index_num – we want profit, the 4th row in our table.

Range_lookup – FALSE, for an exact match.

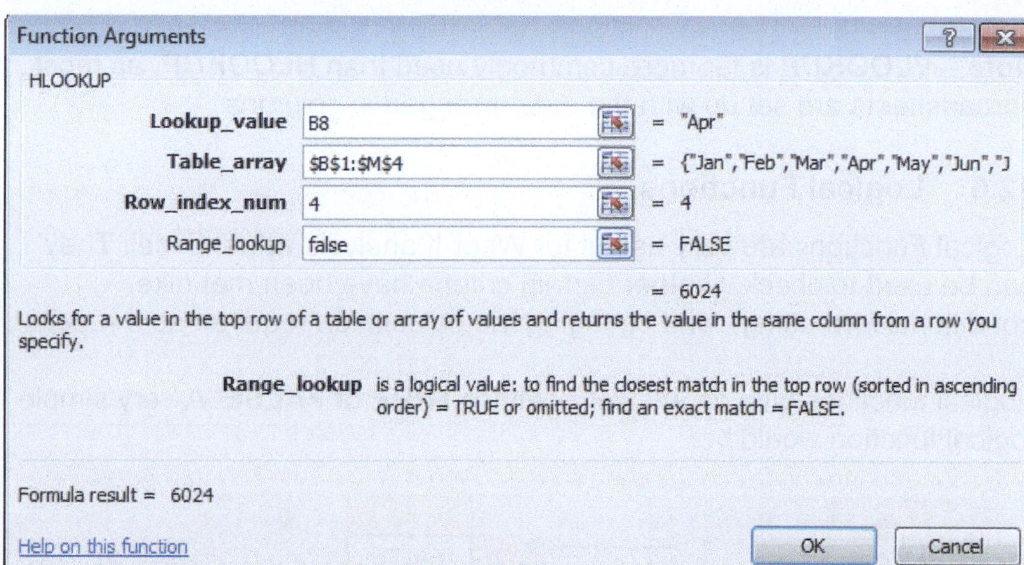

B9 | =HLOOKUP(B8,$B$1:$M$4,4,FALSE)

	A	B	C	D	E	F	G	H	I	
1		Jan	Feb	Mar	Apr	May	Jun	Jul	Aug	Sep
2	Sales	10,810	10,418	12,530	11,479	14,062	13,303	13,887	14,356	
3	Costs	6,376	7,183	6,017	5,455	5,542	6,218	6,232	7,151	
4	Profit	4,434	3,235	6,513	6,024	8,520	7,085	7,655	7,205	
5										
6										
7										
8	Month	Apr								
9	Profit	6,024								
10										

The lookup is complete – if the month is changed, the profit will update accordingly:

B9 | =HLOOKUP(B8,$B$1:$M$4,4,FALSE)

	A	B	C	D	E	F	G	H	I	
1		Jan	Feb	Mar	Apr	May	Jun	Jul	Aug	Sep
2	Sales	10,810	10,418	12,530	11,479	14,062	13,303	13,887	14,356	1
3	Costs	6,376	7,183	6,017	5,455	5,542	6,218	6,232	7,151	
4	Profit	4,434	3,235	6,513	6,024	8,520	7,085	7,655	7,205	
5										
6										
7										
8	Month	Mar								
9	Profit	6,513								
10										

Note – **VLOOKUP** is far more commonly used than **HLOOKUP**, as most spreadsheets are set up with the data arranged in columns.

12.6 Logical Functions

Logical Functions are very useful for What-If analysis within Excel. They can be used to check whether certain criteria have been met (like conditional formatting), and changing the calculation required as a result.

Logical functions give an answer of either **TRUE** or **FALSE**. A very simple logical function would be:

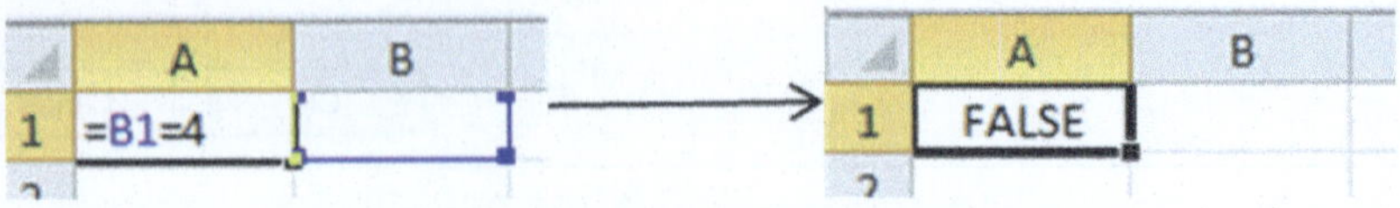

The first '=' is just there to tell Excel that this is a formula. The logical test is **B1=4**. This can either be TRUE – if B1 does equal 4, or FALSE, if it does not. As there's no value in cell B1, the answer is FALSE.

A1 | fx =B1=4

	A	B	C	D
1	TRUE	4		

If you enter 4 into B1, the answer changes to TRUE.

This is very useful for checking if two cells which should have the same value do have the same value!

Other checks

The full list of logical checks is as follows:

Check	Symbol
Equal to	=
Less than	<
Less than or equal to	<=
Greater than	>
Greater than or equal to	>=
Not equal to	<>

Note the 'Not equal to' and 'Less/greater than or equal to' – the order of the symbols is important.

B17 | fx =B14>=B16

	A	B	C	D
1		Sales		
2	Jan	6,672		
3	Feb	6,821		
4	Mar	6,733		
5	Apr	7,447		
6	May	7,337		
7	Jun	9,646		
8	Jul	7,979		
9	Aug	7,048		
10	Sep	7,172		
11	Oct	8,884		
12	Nov	5,834		
13	Dec	9,953		
14	**Total**	91,526		
15				
16	Target Sales	100,000		
17	Target met	FALSE		
18				

Here, we are checking whether a target has been met – is the value in B14, total sales, at least as big as the target.

It is not, so the value is FALSE.

12.7 IF

Logical checks are very useful, but it may be more appropriate to have something other than TRUE or FALSE as a response, an IF function can do this.

The **IF** function has 3 arguments, as follows:

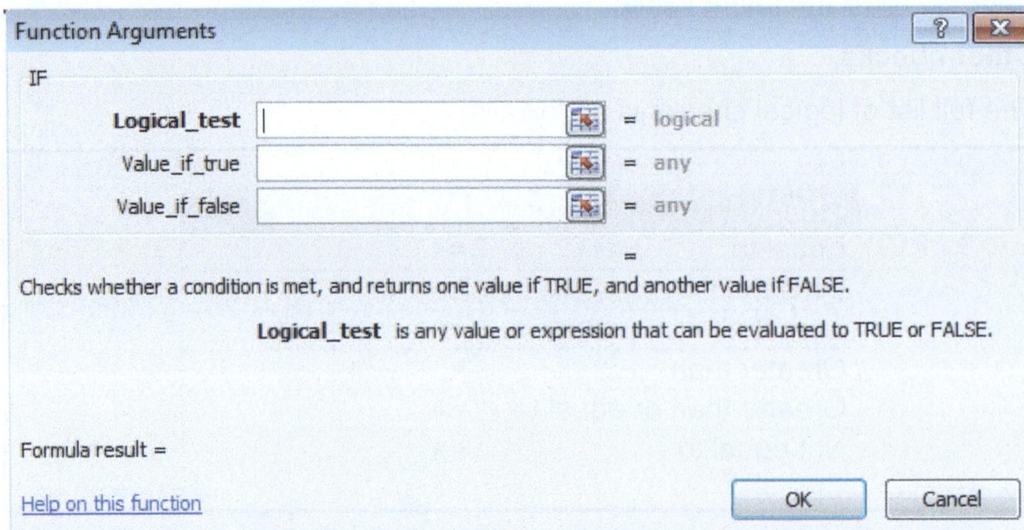

Logical_test – as above, a logical test is a test that will have the value TRUE or FALSE

Value_if_true – enter here what you would like to do if the test is true – this could be a calculation, some text or even another Excel function.

Value_if_false – enter here what to do if the test is false, in the same way.

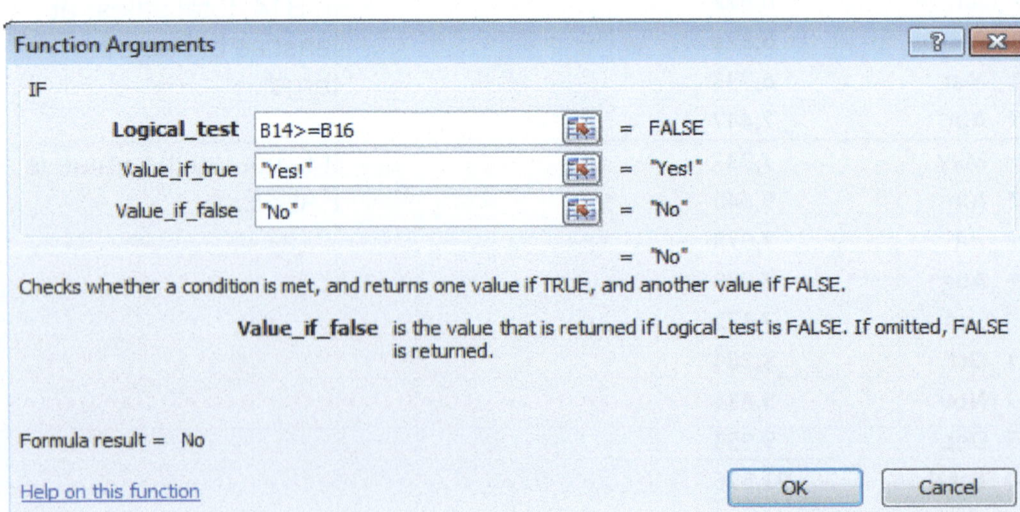

The logical test is as it was in the previous example – have the target sales been met? If they have, we want text saying “Yes!”, otherwise “No”. Note that the quote marks (“”) are required to tell Excel to show text.

B17 | =IF(B14>=B16,"Yes!","No")

	A	B	C	D	E	F
13	Dec	9,953				
14	**Total**	91,526				
15						
16	Target Sales	100,000				
17	Target met	No				

If the target changed to 90,000:

B17 | =IF(B14>=B16,"Yes!","No")

	A	B	C	D	E	F
13	Dec	9,953				
14	**Total**	91,526				
15						
16	Target Sales	90,000				
17	Target met	Yes!				

To summarise,

(1) **What are we testing**

(2) **What to do if the test is true**

(3) **What to do if the test is false**.

You can then bring in more complicated calculations:

B18 | =IF(B17="Yes!",B14*10%,0)

	A	B	C	D	E	F
10	Sep	7,172				
11	Oct	8,884				
12	Nov	5,834				
13	Dec	9,953				
14	**Total**	91,526				
15						
16	Target Sales	90,000				
17	Target met	Yes!				
18	10% Bonus	9,153				

So here, if B17 equals "Yes!", multiply B14 by 10%, otherwise the bonus is zero.

Going back to the **VLOOKUP** example, we might want to check that we have enough stock.

	A	B	C	D	E	F	G	H	I	J	K
1	Code	Product	Number in stock	Price							
2	Z101	Red pen	3	£9.00							
3	Z102	Yellow pen	7	£7.88			Invoice				
4	Z103	Purple pen	17	£5.86		Code	Product	Order Size	Unit Price	Total Price	Stock check
5	Z104	Green pen	13	£1.19		Z105	Red crayon	5	9.56	£47.80	
6	Z105	Red crayon	20	£9.56		Z107	Purple crayon	2	1.86	£3.72	
7	Z105	Yellow crayon	4	£7.27		Z110	Yellow ruler	1	0.56	£0.56	
8	Z107	Purple crayon	9	£1.86		Z113	Blue calculator	8	3.53	£28.24	
9	Z108	Green crayon	17	£0.86					Total	£80.32	
10	Z109	Red ruler	17	£4.55							
11	Z110	Yellow ruler	20	£0.56							
12	Z111	Green ruler	12	£5.35							
13	Z112	Purple ruler	4	£4.88							
14	Z113	Blue calculator	12	£3.53							
15	Z114	Orange calculator	6	£7.16							

To start an IF formula, think "What do I need to compare or check?" Here, we need to see if the order size is less than or equal to the number in stock (note that you could check the other way round – is the number in stock greater than or equal to the order size – it does not matter). The order size is easy – cell H5. The number in stock depends on the product code in cell F5 though – we need to do a **VLOOKUP** to find this. This leads to a very big formula, but if you break it down step by step it is things we have already used. One way to go about this is to do the logical test first, and build the IF formula around it. So, we need a **VLOOKUP** to find the stock levels:

K5 fx =VLOOKUP(F5,$A$1:$D$15,3,FALSE)

	A	B	C	D	E	F	G	H	I	J	K
1	Code	Product	Number in stock	Price							
2	Z101	Red pen	3	£9.00							
3	Z102	Yellow pen	7	£7.88			Invoice				
4	Z103	Purple pen	17	£5.86		Code	Product	Order Size	Unit Price	Total Price	Stock check
5	Z104	Green pen	13	£1.19		Z105	Red crayon	5	9.56	£47.80	20
6	Z105	Red crayon	20	£9.56		Z107	Purple crayon	2	1.86	£3.72	
7	Z105	Yellow crayon	4	£7.27		Z110	Yellow ruler	1	0.56	£0.56	
8	Z107	Purple crayon	9	£1.86		Z113	Blue calculator	8	3.53	£28.24	
9	Z108	Green crayon	17	£0.86					Total	£80.32	

Similar to the earlier price example; we need to compare this to cell H5 – either click in the formula bar at the top, or press F2 to edit the cell.

IF =h5<=VLOOKUP(F5,$A$1:$D$15,3,FALSE)

	A	B	C	D	E	F	G	H	I	J	K
1	Code	Product	Number in stock	Price							
2	Z101	Red pen	3	£9.00							
3	Z102	Yellow pen	7	£7.88			Invoice				
4	Z103	Purple pen	17	£5.86		Code	Product	[illegible]	Unit Price	Total Price	Stock check
5	Z104	Green pen	13	£1.19		Z105	Red crayon	5	9.56	£47.80	=h5<=VLOOK
6	Z105	Red crayon	20	£9.56		Z107	Purple crayon	[illegible]	1.86	£3.72	
7	Z105	Yellow crayon	4	£7.27		Z110	Yellow ruler	1	0.56	£0.56	
8	Z107	Purple crayon	9	£1.86		Z113	Blue calculator	8	3.53	£28.24	
9	Z108	Green crayon	17	£0.86					Total	£80.32	

A box appears around the cell to show which one is being used.

	Invoice				
Code	Product	Order Size	Unit Price	Total Price	Stock check
Z105	Red crayon	5	9.56	£47.80	TRUE
Z107	Purple crayon	2	1.86	£3.72	TRUE
Z110	Yellow ruler	1	0.56	£0.56	TRUE
Z113	Blue calculator	8	3.53	£28.24	TRUE
			Total	£80.32	

All the logical checks are TRUE – we have enough of each product. Changing one of the product codes shows how this will update:

	A	B	C	D	E	F	G	H	I	J	K
1	Code	Product	Number in stock	Price							
2	Z101	Red pen	3	£9.00							
3	Z102	Yellow pen	7	£7.88			Invoice				
4	Z103	Purple pen	17	£5.86		Code	Product	Order Size	Unit Price	Total Price	Stock check
5	Z104	Green pen	13	£1.19		Z101	Red pen	5	9	£45.00	FALSE
6	Z105	Red crayon	20	£9.56		Z107	Purple crayon	2	1.86	£3.72	TRUE
7	Z105	Yellow crayon	4	£7.27		Z110	Yellow ruler	1	0.56	£0.56	TRUE
8	Z107	Purple crayon	9	£1.86		Z113	Blue calculator	8	3.53	£28.24	TRUE
9	Z108	Green crayon	17	£0.86					Total	£77.52	

There are only 3 red pens in stock, so the order size is too big.

Now we have the logical check, the IF function can be built around it. Remember how the IF function works - =IF(logical test, value_if_true, value_if_false), if we edit the formula, and type **"IF("** in front of the logical test (but after the first equals sign).

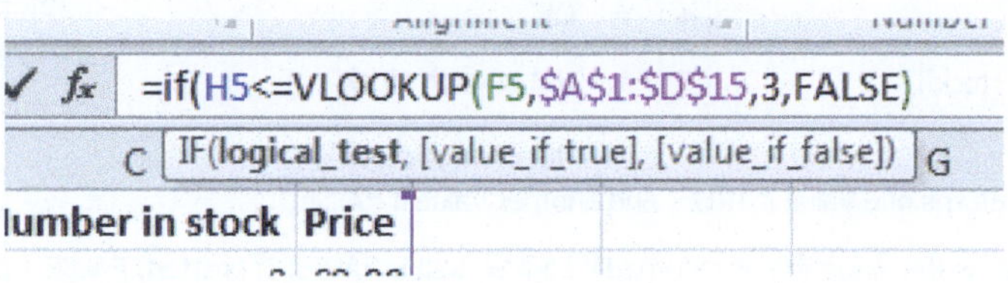

Notice how **logical_test** is in bold – Excel is showing which argument is being entered.

You can then either manually enter the comma after the logical test and enter the other arguments; or click the **Insert Function** button to bring up the appropriate menu:

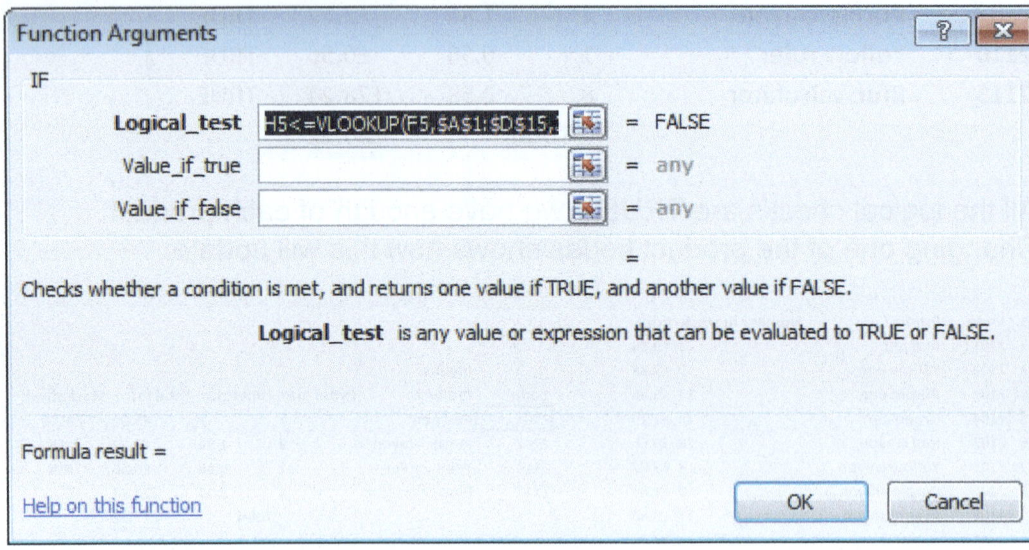

Enter the other two arguments as required:

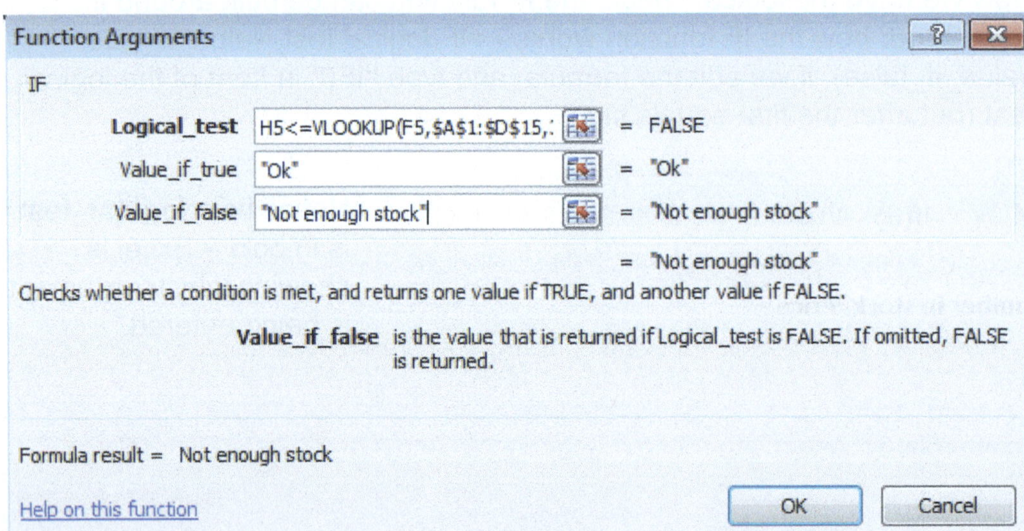

	Invoice				
Code	**Product**	**Order Size**	**Unit Price**	**Total Price**	**Stock check**
Z101	Red pen	5	9	£45.00	Not enough stock
Z107	Purple crayon	2	1.86	£3.72	Ok
Z110	Yellow ruler	1	0.56	£0.56	Ok
Z113	Blue calculator	8	3.53	£28.24	Ok
			Total	£77.52	

12.8 AND

AND is used when you want to check more than one thing is true. As it is a logical function, the result of an **AND** function will be TRUE or FALSE. The basic idea is to say:

Is this true **and** is this true **and** is this true **and**…

The **AND** function will return a value of TRUE if **ALL** of the checks are TRUE. If any are FALSE, then the answer will be FALSE.

You can test up to 255 logical checks. Let us look at a few examples:

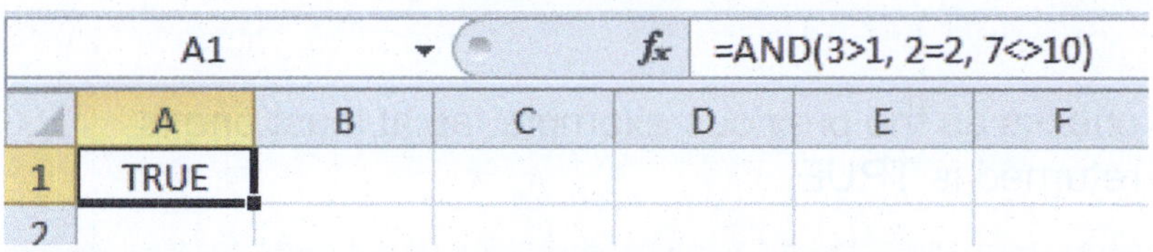

In this example, three things are being checked – is 3 greater than 1, is 2 equal to 2 and is 7 not equal to 10. Obviously all three are true, so the value in the cell is also TRUE. Clicking on the Insert Function button breaks this down nicely:

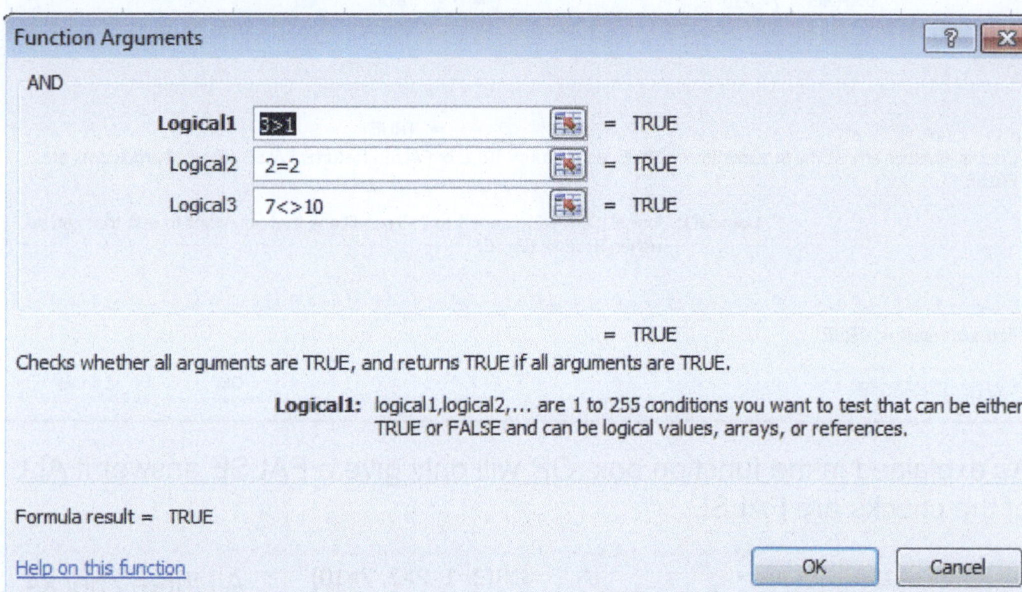

If we change the arguments so that only one is false, this will affect the outcome:

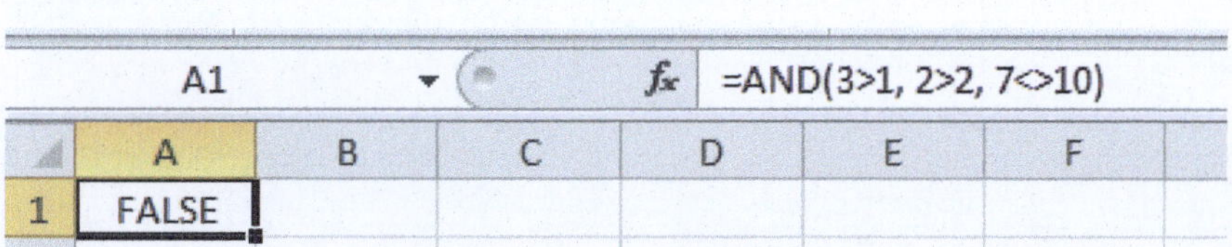

2 is not greater than 2, so the value is FALSE!

12.9 OR

OR works in a similar way to **AND**, but this time we are checking:

Is this true **OR** is this true **OR** is this true….

As a result only ONE of the logical checks needs to be true for the value to be TRUE.

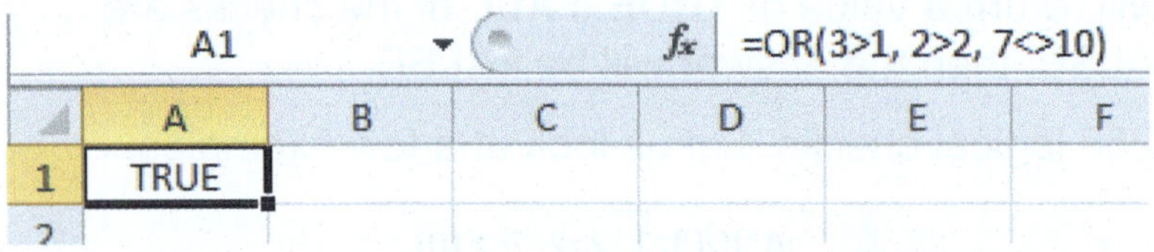

Taking the same checks as the previous example, as at least one is TRUE, the value returned is TRUE.

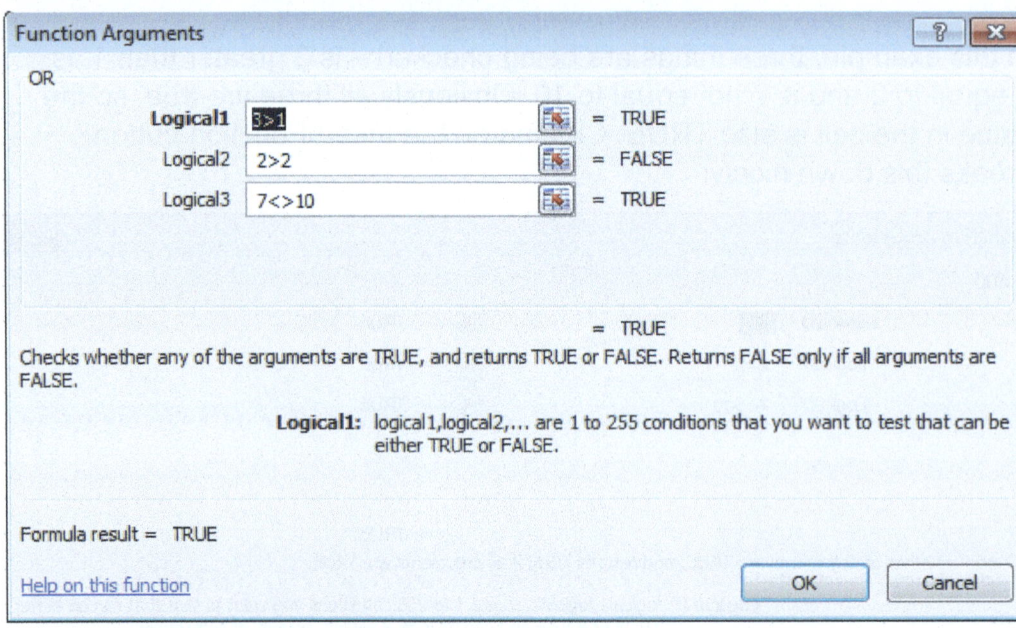

As explained in the function box, OR will only give a FALSE answer if ALL of the checks are FALSE.

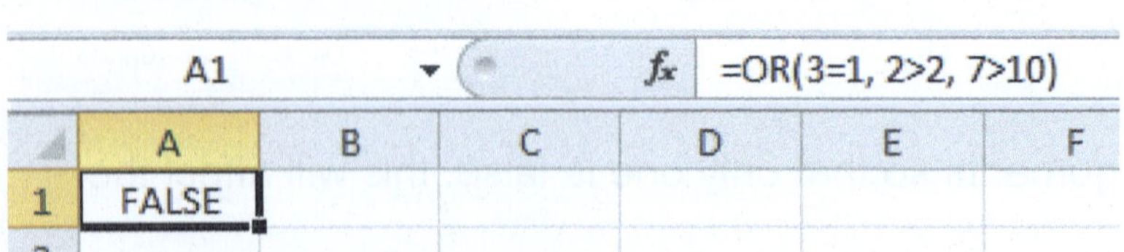

All three checks are FALSE.

12.10 Using AND and OR

The main use of these will be within an **IF** statement. If, for example, you wish to check two things, the logical test part of the **IF** formula would be an **AND** function. Remember, the first argument in an **IF** statement is a logical test with the answer TRUE or FALSE – an **AND** function will give this.

	A	B	C	D
1	Day	Weather	Picnic?	
2	Monday	Rainy		
3	Tuesday	Cloudy		
4	Wednesday	Sunny		
5	Thursday	Sunny		
6	Friday	Rainy		
7	Saturday	Sunny		
8	Sunday	Cloudy		
9				

We might want to check that the weather is going to be sunny or cloudy for our picnic.

Set up the logical check first.

C2 =OR(B2="Cloudy",B2="Sunny")

	A	B	C	D	E	F
1	Day	Weather	Picnic?			
2	Monday	Rainy	FALSE			
3	Tuesday	Cloudy	TRUE			
4	Wednesday	Sunny	TRUE			
5	Thursday	Sunny	TRUE			
6	Friday	Rainy	FALSE			
7	Saturday	Sunny	TRUE			
8	Sunday	Cloudy	TRUE			

This OR function can be used as the logical check in an IF statement:

=If(OR(B2="Cloudy",B2="Sunny")

IF(**logical_test**, [value_if_true], [value_if_

B	C
Weather	Picnic?
Rainy	=If(OR(B2="Cloud
Cloudy	TRUE

Start entering the IF statement, with the open bracket.

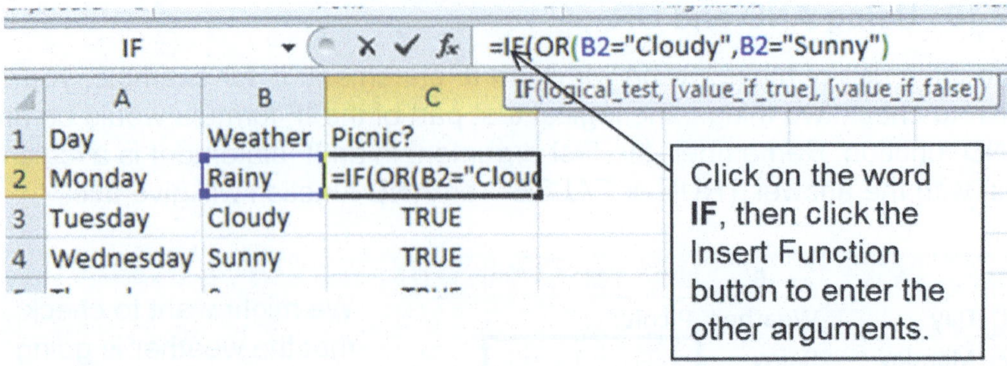

	A	B	C
1	Day	Weather	Picnic?
2	Monday	Rainy	=IF(OR(B2="Cloud
3	Tuesday	Cloudy	TRUE
4	Wednesday	Sunny	TRUE

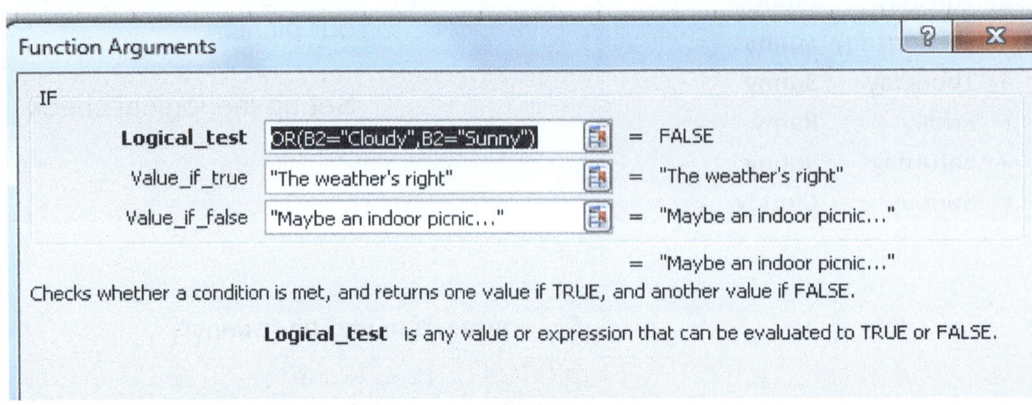

This is easier to understand than TRUE/FALSE and although it creates a long formula, it is no more complicated than any of the previous examples.

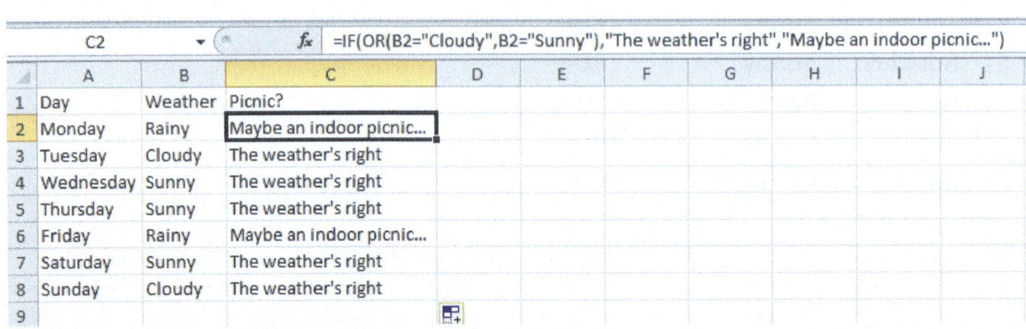

C2 =IF(OR(B2="Cloudy",B2="Sunny"),"The weather's right","Maybe an indoor picnic...")

	A	B	C
1	Day	Weather	Picnic?
2	Monday	Rainy	Maybe an indoor picnic...
3	Tuesday	Cloudy	The weather's right
4	Wednesday	Sunny	The weather's right
5	Thursday	Sunny	The weather's right
6	Friday	Rainy	Maybe an indoor picnic...
7	Saturday	Sunny	The weather's right
8	Sunday	Cloudy	The weather's right

We might only want to go for a picnic on a sunny Saturday, for example. The idea is exactly the same – our logical test is “Is the day Saturday **AND** is the weather sunny?”

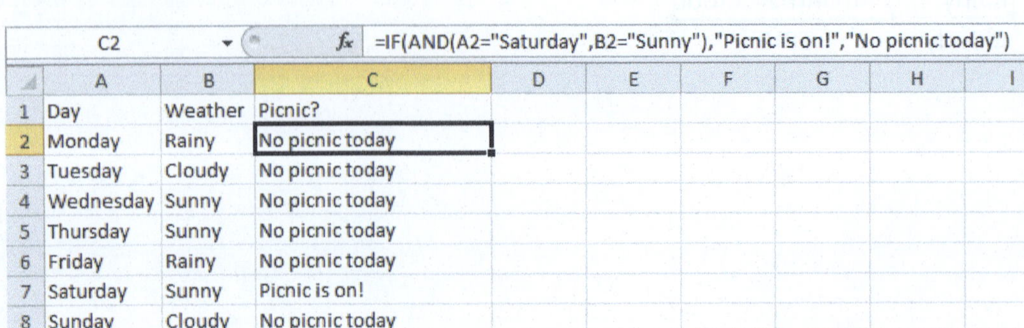

C2 =IF(AND(A2="Saturday",B2="Sunny"),"Picnic is on!","No picnic today")

	A	B	C
1	Day	Weather	Picnic?
2	Monday	Rainy	No picnic today
3	Tuesday	Cloudy	No picnic today
4	Wednesday	Sunny	No picnic today
5	Thursday	Sunny	No picnic today
6	Friday	Rainy	No picnic today
7	Saturday	Sunny	Picnic is on!
8	Sunday	Cloudy	No picnic today

12.11 Date functions

Date functions can be used to insert dates into worksheets so that they are always current or they can be used in formulas to help calculations.

To deal with dates, Excel treats every date as a number – how it is displayed is based on the format you choose in the Format Cells menu.

Dates 'start' from 1 January 1900, i.e. this day is represented by the number 1. Every day beyond this the number increases by 1. For example:

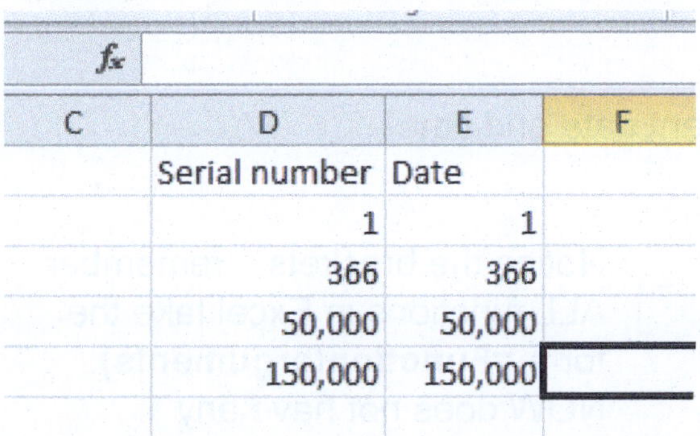

These two columns are identical. However, if we change the FORMAT of the 2nd column to be dates, they can be viewed as required.

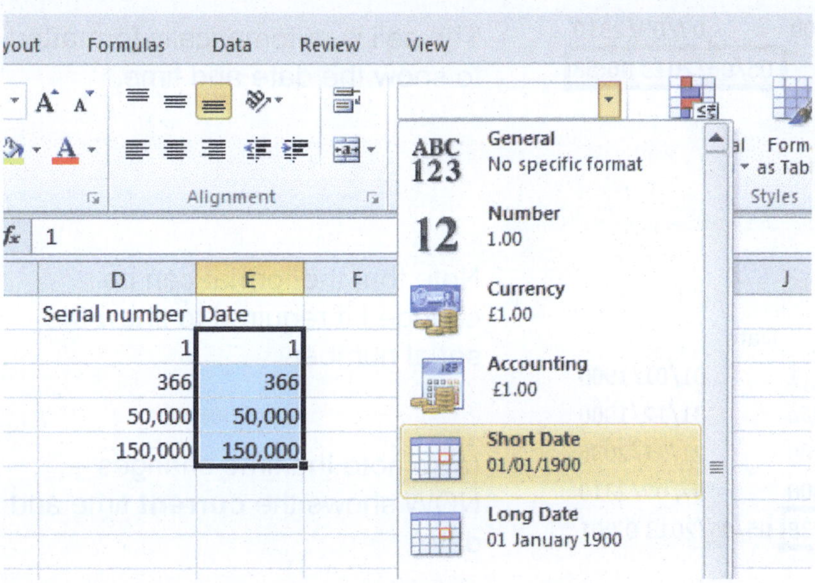

Select the cells, then either use the format cells option, or the drop down box in the **Home Menu**, under **Number**.

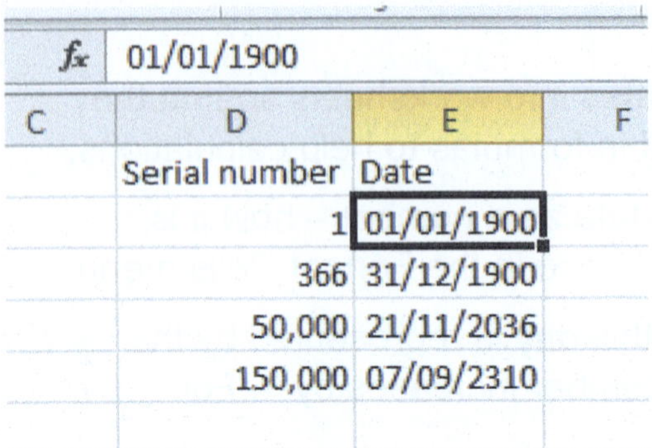

The dates are shown as required. Notice that they have been updated in the formula bar too.

NOW

The **NOW** function returns the current date and time.

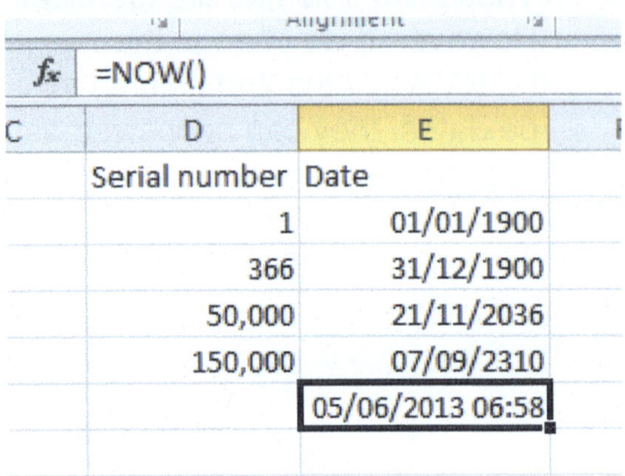

Notice the brackets – remember ALL functions in Excel take the form **=Function(arguments)**. NOW does not have any arguments, but still requires the brackets.

The cell is automatically formatted to show the date and time.

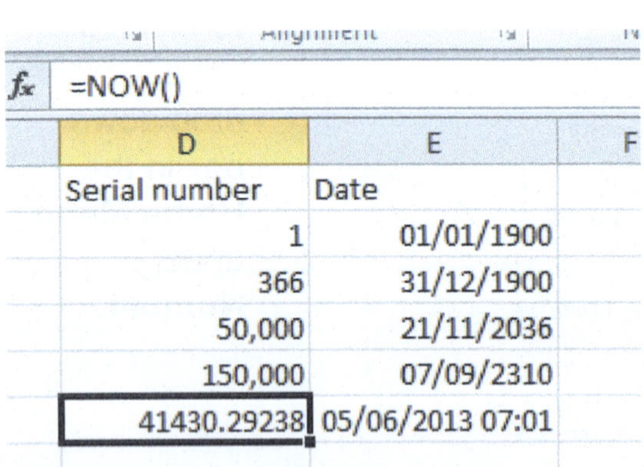

Note that the format can be changed if required to show the serial number.

(also note the time changes – NOW shows the **current** time and date)

If you wish to 'fix' the value in the cell, use **copy** and **paste values** from the **Paste Special** menu.

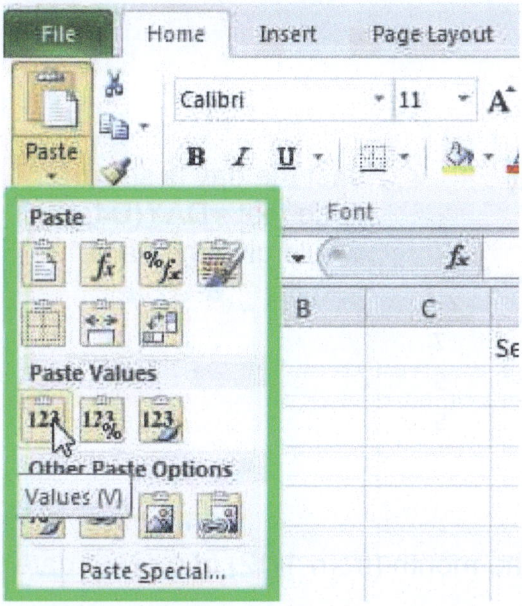

Paste values will remove the formulas from the cells.

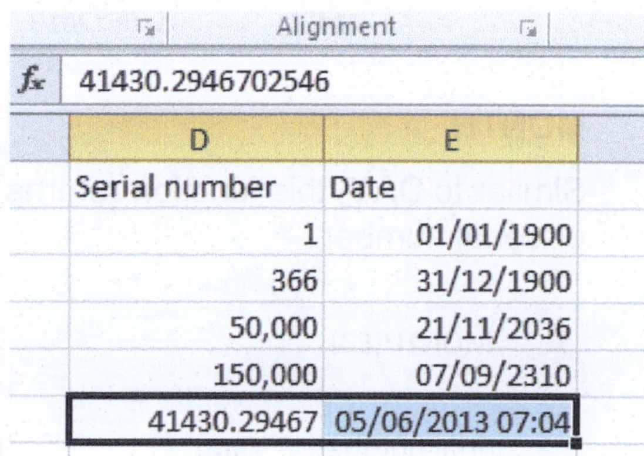

f_x 41430.2946702546

D	E
Serial number	Date
1	01/01/1900
366	31/12/1900
50,000	21/11/2036
150,000	07/09/2310
41430.29467	05/06/2013 07:04

Now the date/time is fixed.

TODAY

TODAY is very similar to **NOW**, except that only todays date is shown, not the time.

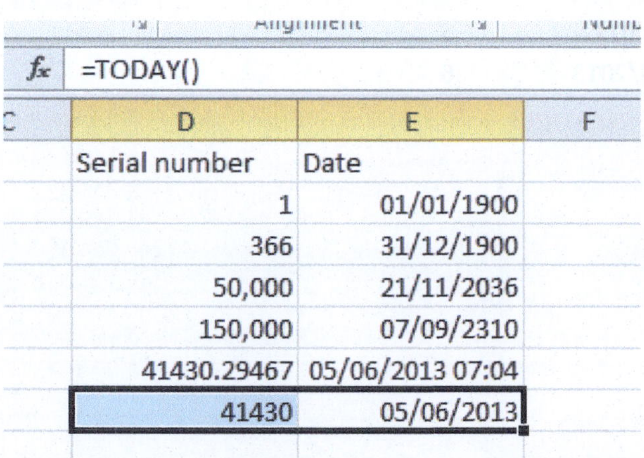

f_x =TODAY()

D	E
Serial number	Date
1	01/01/1900
366	31/12/1900
50,000	21/11/2036
150,000	07/09/2310
41430.29467	05/06/2013 07:04
41430	05/06/2013

The format is set as a date, but can be changed if necessary.

DAY

The **DAY** function returns the day in the month of a given date or serial number.

fx =DAY(E4)

Serial number	Date	Day
1	01/01/1900	1
366	31/12/1900	31
50,000	21/11/2036	21
150,000	07/09/2310	7
41430.29467	05/06/2013 07:04	5
41430	05/06/2013	5

Just the day is shown. Note that **=DAY(D4)** would give the same result.

MONTH

Similar to **DAY**, this function returns the month (from 1-12) of a given date or serial number.

fx =MONTH(E3)

Serial number	Date	Month
1	01/01/1900	1
366	31/12/1900	12
50,000	21/11/2036	11
150,000	07/09/2310	9
41430.29467	05/06/2013 07:04	6
41430	05/06/2013	6

If you wanted to show this as "January", rather than 1, you could use **VLOOKUP**.

	A	B	C	D	E	F
1	Number	Month		Serial number	Date	Month
2	1	January		1	01/01/1900	1
3	2	February		366	31/12/1900	12
4	3	March		50,000	21/11/2036	11
5	4	April		150,000	07/09/2310	9
6	5	May		41430.29467	05/06/2013 07:04	6
7	6	June		41430	05/06/2013	6
8	7	July				
9	8	August				
10	9	September				
11	10	October				
12	11	November				
13	12	December				

The VLOOKUP formula would then be:

F2 =VLOOKUP(MONTH(E2),$A$1:$B$13,2,FALSE)

	A	B	C	D	E	F
1	Number	Month		Serial number	Date	Month
2	1	January		1	01/01/1900	January
3	2	February		366	31/12/1900	December
4	3	March		50,000	21/11/2036	November
5	4	April		150,000	07/09/2310	September
6	5	May		41430.29467	05/06/2013 07:04	June
7	6	June		41430	05/06/2013	June
8	7	July				
9	8	August				
10	9	September				
11	10	October				
12	11	November				
13	12	December				

Our **lookup_value** is MONTH(E2) – i.e. a number from 1-12. The formula will then search for this number is cells A1:A13, and give the value in the corresponding row of column B (the second column).

Note that this is not the only way to achieve this result – in Excel there is usually more than one way to achieve a desired result (for example using **SUM** or +) – if it works, it is correct!

YEAR

This function returns the year of a given date or serial number.

fx =YEAR(E4)

C	D	E	F
	Serial number	Date	Year
	1	01/01/1900	1900
	366	31/12/1900	1900
	50,000	21/11/2036	2036
	150,000	07/09/2310	2310
	41430.29467	05/06/2013 07:04	2013
	41430	05/06/2013	2013

Again, it does not matter whether column D or E is used – the same result would be given.

DATE

The DATE function converts numbers into a date. It is written as follows:

=DATE(Year,Month,Day)

fx =DATE(1978,11,23)

C	D
	23/11/1978

Each argument can be a number, cell reference or calculation, as usual.

For example, you might want to find the first day of the month of a given date:

fx =DATE(YEAR(E2),MONTH(E2),1)

C	D	E	F
	Serial number	Date	1st Day of Month
	1	01/01/1900	01/01/1900
	366	31/12/1900	01/12/1900
	50,000	21/11/2036	01/11/2036
	150,000	07/09/2310	01/09/2310
	41430.29467	05/06/2013 07:04	01/06/2013
	41430	05/06/2013	01/06/2013

WEEKDAY

This useful function returns the day of the week of a given date – from 1-7, with 1 being Sunday, 2 Monday, etc.

fx =WEEKDAY(E3)

C	D	E	F
	Serial number	Date	Weekday
	1	01/01/1900	1
	366	31/12/1900	2
	50,000	21/11/2036	6
	150,000	07/09/2310	4
	41430.29467	05/06/2013 07:04	4
	41430	05/06/2013	4

Again, it would be more use to see "Saturday" etc.

F3 fx =VLOOKUP(WEEKDAY(E3),$A$2:$B$8,2,FALSE)

	A	B	C	D	E	F
1	Number	Day		Serial number	Date	Weekday
2	1	Sun		1	01/01/1900	Sun
3	2	Mon		366	31/12/1900	Mon
4	3	Tue		50,000	21/11/2036	Fri
5	4	Wed		150,000	07/09/2310	Wed
6	5	Thu		41430.29467	05/06/2013 07:04	Wed
7	6	Fri		41430	05/06/2013	Wed
8	7	Sat				
9						

Note in this example the **table_array** does not include the headers (row 1). It does not matter whether these are included or not.

12.12 Activities

The activities in this guide are designed to test your knowledge on the techniques shown in this chapter. They may also use techniques used in previous chapters, to build up your knowledge. Suggested answers are available on MyKaplan, although it is better to refer to the notes and try to understand the methods than look straight at the answers.

Activity 12-1

This activity mainly tests use of the **ROUND** function, along with some conditional formatting and simple functions.

(a) Open the **Stock list** file in the **Activities** folder.

(b) Note the information – we have a list of stock items, the amount in stock and the total value of the stock. In column E, we need to calculate the cost per unit.

(c) In column E, calculate the **cost per unit**, rounded to **2 decimal places**.

(d) Format the figures in column E showing the figures to **3 decimal places**, with a **£** sign in front of the numbers (currency format).

(e) In cells E16, E17 and E18, enter formulas to show the **average**, **smallest** and **largest** cost per unit respectively.

(f) Label these as Average, Lowest and Highest in cells D16-D18.

(g) Use conditional formatting to fill the largest value in cells E2:E15 in yellow.

(h) Change the value in cell **C3** to **5** – Note that this should change the value in D18 to £45.60 and the E3 should fill yellow.

(i) Save the file in the **Solutions** folder as **Activity 12-1** and close it.

Activity 12-2

This is a normal **VLOOKUP**, with a date function.

(a) Open the **Stock Checker** workbook from the **Activities** folder.

(b) This is a simple stock checker – the product can be selected from a drop down menu in Cell A3. We need the number in stock to be returned from column D on the stock sheet.

(c) Use a **VLOOKUP** formula in **B3** to find the stock level based on the value in **A3**).

(d) Change the product in **A3** to '**Doodad 2**'. Click in A3 and select the drop down menu to change the product.

(e) The value in **B3** should change to **99**.

(f) Enter a formula to put **today's date** into **B1**.

(g) **Left-Align** and **Bold** cell **B1**.

(h) Save the file as **Activity 12-2** in the **Solutions** folder and close it.

Activity 12-3

This exercise requires the use of an **IF** function to check whether a target profit margin has been met.

(a) **Open** the **Target GP** file from the **Activities** folder.

(b) We need to calculate the Gross Profit in column D, and then GP % in column E. GP% is Gross Profit as a percentage of sales.

(c) **Format** the values in column E as **percentage** format to **1 decimal place**.

(d)

E4 | fx =D4/B4

	A	B	C	D	E	F
1	Target Gross	15.0%				
2						
3		Sales	Cost of Sales	Gross Profit	Gross Profit %	Target GP % Met?
4	January	534	454	80	15.0%	
5	February	997	877	120	12.0%	

Your spreadsheet should look like this.

(e) Using an **IF** statement, return 'Yes' if the GP% is greater than or equal to the target in B1 and 'No' if it is not.

(f) Sense check your results – are you getting the results you expect?

(g)

	A	B	C	D	E	F
1	Target Gros:	15.0%				
2						
3		Sales	Cost of Sales	Gross Profit	Gross Profit %	Target GP % Met?
4	January	534	454	80	15.0%	No

You may find you get the above – this should be Yes – the target has been met! Let us see why it is not working.

(h) Change the **format** in column E to **2 decimal places**.

(i)

Gross Profit %	Target GP % Met?
14.98%	No

As this calculation is unrounded, the target has not been met.

(j) Use the **ROUND** function in column E to round the calculation to 3 **decimal places.** Note that for percentages, 14.98% is equivalent to 0.1498, so we need to round to 3 decimal places.

(k) Your Formulas should now work. If you are not getting the results you expect, check the formula that is not working – see which cells are being used. It is usually a problem with absolute/relative references.

(l) **Change** the value in **B1** to 20% – see how column F changes.

(m) **AutoFit** the column widths and save as **Activity 12-3** in the Solutions folder. Close the file.

Activity 12-4

This example uses calculations across worksheets, as well as requiring an **IF** formula.

(a) **Open** the **Boat sales** file from the **Activities** folder.

(b) This workbook contains four worksheets:

Sales Volume – shows the sales to four customers of four different products.

Pricing – shows the price of the four products.

Discounting – shows the discount offered to each customer if target sales are met.

Monthly sales – calculates revenue, and any discount offered.

The calculations are required on the **Monthly Sales** worksheet.

(c) On the Monthly Sales sheet, in cells **C4:F7**, calculate the sales revenue from each product by customer (volume*price). Note that a combination of relative and mixed referencing is required.

(d) Calculate the totals by product and customer in cells **G4:G7** and **C9:G9**.

(e) In cells **H4:H7** we need to calculate the value of the discount. A discount is given **IF** the actual sales (from the Sales Volume sheet) are greater than or equal to the volume target for each customer – in cells B4:B7.

The discount offered will be the total sales figure multiplied by the discount on the Discounting sheet.

(f) Calculate the **discounted sales in column I** as Total sales-Discount, and **copy the totals across** in row 9.

(g) In **J4:J7** you need a formula to say 'Yes' if a discount has been given and 'No' if it has not. There are several ways to achieve this.

(h) Save the file as **Activity 12-4** in the **Solutions** folder and close it.

Activity 12-5

This example builds on the last example, but requires the use of an AND formula.

(a) **Open** the **Boat sales Two** file from the **Activities** folder.

(b) This workbook contains four worksheets:

Sales Volume – shows the sales to four customers of four different products.

Pricing – shows the price of the four products.

Discounting – shows the discount offered to each customer if target sales are met.

Monthly sales – calculates revenue, and any discount offered.

The calculations are required on the **Monthly Sales** worksheet.

(c) On the Monthly Sales sheet, in cells **C4:D7**, calculate the sales revenue from each product by customer (volume*price). Note that a combination of relative and mixed referencing is required.

(d) Calculate the totals by product and customer in cells **E4:E7** and **C9:E9**.

(e) In cells **F4:F7** we need to calculate the value of the discount. A discount is now given **IF** the actual sales (from the Sales Volume sheet) **FOR EACH PRODUCT** are greater than or equal to the volume target for each customer – in cells B4:B7. So the sales for SuperCruise AND the sales for Windrush must be bigger than target – this will form your logical test.

The discount offered will be the total sales figure multiplied by the discount on the Discounting sheet.

(f) Calculate the discounted sales in column I as Total sales-Discount, and copy the totals across in row 9.

(g) In **H4:H7** you need a formula to say 'Yes' if a discount has been given and 'No' if it has not. There are several ways to achieve this.

(h) Save the file as **Activity 12-5** in the **Solutions** folder and close it.

Activity 12-6

This example builds on the last example, but requires the use of an **OR** formula.

(a) **Open** the **Boat sales Three** file from the **Activities** folder.

(b) This workbook contains four worksheets:

Sales Volume – shows the sales to four customers of four different products.

Pricing – shows the price of the four products.

Discounting – shows the discount offered to each customer if target sales are met.

Monthly sales – calculates revenue, and any discount offered.

The calculations are required on the **Monthly Sales** worksheet.

(c) On the Monthly Sales sheet, in cells **C4:D7**, calculate the sales revenue from each product by customer (volume*price). Note that a combination of relative and mixed referencing is required.

(d) Calculate the totals by product and customer in cells **E4:E7** and **C9:E9**.

(e) In cells **F4:F7** we need to calculate the discounted sales. A discount is now given IF the actual sales (from the Sales Volume sheet) **FOR EITHER PRODUCT** are greater than or equal to the volume target for each customer – in cells B4:B7. So the sales for SuperCruise OR the sales for Windrush must be bigger than target – this will form your logical test.

As we are now calculated discounted sales, we cannot just multiply sales*discount like in the previous two examples. The discounted sales will be Total Sales-(Discount*Total Sales).

(f) Copy the **totals** across in row 9.

(g) In **G4:G7** you need a formula to say 'Yes' if a discount has been given and 'No' if it has not. There are several ways to achieve this.

(h) Save the file as **Activity 12-6** in the **Solutions** folder and close it.

Activity 12-7

This is an example of a **VLOOKUP** requiring the use of **TRUE** rather than FALSE as the final argument, included for illustration purposes.

(a) **Open** the **Salary VLookup** file from the **Activities** folder.

(b) This workbook contains two worksheets:

Lookup Table – Shows a range of sales targets, along with the basic salaries, commission and bonus which would be paid at those levels.

Salary Calculator – based on the salary entered in cell D5, the basic wage, commission and bonus should be calculated using the information in **Lookup Table**.

(c) On the **Salary Calculator** worksheet, enter a test value for sales of **15000** in **D5**.

(d) We now need to populate the Basic Wage in **D9**. This requires the **Lookup Table**.

(e) We need a formula to 'find' the appropriate sales range (in this case 0-20000), and return the value in column C, the basic. This is done using **VLOOKUP**. Enter a **VLOOKUP** formula in cell **D9** on Salary Calculator. Note you will need to make the **Range_lookup TRUE** (see note at the end of the activity)

(f) With a correct formula you should get a basic wage of £1,000. Change the 15000 in D5 to 75000 and the basic should change to £1,100.

(g) We need a similar lookup for commission in **E9** on **Salary Calculator**. We need the lookup to calculate the value of the salary so remember to multiply the % by the monthly sales figure.

(h) Put a similar formula in to **F9** to calculate the bonus (as a percentage of monthly sales) and find the **total** in **G9**.

(i) Save the file in the **Solutions** folder as **Activity 12-7** and close it.

Note: If we had used FALSE instead of TRUE in this activity, the formula would 'look' down cells A1:A8 of the table to try and find 15,000, but it is not there, so a #N/A error would be shown.

TRUE finds the nearest match which is smaller than the lookup value, again working down the column. So A1='Sales' – this would be ignored as it is not a number. A2=0 – 15000 is bigger than zero, so try the next. A3=20,001 – this is bigger than 15000, so use the data in row 2, and give a Basic of 1000.

When we changed sales to 75000, the nearest match which is smaller than 75000 is 50000, so a basic of 1100 is given, as required.

Activity 12-8

This is the same example as Activity 12-7, but using **HLOOKUP**

(a) **Open** the **Salary HLookup** file from the **Activities** folder.

(b) Following the steps in **activity 12-7**, use **HLOOKUP** to find a Basic Wage, Commission and Bonus based on the Monthly Sales in cell D5, along with a total.

(c) Make sure the value in **D5** is **zero** – You should see **#N/A** errors:

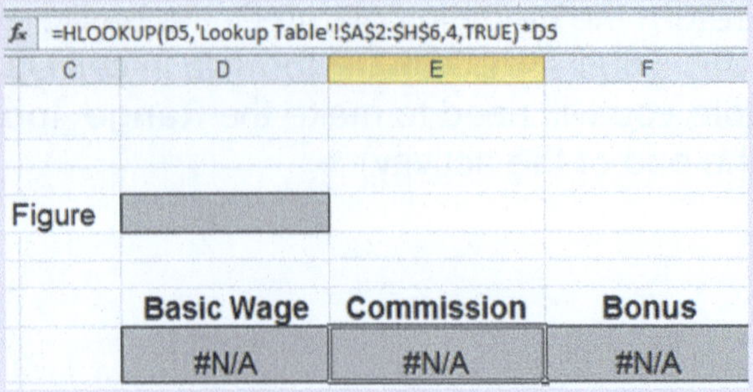

(d) This is because of the Lookup Table. Notice that the first salary is £1. The lookup looks for the nearest value less than or equal to zero – as there are no values less than or equal to zero, #N/A is returned. **Change the sales figure to 1**, and the lookups will work

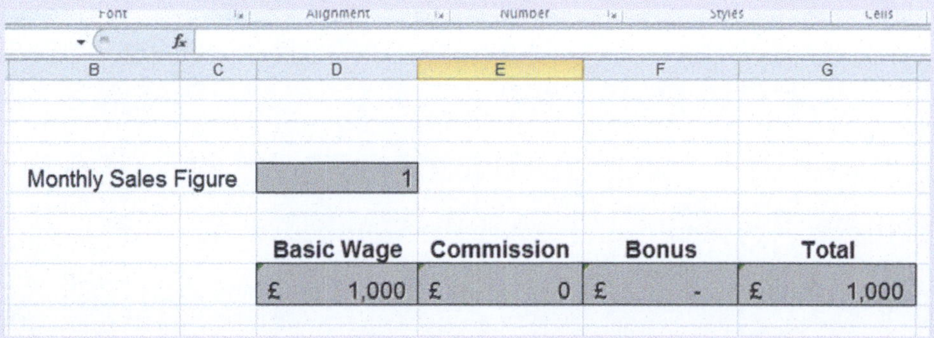

(e) #N/A errors do not look very professional. We could use an IF statement to remove them. The idea would be IF the value in D5 is zero, show zero, otherwise do the lookup.

Add IF statements to cells D9, E9 and F9 to remove the #N/A errors

(f) Change the sales back to zero to check that the errors do not appear.

(g) Save the file as **Activity 12-8** in the **Solutions** folder and close it.

Tracing errors in formulas

13

13.1 Introduction

This chapter will help you to understand the types of errors that can occur and learn how to trace errors in the spreadsheets.

KNOWLEDGE

3.5 Explain how to find and sort errors in formulas.

3.6 Check spreadsheet information meets needs, using IT tools and making corrections as necessary.

In this chapter you will learn how to trace errors in formulas and use some of Excel's tools to find and them. In this chapter you will be looking at different types of error and some useful ways to track down any problems you may be having with your formulas.

13.2 Types of error

You need to be aware of a number of different types of error. The errors below will be displayed in the cell where the problem is.

Error	Description
#DIV/0!	This occurs if we have tried to divide by zero or a blank cell.
#N/A	This occurs if data is not available. It is common in LOOKUP functions.
#NAME?	This occurs if we use a name that Excel doesn't recognise. This is common in incorrectly spelled function names.
#NUM!	This occurs if you place an invalid argument in a function.
#REF!	This occurs if a formula uses an invalid cell reference.
#VALUE!	This occurs if we attempt to use an incorrect data type.

Tip

When you are editing a cell that contains a formula, Excel colour codes the formula and then places a coloured border around cells that make up the formula.

13.3 Formula AutoCorrect

When writing formulas sometimes parentheses (Brackets) get left out or placed in the wrong order, or you might enter the wrong number of arguments (syntax error). **Formula AutoCorrect** will pop up on screen and offer to correct the problem. Whilst Excel is very good at finding errors you do need to be careful as it sometimes guesses incorrectly.

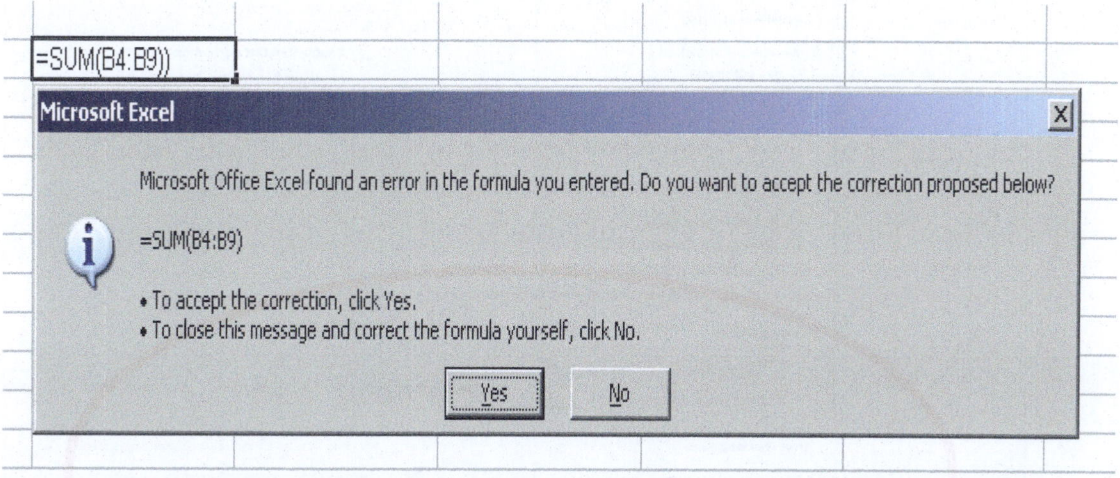

In the example above Excel has correctly determined that one too many brackets have been placed in the formula. In this instance you can accept the offered solution.

13.4 Error checking

Excel can be set up to check for errors, and highlight problem cells. The settings can be found in the **File** tab, under **Options, Formulas.**

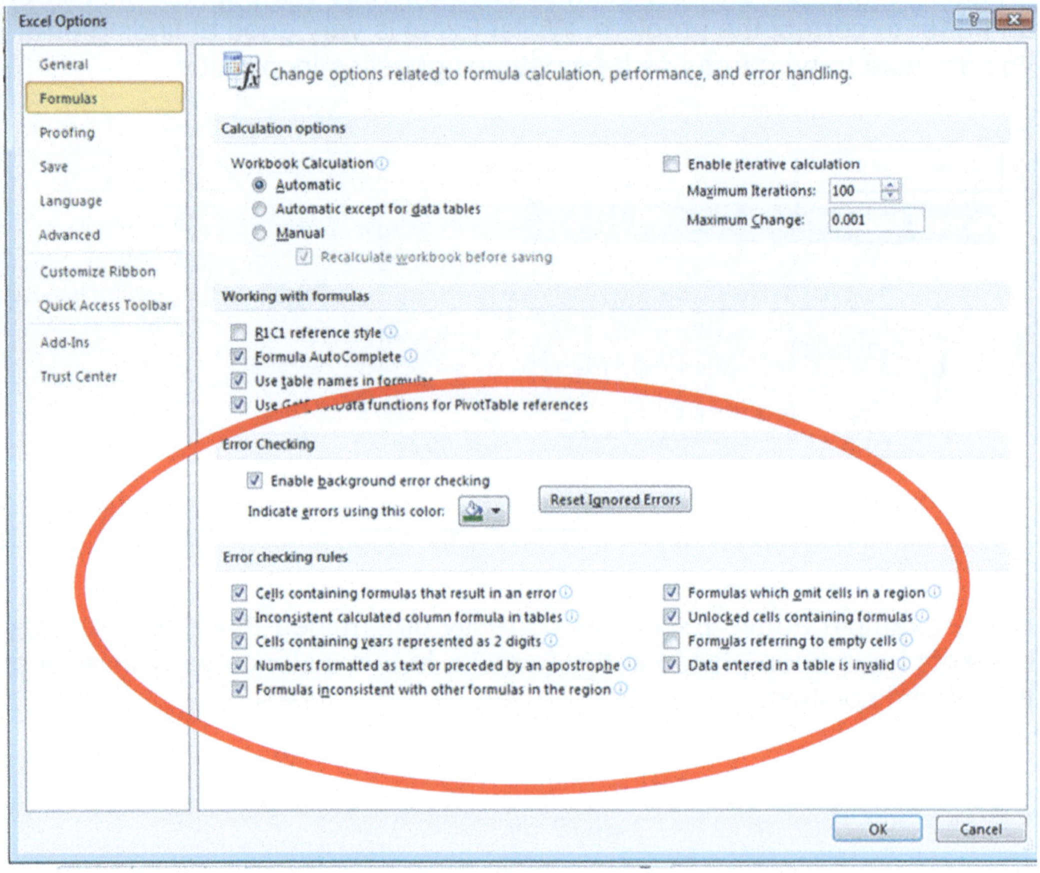

These options allow you to set your own rules for error checking. It is probably best left in its default setting.

If Error Checking is turned on, when a problem is found with a formula, Excel will place a green 'flag' in the cell.

Excel also has a more local error checking tool. When you enter a formula Excel will place a flag in a cell if it thinks you are making an error.

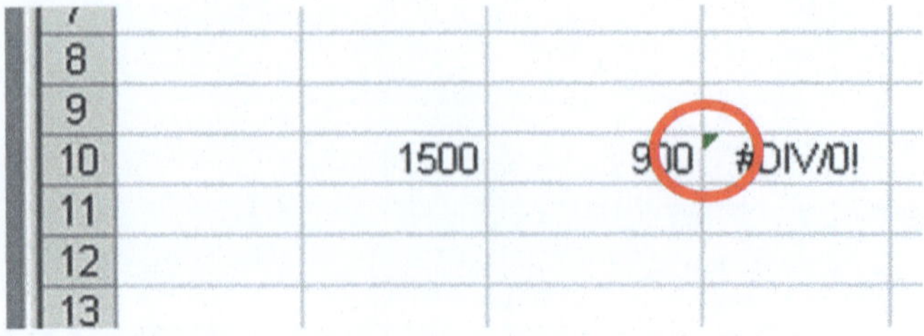

In the above example Excel has put a flag in the cell where it thinks there is an error. If you click into the error cell you will be given the option to review and deal with the error.

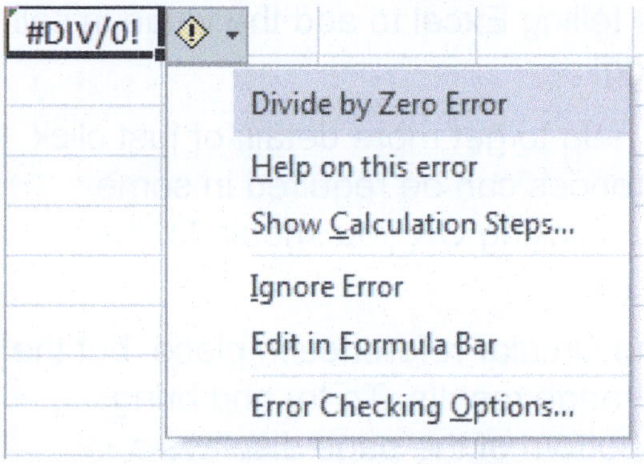

Above you can see a **Divide by zero error**. You now have the opportunity to get help from a number of sources, or ignore the error.

- If you click Help on this error the Excel Help system will pop up and you can ask questions and seek help from here
- 'Show calculation steps' is dealt with later in the chapter under **Evaluate Formula**.
- You can choose to ignore the error. This is fine if you know what the problem is and can fix it, but you should not simply ignore the error as you will create problems elsewhere.
- Edit in formula bar puts the cursor in the formula bar, and you can fix your problem directly.
- Error checking options will bring up the menu shown above.

13.5 Circular references

A circular reference is a common error and occurs when you try to include the cell that we are writing a formula in as part of the formula. For example:

If you typed the following formula into Cell A3, you would get a circular reference message.

=SUM(A1:A3)

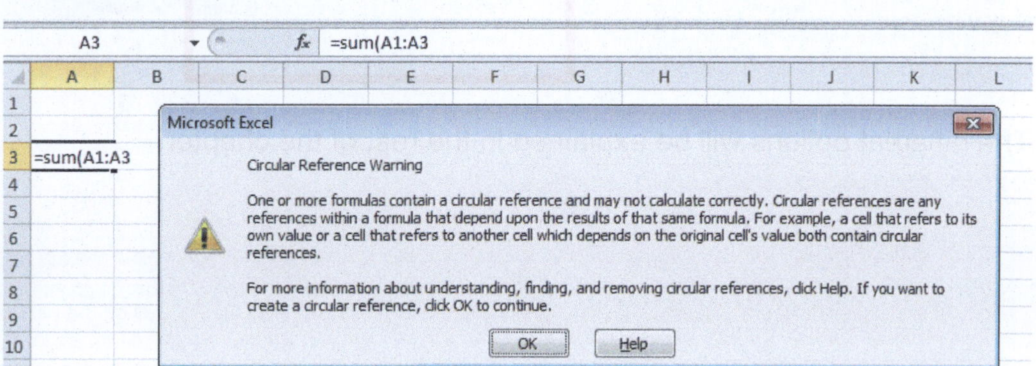

This is a circular reference, as you are telling Excel to add the value in cell A3 to cell A3 – it should keep increasing!

As the warning says, you can click on help to get more detail, or just click OK to continue. Although circular references can be required in some situations, it is very rare, therefore after clicking OK you should fix the formula.

Excel will allow you to continue with the circular reference in place, but the formula will not work and can cause strange results. To try and bring attention to this, the Status Bar at the bottom of the page displays a warning if a circular reference is in place.

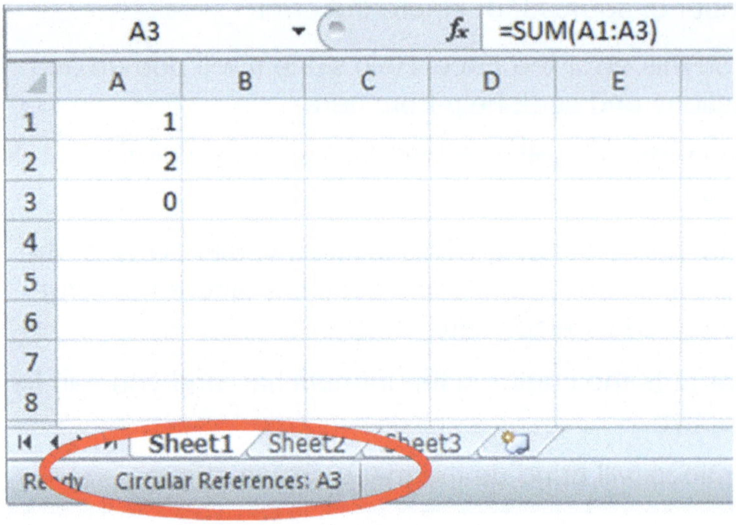

13.6 Formula Auditing Toolbar

The **Formula Auditing Toolbar** is a very useful tool for finding and controlling errors in spreadsheets – especially complex ones. It is found in the **Formulas** tab.

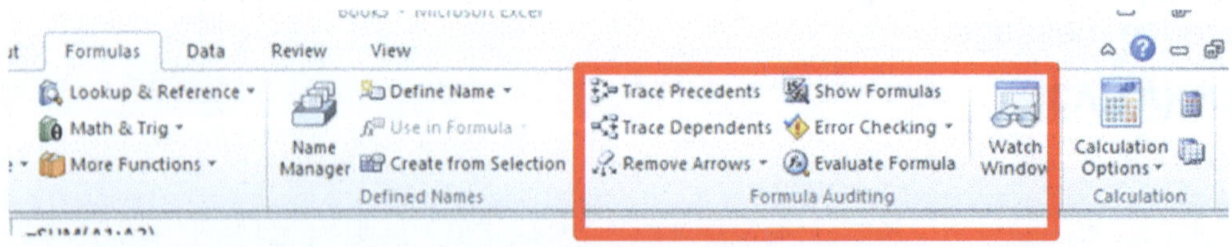

The different options will be explained in the rest of the chapter.

13.7 Trace precedents

This useful tool allows you to see which cells are used in the calculation of your selected cell. This is helpful if you are trying to work out why a formula is giving an unexpected value or error.

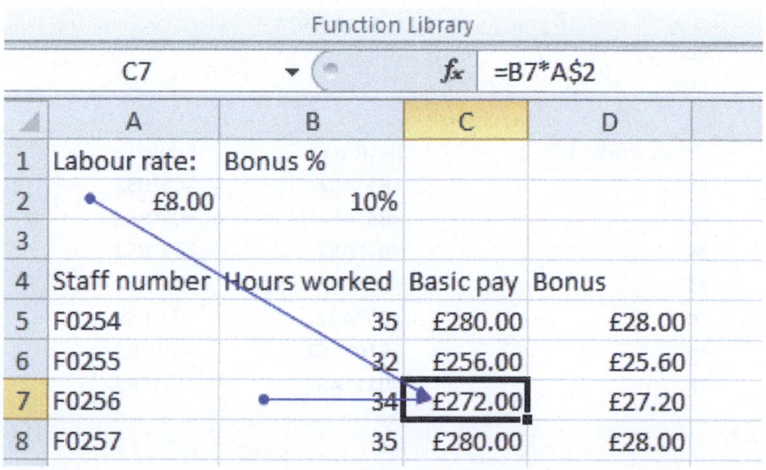

Function Library

C7 | =B7*A$2

	A	B	C	D
1	Labour rate:	Bonus %		
2	£8.00	10%		
3				
4	Staff number	Hours worked	Basic pay	Bonus
5	F0254	35	£280.00	£28.00
6	F0255	32	£256.00	£25.60
7	F0256	34	£272.00	£27.20
8	F0257	35	£280.00	£28.00

Clicking the 'Trace Precedents' button with C7 selected will show which cells are being used.

13.8 Trace dependents

Similar to trace precedents, clicking this button will show all the cells which are referring to this cell in a formula.

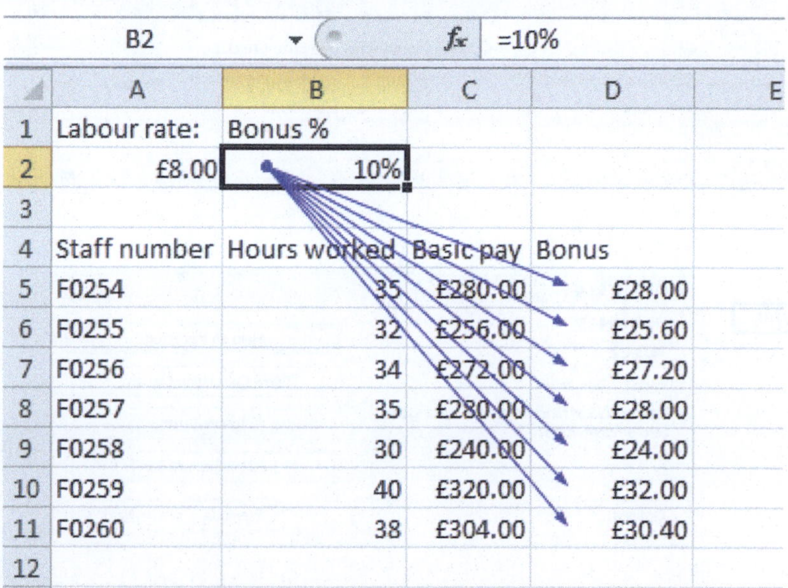

B2 | =10%

	A	B	C	D	E
1	Labour rate:	Bonus %			
2	£8.00	10%			
3					
4	Staff number	Hours worked	Basic pay	Bonus	
5	F0254	35	£280.00	£28.00	
6	F0255	32	£256.00	£25.60	
7	F0256	34	£272.00	£27.20	
8	F0257	35	£280.00	£28.00	
9	F0258	30	£240.00	£24.00	
10	F0259	40	£320.00	£32.00	
11	F0260	38	£304.00	£30.40	
12					

13.9 Remove arrows

If you have been using Trace Precedents/Dependents, this button will remove all of the arrows from the spreadsheet. There are two options within this button – to just remove precedent or dependent arrows.

13.10 Show formulas

This has already been seen in a previous chapter – this button toggles between showing the results of the formula in a cell, and showing the formula itself.

	A	B	C	D
1	Labour rate:	Bonus %		
2	8	=10%		
3				
4	Staff number	Hours worked	Basic pay	Bonus
5	F0254	35	=B5*A$2	=C5*B$2
6	F0255	32	=B6*A$2	=C6*B$2
7	F0256	34	=B7*A$2	=C7*B$2
8	F0257	35	=B8*A$2	=C8*B$2
9	F0258	30	=B9*A$2	=C9*B$2
10	F0259	40	=B10*A$2	=C10*B$2
11	F0260	38	=B11*A$2	=C11*B$2
12				

13.11 Error checking

This button checks the spreadsheet for cells with errors, and gives more help on the options you have.

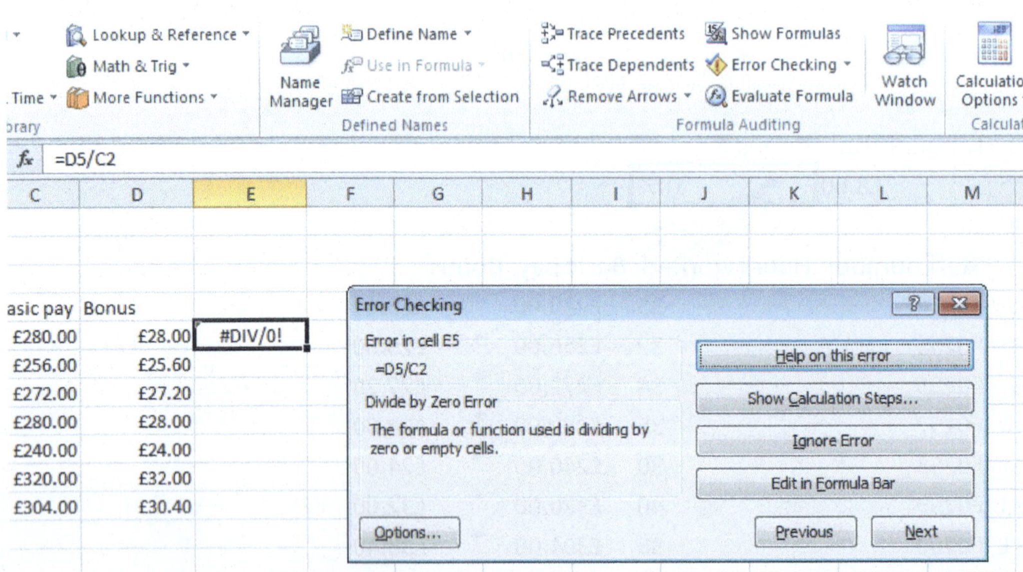

Here, we have a Divide by Zero error which has been highlighted. The options are:

- **Help on this error** – brings up the Help Function.
- **Show Calculation Steps** – performs the **Evaluate Formula** function (see below) on the cell.
- **Ignore Error** – moves on to the next error on the sheet.
- **Edit in Formula Bar** – allows you to correct the error.
- **Options** – brings up the menu shown in **Section 12.4**.
- **Previous** – move back to the last error found.
- **Next** – move on to the next error in the sheet (same as **Ignore**).

There are two other options available within the Error Checking button:

Trace error

This works in the same way as **Trace Precedents**, allowing you to see which cells are being used in order to help find where the error is coming from.

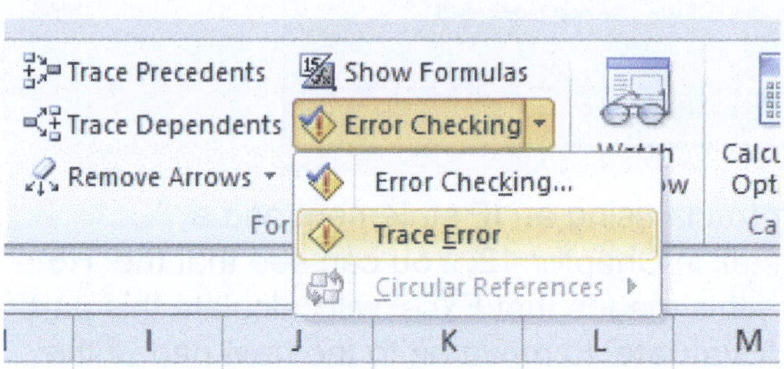

If the Active Cell contains an error, then clicking this will show the cells used in the formula.

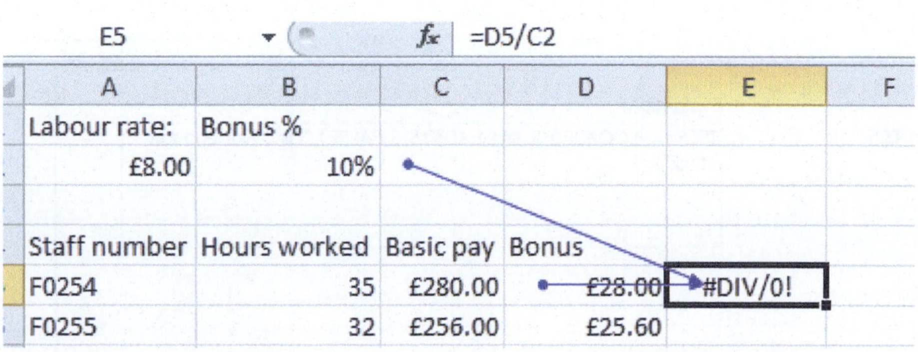

Circular references

If there are circular references in your workbook, this menu allows you to identify and navigate to them quickly. If there are no circular references it will be greyed out – unavailable for selection.

13.12 Evaluate formula

This may be the most useful function within the Formula Auditing toolbar – it allows you to work through a formula step by step to see how the result is being calculated. It is especially useful for more complicated formulas like **VLOOKUP** and **IF** statements.

To Evaluate a Formula, select the cell and click '**Evaluate Formula**'.

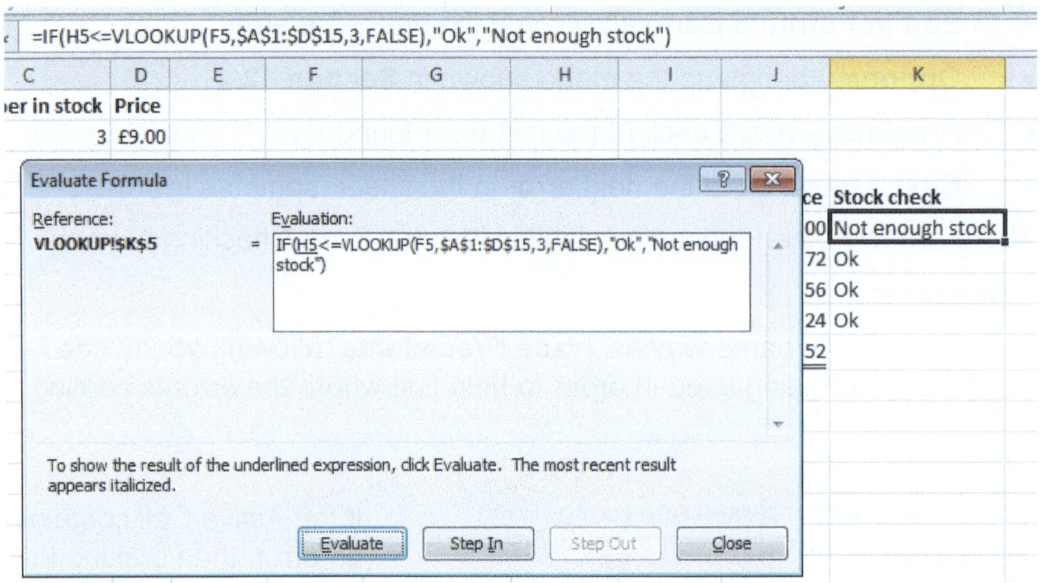

This is a fairly complicated formula using an **IF** statement and a **VLOOKUP** – explained in detail in Chapter 12. You can see that the '**H5**' in the formula is underlined – this means that Excel will calculate this part of the formula first. Click on '**Evaluate**' to move on to the next part of the calculation.

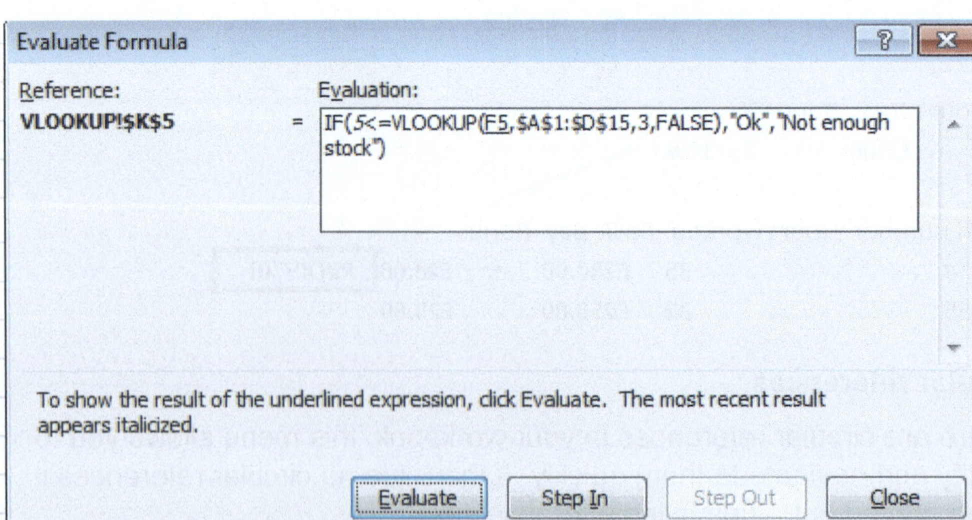

The value in cell H5 is 5. The next part of the evaluation is '**F5**'. Keep clicking '**Evaluate**' to see how the calculation works.

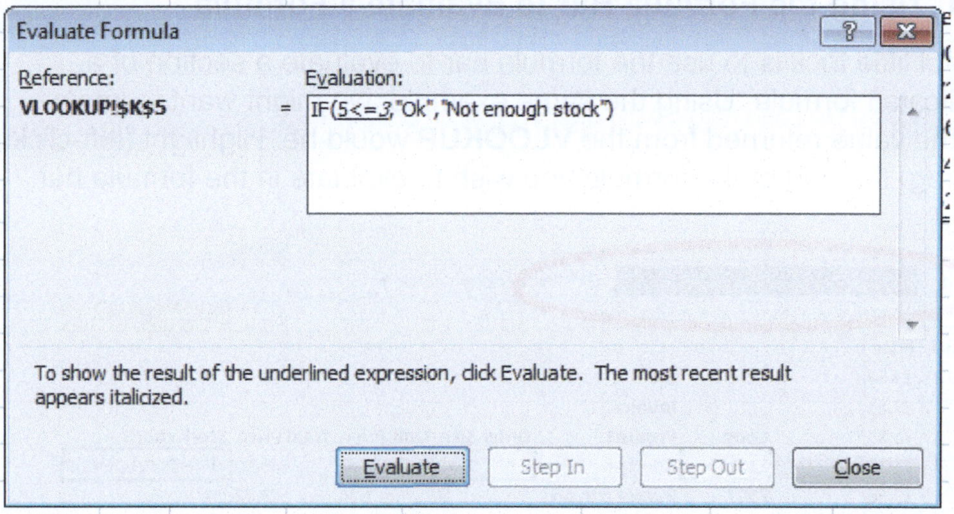

After a few clicks, we have the expression above. '3' is the value of the VLOOKUP part of the formula – this is now a simple IF function – IF 5 is less than or equal to 3, then put "Ok", otherwise put "Not enough stock".

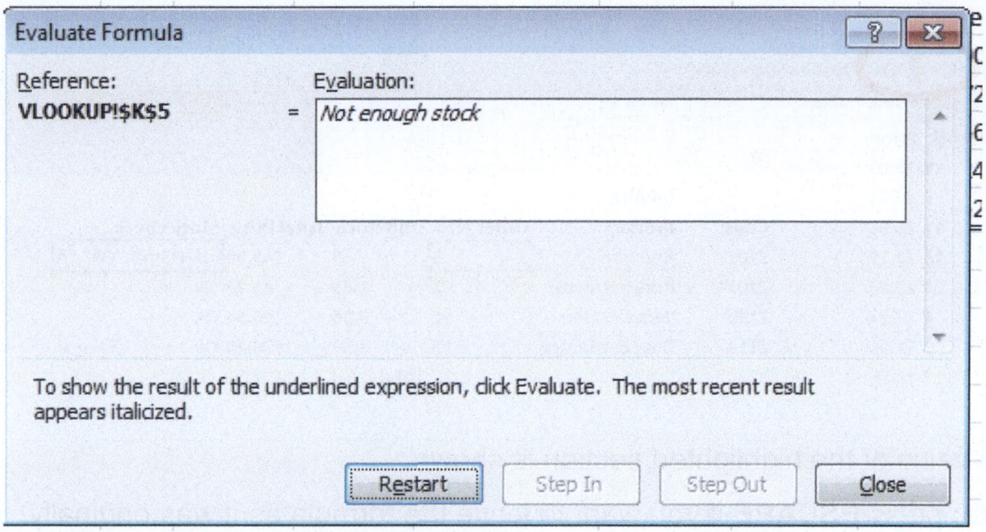

5 is obviously not less than or equal to 3, so the final result is shown. This can make finding errors in your formulas very easy to find.

13.13 Using the Formula Bar to Evaluate a Formula

A useful little trick is to use the formula bar to evaluate a section of a complicated formula. Using the same example, we might want to know what the value returned from the **VLOOKUP** would be. Highlight (left-click and drag) the part of the formula you wish to evaluate in the formula bar:

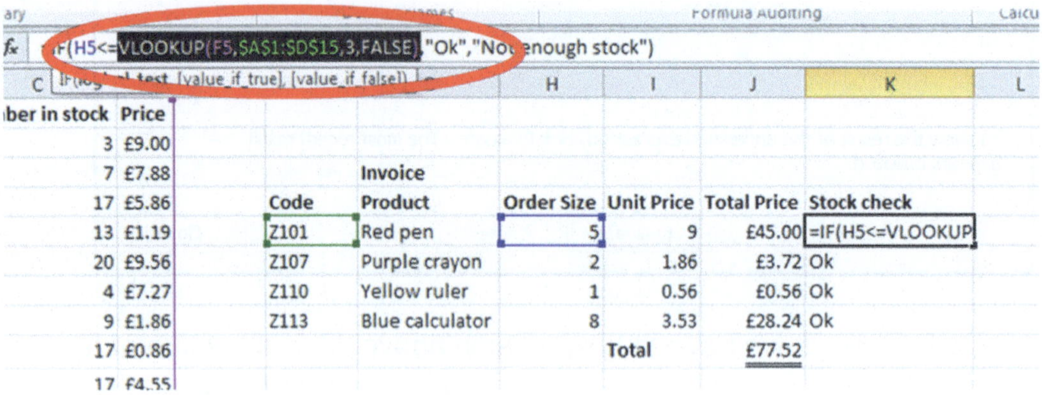

Press **F9** to evaluate this part of the Formula.

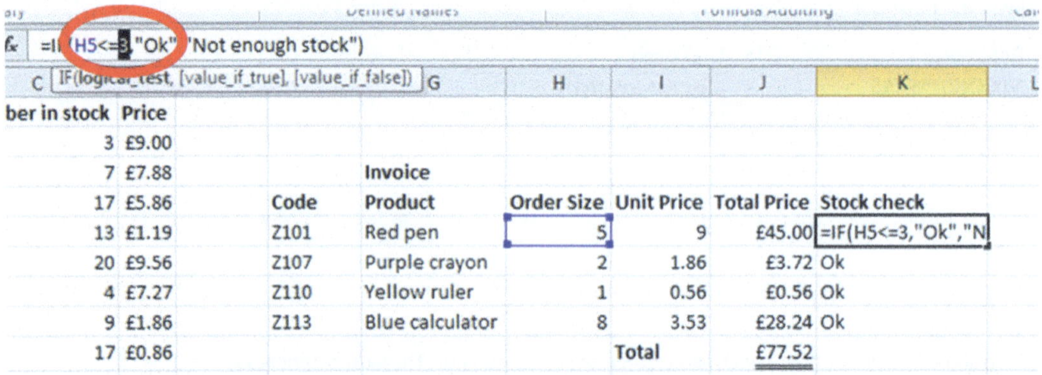

The value of the highlighted section is shown.

Note: press **ESCAPE** if you want to leave the formula as it was originally. If you press Enter then the formula will be shown as above, with the value in instead of the formula. Of course if you do this, pressing **Ctrl-Z** (undo) will correct the mistake.

13.14 Watch Window

This tool is most useful when dealing with formulas that reference across multiple worksheets or workbooks. It allows you to 'watch' a cell or cells, without having to have that cell visible on your worksheet.

To select a cell to 'watch', click on the **'Watch Window'** button, then '**Add Watch**', and select the cell you wish to watch. The window will then show the cell's formula and value even if you don't have that sheet visible.

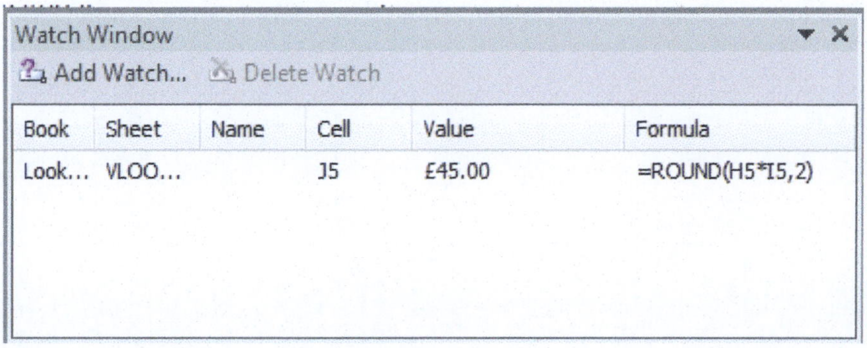

13.15 Activities

These techniques can be applied to any spreadsheet – try to use them wherever possible. Complicated formulas often don't work the first time you try them – use error checking techniques to try and find where the problem is.

Charts and graphs

14

14.1 Introduction

This chapter will guide you on how to create a number of different graphs and how to move and change these charts and graphs within the spreadsheet.

KNOWLEDGE

3.3 Select and use appropriate tools and techniques to generate, develop and format charts and graphs.

In this session we will be examining Charts and Graphs. We will be looking at several types of charts and their construction, formatting and location.

In essence there is very little difference between a chart and a graph and the term is interchangeable. One minor difference is that some charts do not have axes, whilst graphs always do.

14.2 Chart and graph terminology

Listed below are the more common charting terms:

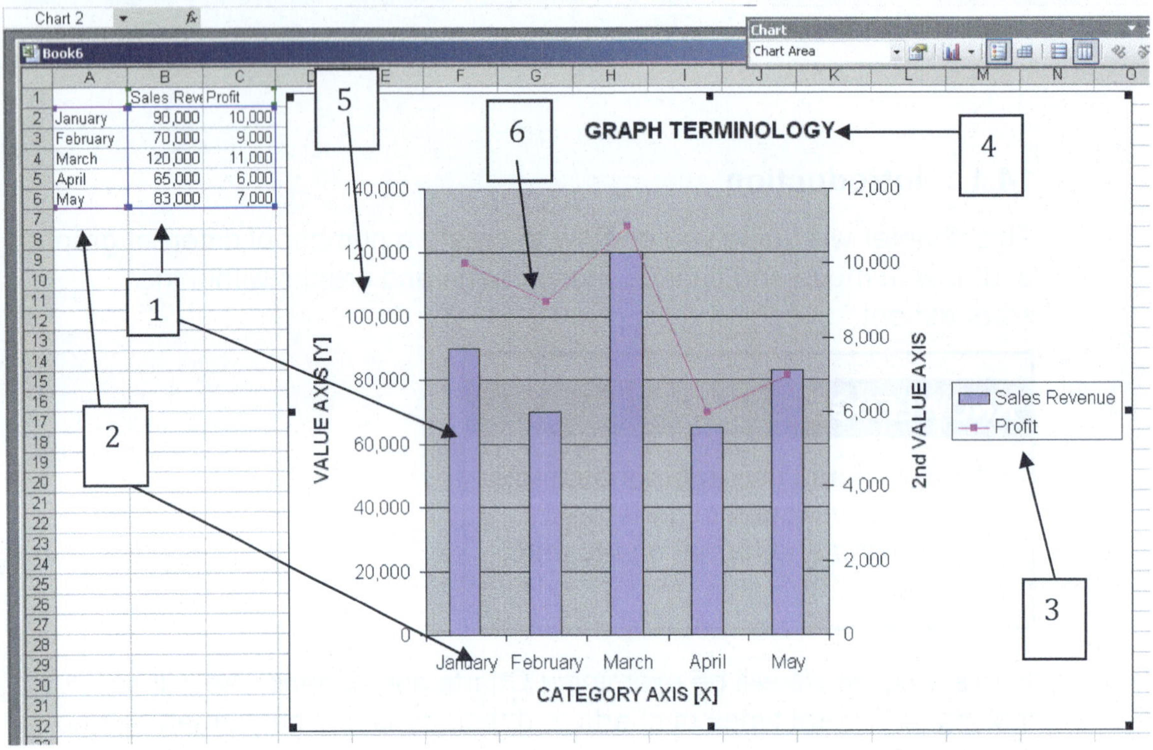

1 **Data Series** – these are the numbers **[values]** from which Excel is creating the graph. These are plotted on the **Value or 'Y' axis**.

2 **Category** – the information that identifies the data series. This is plotted along the **Category or 'X' axis**.

3 **Legend** – this identifies the different data series.

4 **Title** – gives meaning to the graph.

5 **Scale** – both the 'X' and the 'Y' axis (if numerical) can have a scale. These identify the range of values in the data series.

6 **Data Point** – this denotes the value of a particular data series. **Data Labels** can be placed next to data points to give greater meaning. Data Points have Data Markers. **Data Markers** are different shapes and colours for each data series.

14.3 Creating charts and graphs

Within Excel there are two basic ways to display charts and graphs. There is no right or wrong way, it is down to user preference. It is also a simple matter to switch between the two types.

1 **Chart Sheet** – here the chart or graph becomes the entire worksheet.

2 **Embedded** – here the chart or graph is located on the sheet that contains the data. The chart can be moved around to suit the user.

The easiest way to create a chart in Excel is to **Select** the **Data** you wish to chart, then go to the **Insert** tab, and select the **Chart** you wish to insert.

You can also highlight the data you want in your chart and **press F11**. Excel will create a default (column) chart on a chart sheet.

14.4 Types of charts and graphs

You need to be aware of the following types of graph:

- Bar and Column charts.
- Pie and Doughnut charts.
- Scatter graph.
- Bubble chart.
- Single and double line graphs.
- Multiple graph types on one chart.

Bar and Column charts

Bar and column charts are used to display and compare the number, frequency or other measure for different discrete categories of data. They are one of the most commonly used types of graph because they are simple to create and very easy to interpret. They are also a flexible chart type and there are several variations of the standard bar chart including component bar charts, and compound bar charts.

Bar charts are useful for displaying data that are classified into categories.

Bar charts are also useful for displaying data that include categories with negative values, because it is possible to position the bars below and above the x-axis.

The chart is constructed such that the lengths of the different bars are proportional to the size of the category they represent. The x-axis represents the different categories and so has no scale. In order to emphasise the fact that the categories are discrete, a gap is left between the bars on the x-axis. The y-axis does have a scale and this indicates the units of measurement.

A column chart has vertical columns to represent the data and bar charts have horizontal columns.

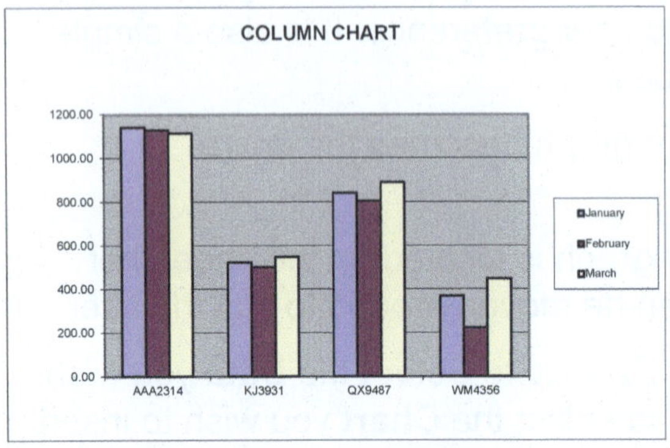

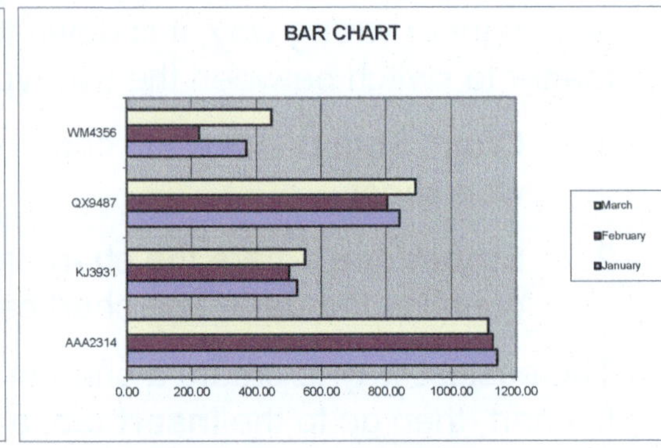

Pie and Doughnut charts

A pie chart is a circular graph that shows the relative contribution that different sub-groups contribute to an overall category. A wedge of the circle represents each sub-groups contribution. Every 1% contribution that a sub-group contributes to the total corresponds to an angle of 3.6 degrees.

Pie charts are generally used to show percentage or proportional data, but they can only represent one category split into its sub-groups. This makes it harder to draw any comparisons between either products or areas without producing multiple pie charts. It is also not possible to 'read off' the actual data unless data labels are added, which is possible with other forms of graphical representation.

Pie charts are good for displaying data for around 6 sub-groups or fewer. When there are more sub-groups it is difficult for the eye to distinguish between the relative sizes of the different sectors and so the chart becomes difficult to interpret.

Pie and Doughnut charts are very similar. They both represent proportions of a whole and neither of them have axes. The major difference between the two is that a Pie Chart can only have one data series whilst a Doughnut can have two or more.

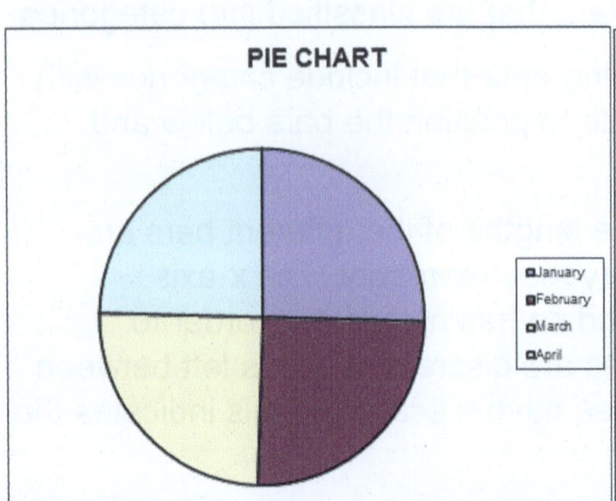

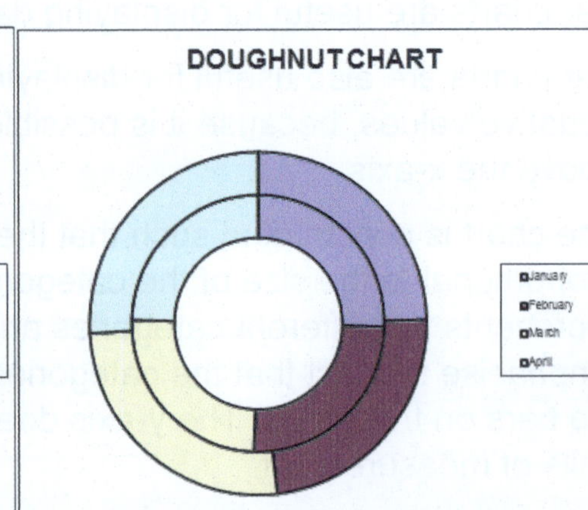

Scatter graph (XY)

Scatter diagrams are used to show the relationship between pairs of quantitative measurements made for the same object or individual. For example, a scatter diagram could be used to present information about production levels and costs.

In a scatter diagram a dot or cross represents each data set and is plotted on the graph with reference to the x-axis and y-axis, each of which represent one of the two measurements. On a scatter diagram both the x and y-axis have scales. By analysing the pattern of dots that make up a scatter diagram it is possible to identify whether there is any relationship (correlation) between the two measurements. Regression lines, lines of best fit, can also be added to the graph and used to decide whether the relationship between the two sets of measurements can be explained or if it is due to chance.

In the example below the relationship is of sales volume to sales revenue. The data points (represented by diamonds) show the intersection of the two sets of numbers.

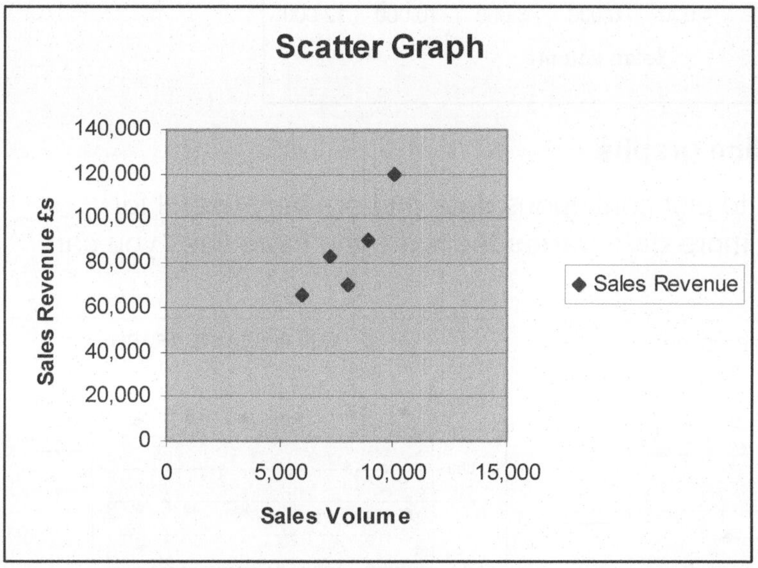

Bubble chart

A Bubble chart is very similar to a scatter graph in that it compares values. The difference here is that a third data series is added. The third data series is represented by the size of the bubble. In our example below the bubble represents profit.

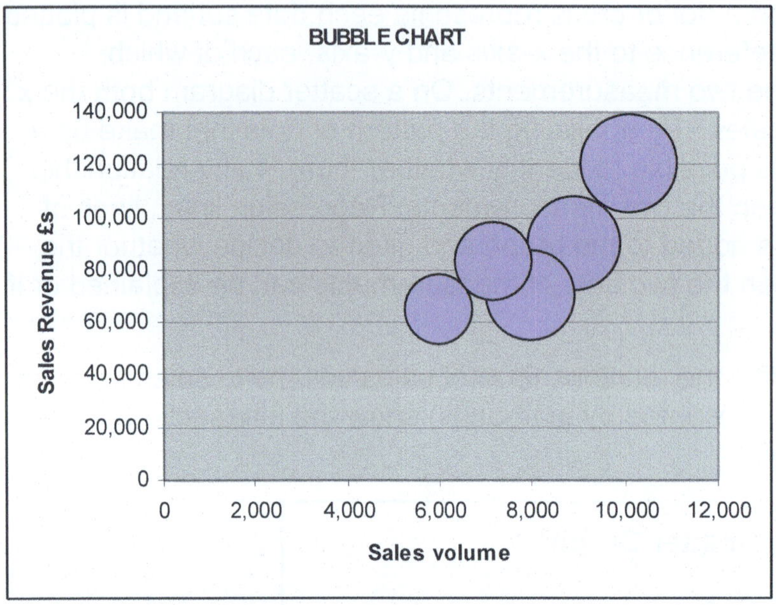

Single and double line graphs

Line charts are used to plot continuous data and are very useful for showing trends. The more **data series** there are the more lines you can have on your graph.

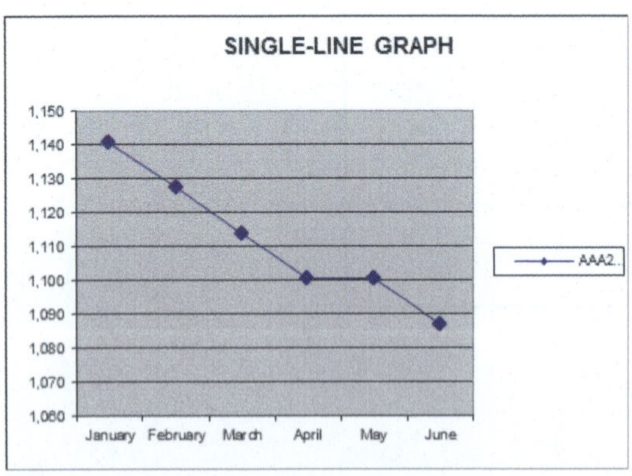

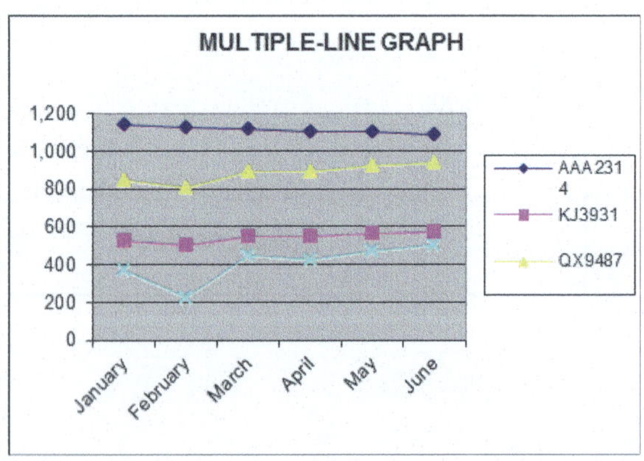

Multiple graph types on one chart

Also known as **Combination Charts** these charts must consist of at least two data series. With this chart type you can have either two graph types on **one** axis or insert a second **value** or **'Y'** axis.

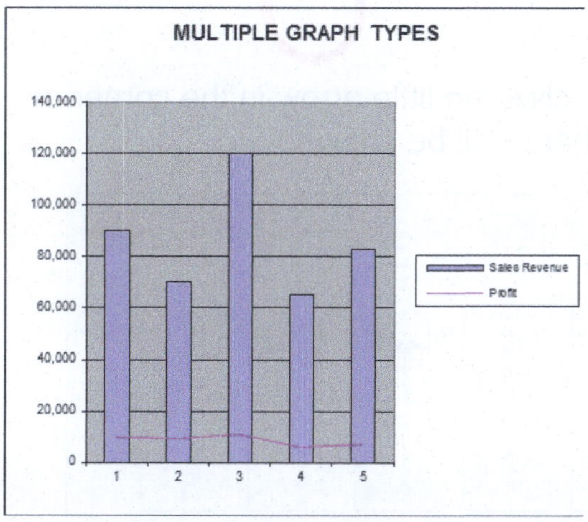

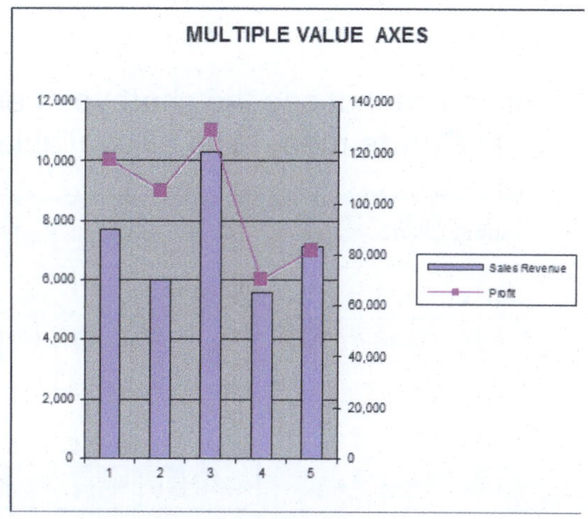

14.5 Creating a chart or graph

Select the data you wish to graph, and on the **Insert** tab, select the chart type you want.

B1 | *fx* Product

	A	B	C	D	E
1	Code	Product	Number in stock	Price	
2	Z101	Red pen	3	£9.00	
3	Z102	Yellow pen	7	£7.88	
4	Z103	Purple pen	17	£5.86	
5	Z104	Green pen	13	£1.19	
6	Z105	Red crayon	20	£9.56	
7	Z105	Yellow crayon	4	£7.27	
8	Z107	Purple crayon	9	£1.86	
9	Z108	Green crayon	17	£0.86	
10	Z109	Red ruler	17	£4.55	
11	Z110	Yellow ruler	20	£0.56	
12	Z111	Green ruler	12	£5.35	
13	Z112	Purple ruler	4	£4.88	
14	Z113	Blue calculator	12	£3.53	
15	Z114	Orange calculator	6	£7.16	
16					

Select the data, then find the chart type you are after.

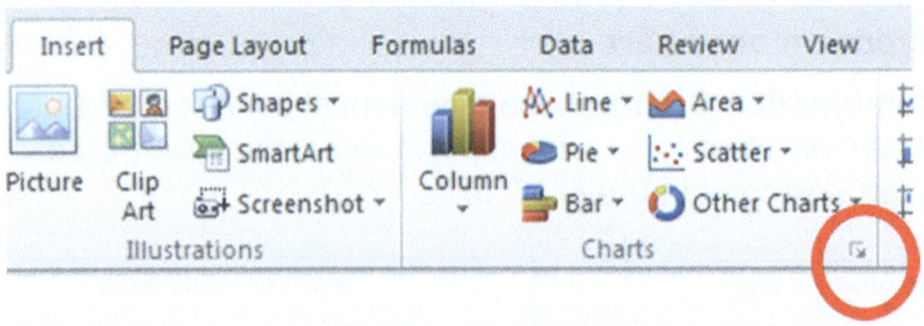

If you cannot see the chart you need, click the little arrow in the corner of the **Charts** menu, and all available charts will be shown.

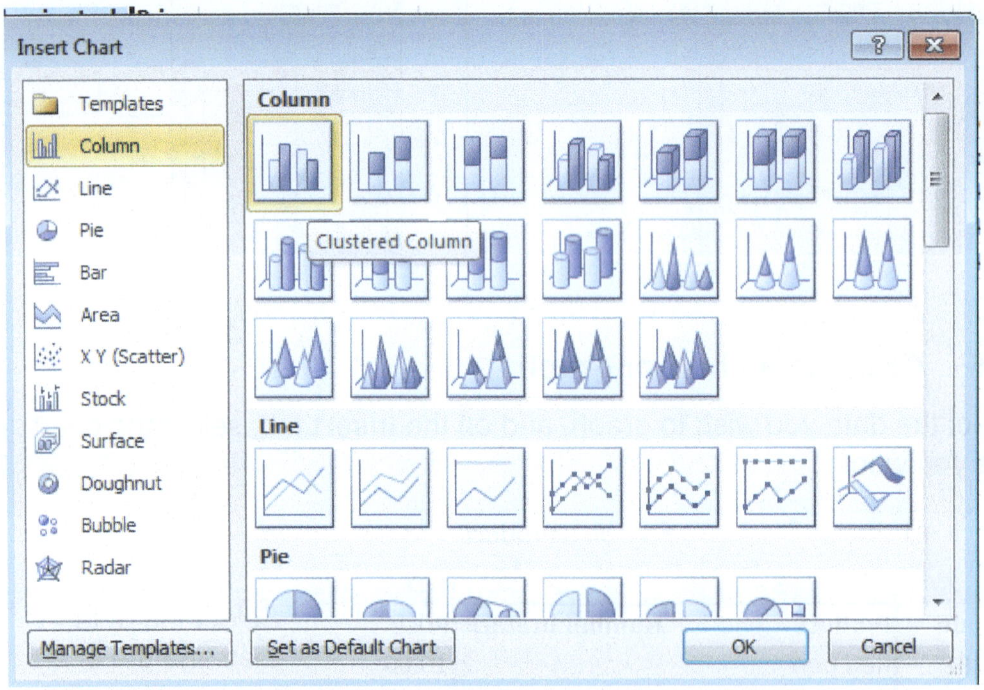

So, if you are asked for a **Clustered Column chart**, and do not know what it is – go into this menu and hover over the options to find what you need. Click **OK** once you have found what you need, and the chart will be shown.

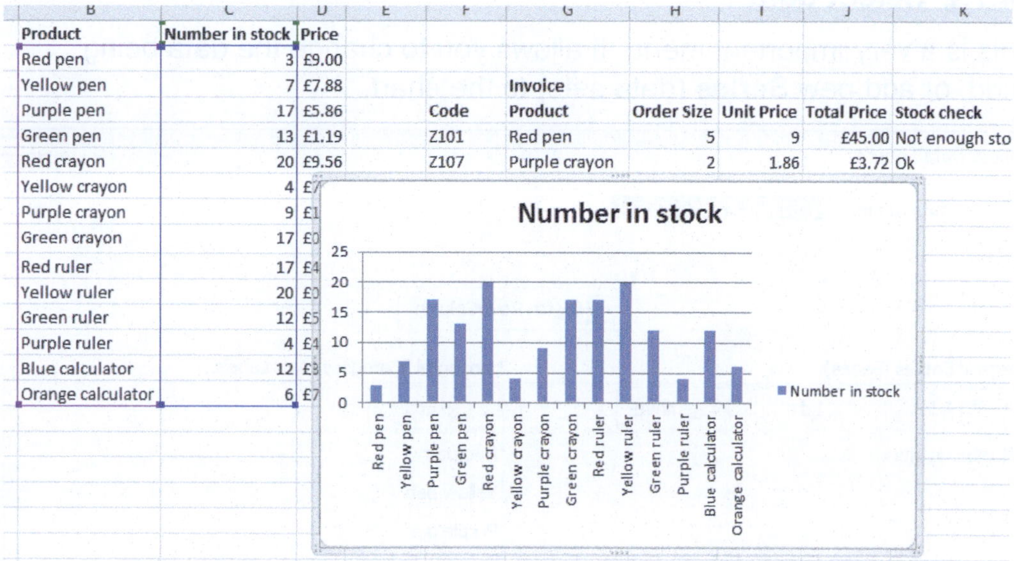

You can also see that the data being used is also highlighted.

As shown, creating a chart is not difficult – what may prove more difficult is getting it to look exactly how you want it to. There are many options available, and these will be dealt with in turn.

14.6 The chart tools tabs

When you create a chart, or have one selected, the chart tools tabs will become available on the Ribbon. These will allow you to change the features of your chart.

There are 3 tabs within the Chart Tools menu, as follows:

14.7 Design Tab

This is to do with the fundamental features of your chart – what sort of chart it is, the data used and where it is shown on your spreadsheet. The main options are:

14.7.1 Change chart type

This allows you to change the type of chart you are using. The menu showing all available charts is shown, and can be selected in the same way as a new chart.

14.7.2 Select data

This is a very important menu. It allows you to change the data being used, or add new **Series** (data sets) to the chart.

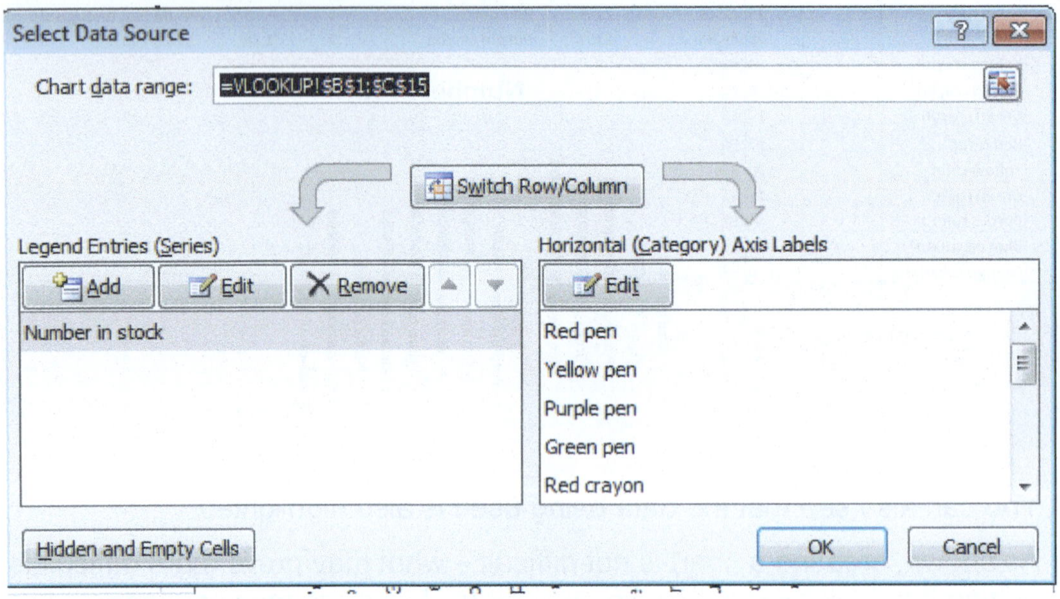

The data range, as shown here, is the original data that was selected to draw the graph. This can be edited if more data is added, or if you wish to add another set of data to the graph.

14.7.3 Move chart

This allows you to switch between an **embedded** chart and a **Chart Sheet**. Simply click on the **Move Chart** button to change the location of your chart.

14.8 Layout Tab

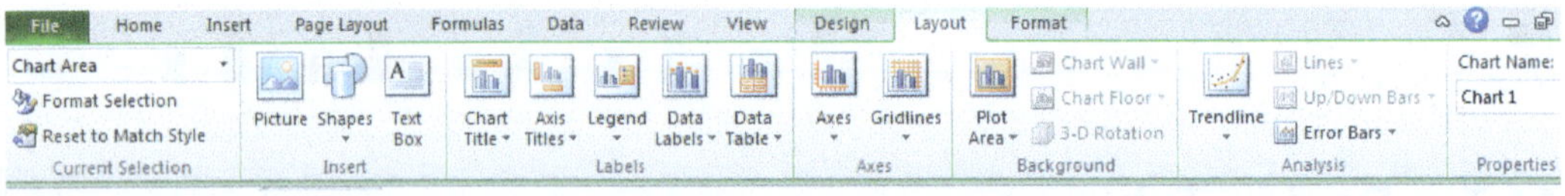

From the point of view of the SDST assessment, this is probably the most important menu. This is where you can change many of the key visual features of your chart, such as titles and legends.

14.8.1 Chart title

As the name suggests, this allows you to add or remove a main Title for your chart. There are also options as to where and how the title is displayed.

14.8.2 Axis titles

Again, this option allows you to add or remove titles for both axes.

14.8.3 Legend

As explained earlier, the **Legend** is the 'key' which explains what the different colours or bars on the graph correspond to. Use this button to add or remove a **Legend**, as well as change the location of the **Legend**.

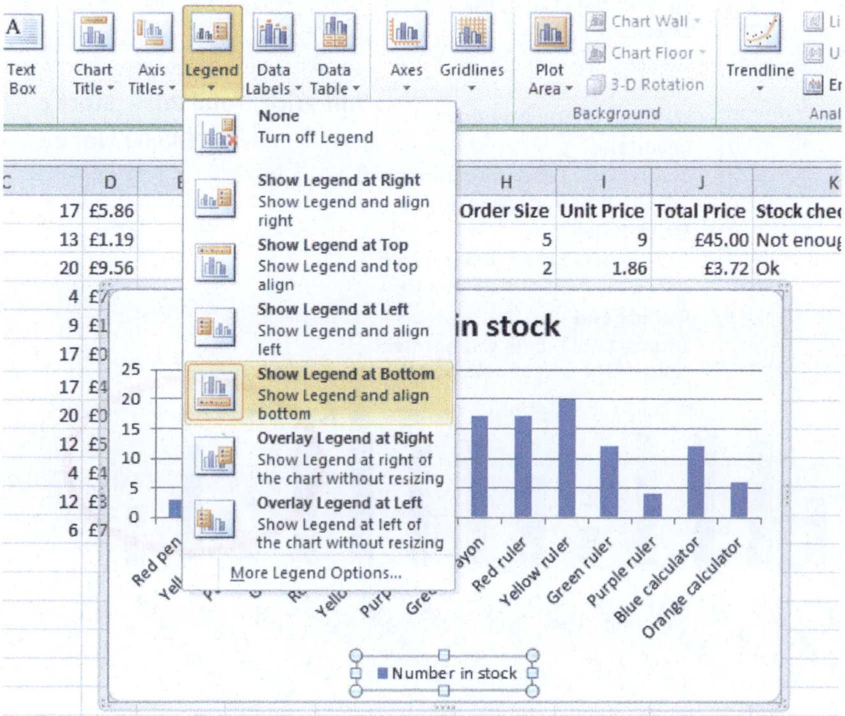

14.8.4 Data labels

These show the actual values of the data points on the graph. You can turn them on or off, as well as where they appear on the chart.

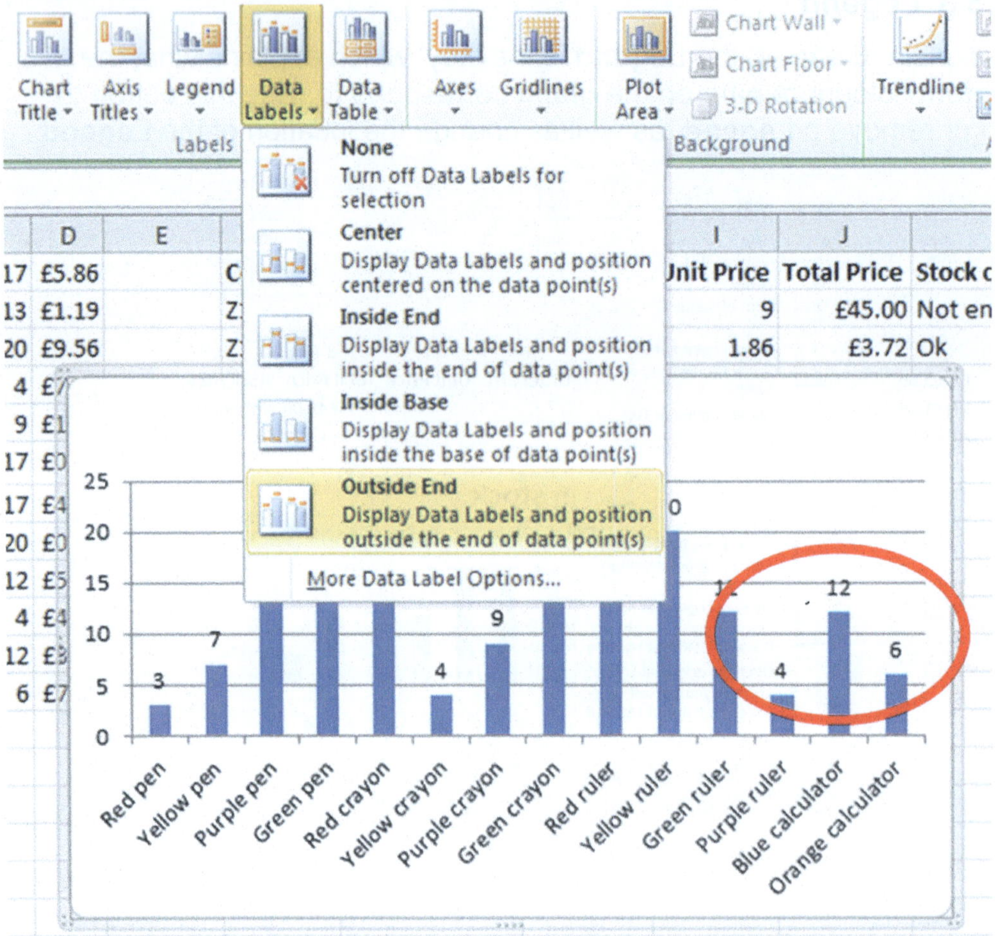

14.8.5 Data table

A data table shows the actual data points being used to make the chart – like data labels but shown beneath the chart. Use this option to add/remove a data table, with or without a legend (key). The example below shows a data table with a legend key.

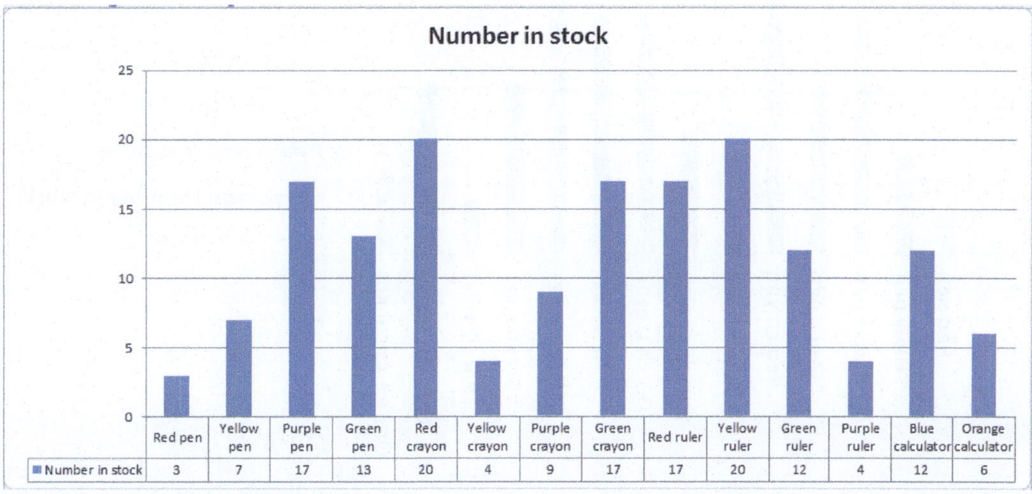

14.8.6 Trend lines

A trend line shows the general pattern of movement in your data set. Use the **Trend Line** button to do this. You will be presented with several options – normally you will choose **Linear Trendline**. The trendline will be added.

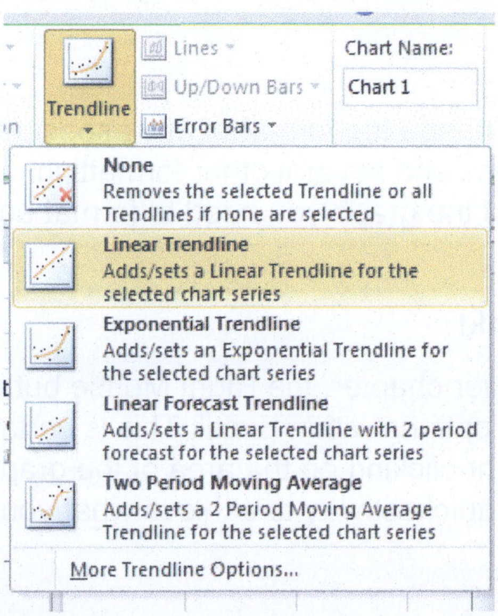

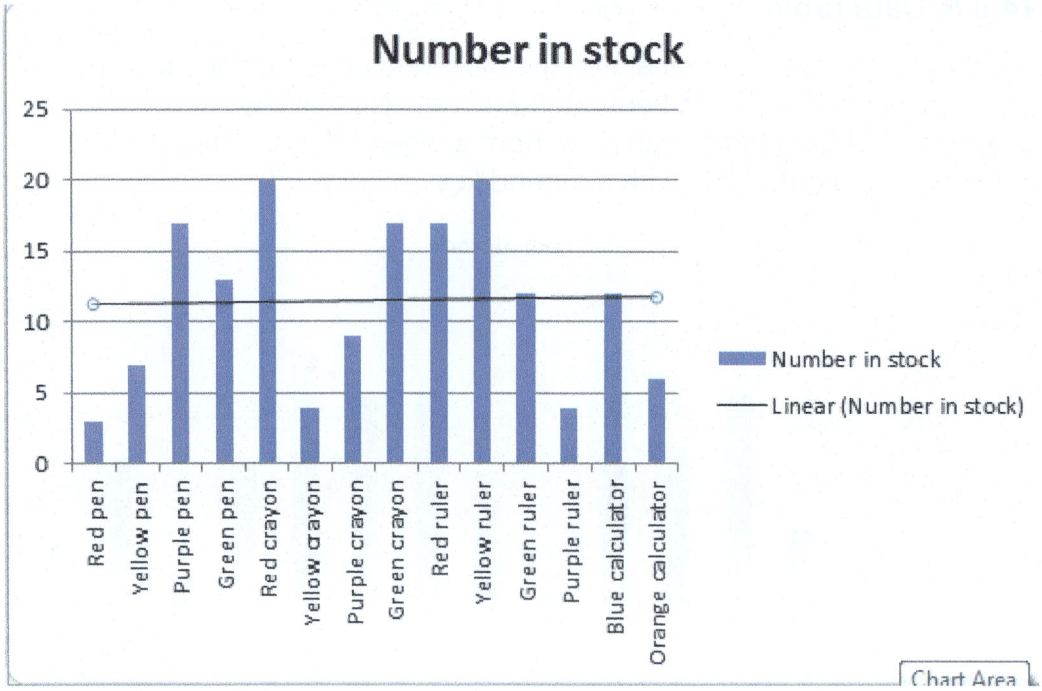

The trendline is shown. There's no real trend in this data set, hence the flat line.

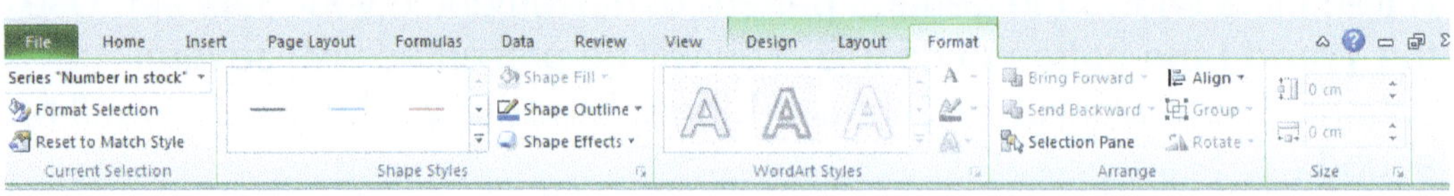

14.9 Format Tab

This tab allows you to change the format of any aspect of your graph – colours, thickness of lines and several other formatting options. Select (left-click on) the area of the graph you need to format and then select the option you need.

14.10 Just right click!

As mentioned in an earlier chapter, the Right Mouse button brings up many context-sensitive options within Excel. This is certainly true when dealing with charts. Right-clicking on the area of the graph you wish to manipulate is often the quickest way to achieve what you need to achieve.

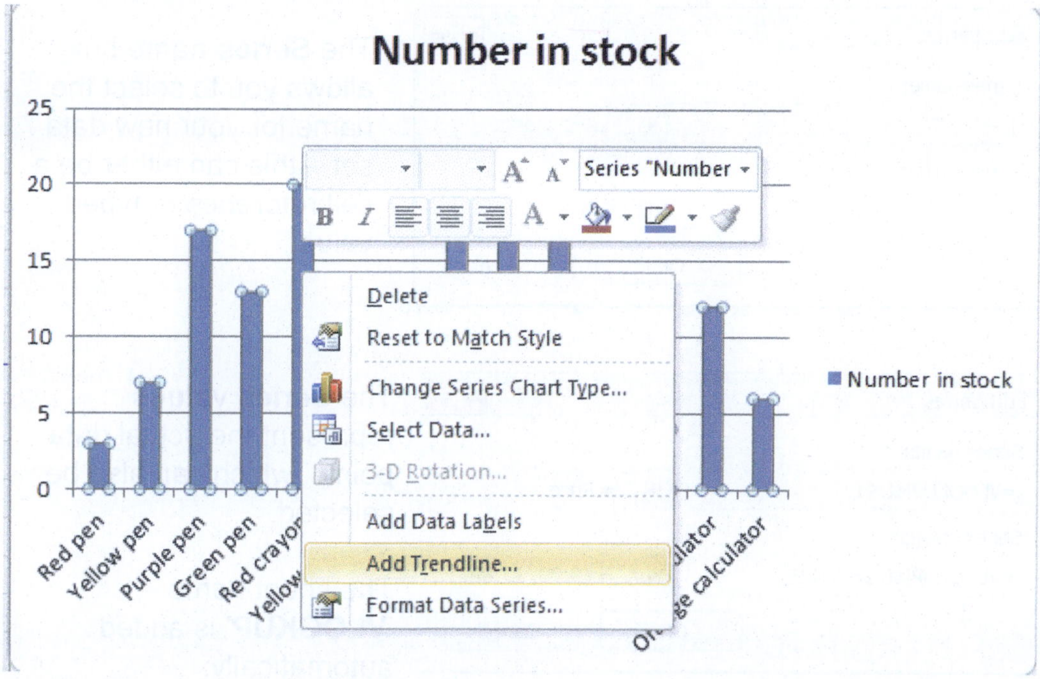

Here, right-clicking on a data point gives options to change the chart type, or add a trend line, as well as a few others.

14.11 Adding another data set

As mentioned in **Section 14.7.2**, more data series can be added if you want to show more information on your graph. This is done within the **Select Data** option. Click **Add** to add more data.

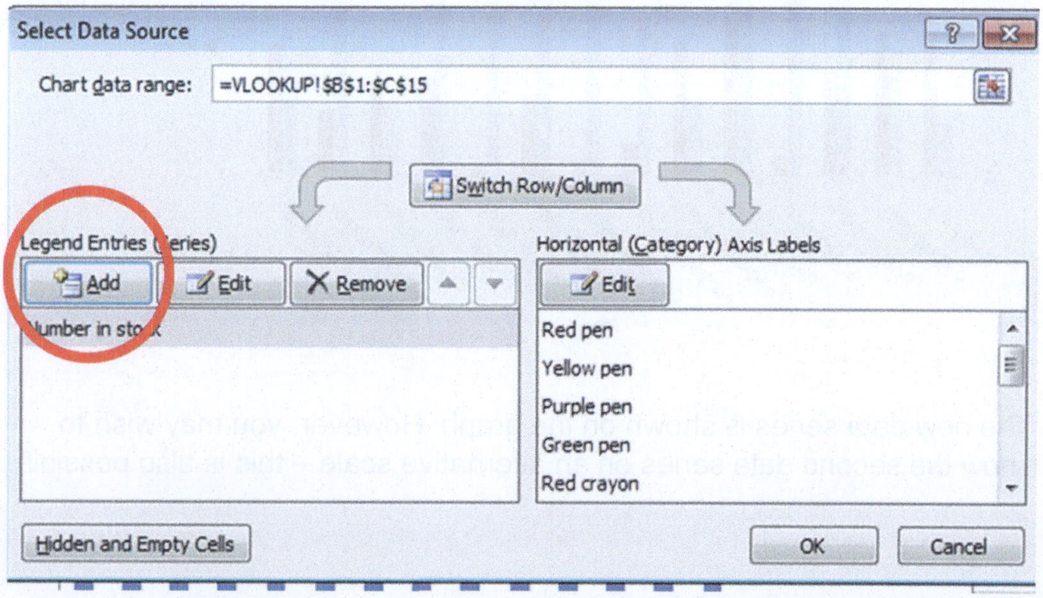

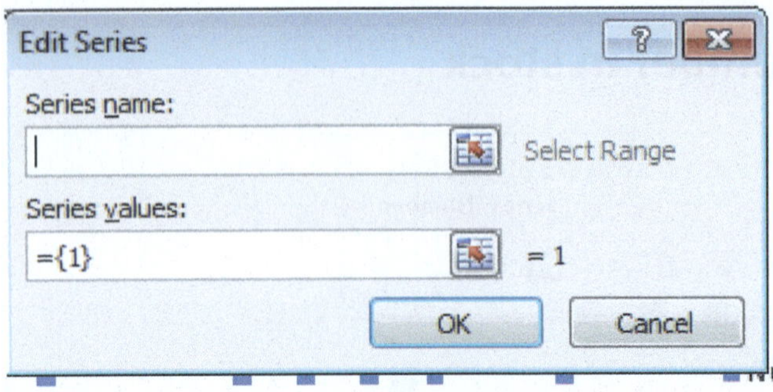

The **Series name** box allows you to select the name for your new data set – this can either be a cell reference or typed value.

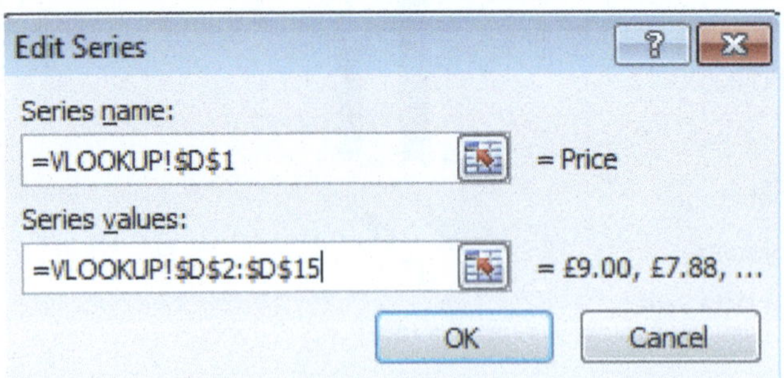

The **Series values** represent the actual data points, which can also be selected.

The sheet name – '**VLOOKUP**' is added automatically.

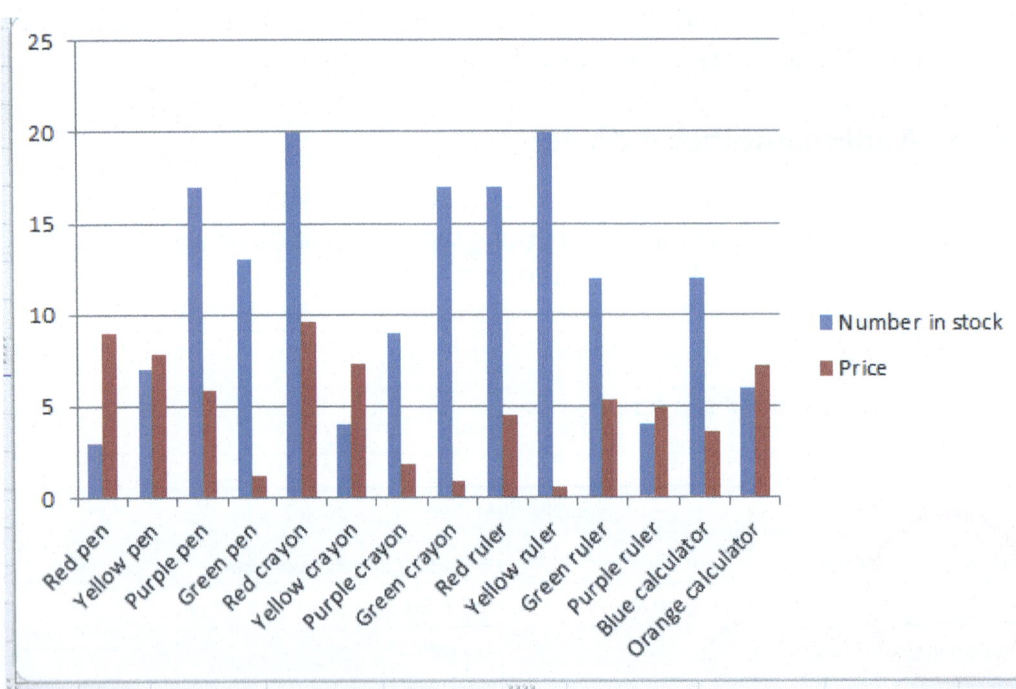

The new data series is shown on the graph. However, you may wish to show the second data series on an alternative scale – this is also possible.

You need to **Format** the data series. This can be done by either:

- **Right-Clicking** on the data series on the graph itself, and selecting **Format Data Series**.

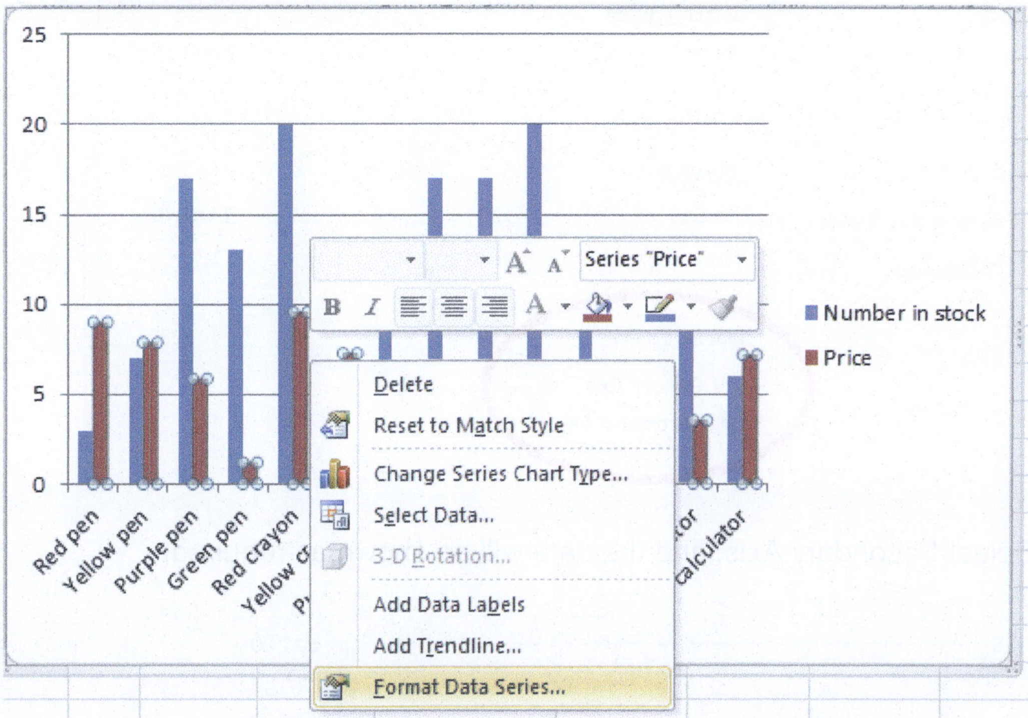

- Or select (left-click on) the data series, and in the **Layout** tab of Chart Tools, select **Format Selection**.

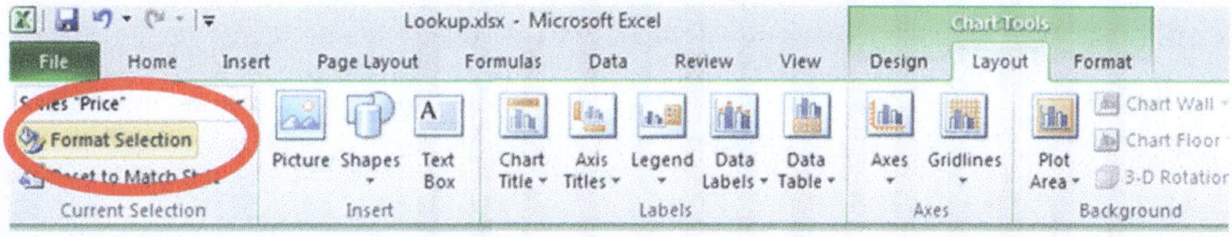

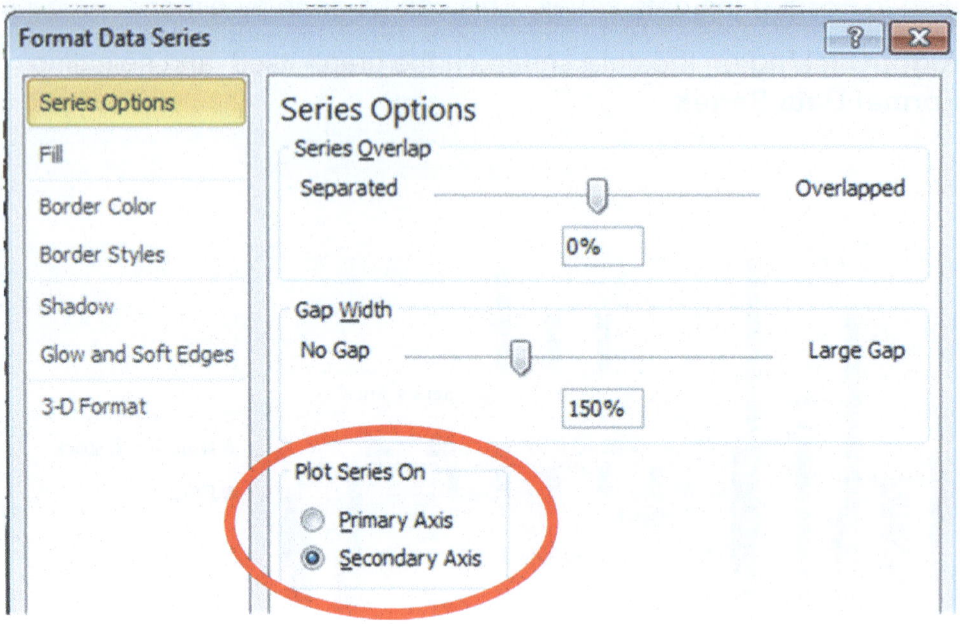

Select Secondary Axis, and the data will be shown as required.

However, this may not be exactly what you want – remember that the chart function is very flexible. You could, for example, select the data set again and change the chart type to 'Line'.

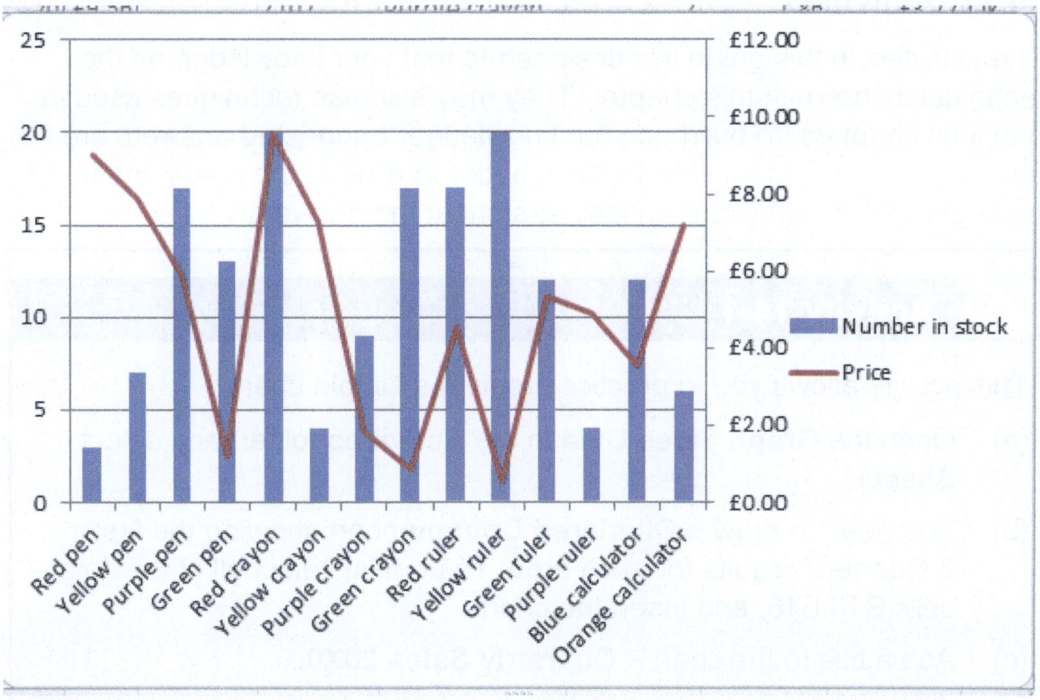

Remember, if you change the chart type and it doesn't appear as you would like, use the **undo** button.

14.12 Activities

The activities in this guide are designed to test your knowledge on the techniques shown in this chapter. They may also use techniques used in previous chapters, to build up your knowledge. Suggested answers are available on MyKaplan, although it is better to refer to the notes and try to understand the methods than look straight at the answers.

Activity 14-1

This activity allows you to practice creating a simple chart.

(a) Open the **Graph Sales Data** in the **Activities** folder, and select **Sheet1**.

(b) You need to draw a **Clustered Column** chart showing the first 3 Quarters' results for each area. To do this, select all of the data – cells B13:E16, and insert the chart.

(c) Add a title to the chart – **Quarterly Sales 20X0**.

Add a title to the y-axis – **£000**.

Delete the Legend.

Add a data table to the graph – with a legend.

(d) Move the chart to the right of the data so everything is visible.

(e) Save the file as **Activity 14-1** in the **Solutions** folder.

Activity 14-2

This activity allows you to edit an existing chart. It follows directly on from **Activity 14-1**.

(a) If it is not already open, open **Activity 14-1** from the **Solutions** folder.

(b) The aim of this exercise is to add the Quarter 4 Forecast information to the chart. To do this, **Select** the chart, and use **Select Data** from the **Design** tab. Notice the Chart data range:

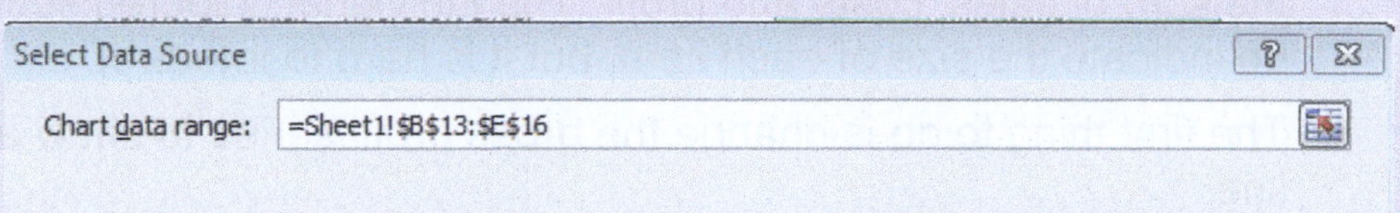

(c) We need to extend the data range to include the Quarter 4 forecast – F13:F16.

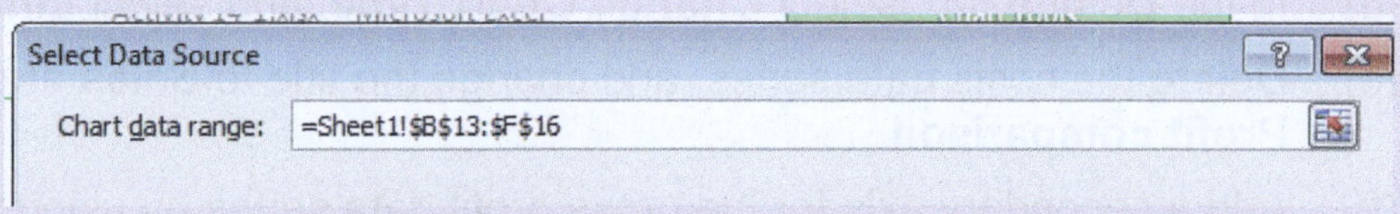

(d) Change the **Forecast Increase** figure in cell A2 to 100%. The Quarter 4 forecast is based on this – the figures, and the chart, will update. Change it back to 10%.

(e) **Move** the chart to a chart sheet.

(f) Save the workbook as **Activity 14-2** in the **Solutions** folder.

Activity 14-3

This activity allows you to change the chart type being used, add a trendline, and deal with formatting of chart items.

(a) Open the **Graph Sales Data** workbook from the **Activities** folder, and select **Sheet2**.

(b) This is a stacked column chart, showing sales, costs and gross profit. It is not a meaningful representation of the data. For example, the first bar, for January, shows a total of £20,000. This is the sum of sales, costs and profit. The individual coloured sections do indicate the size of each item, but it is hard to interpret.

The first thing to do is change the gross profit series to show as a line.

(c) **Select** the gross profit data series (click on any part of the chart coloured in cream).

(d) In the **Design** tab, select **Change Chart Type**, and select **Line.**

(e) **Delete** the costs data series, and change the title to **Sales and Profit comparison**.

(f) Add a secondary axis for the gross profit data series by using the **Format Data Series** menu.

(g) Add a **linear trendline** to the gross profit data series.

(h) **Select** the trendline. Change the format so that it is a thick line (3pt), coloured bright green.

(i) Save the file as **Activity 14-3** in the **Solutions** folder.

Data validation

15.1 Introduction

This chapter will explain how to restrict data within cells and give a brief introduction to named ranges.

KNOWLEDGE

1.1 Identify what numerical and other information is needed in the spreadsheet and how it should be structured.

Data validation allows a user to restrict what values can be entered into a cell. This can prevent incorrect data entry, or allow another user to select from a Dropdown list, making data entry easier.

15.2 Data validation

To add data validation, select the cell(s) required, then in the **Data** tab, select **Data Validation**.

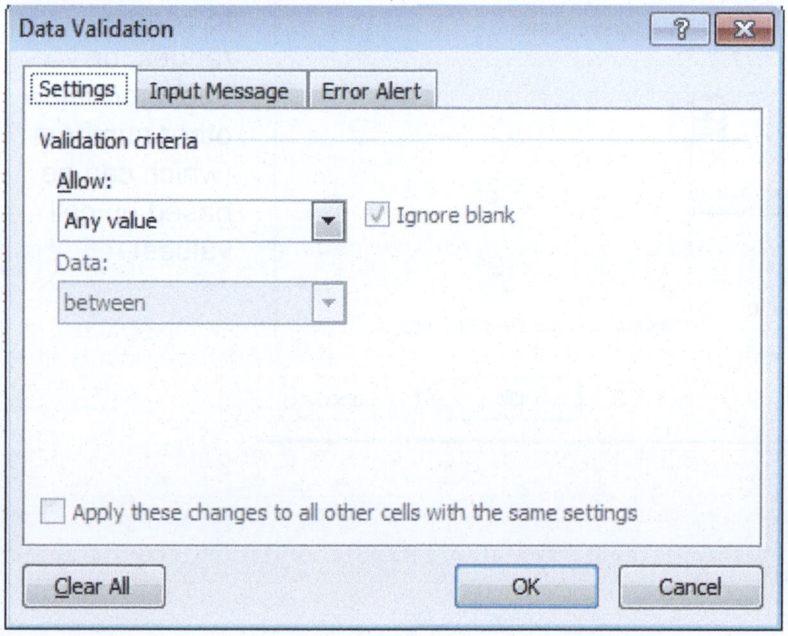

The Data Validation menu has three tabs – Settings, Input Message and Error Alert

15.2.1 Settings

This is where you define exactly how you would like to restrict your cell entry. The default is as shown above – **Allow any value**. Selecting this dropdown box shows the options available.

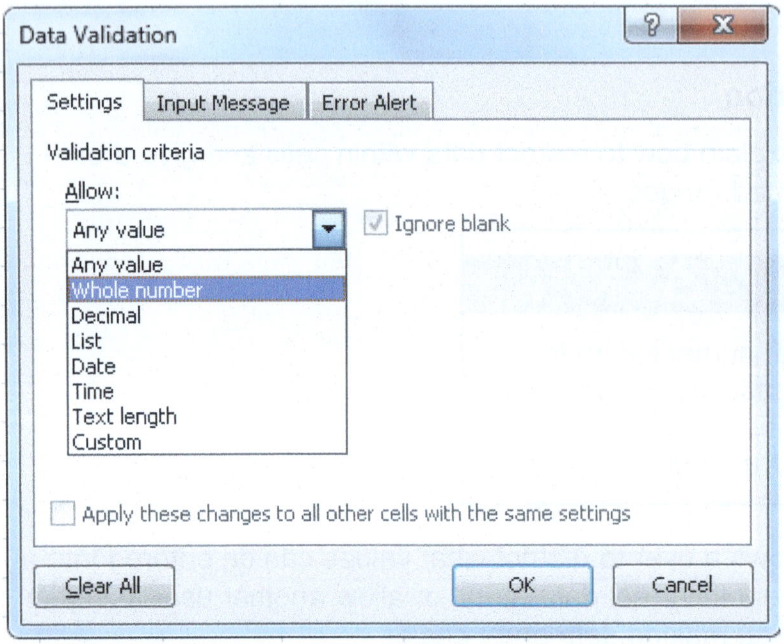

When an option is selected, more options become available. For example, whole number only allows whole numbers, but you can further restrict the range.

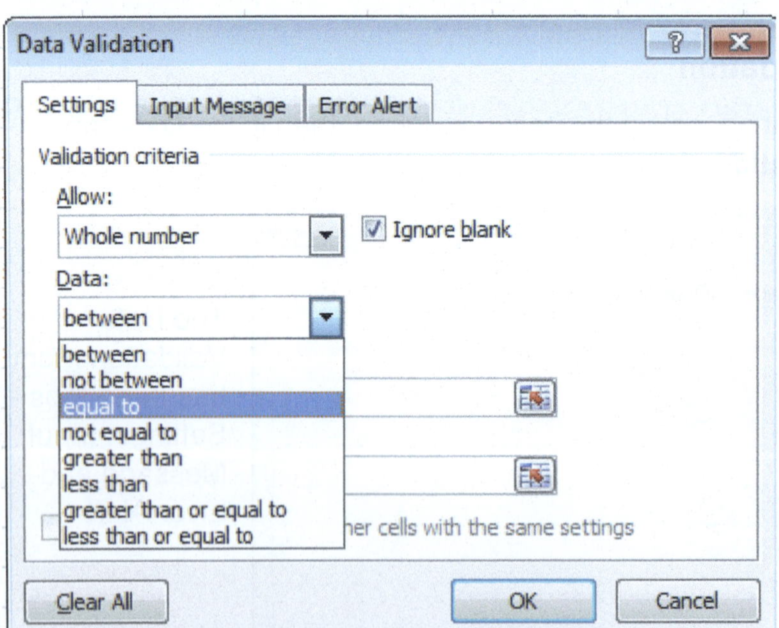

As on many other options, you can restrict to certain ranges, or above or below other numbers (which can be based on cell values).

You can also restrict to a list of options. This is very useful when a cell should only contain certain entries.

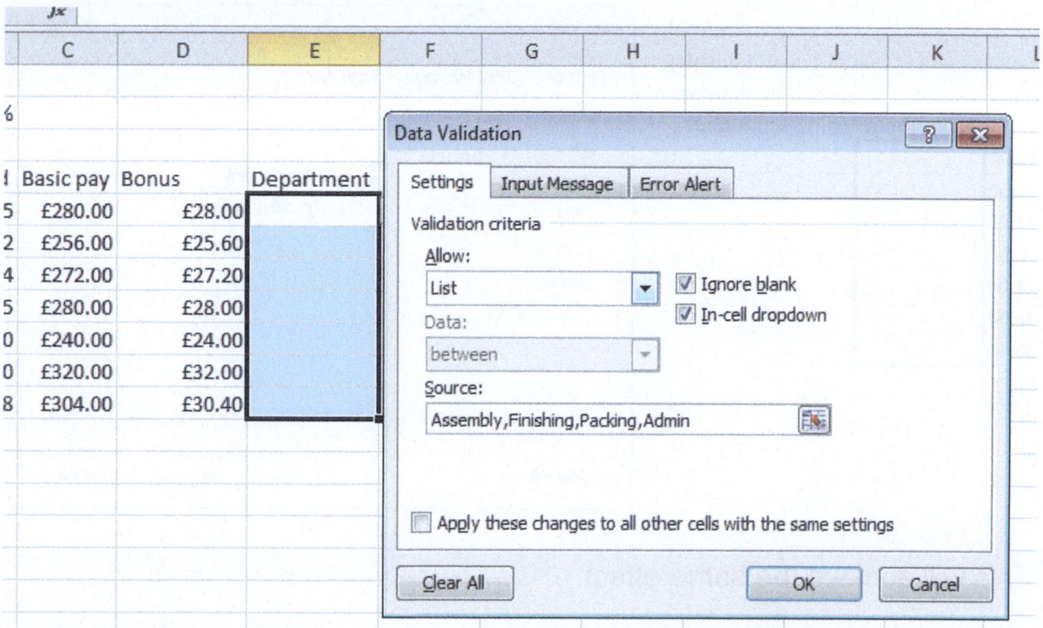

In the Data Validation menu, select Allow **List**, and type the possible options in the box, separated by a comma. Notice the **In-cell dropdown** option is checked. Click **OK**.

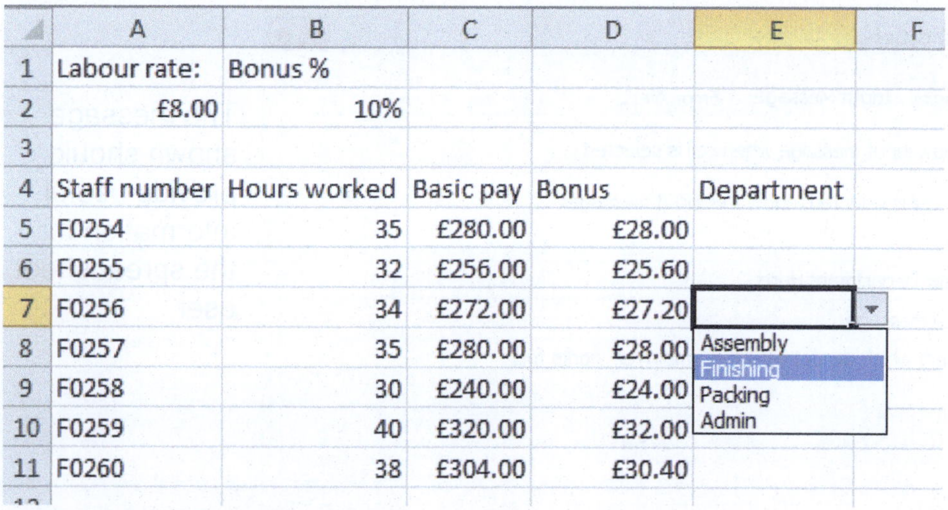

Now, when the cell is clicked on, the four options are shown. You can still type in the cell, as well as using the dropdown. If you type something that is not in the list an error message will show.

Rather than typing the values in, you can also refer to a range of cells.

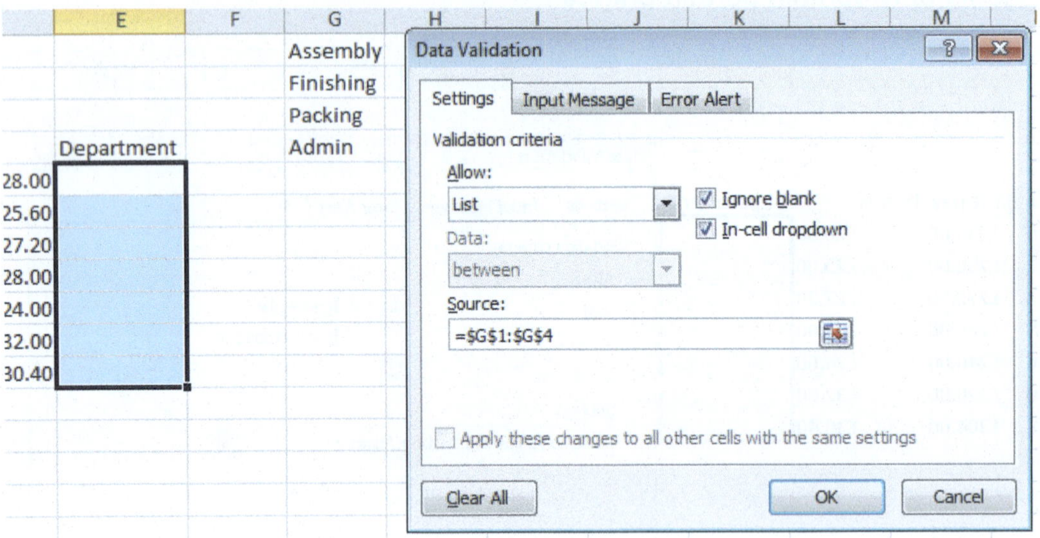

This will achieve the same effect.

15.2.2 Input message

This option is again useful for helping other users of the spreadsheet to enter the correct data. If activated, when the cell is selected a message will be displayed giving help on what can be entered.

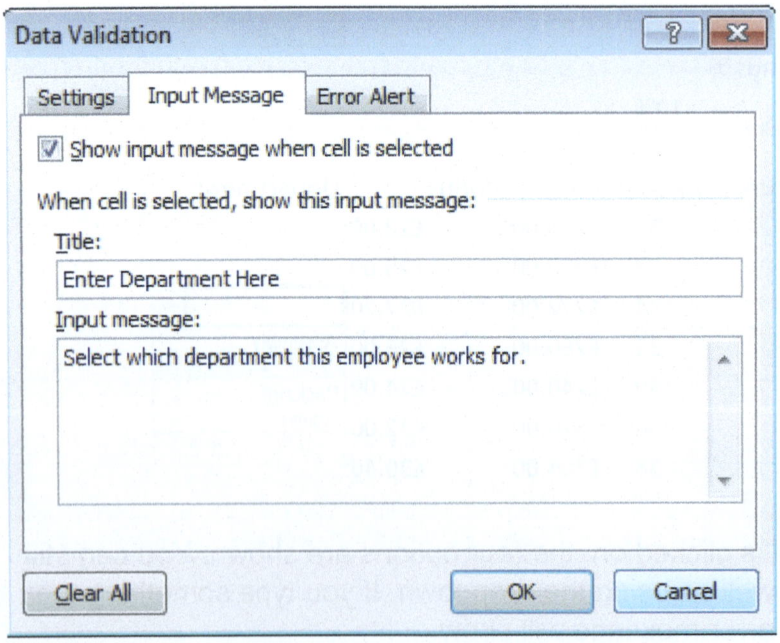

The message shown should provide useful information for the spreadsheet user.

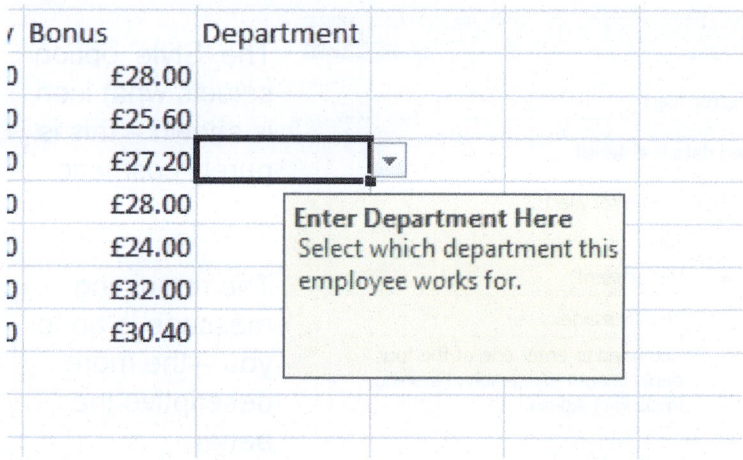

When the cell is selected, the message is shown.

15.2.3 Error alert

This tab allows you to select the error message that is shown if incorrect data is entered. By default, if the data validation restrictions are not met, the following error is shown:

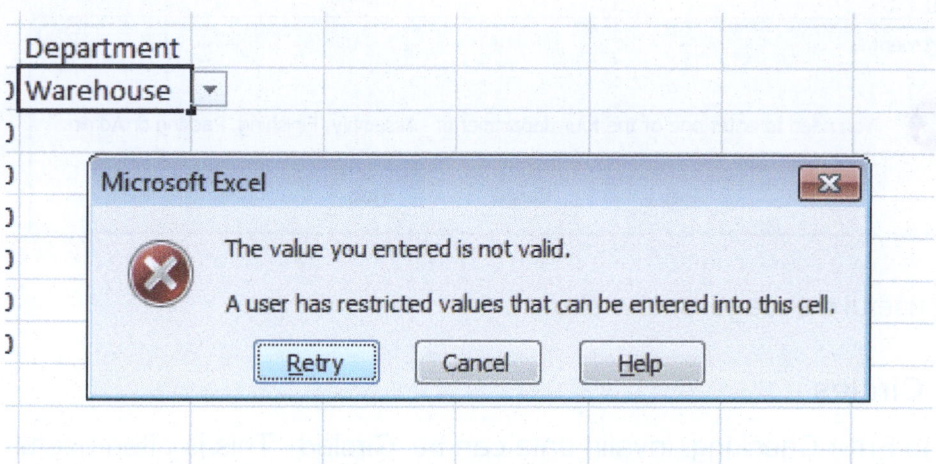

This is not particularly helpful to a user, as they may not know what they have done wrong. Use the Error Alert tab to change this message.

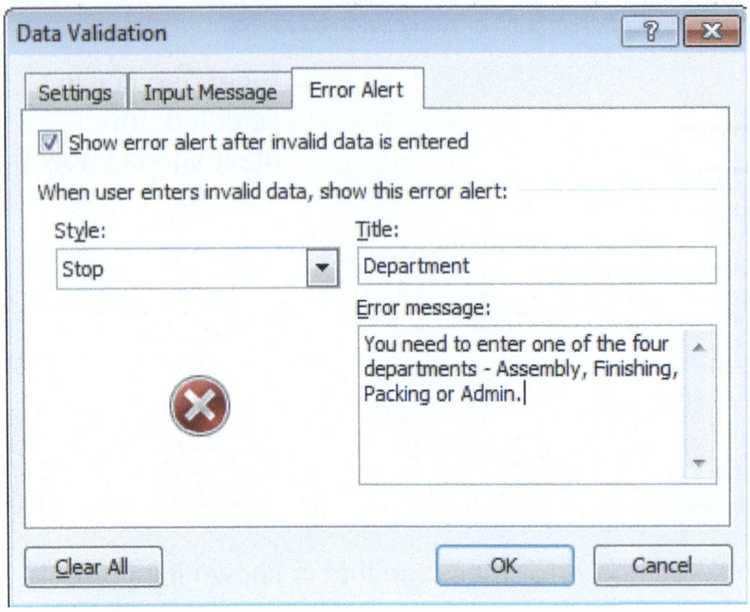

The 'Style' option selects what icon is shown – this is purely cosmetic

The remaining message is up to you – the more descriptive the better.

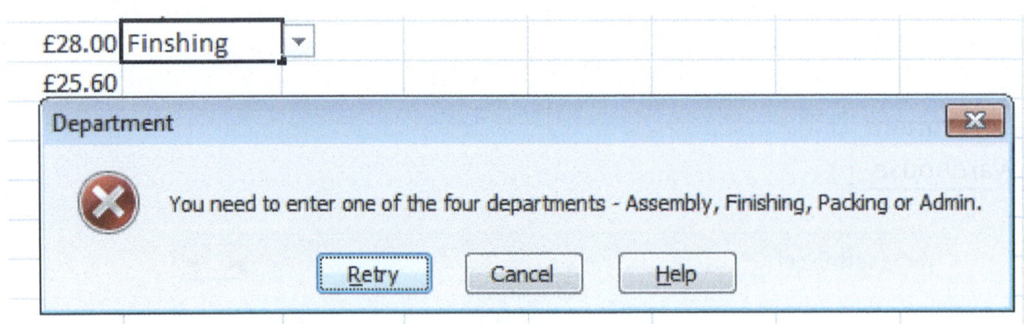

A more useful message is now shown.

15.3 Circles

Similar to Error Checking, invalid data can be 'Circled'. This is often useful if the data validation is added after the data has been entered.

Labour rate:	Bonus %			
£8.00	10%			
Staff number	Hours worked	Basic pay	Bonus	Department
F0254	35	£280.00	£28.00	Finishing
F0255	32	£256.00	£25.60	Finishing
F0256	34	£272.00	£27.20	Maintenance
F0257	35	£280.00	£28.00	Assembly
F0258	30	£240.00	£24.00	Admin
F0259	40	£320.00	£32.00	Maintenance
F0260	38	£304.00	£30.40	Packing

This is the data set – if we add the data validation as before, no error is shown.

However, if we then select **Circle Invalid Data** from the **Data Validation** menu:

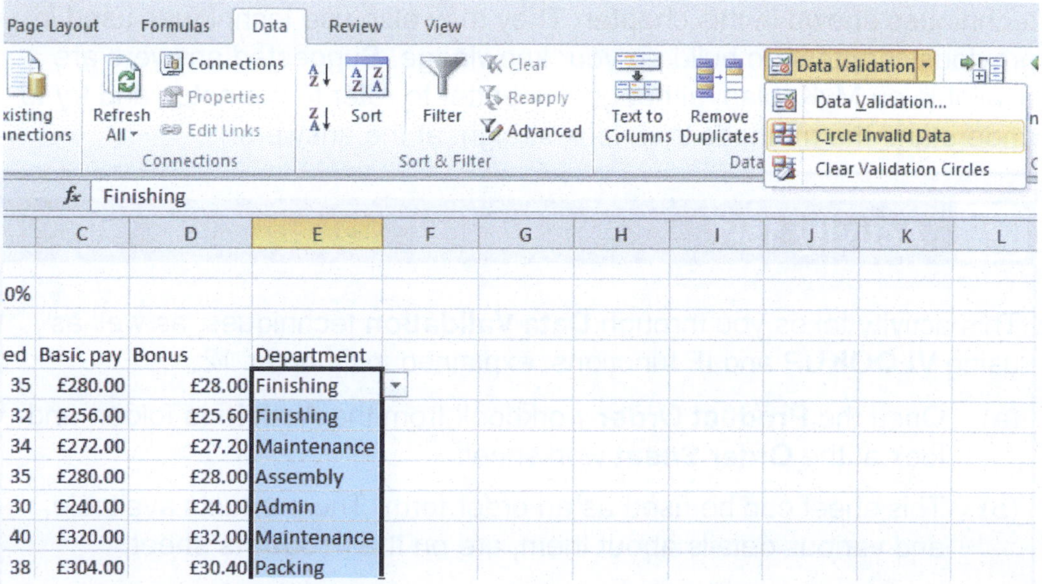

The invalid data will be circled.

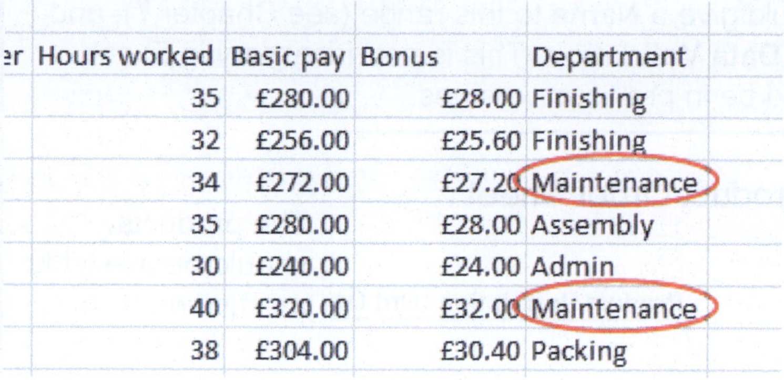

This may indicate that we need to change the validation rules, or change the data.

15.4 Activity

The activities in this guide are designed to test your knowledge on the techniques shown in this chapter. They may also use techniques used in previous chapters, to build up your knowledge. Suggested answers are available on MyKaplan, although it is better to refer to the notes and try to understand the methods than look straight at the answers.

Activity 15-1

This activity takes you through **Data Validation** techniques, as well as using **VLOOKUP** and **IF** functions, explained in Chapter 12.

(a) Open the **Product Order** workbook from the **Activities** folder, and look at the **Order Sheet** worksheet.

(b) This sheet can be used as an order form. The products available, and various details about them, are on the **Products** sheet.

(c) In cell A12, use **Data Validation** to restrict entry to the available product codes found on the Products Sheet.

Note – you could give a **Name** to this range (see Chapter 7), and use that in the **Data Validation**. This is not necessary in Excel 2010, but would be in previous versions.

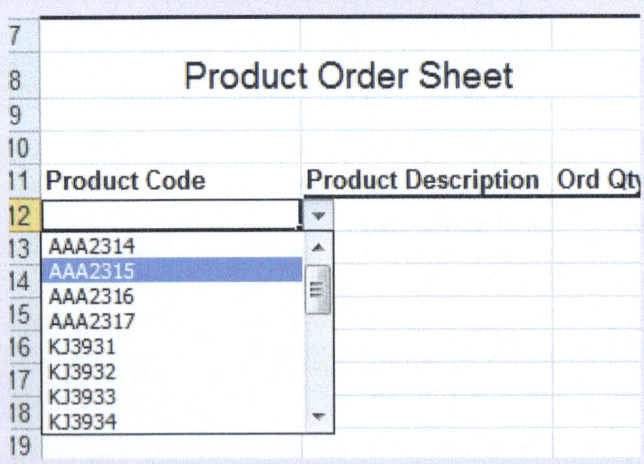

The products should be available as shown.

(d) Copy the Validation from cell A12 into cells A13:A40. This can be performed using **Paste Special**, and selecting **Validation**.

Select AAA2315 in Cell A12.

(e) In cell B12, use a **VLOOKUP** formula to return the description. Add an **IF** function to return a blank cell if the value in column A is also blank.

(f) Copy the formula down into cells B13:B40.

(g) In Cell C12, use data validation to restrict the order quantities to whole numbers greater than or equal to the minimum order quantity in cell B1 (consider cell referencing. Add an error alert explaining that the value in the cell must be greater than or equal to the minimum order quantity.

(h) Copy the validation into cells C13:C40.

(i) Enter 20 in cell C12. An error should appear. Click Cancel. Enter 25 in C12. The order value should update.

(j) Select product KJ3932 in A13, QX9489 in A14 and WM4361 in A15. Enter order quantities of 35, 28 and 40 respectively.

(k) Change the value in cell B1 to 30.

(l) In the **Data** tab, select **Data Validation,** and **Circle Invalid Data.**

(m) The values below 30 should be circled.

Product Order Sheet — Date

Product Code	Product Description	Ord Qty	List Price	Order Value
AAA2315	Widget White	25	£6.00	£150.00
KJ3932	Wotsit White	35	£3.00	£105.00
QX9489	Thingy Blue	28	£10.00	£280.00
WM4361	Youknow Orange	40	£6.00	£240.00

Save the file as **Activity 15-1** in the **Solutions** folder. Note: when the spreadsheet is saved the validation circles will be cleared.

Spreadsheet templates

16

16.1 Introduction

This chapter will help you to understand what a template does, where to store it, and how to retrieve it.

KNOWLEDGE
1.4 Store and retrieve spreadsheet files effectively, in line with company guidelines and conventions where applicable.

Templates are useful tools for creating and storing workbooks that are used constantly. The most used templates are the Excel workbooks that contain three sheets that we use all the time. There are also a number of templates readily available in Excel.

When you create a template you should save it to a special template folder. Excel will add an .xlt or.xltx extension to the workbook.

The next time you want to open the template, you open it from the template folder and Excel will create the new workbook with the same name as the template – but it will add a number to it.

16.2 Activity

This activity takes you through the steps required to create a template.

Activity 16-1

(a) Open the **Product Order** workbook in the **Activities** folder.

This spreadsheet could be used regularly as an order form.

(b) Choose **Save As** from the **File** tab.

(c) Select the **Excel Template** option in the **Save as type** dropdown menu.

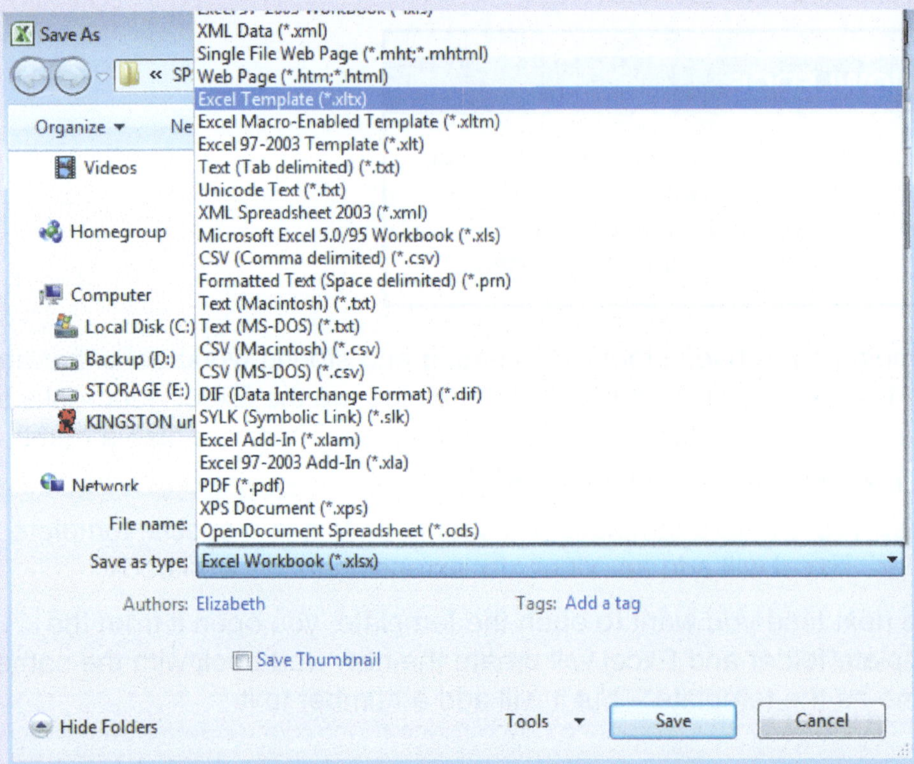

(d) 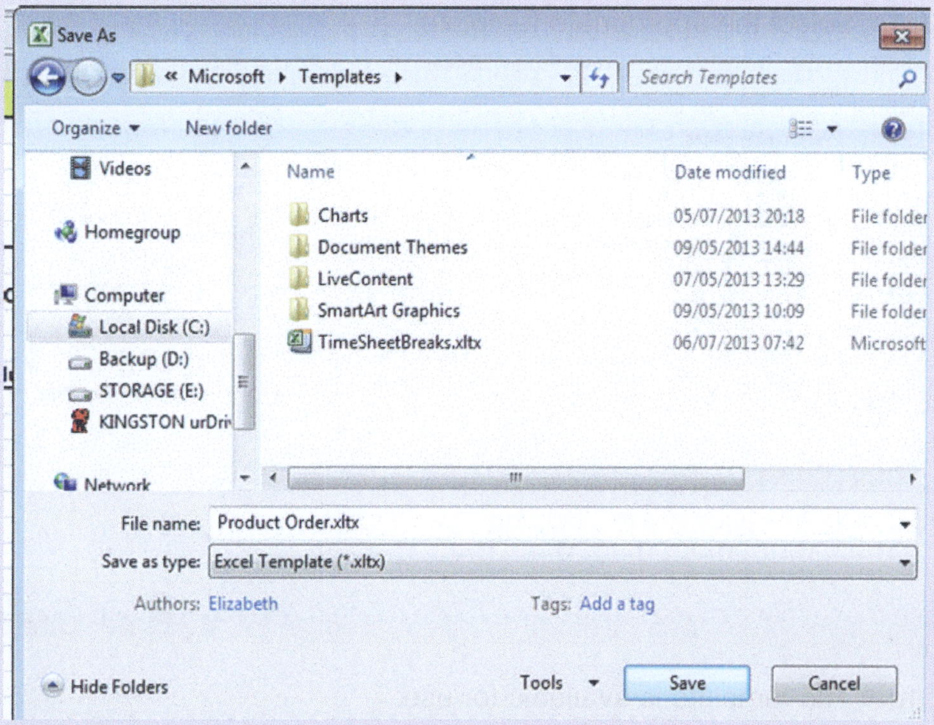

The default template folder will automatically be selected. Click **Save**.

(e) Close the file

(f) To use the template, go to the **File** tab, and select **New,** and **My Templates**.

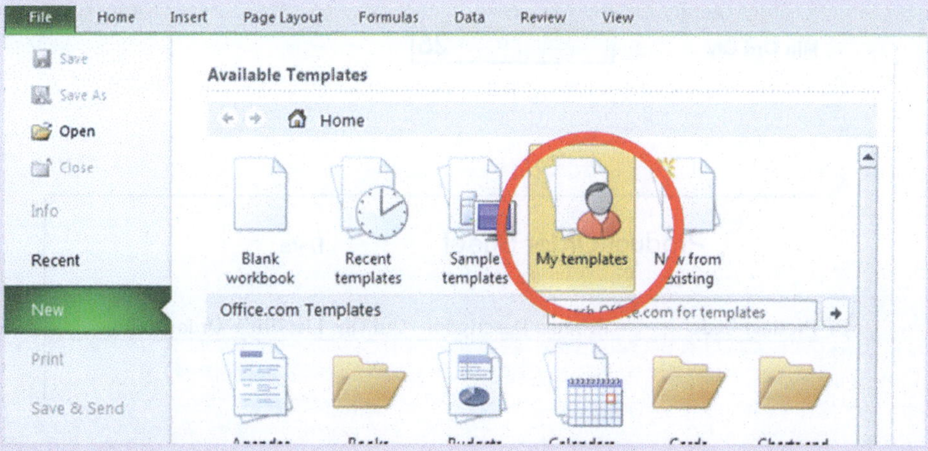

(g) Select the appropriate template.

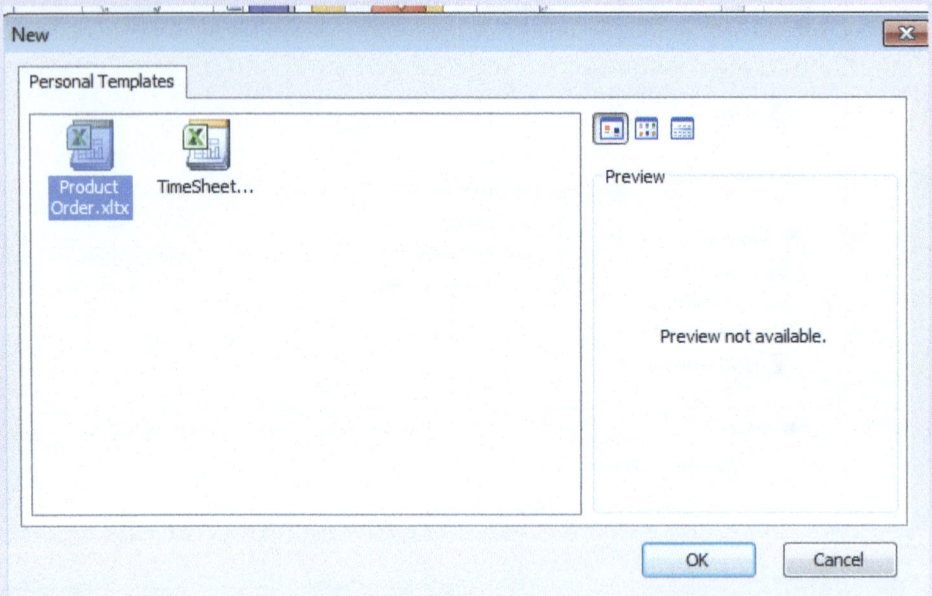

(h) The template is available for use:

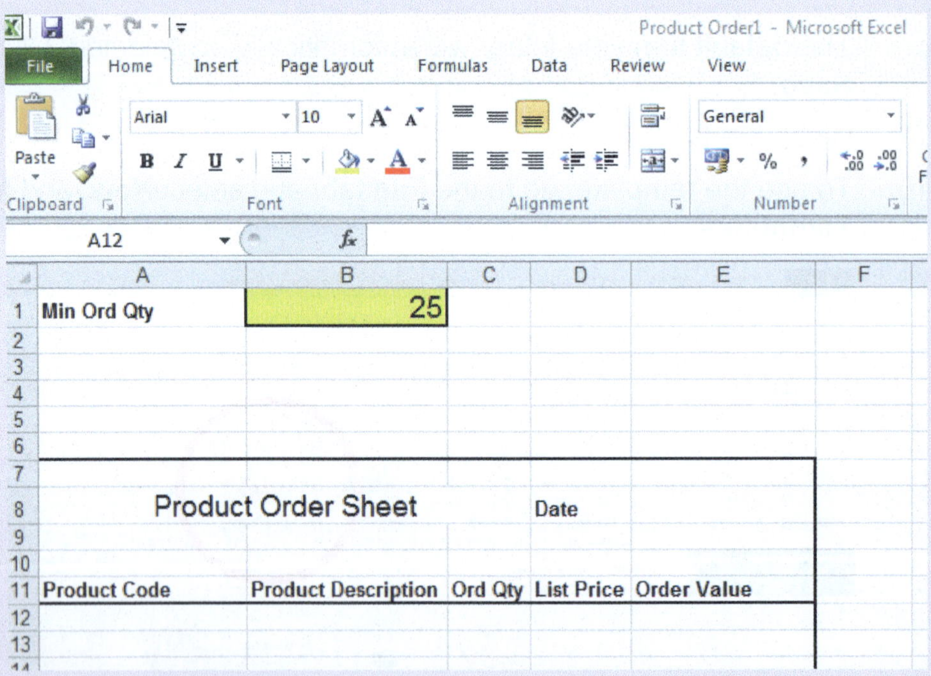

Spreadsheet protection

17

17.1 Introduction

This chapter will show you how to protect your spreadsheets so that no other user can change the content of the spreadsheet.

KNOWLEDGE

1.4 Store and retrieve spreadsheet files effectively, in line with company guidelines and conventions where applicable.

In this session you will learn how to:

- How to hide formulas.
- How to lock cells.
- How to protect a worksheet.
- How to protect a workbook.

17.2 Worksheet protection

To prevent accidental/unauthorised changes to a worksheet, it must be protected. This is performed in the **Review** tab.

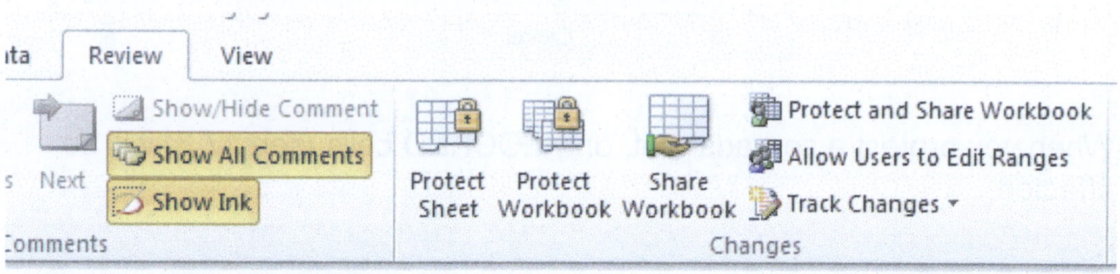

Click **Protect Sheet** to protect the sheet. You are then presented with a series of options giving you the power to restrict various activities.

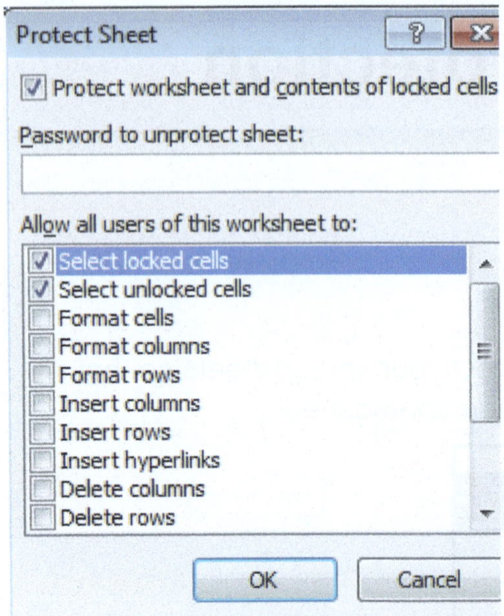

Check/uncheck the boxes as required, depending on what access you wish to give/remove.

You can also set a password if required. If you enter a password you will be required to confirm it. This password will then be required to unprotect the sheet.

Note the warning. If you forget the password to unprotect a worksheet, then it cannot be recovered.

If the password is forgotten then copy and paste the locked spreadsheet into a new, unlocked sheet.

When you protect a spreadsheet, only LOCKED cells (see 17.3) will be affected.

If a sheet is protected, then use the **Unprotect Sheet** option to remove protection.

17.3 Cell protection

To prevent unauthorised/accidental changes to a cell, it must first be protected. This can be done in the **Format cells** menu – all cells are protected by default.

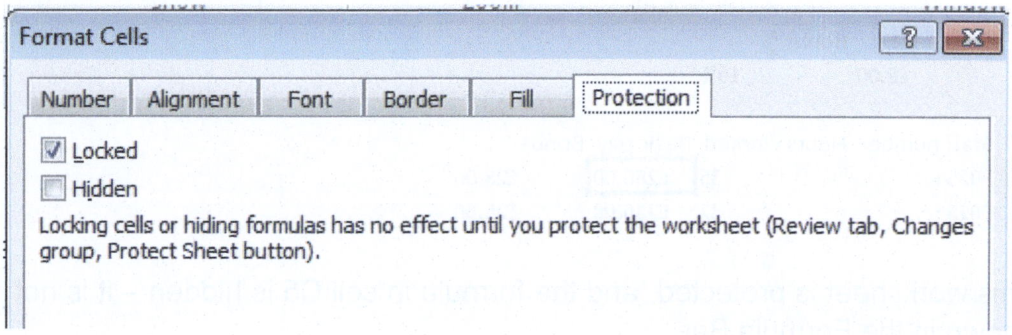

As explained in the menu – this will have no effect until the worksheet is protected – however, if a worksheet is protected, you cannot lock/unlock cells, so unprotect it first. If you wish to unlock a cell to allow data entry, then uncheck this tick box.

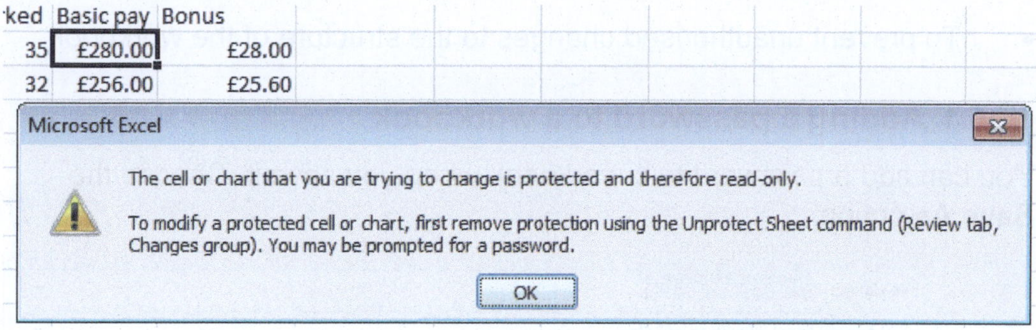

If you try to edit a locked cell, the above warning will be shown.

17.4 Hide formulas

Again, this is done in the **Format Cells** menu, under **Protection**. Check or uncheck the tickbox as required, and the formulas will be hidden.

To hide formulas you will need to go to the **Format Cells** dialogue box, open the protection tab and click **hidden**. It must be stressed that the formulas will only become hidden when the worksheet is protected.

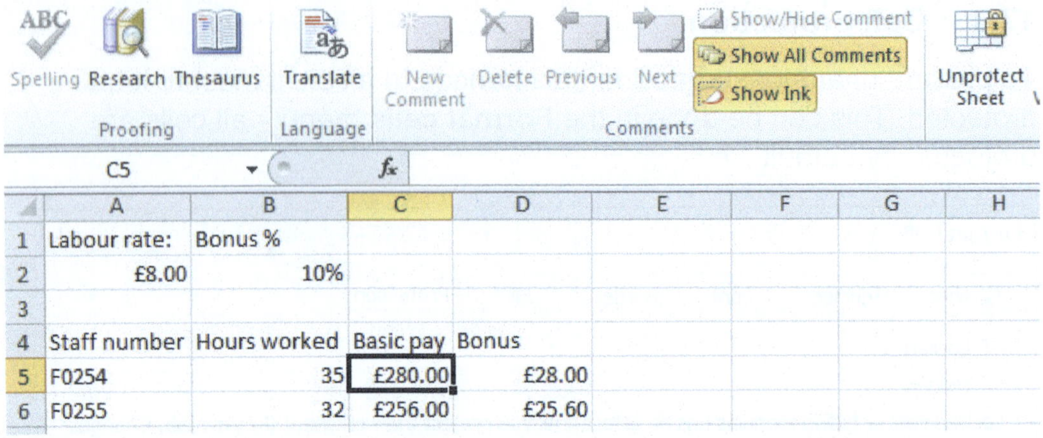

This worksheet is protected, and the formula in cell C5 is hidden – it is not shown in the Formula Bar.

17.5 Workbook protection

There are two main options regarding workbook protection:

- To prevent unauthorised access/changes to the workbook itself.
- To prevent unauthorised changes to the structure of the workbook.

17.5.1 Adding a password to a workbook

You can add a password to a workbook when you save it. Choose the **Save As** option.

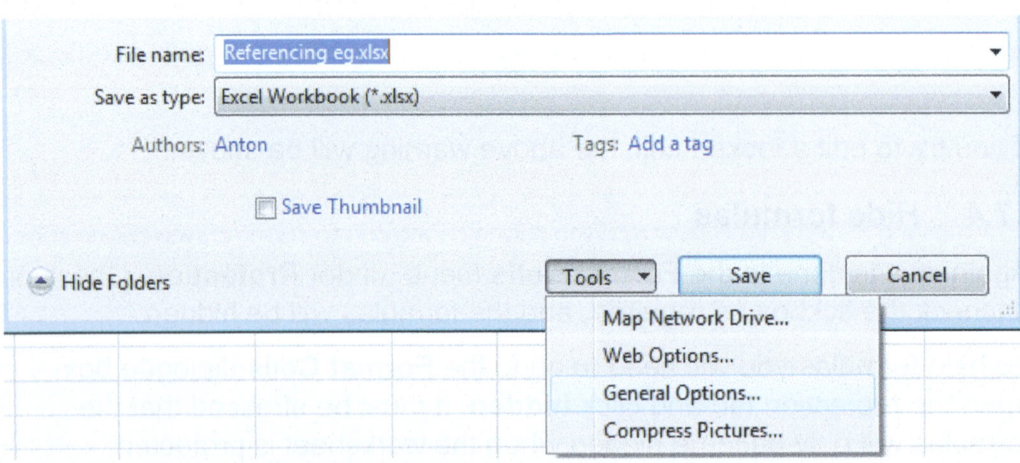

At the bottom of the window is the **Tools** option. Select **General Options.**

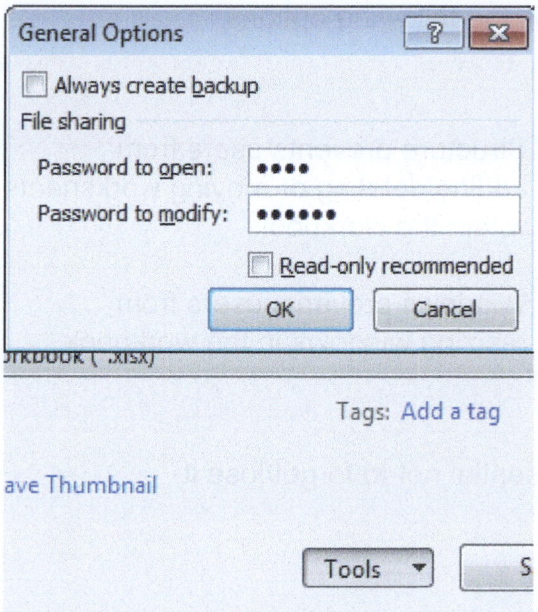

There are two main options – Password to open means a password is required to access the document.

Password to modify allows users to view the document, but requires a password to make any changes.

Any passwords used will require verification and must not be forgotten or lost.

17.5.2 Protecting the workbook structure

This is performed within the **Review** tab, in the **Changes menu.**

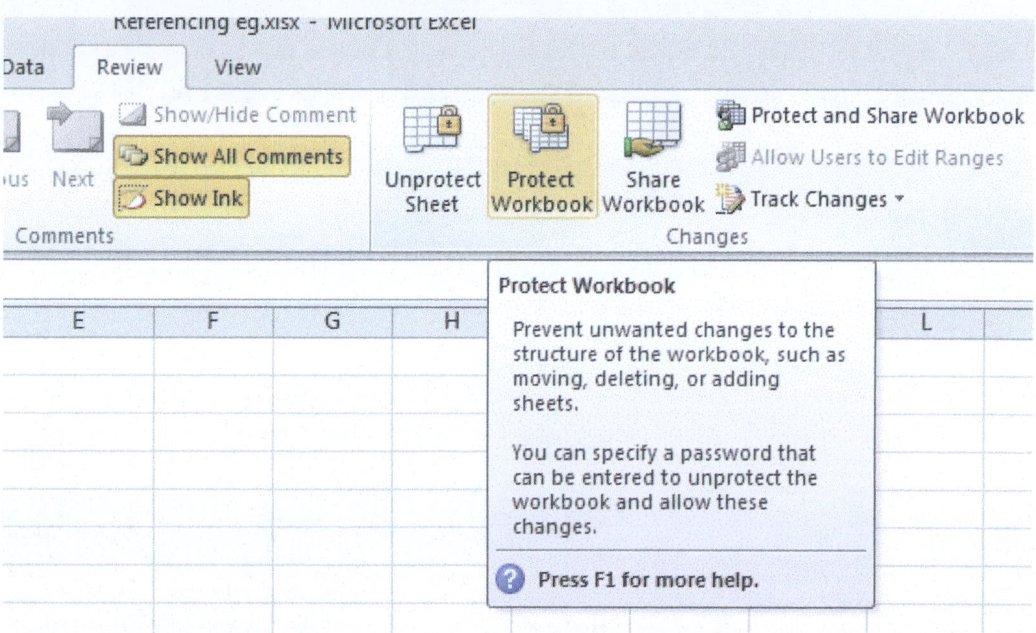

As explained in the picture, a user cannot change the order of worksheets, or add or delete sheets.

Clicking on the Protect buttons brings the following options:

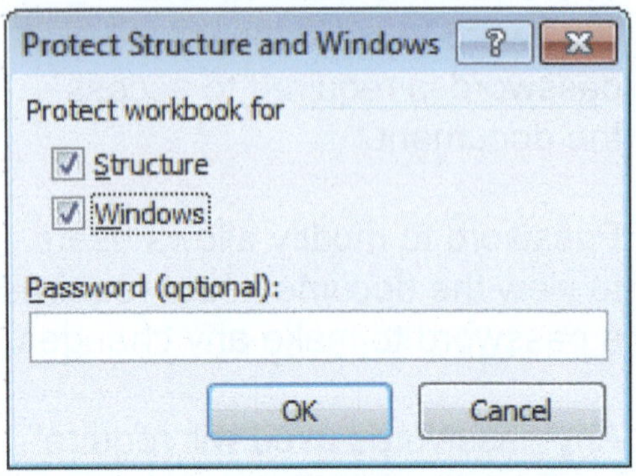

Structure prevents users from adding/deleting or moving worksheets within the workbook.

Windows prevents users from resizing windows in the workbook.

Again, if a password is used, it is essential not to forget/lose it.

18 Sharing workbooks

18.1 Introduction

This chapter will show you the function of 'read only' spreadsheets and how to share workbooks.

KNOWLEDGE

1.4 Store and retrieve spreadsheet files effectively, in line with company guidelines and conventions where applicable.

18.2 Sharing a workbook

Normally when a user tries to open a workbook that is in use already they are presented with the dialogue box below. Here they have three options.

1 They could open the file **Read-Only**. They can have access to the file, but they can only save changes they make if they use **Save-as** and give the file a new name.

2 They could open the file with the **Notify** button. Here they can view the file and when presented with another dialogue box informing them that the file is available for **read-write** they can make their changes.

3 They can click **Cancel** to close the dialogue box without opening the file.

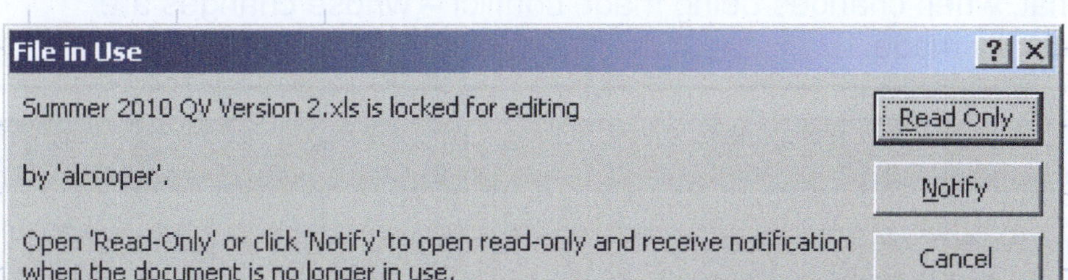

Excel cannot be considered a multi-user application. It does, however, have a feature called **Share Workbook** that does allow more than one user on a **network** to update a spreadsheet at the same time.

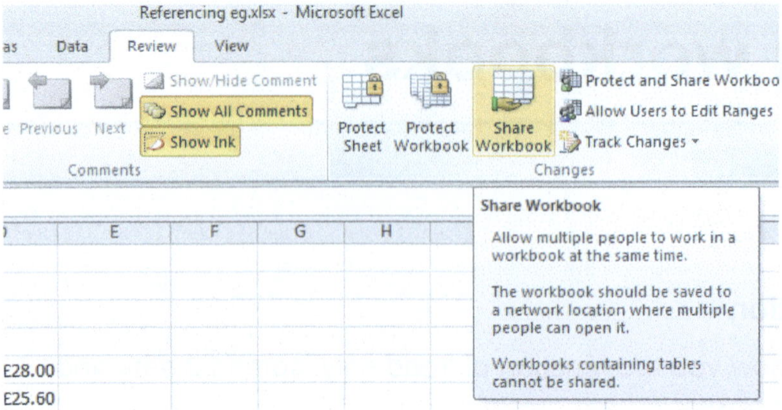

If the writer follows the path above they will be presented with the following dialogue box. If they tick the **Allow Changes** box the workbook will allow multiple users. When in this mode Excel keeps a track of the changes that have been made. Also the 2nd tab becomes available.

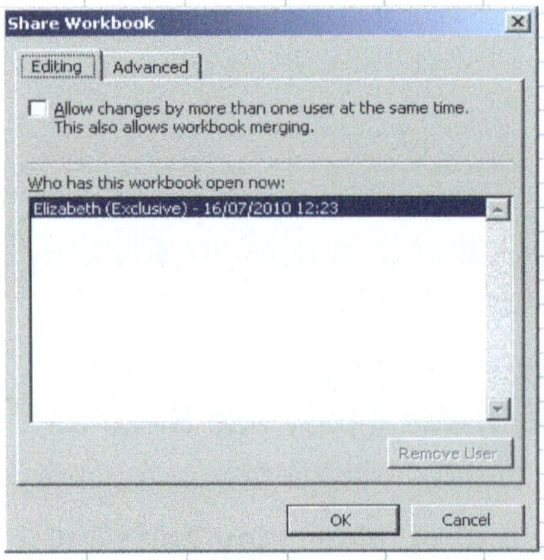

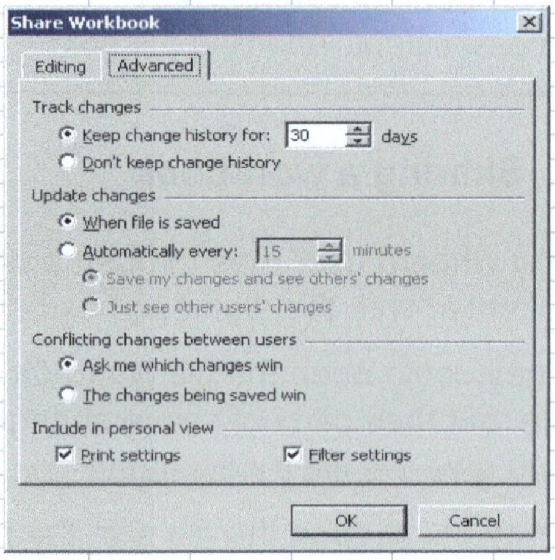

The writer can then stipulate:

- If changes should be recorded and for how long.
- When the changes will come into effect.
- That, when changes being made conflict – whose changes are actually made.

Note

When a workbook is shared most of the functionality of the spreadsheet is impaired. For instance: deleting; merging, insert charts and objects, conditional formats, data validation and subtotals, to name but a few. If any of these are required, sharing must be turned off, the task performed, then sharing can be resumed.

Consolidating worksheets

19

19.1 Introduction

This chapter will show you how to join one or more workbooks together using the consolidation tool and to understand the various aspects of this function.

KNOWLEDGE	
2.3	Select and use a range of tools and techniques to analyse and interpret data to meet requirements.

19.2 The consolidation tool

We have seen previously (Chapter 7) how to link two or more worksheets/workbooks together to when referencing to cells/worksheets in calculations. Excel comes equipped with a **Consolidation** tool to aid us in this task.

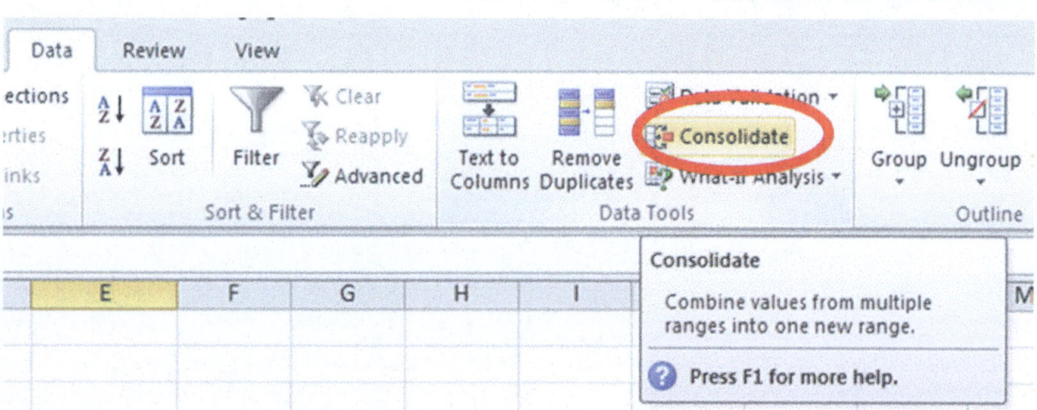

Consolidation can be done with or without creating links to the source data. With a link means any updates in the source data will also update the consolidation, without links and any updates in the source data will not show in the consolidation.

Links to source data can be set up without the source data being open but it is often easier if it is.

The consolidation tool is very useful as it allows you to use row and column headings to perform the consolidation. This is very effective as the row and column labels do not need to be in the same position in the worksheets. However, the row and column labels MUST be spelt exactly the same (they are not case sensitive).

The **Consolidation Tool** when opened presents you with the following dialogue box.

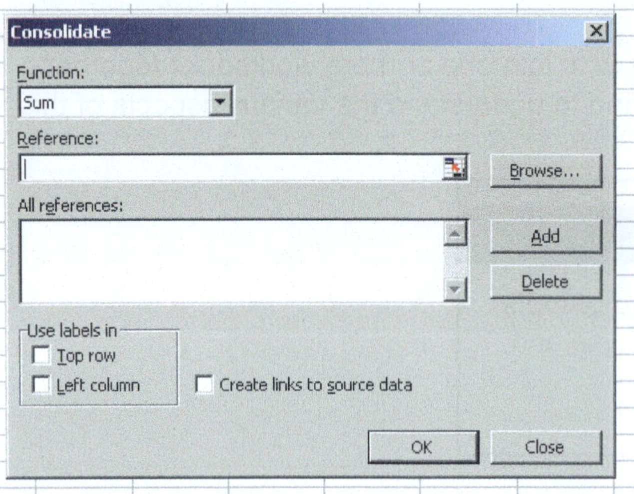

You select the data you wish to consolidate in the **Reference** box, then click **Add**. Add all the data sources you wish to consolidate, then click **OK**. The data will be consolidated.

You can also choose the function – **SUM**, **AVERAGE**, **MIN** or **MAX** – depending on what you want Excel to do.

19.3 Activities

The activities in this guide are designed to test your knowledge on the techniques shown in this chapter. They may also use techniques used in previous chapters, to build up your knowledge. Suggested answers are available on MyKaplan, although it is better to refer to the notes and try to understand the methods than look straight at the answers.

Activity 19-1

This activity demonstrates the use of the **Consolidation** tool.

(a) Open the following workbooks from the **Activities** folder:

- NorthvSouth Consolidation
- Southern
- Northern.

(b) The aim is to consolidate the data on the Southern and Northern workbooks into the NorthvSouth Consolidation workbook.

(c) Select cell **B2** in the NorthvSouth Consolidation workbook. This is where we need to consolidate our data.

(d) Select the **Consolidation** tool from the **Data** tab.

(e) You need to add two references – one each from the Northern and Southern workbooks. Use the reference button at the end of the Reference box, select the required data, and click the reference button again:

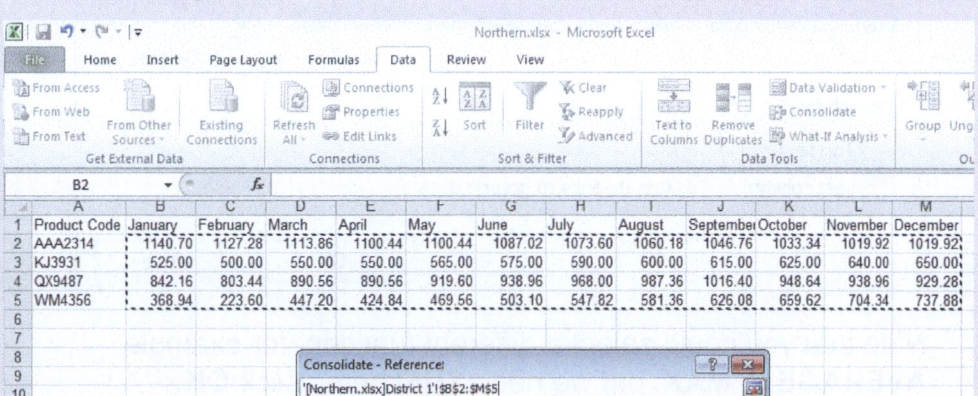

(f) Once the data is selected, click **Add** to add it to the consolidation.

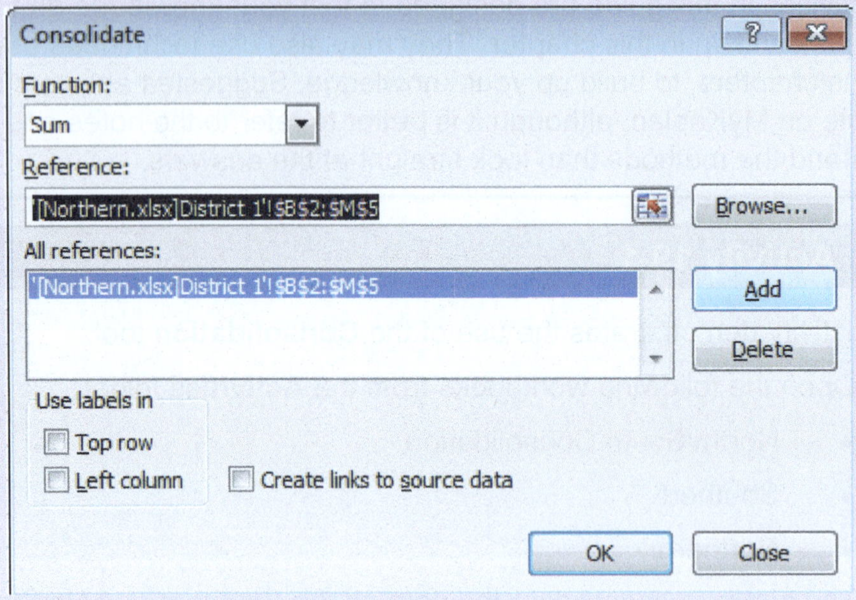

(g) Repeat for the other data set.

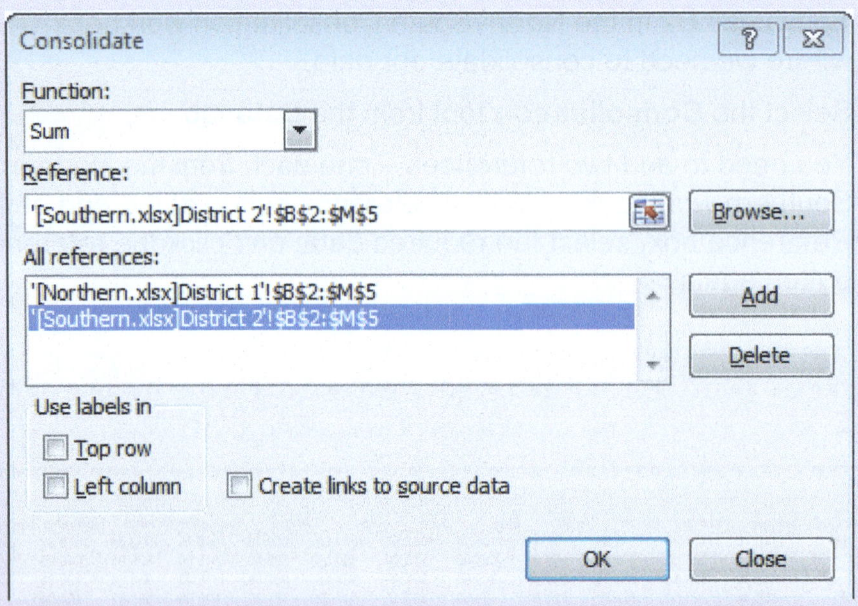

Note that you could select a different function, for example **AVERAGE** or **MAX**, but we need **SUM** here. Click **OK.**

(h) The data is consolidated (added up).

B2 | f_x 2509.54

	A	B	C	D	E	F
1	Product Code	January	February	March	April	May
2	AAA2314	2509.54	2482.70	2455.86	2415.60	2415.60
3	KJ3931	1060.00	1010.00	1110.00	1110.00	1140.00
4	QX9487	1703.68	1626.24	1800.48	1800.48	1858.56
5	WM4356	726.70	436.02	883.22	838.50	927.94

(i) Note that if you select the "Create links to source data" in part f, formulas are created so that the figures will be updated if the original data changes, as well as subtotals created.

B2 | f_x ='[Northern.xlsx]District 1'!$B$2

	A	B	C	D	E
1	Product Code	January	February	March	April
2		1140.70	1127.28	1113.86	1100.44
3		1368.84	1355.42	1342.00	1315.16
4	AAA2314	2509.54	2482.70	2455.86	2415.60
7	KJ3931	1060.00	1010.00	1110.00	1110.00
10	QX9487	1703.68	1626.24	1800.48	1800.48
13	WM4356	726.70	436.02	883.22	838.50
14					

(j) Save as **Activity 19-1** in the **solutions** folder.

Activity 19-2

This activity also uses the **consolidation** tool, but demonstrates how it is more flexible than using SUM or other functions if the data is in different locations on the source worksheets. The approach is very similar to Activity 19-1, but labels must be used for the consolidation.

(a) Open the following workbooks from the **Activities** folder:

- EastvWest Consolidation
- Eastern
- Western.

(b) As in Activity 19-1, we need to consolidate (**SUM**) the data on the two data workbooks – Eastern and Western. Notice though, that the data is laid out differently – the Months and products are in a different order on the two sheets.

(c) Select cell **A1** in the EastvWest Consolidation workbook, and select the Consolidation tool.

(d) Add the two references as before – except that the data **AND** row and column headings must be selected – i.e. from cell A1 to the corner of the data. Also select the options to use labels.

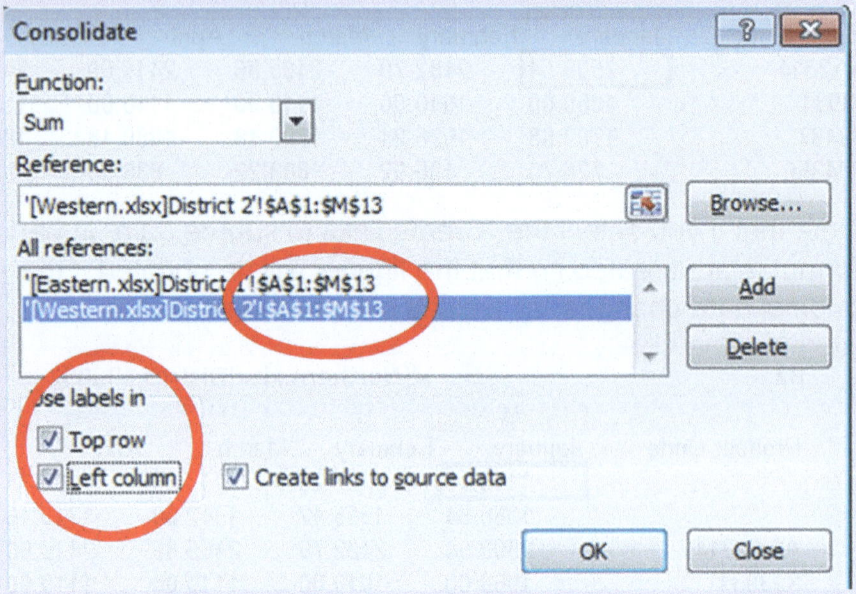

(e) When the consolidation is complete, the formulas will allow for the fact that the labels are in different places on each sheet.

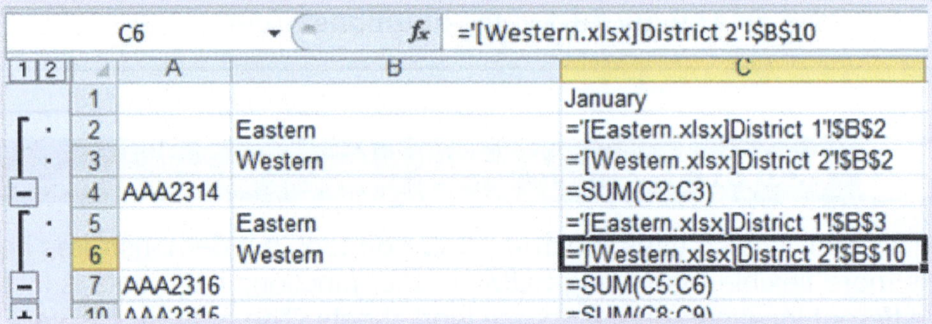

For example, product AAA2314 is in row 3 on the Eastern Spreadsheet, and row 10 on the Western, as shown here.

(f) Save as **Activity 19-2** in the **solutions** folder.

Creating simple pivot tables

20

20.1 Introduction

This chapter will show you how to use the function of pivot tables as a form of consolidation, how to insert formulas into these pivot tables, and how to create charts from pivot tables.

KNOWLEDGE

2.3 Select and use a range of tools and techniques to analyse and interpret data to meet requirements.

3.3 Select and use appropriate tools and techniques to generate, develop and format charts and graphs.

In this session we will be covering:

- Construction of Pivot Tables.
- Pivot Table tools
  - (i) Formatting.
  - (ii) Grand Totals and Sub-totals.
  - (iii) Grouping and Ungrouping.
  - (iv) Refreshing data.
  - (v) Changing the calculation function.
  - (vi) Adding Formulas to Pivot Tables.
- Pivot Charts

20.2 An important point about pivot tables

Pivot Tables may seem a bit confusing when you first use them – there are a lot of options to choose from and they might not do what you want them to first time. The important point is that **you cannot break a pivot table**! Aside from the ability to use Ctrl-Z to undo any mistakes, a pivot table **will never change the original data**. So if it all goes wrong, just delete the table and start again (charts are similar in this way – very easy to create a new one, so just do that).

20.3 Construction of pivot tables

A **Pivot Table** is a tool used for turning tables of data into meaningful reports. The tool can be used to create reports from external sources, multiple-workbooks (another consolidation tool) and workbooks.

In essence a **Pivot Table** is a means of taking raw data and presenting it so that the user can understand what they are looking at. It is often best to think in terms of 'what would I want a report on this data to look like?' You can then set your pivot table to look like this.

To create a pivot table, select the data (**including headers**) you wish to use, then in the **Insert** tab, select **Pivot Table.**

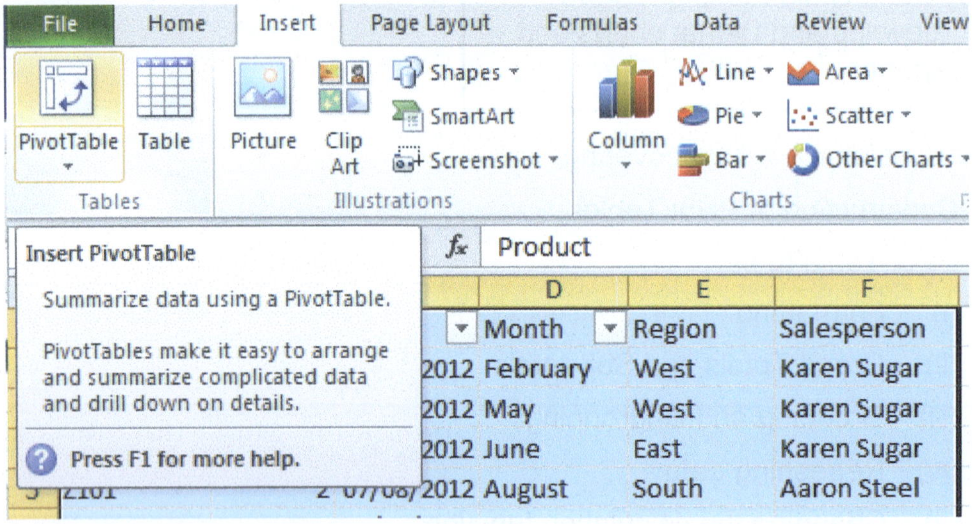

This opens the **PivotTable Wizard**.

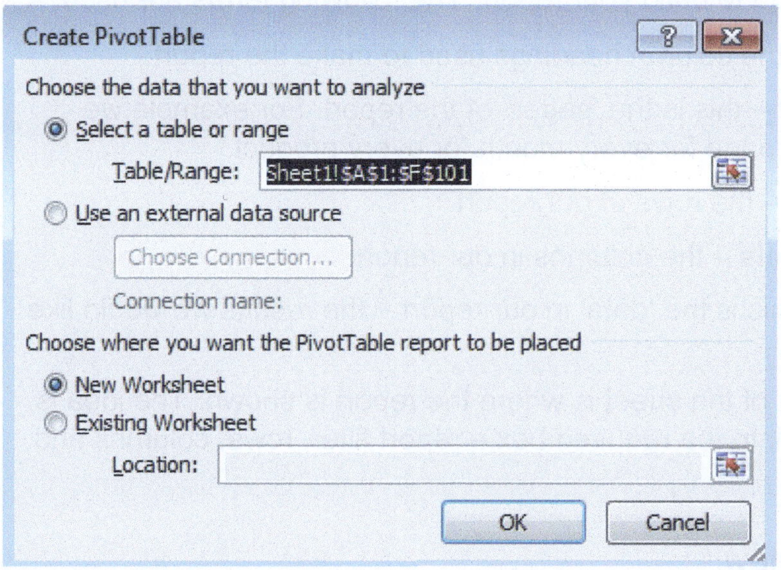

You can also choose whether to create the table in a new worksheet or place it somewhere on your existing sheet.

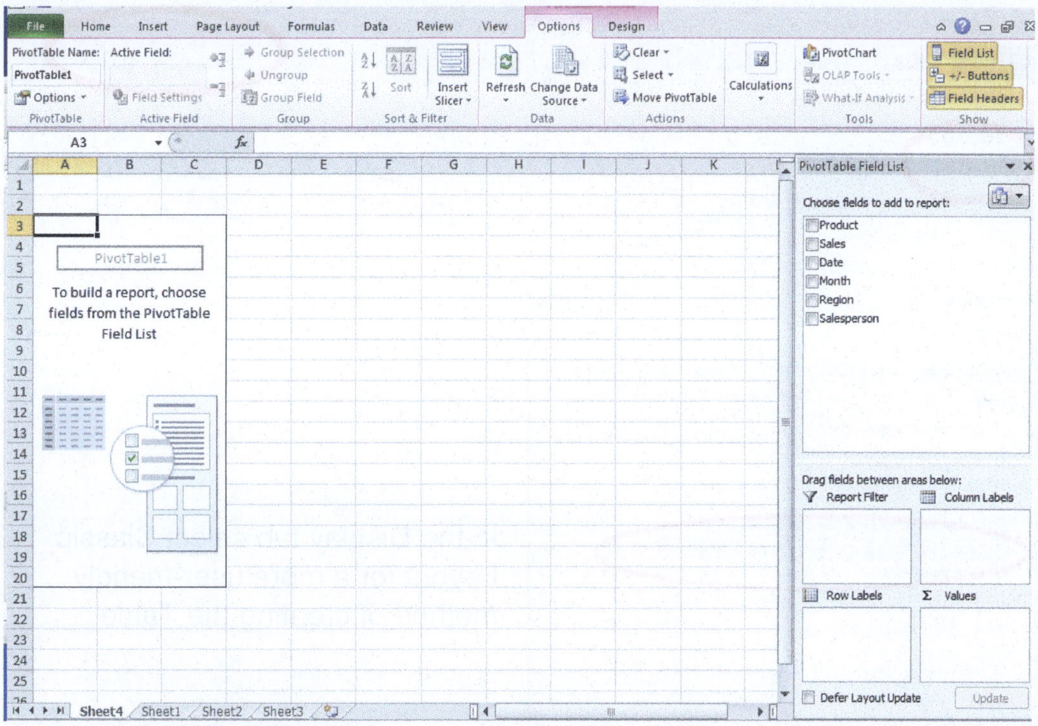

This view allows you to build your report. The following terms are used:

- **Fields** – are the column headings used to make the report.
- **Report Filter** – this is the 'pages' of the report. For example we might have a page for every month, or every product.
- **Row Labels** – the rows of our report.
- **Column Labels** – the columns in our report.
- ∑ **Values** – this is the 'data' in our report – the results we would like to show.

The box on the left of the sheet is where the report is shown. The idea is to 'drag' the fields into the required box – report filter, rows, columns and values.

20.4 Classic view

There is an alternative way to create a Pivot Table, which many people feel is more user-friendly. This may be displayed by default, but if your screen looks like the screenshot on the previous page, you could try Classic View, in the **Options** tab, select **Options.**

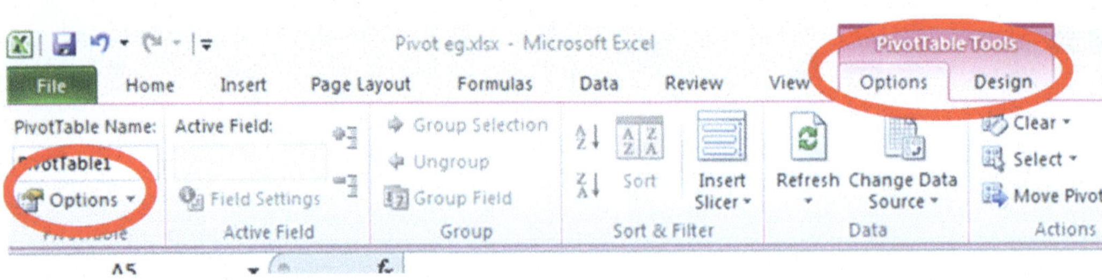

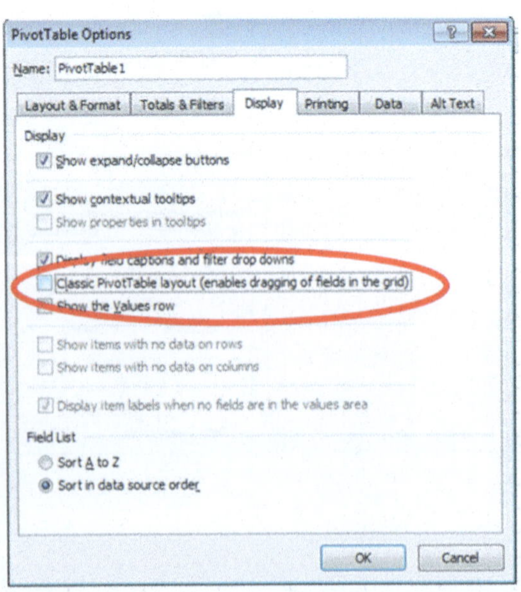

In the Display tab select Classic Layout for a more user-friendly method of creating the Table.

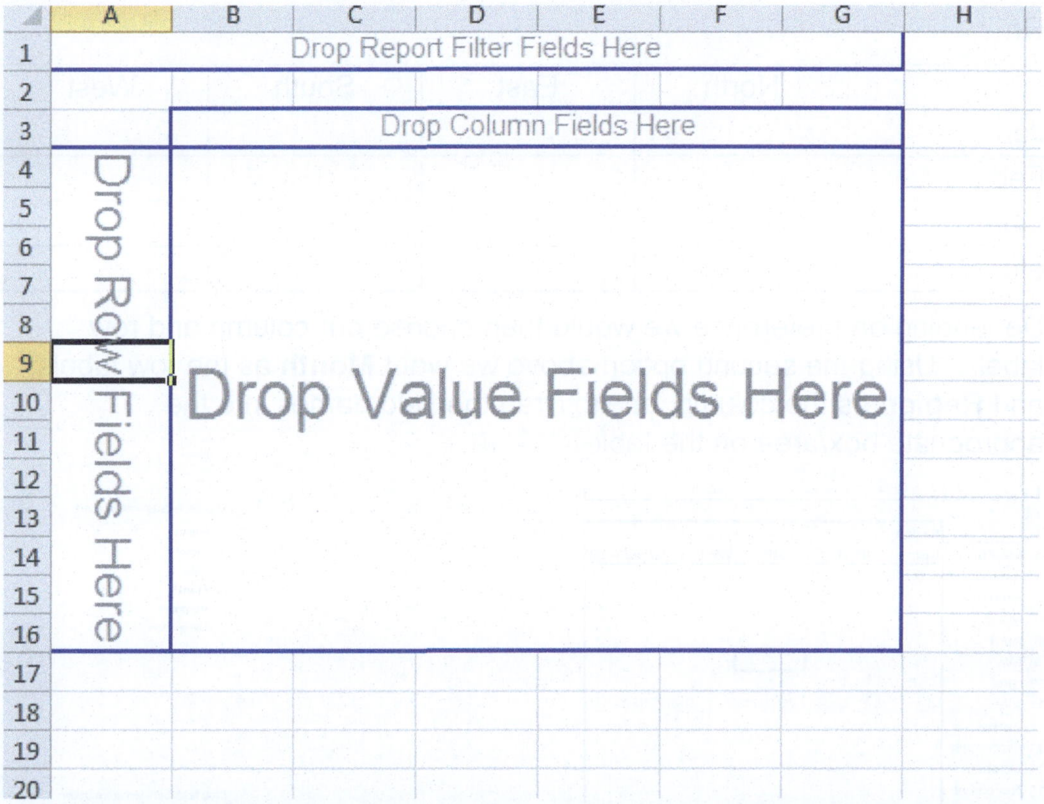

The appearance of the table changes – as it says, you can now 'drag and drop' the field names onto the table if you prefer. There is no difference in terms of the final appearance, but many people prefer this method.

20.5 Creating a report

We need to create a report showing total sales for each month, split by region. We can use the **Pivot Table** to show this very easily, but how do we do it. We could have a simple report looking like this:

January – North

January – East

January – South

Etc

This would give the results we want, but not in a very user- friendly way. We could have the following:

Region	Jan	Feb	Mar	Apr	May	Jun	...
North							
East							
South							
West							

Or:

	North	East	South	West
Jan				
Feb				
Mar				
etc				

Depending on preference we would then choose our column and row labels. Using the second option above we want **Month** as the row labels, and **Region** as the column labels. Drag the field names into the appropriate box/area on the table.

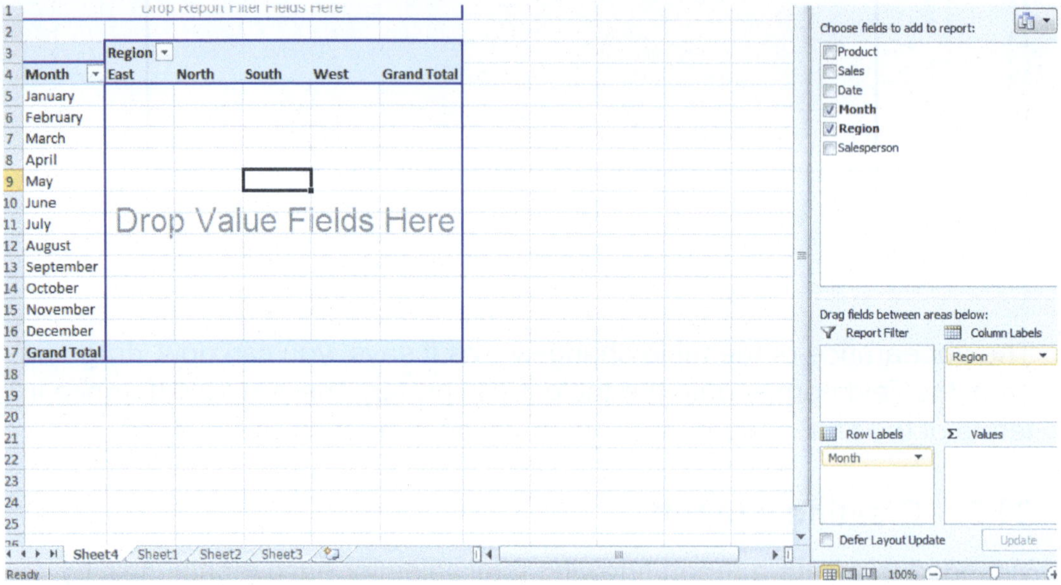

Our report is starting to take shape. We need some data though – that is the **value field.** We would like to know sales by month, so drag the sales field into the value area.

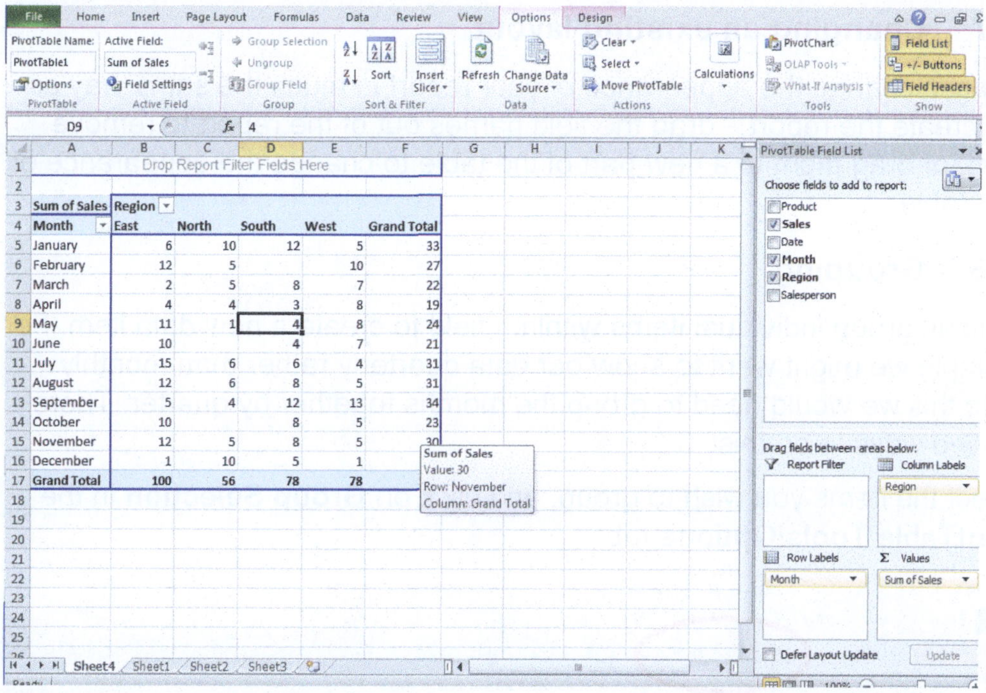

The report is complete.

20.6 Further report options

Pivot Tables are very versatile. You are not restricted to one field in the row labels, for example – if we wanted to show each individual's sales by month, drag the salesperson field over to the row labels and see what happens:

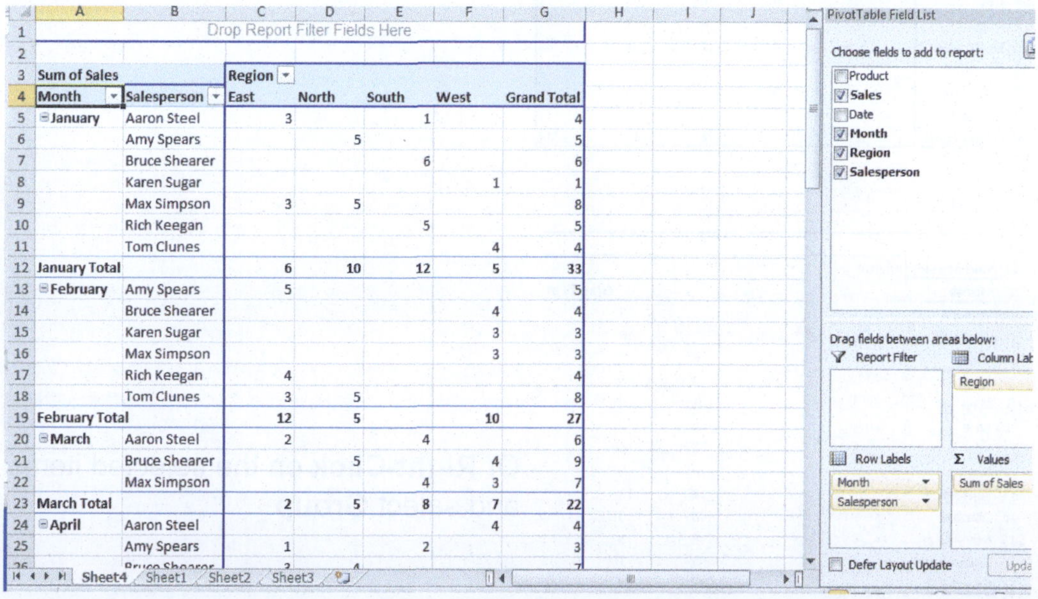

We have now got the detail we wanted. The best thing to do is to play with all the different layouts and see what suits your needs the best.

20.7 Changing an existing layout

You can change the appearance of your report in much the same way as you create the report – drag the field names out of the report to remove them, or drag them to a new part of the table to change the appearance of your table.

20.8 Grouping

You can group individual items within a field to create a new data item. For example we might want to show our data quarterly rather than monthly – to do this we would need to group the months together by quarter. There are two ways to do this:

Select the items you wish to group, and click on **Group Selection** in the **PivotTable Tools/Options** tab.

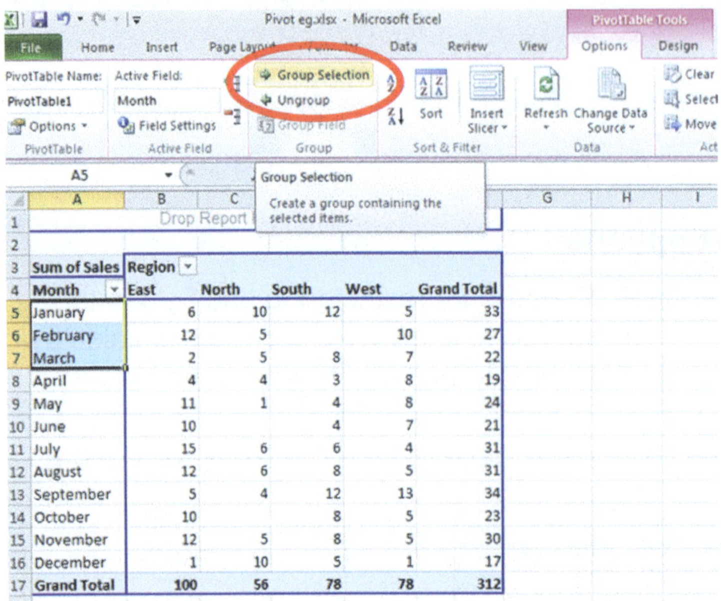

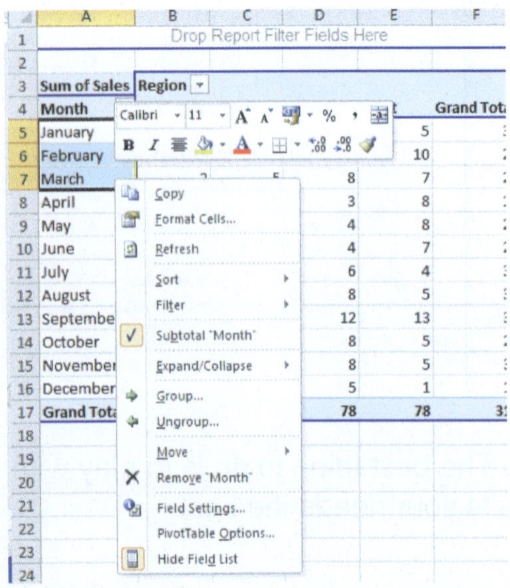

Or **Right-Click** on the selected items and select **Group**.

The field is split and the new group shown. This can be renamed by typing the new name in the cell.

Sum of Sales		Region				
Month2	Month	East	North	South	West	Grand Total
⊟Group1	January	6	10	12	5	33
	February	12	5		10	27
	March	2	5	8	7	22
⊟April	April	4	4	3	8	19
⊟May	May	11	1	4	8	24
⊟June	June	10		4	7	21
⊟July	July	15	6	6	4	31
⊟August	August	12	6	8	5	31
⊟September	September	5	4	12	13	34
⊟October	October	10		8	5	23
⊟November	November	12	5	8	5	30
⊟December	December	1	10	5	1	17
Grand Total		100	56	78	78	312

Drop Report Filter Fields Here

Sum of Sales		Region				
Month2	Month	East	North	South	West	Grand Total
⊟Q1	January	6	10	12	5	33
	February	12	5		10	27
	March	2	5	8	7	22
⊟Q2	April	4	4	3	8	19
	May	11	1	4	8	24
	June	10		4	7	21
⊟Q3	July	15	6	6	4	31
	August	12	6	8	5	31
	September	5	4	12	13	34
⊟Q4	October	10		8	5	23
	November	12	5	8	5	30
	December	1	10	5	1	17
Grand Total		100	56	78	78	312

Clicking on the – boxes next to the field items allows you to expand/contract the data – similar to subtotals.

We could remove the individual months' data by removing that field from the table:

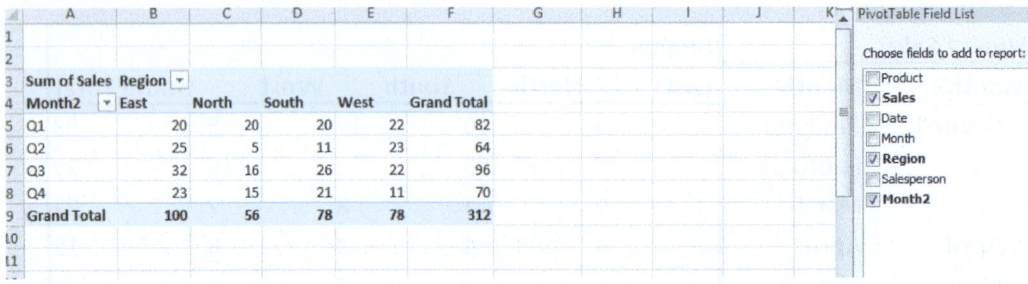

To remove grouping(s), select the grouping(s), and click **Ungroup.**

20.9 Dealing with totals

Totals and subtotals can be added and removed from your **Pivot Table**. As is often the case, right-clicking on the subtotal you want to add/remove is often the easiest way, but here are the key methods.

Subtotals

You may require subtotals for individual fields. For example, we might want to see a quarterly subtotal. This would be the Month2 field.

Select the field by clicking anywhere within it. Then, in the **PivotTable Tools/Options** tab, choose **Field Settings**.

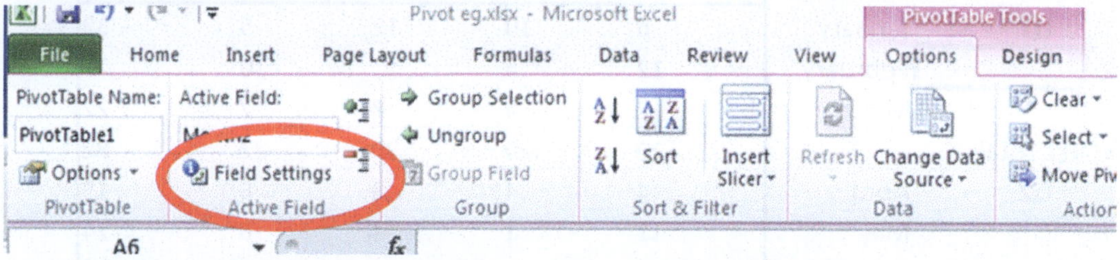

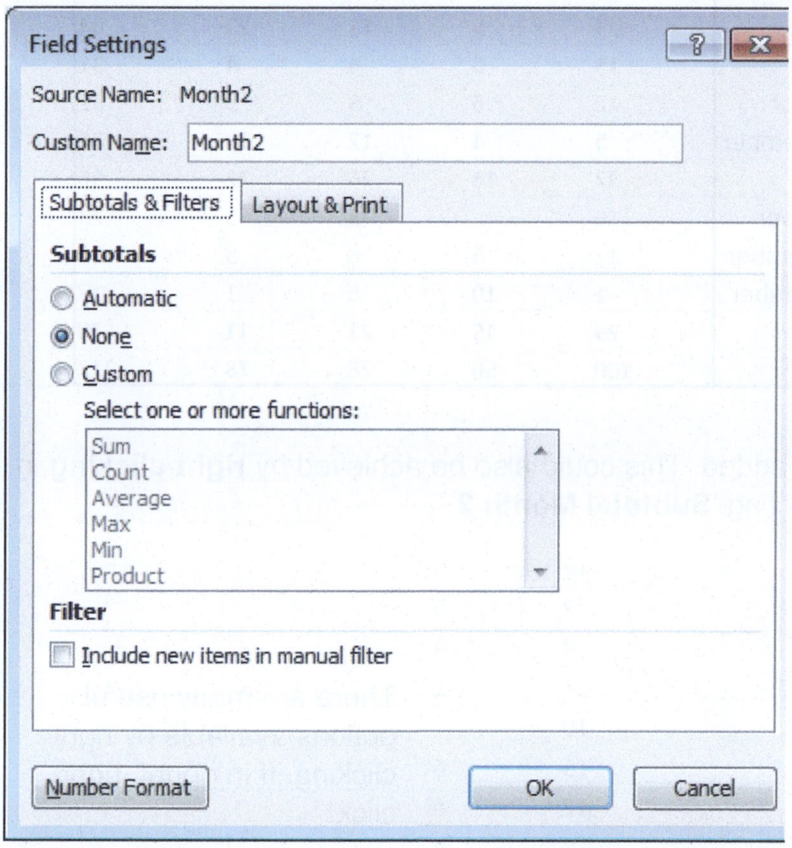

This will bring the appropriate menu up:

Select **Automatic** to add subtotals, or **None** to remove existing subtotals. You could use custom for more advanced subtotals using different functions.

Sum of Sales		Region				
Month2	**Month**	**East**	**North**	**South**	**West**	**Grand Total**
⊟Q1	January	6	10	12	5	33
	February	12	5		10	27
	March	2	5	8	7	22
Q1 Total		**20**	**20**	**20**	**22**	**82**
⊟Q2	April	4	4	3	8	19
	May	11	1	4	8	24
	June	10		4	7	21
Q2 Total		**25**	**5**	**11**	**23**	**64**
⊟Q3	July	15	6	6	4	31
	August	12	6	8	5	31
	September	5	4	12	13	34
Q3 Total		**32**	**16**	**26**	**22**	**96**
⊟Q4	October	10		8	5	23
	November	12	5	8	5	30
	December	1	10	5	1	17
Q4 Total		**23**	**15**	**21**	**11**	**70**
Grand Total		**100**	**56**	**78**	**78**	**312**

The subtotals are added. This could also be achieved by **right-clicking** in the field, and selecting '**Subtotal Month 2**'

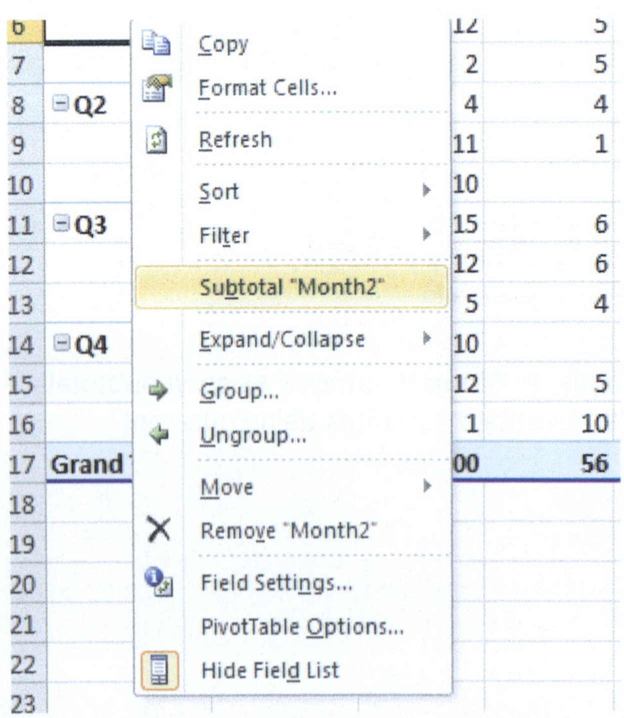

There are many useful options available by right-clicking. If in doubt, right-click!

Grand totals

Grand Totals at the bottom/end of your table can also be added or removed. To remove them right click on the total, and select **Remove Grand Total**.

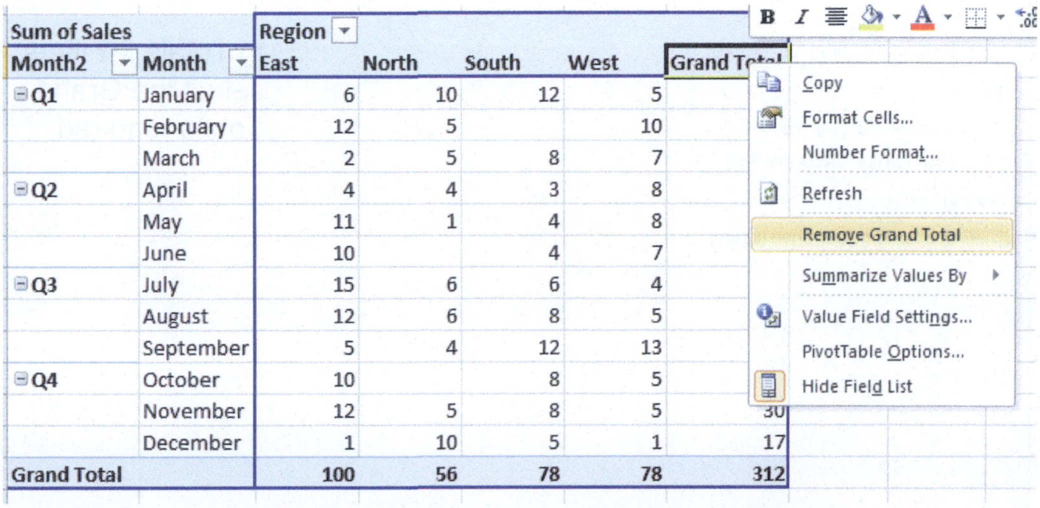

Sum of Sales		Region				
Month2	Month	East	North	South	West	Grand Total
Q1	January	6	10	12	5	
	February	12	5		10	
	March	2	5	8	7	
Q2	April	4	4	3	8	
	May	11	1	4	8	
	June	10		4	7	
Q3	July	15	6	6	4	
	August	12	6	8	5	
	September	5	4	12	13	
Q4	October	10		8	5	
	November	12	5	8	5	30
	December	1	10	5	1	17
Grand Total		100	56	78	78	312

To add Grand Totals you need the **PivotTable Options** menu.

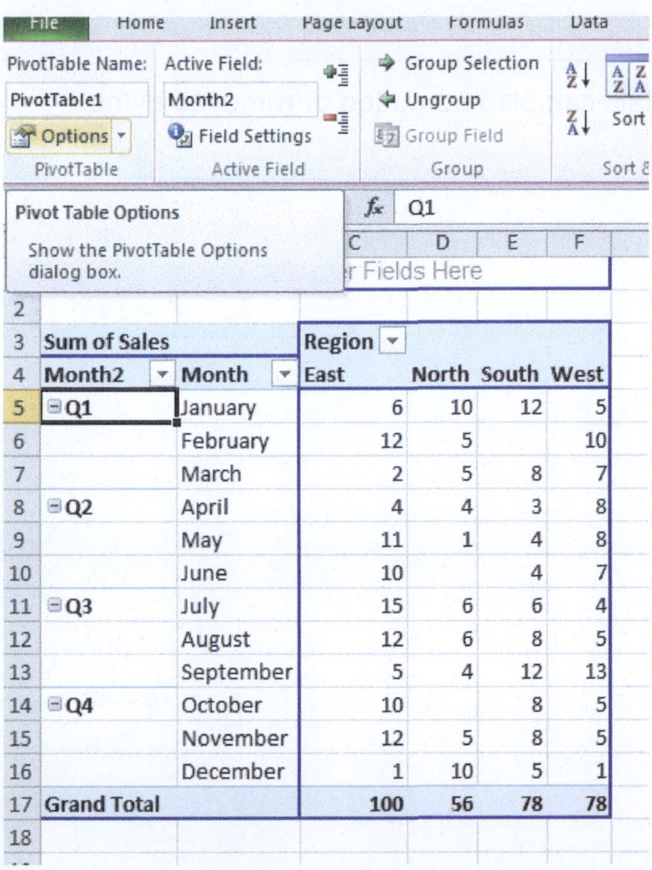

Sum of Sales		Region			
Month2	Month	East	North	South	West
Q1	January	6	10	12	5
	February	12	5		10
	March	2	5	8	7
Q2	April	4	4	3	8
	May	11	1	4	8
	June	10		4	7
Q3	July	15	6	6	4
	August	12	6	8	5
	September	5	4	12	13
Q4	October	10		8	5
	November	12	5	8	5
	December	1	10	5	1
Grand Total		100	56	78	78

This can be found in the Ribbon, or by right-clicking on the table and select **PivotTable Options**.

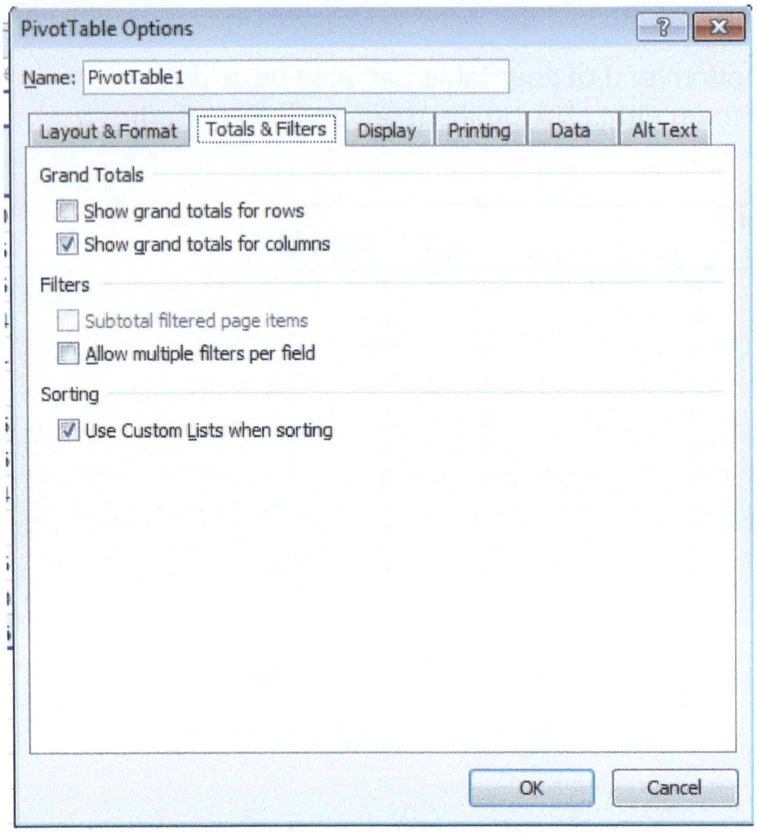

In Totals & Filters, select the Grand Totals required.

Both subtotals and grand totals can also be added or removed in the **PivotTable Tools/Design** tab.

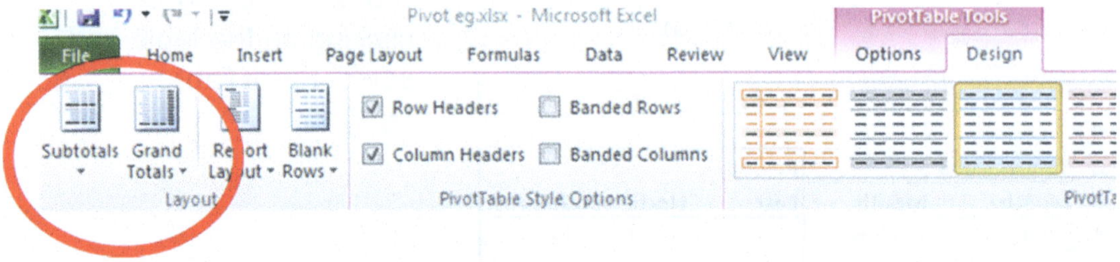

20.10 Filters

You may have already noticed the **filter** buttons on each field. This allows you to further customise your table to show what you want. These are used in the same way as AutoFilters, explained in **Chapter 4**. Click on the box to apply a filter.

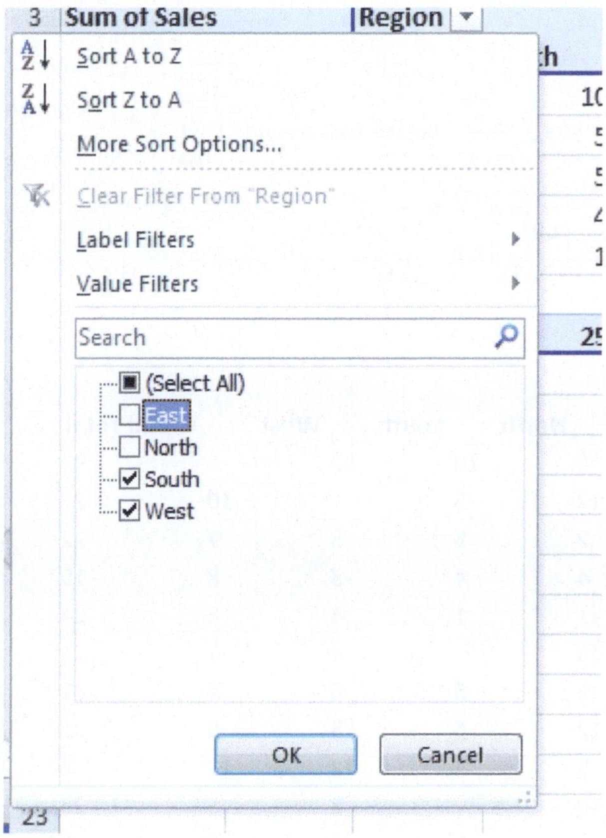

A filter has been applied to only show the South and West's results.

Sum of Sales		Region		
Month2	Month	South	West	Grand Total
⊟Q1	January	12	5	17
	February		10	10
	March	8	7	15
⊟Q2	April	3	8	11
	May	4	8	12
	June	4	7	11
Grand Total		31	45	76

You can see from the icons that Month2 and Region both have filters applied. The totals are updated accordingly.

20.11 Report filter

This is just another part of the report – as explained earlier it acts as 'pages' of your report 'book'. We could use 'Salesperson' as our pages – drag the Salesperson field into the report filter box.

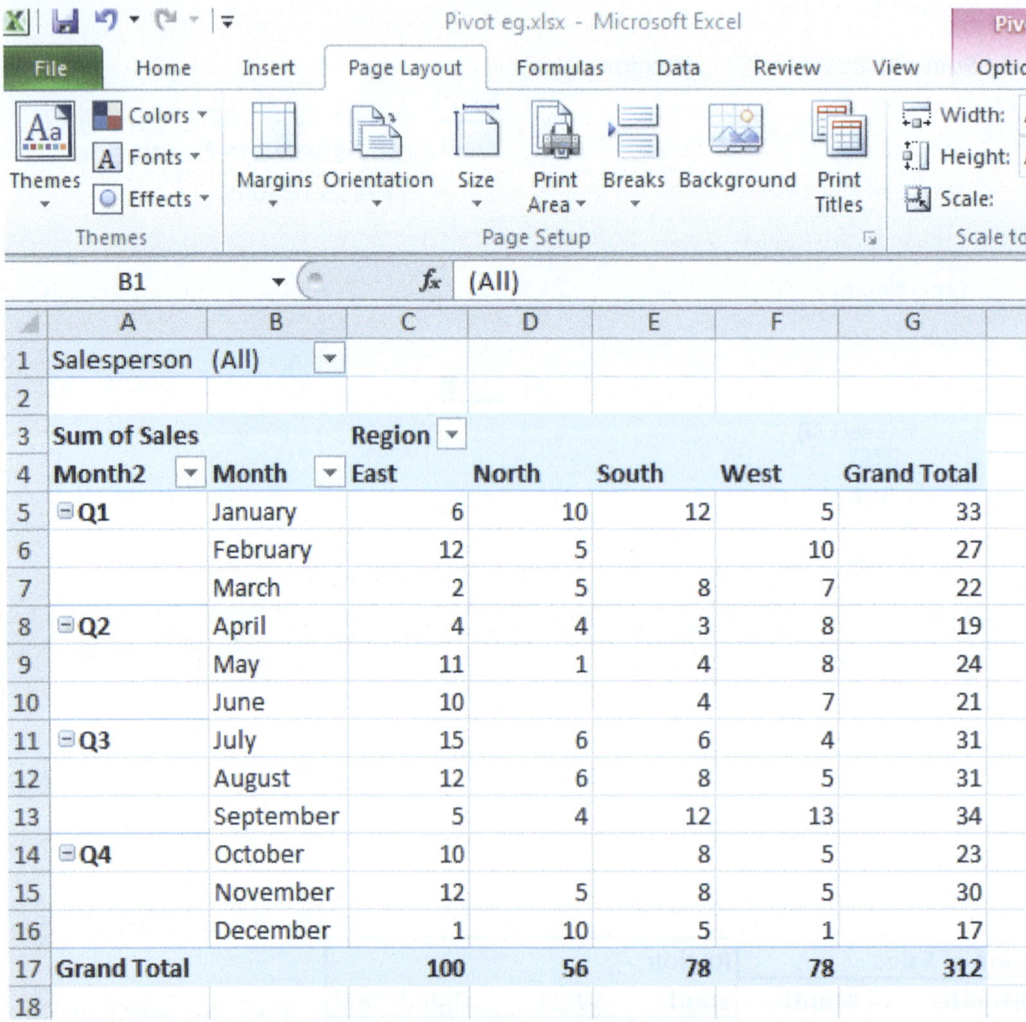

	A	B	C	D	E	F	G
1	Salesperson	(All)					
2							
3	**Sum of Sales**		**Region**				
4	**Month2**	**Month**	**East**	**North**	**South**	**West**	**Grand Total**
5	**Q1**	January	6	10	12	5	33
6		February	12	5		10	27
7		March	2	5	8	7	22
8	**Q2**	April	4	4	3	8	19
9		May	11	1	4	8	24
10		June	10		4	7	21
11	**Q3**	July	15	6	6	4	31
12		August	12	6	8	5	31
13		September	5	4	12	13	34
14	**Q4**	October	10		8	5	23
15		November	12	5	8	5	30
16		December	1	10	5	1	17
17	**Grand Total**		**100**	**56**	**78**	**78**	**312**
18							

Nothing has changed, but we have the option to further summarise our data by using the filter on that field.

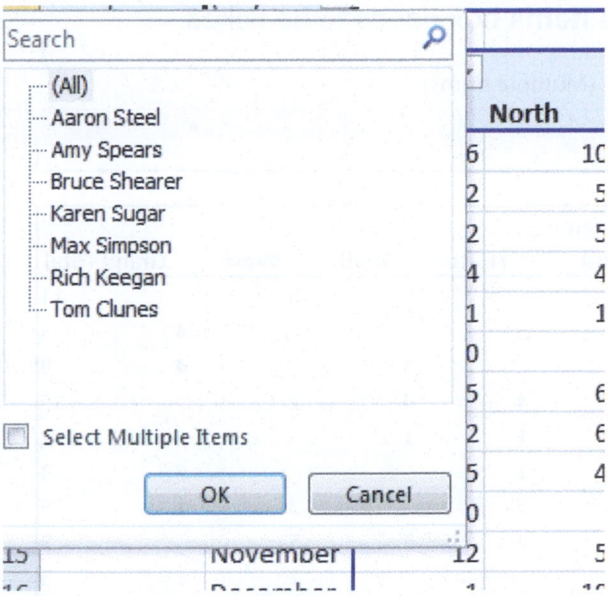

Clicking the **Filter** button allows us to select the salesperson we wish to view the data for.

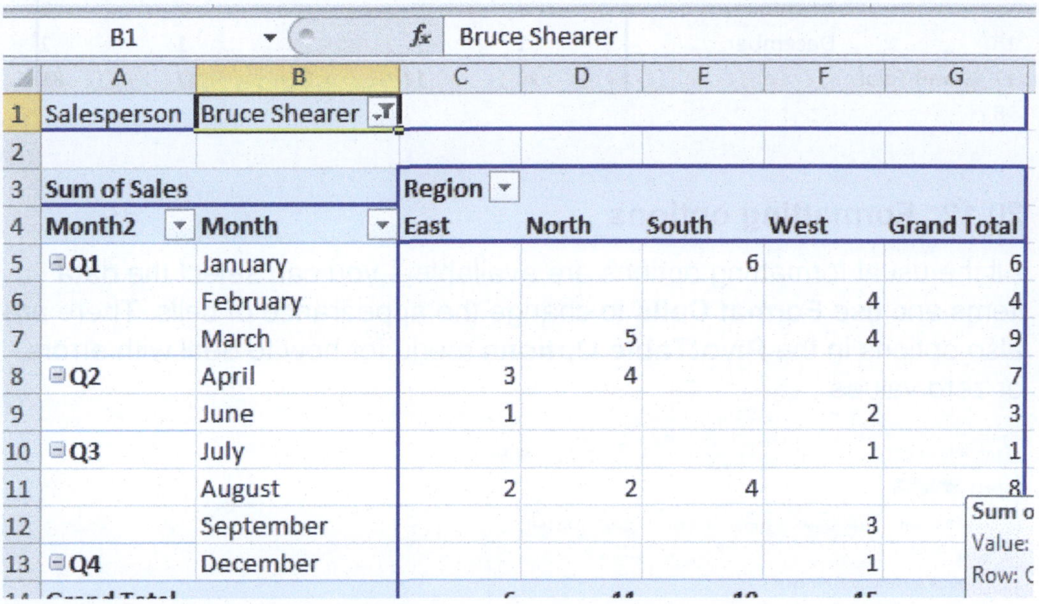

Salesperson	Bruce Shearer					
Sum of Sales		Region				
Month2	Month	East	North	South	West	Grand Total
Q1	January			6		6
	February				4	4
	March		5		4	9
Q2	April	3	4			7
	June	1			2	3
Q3	July				1	1
	August	2	2	4		8
	September				3	
Q4	December				1	

Selecting one field item just shows the information for that person. We could pick more than one.

Notice that the **Select Multiple Items** box needs to be ticked.

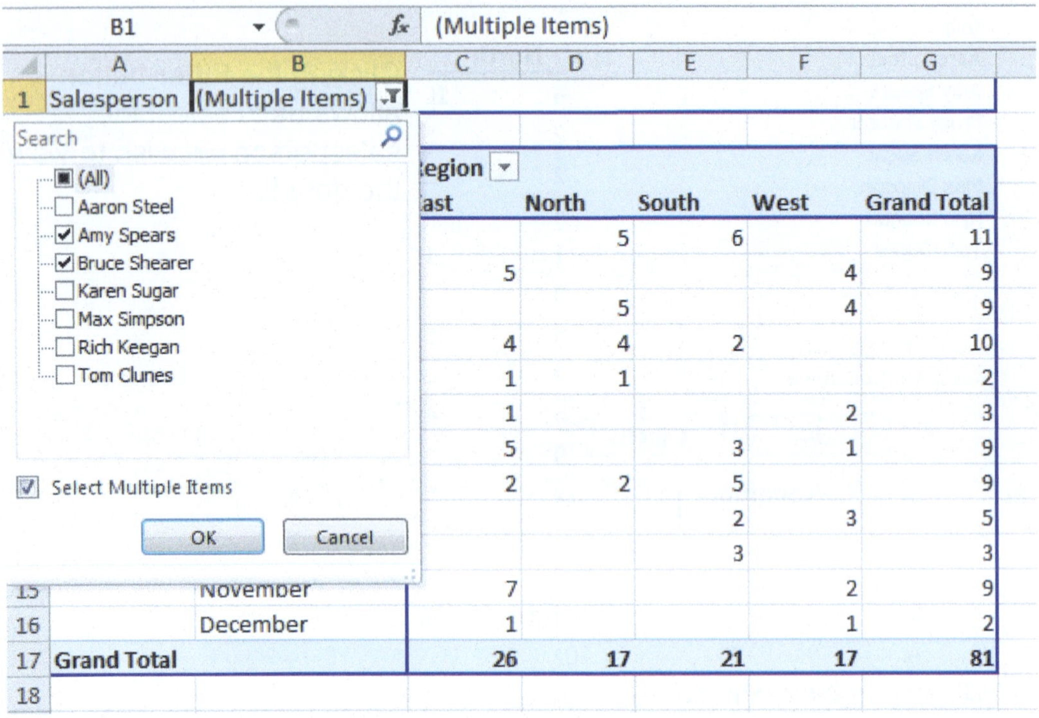

20.12 Formatting options

All the usual formatting options are available – you can select the data items and use **Format Cells** to change the appearance of cells. There are also options in the **PivotTable Options** menu for how to deal with errors or zero values.

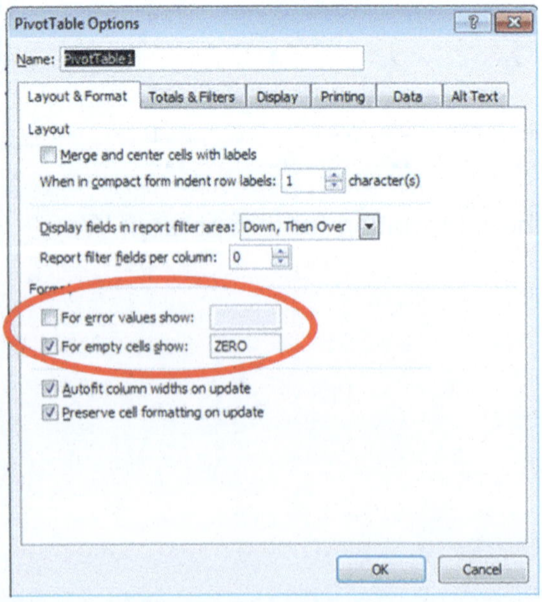

Here, I have selected that empty cells be filled with the text "ZERO" – to show the effect. You can also specify what to do if a cell contains an error.

Salesperson	(All)					
Sum of Sales		Region				
Month2	Month	East	North	South	West	Grand Total
⊟Q1	January	6	10	12	5	33
	February	12	5	ZERO	10	27
	March	2	5	8	7	22
⊟Q2	April	4	4	3	8	19
	May	11	1	4	8	24
	June	10	ZERO	4	7	21
⊟Q3	July	15	6	6	4	31
	August	12	6	8	5	31
	September	5	4	12	13	34
⊟Q4	October	10	ZERO	8	5	23
	November	12	5	8	5	30
	December	1	10	5	1	17
Grand Total		**100**	**56**	**78**	**78**	**312**

Note – usually a blank, hyphen or 0 would be used.

20.13 Changing the calculation function

Most of the time, **SUM** is the most appropriate function. However, you may wish to use **COUNT** – for example if you want to **COUNT** the number of times something happens, or **MAX/MIN** to find the biggest or smallest amount in your data set.

To change the function you need the **Value Field Settings** menu. This can be found by either **Right-Clicking** in the pivot table, or by going to the **PivotTable Tools/Options** tab.

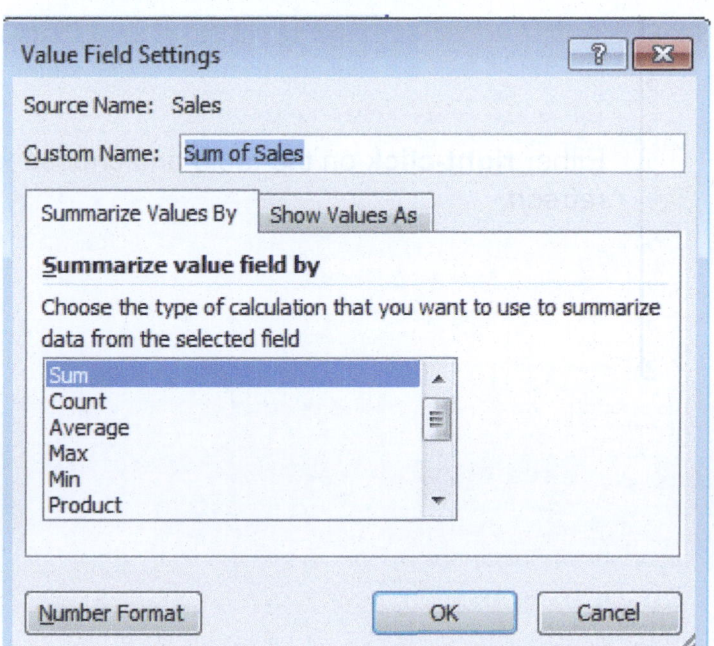

Select the function you want here. For example, **MAX**.

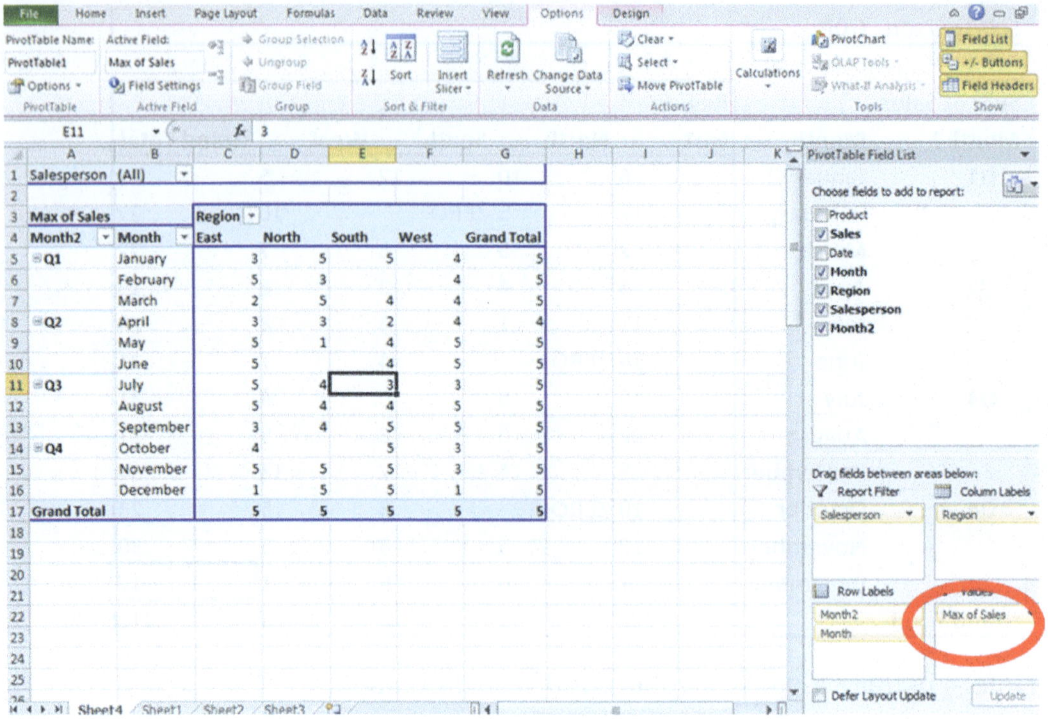

The table now shows the largest number of sales on a single day in each month. You should note too that in the Value field box, **Max of Sales** is shown.

20.14 Refreshing data

If there are any updates to the original data, the **Pivot Table** will need to be updated to reflect this change. Note that this **does not** happen automatically. It is a simple process -

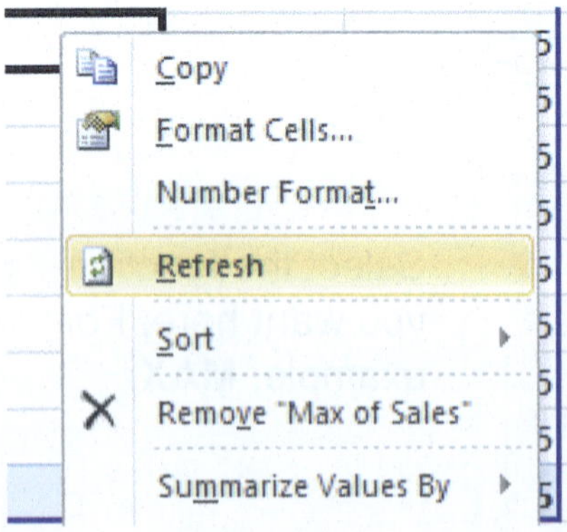

Either **right-click** on the table and choose refresh

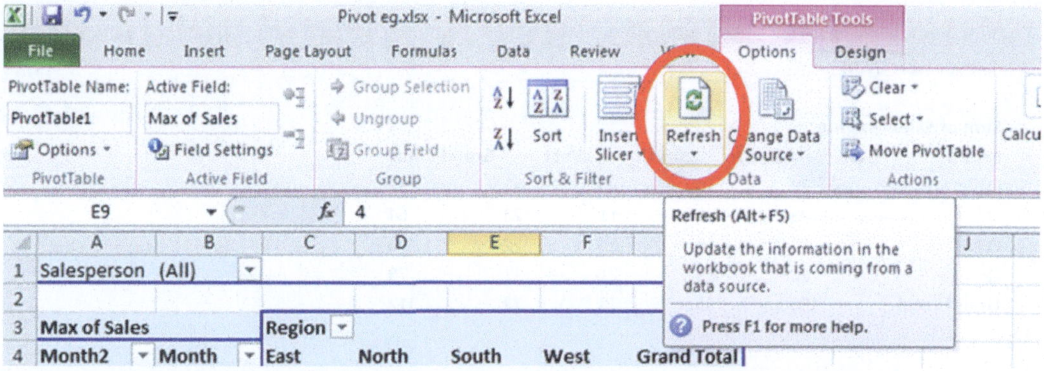

Or use the **Refresh** button in the **PivotTable Tools/Options** tab.

Remember – you cannot change the original data via the Pivot Table.

20.15 Pivot charts

A Pivot Chart is just a chart based on a pivot table. They work in exactly the same way as a normal chart. Pivot Charts change according to the filters applied to your PivotTable.

To insert a Pivot Chart, with the Pivot Table selected, click the **PivotChart** button in the **PivotTable Tools/Options** tab.

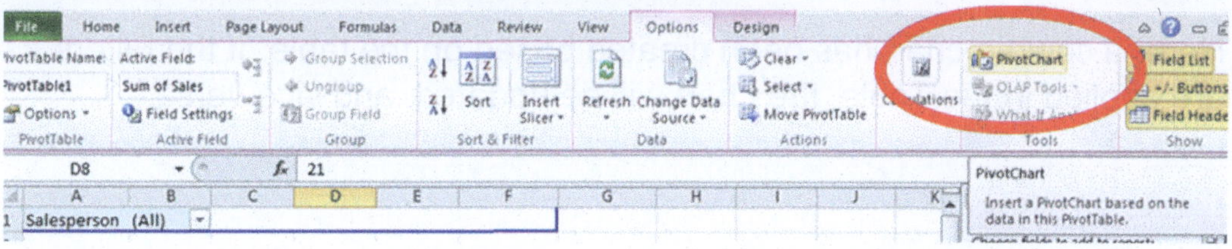

Alternatively, you can use the **Insert** tab, in exactly the same way as creating a normal chart (as long as the Pivot Table is selected). Exactly the same options and chart types are available. It will be created on the same sheet as your Pivot Table by default, although it can be moved to its own sheet in the usual way.

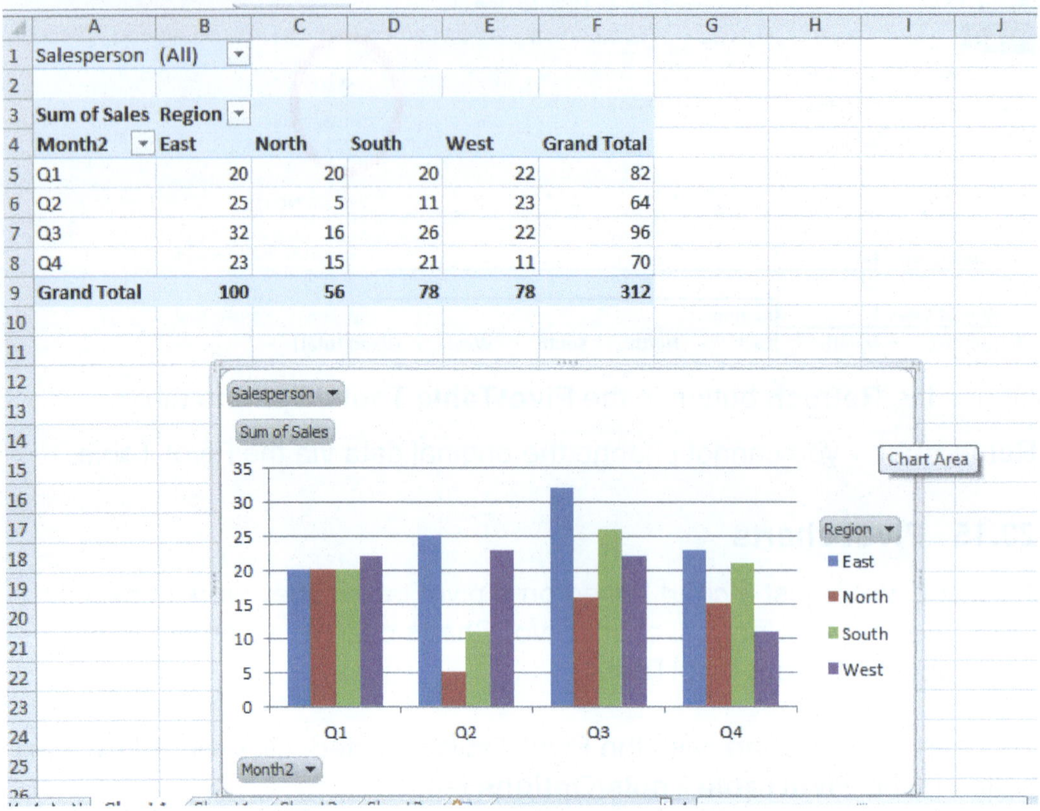

Salesperson	(All)				
Sum of Sales	**Region**				
Month2	**East**	**North**	**South**	**West**	**Grand Total**
Q1	20	20	20	22	82
Q2	25	5	11	23	64
Q3	32	16	26	22	96
Q4	23	15	21	11	70
Grand Total	**100**	**56**	**78**	**78**	**312**

Here, a column chart has been created based on the table. If the Filters are applied in the Table, the chart will be updated, and vice versa.

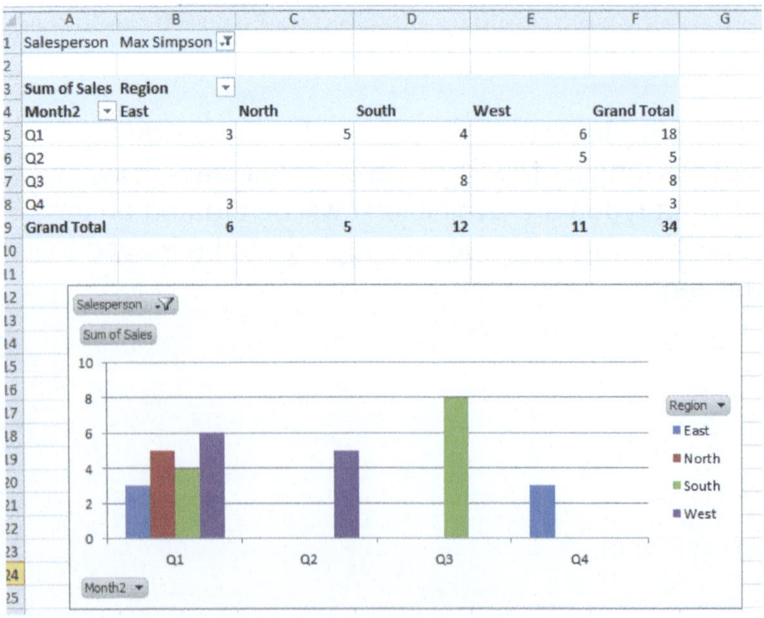

Salesperson	Max Simpson				
Sum of Sales	**Region**				
Month2	**East**	**North**	**South**	**West**	**Grand Total**
Q1	3	5	4	6	18
Q2				5	5
Q3			8		8
Q4	3				3
Grand Total	**6**	**5**	**12**	**11**	**34**

An example filter – note that the graph still shows the data in the Pivot Table.

20.16 Activities

The activities in this guide are designed to test your knowledge on the techniques shown in this chapter. They may also use techniques used in previous chapters, to build up your knowledge. Suggested answers are available on MyKaplan, although it is better to refer to the notes and try to understand the methods than look straight at the answers.

Activity 20-1

This activity allows you to create a **Pivot Table**, and manipulate it as necessary.

(a) Open the **ResultsPivotData** workbook in the **Activities** folder. This only contains one sheet, which contains a data set of exam results.

(b) Create a Pivot Table on a new worksheet that enables us to know how many students were taught by each teacher and sat each exam. We will want to filter our report to show the results (pass or fail).

Result	(All)				
Count of Name	Teacher				
Exam	Graham Rogers	Jim Smith	Mable Thorpe	William Shatner	Grand Total
English			10	21	31
Geography	21	10			31
History		31			31
Maths			31		31
Science			31		31
Sport		31			31
Grand Total	21	72	72	21	186

(c) We now want to use the same Pivot Table to summarise the exam subjects as **Core** subjects (English, Maths and Science), and **Sundry** (everything else). We can **group** the data items to do this.

You will need to hold down **Ctrl** to select the cells as they are not adjacent.

Group these items using **Group Selection** from the **Options** tab.

	A	B	C	D	E	F	G
1	Result	(All)					
2							
3	Count of Name		Teacher				
4	Exam2	Exam	Graham Rogers	Jim Smith	Mable Thorpe	William Shatner	Grand Total
5	⊟Core	English			10	21	31
6		Maths			31		31
7		Science			31		31
8	⊟Sundry	Geography	21	10			31
9		History		31			31
10		Sport		31			31
11	Grand Total		21	72	72	21	186

(d) Move the **Exam 2** field into the **Report Filter** area. Move **Result** into the **Row Labels** (it should be to the right of Exam). You can now select to just see core subjects, sundry subjects, or both. Select **Core**.

(e) Save the file as **Activity 20-1** in the **solutions** folder.

Activity 20-2

This activity continues with the same PivotTable data, and talks you through the steps of creating a **PivotChart**.

(a) Open the **ResultsPivotData** workbook in the **Activities** folder.

(b) Create a **PivotTable** from the data. Use the following settings:

Report Filter = Name

Row Field = Result

Column Field = Exam

Value Field = Score (we want to show the highest percentage formatted to zero decimal places)

(c) Remove the Grand Totals.

	A	B	C	D	E	F	G
1	Name	(All)					
2							
3	**Max of Score**	**Column Labels**					
4	**Row Labels**	**English**	**Geography**	**History**	**Maths**	**Science**	**Sport**
5	Fail	44%	64%	42%	57%	62%	64%
6	Pass	95%	99%	100%	100%	100%	97%
7							
8							

(d) Now, create a **PivotChart**. Make a **clustered bar** chart. The graph will display the data shown in the table.

(e) Add a title to the chart – **Exam Results 2012**.

(f) Change the **Name** to select Gareth Jones and see how the chart changes to show their results.

(g) Save the workbook as **Activity 20-2** in the **Solutions** folder.

Find and replace

21

21.1 Introduction

This chapter will show you how to use a very useful function within Excel, 'find and replace'

KNOWLEDGE

2.2 Select and use a wide range of appropriate functions and formulas to meet calculation requirements.

21.2 Find/Replace

Sometimes you discover that data has been input into a spreadsheet that you need to find or change. This is a fairly simple routine using the **Find and Replace** tool, found in the **Home** tab under **Find & Select**.

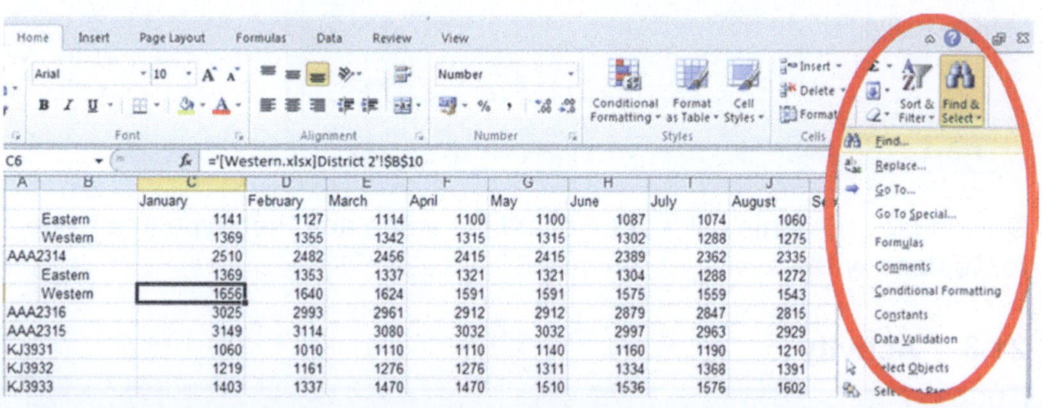

Shortcut

The simplest and fastest way to launch this tool is

Ctrl-f

When the tool is launched the following dialogue box appears:

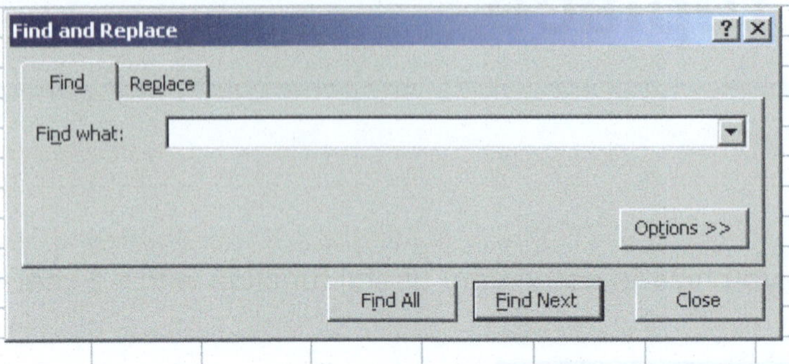

If you are trying to find a value you type it into the **Find what:** field. You can then choose to either find the next version of the value or find them all. If you opt to find them all Excel will present a list that you can scroll through.

There are also options that allow you to choose the case and position if you desire.

If your intention is to find and replace a value then you should select the **Replace** tab. You will then be faced with the following:

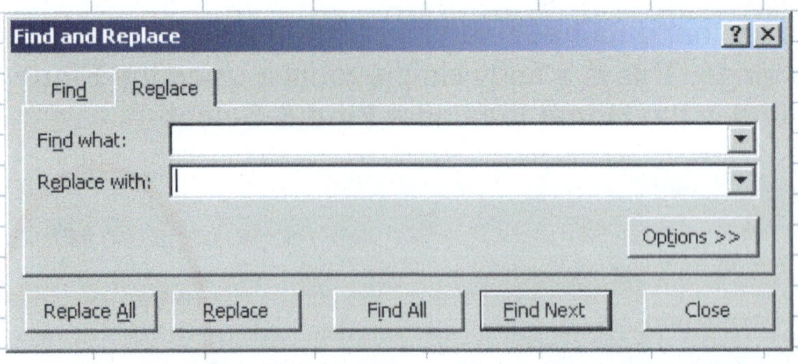

On this tab you again ask Excel to find the value and then type in a value to **Replace with**.

21.3 Activity

Activity 21-1

This activity allows you to practice using the Find and Replace function.

(a) **Open** the **ResultsPivotData** file from the **Activities** folder.

(b) Use the **Find** and **Replace** function to replace all instances of the word **Science** and replace them with **Geology**.

(c) **Find** all instances of Lowther and **replace** them with Luther

(d) Save the file as **Activity 21-1** in the **Solutions** folder and close it.

'What-if' analysis

22

22.1 Introduction

This chapter will show you how to carry out the forecasting technique of 'what-if' analysis.

KNOWLEDGE

2.4 Select and use forecasting tools and techniques.

In this session you will be looking at different methods of **'What-If'** analysis. What-If analysis involves creating a spreadsheet and then asking the question "what if this/these figures were to change". There are a number of tools to look at:

- Creating **Manual** what-if solutions.
- Data Tables.
- Scenario Manager.
- Goal Seek.

With the exception of manual solutions, the above tools can be found in the **Data** tab, in the **Data Tools** section, under What-If Analysis.

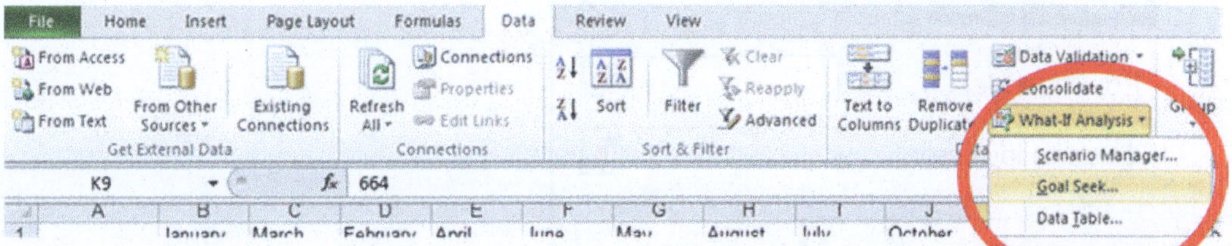

22.2 Creating manual 'What-If' solutions

In previous chapters you have created spreadsheets that used fixed cell references to get their data. These spreadsheets were manual 'what-if' solutions.

The overriding principle for 'what-if' solutions is do not 'hard code' variable data into formulas and functions. If you do this you will be unable to carry out 'what-if' without finding and replacing the hard coded data.

22.3 Data tables

A **Data Table**, as the name suggests, is a table showing how results will change if one or two variables are changed.

There are two types of **Data Table**:

1 **Single Input:** This table allows you to create a spreadsheet with multiple formulas and functions to create a **solution**. The spreadsheet itself can have many variables and you can use a single input **Data Table** to evaluate a change in **one** of these variables – this is its draw back. However, there is nothing to stop you changing any of the other numbers once the table is formed.

2 **Two-Input:** This table works in the same way as above but in this instance you can create a table that allows a change to **two** variables – but only two.

Once your spreadsheet **solution** is created you will be ready create the **Data Table**. Activate the tool as above and you will be presented with the following dialogue box.

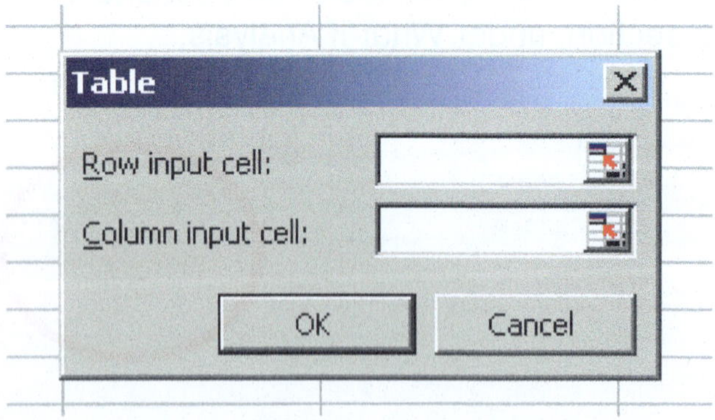

For a **single input** table you will need either a Row or Column input cell, not both. This is determined by the way in which the spreadsheet solution is constructed, either in a Row or a Column. In a single input data table the top-left cell of the table is not used.

For **two input** data tables you will need both Row and Column Inputs. In a two input data table the top-left is used to hold a formula that refers to the solution cell.

22.4 Scenario manager

Scenario manager is a tool that allows you to create scenarios of a particular solution. For example, you are trying to work out your product costs to calculate profits. However, you are uncertain as to the actual costs. You can use **Scenario Manager** to create versions of the potential outcome.

When you are using **Scenario Manager** it will be very useful to **Name** some of the cells to make the reports more understandable. **Naming** cells and ranges is explained in **Chapter 7**.

Using scenario manager

Scenario Manager is used to set up different possible outcomes – you choose which cells (variables) you wish to change, and for each Scenario you set up, you specify the value of these variables – for example you could look at a variety of different sales volumes or prices.

Once all of the different scenarios have been set up, you can run a report to summarise all of the results for your scenarios.

22.5 Goal seek

Goal Seek is 'what-if' in reverse. Here a tool is used to determine a change to a variable that will result in the solution that you want.

For example you may want to make a Net Profit of £10,000 but are unsure of how much a variable such as labour rate will have to change to create this profit.

When you launch **Goal Seek** you are faced with the following dialogue box:

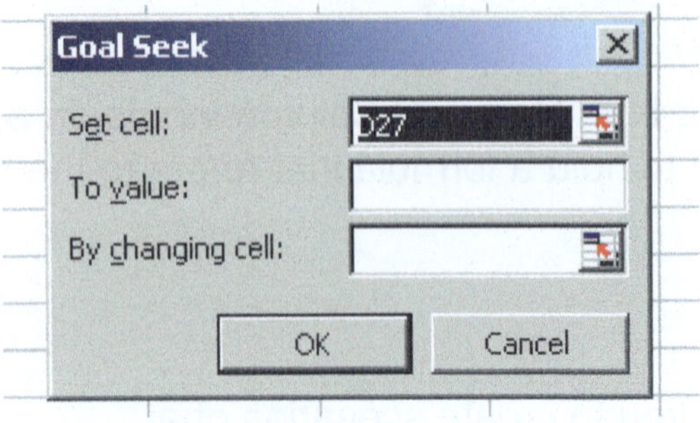

You are asked:

- to **set** a particular cell
- to a particular **value**
- by **changing** a particular cell

Sometimes a solution cannot be found. If this is the case you will need to adjust the values you are asking **Goal Seek** to find till you get a correct answer.

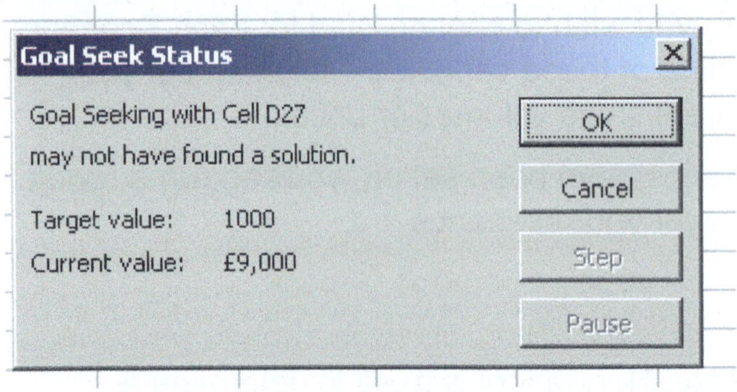

Don't forget to check that the variable is actually involved in the calculation.

22.6 Activities

The following activities are step-by-step examples showing how the techniques described in this chapter work in practice. Suggested answers are available on MyKaplan, although it is better to refer to the notes and try to understand the methods than look straight at the answers.

Activity 22-1

This activity is to show the use of a single input Data Table.

(a) Open the **Data Table 1** file in the **Activities** folder.

(b) The aim is to set up a table which shows how total production costs will change with changing variables – for example if the material cost/kg changes.

(c) In cells D17:D20 we need to calculate full cost for labour, material, fixed costs and full cost. For example, labour will be volume*hourly rate*hours/unit.

Note – for the data table to work, these formulas should use absolute referencing ($ signs).

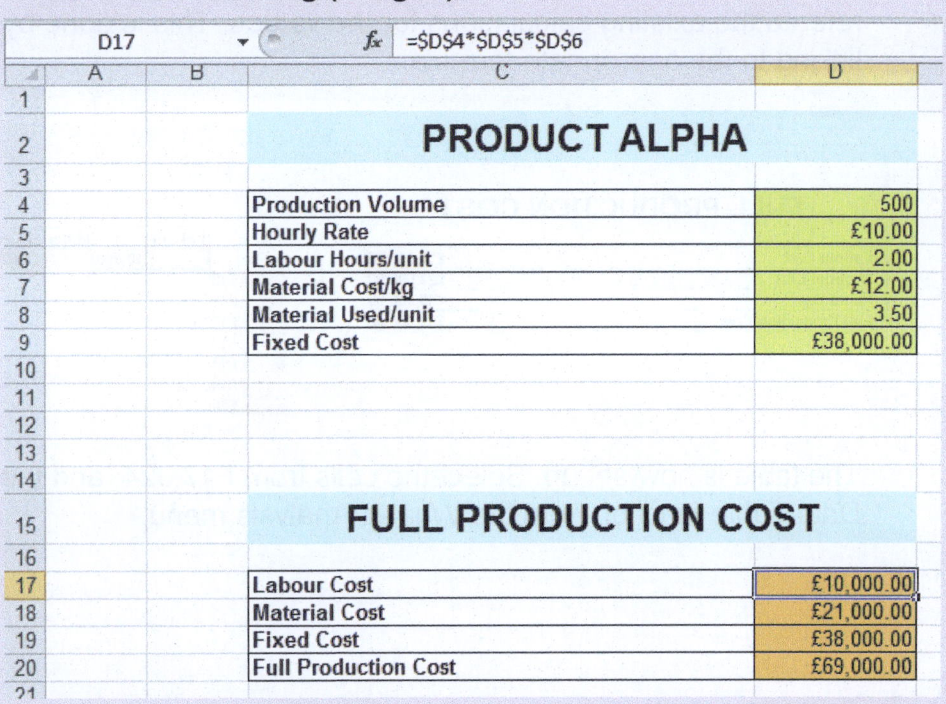

D17 =$D$4*$D$5*$D$6

PRODUCT ALPHA	
Production Volume	500
Hourly Rate	£10.00
Labour Hours/unit	2.00
Material Cost/kg	£12.00
Material Used/unit	3.50
Fixed Cost	£38,000.00

FULL PRODUCTION COST	
Labour Cost	£10,000.00
Material Cost	£21,000.00
Fixed Cost	£38,000.00
Full Production Cost	£69,000.00

(d) We now need to set up the data table – this will go on the right of the sheet where the empty formatting is. The blue shaded part should contain the headings – labour cost, material cost, fixed cost and full cost. The simplest way to achieve this is to copy the headings in C17:C20, then **Paste-Special** in Cell G16 and select transpose.

We also need to put the values for our variable in cells F18:F24. As we will be changing the material cost, enter 10, 11, 12…16 in these cells.

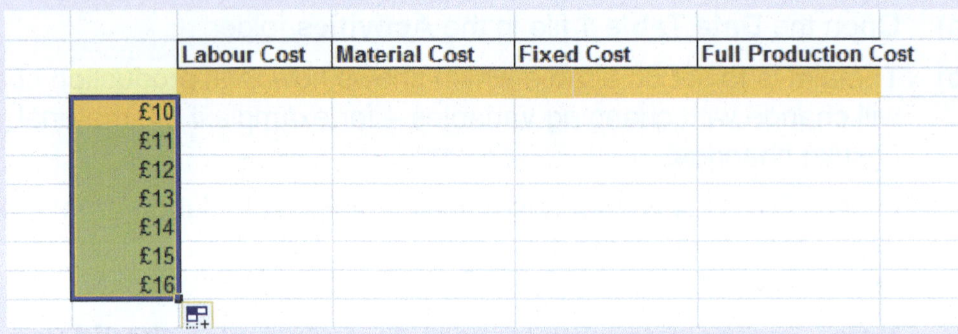

(e) In the top row of the 'table', underneath the headings, we need to refer to the existing calculations for the values. This is done by linking to the appropriate formula.

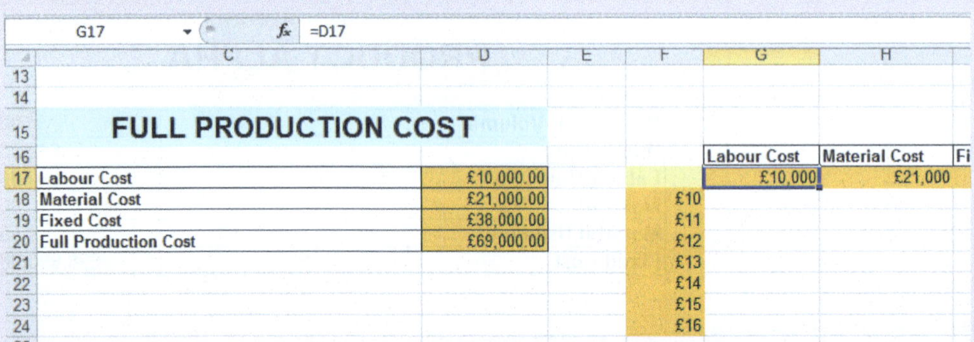

The table is now set up. Select the cells from F17:J24, and the Data Table function from the What-If Analysis menu.

(f) The column input cell is D7 – this is the material cost per unit. If you wish to see how changing other variables will affect the result, select that cell instead. You will probably need to change the values in cells F18:D24 as a result.

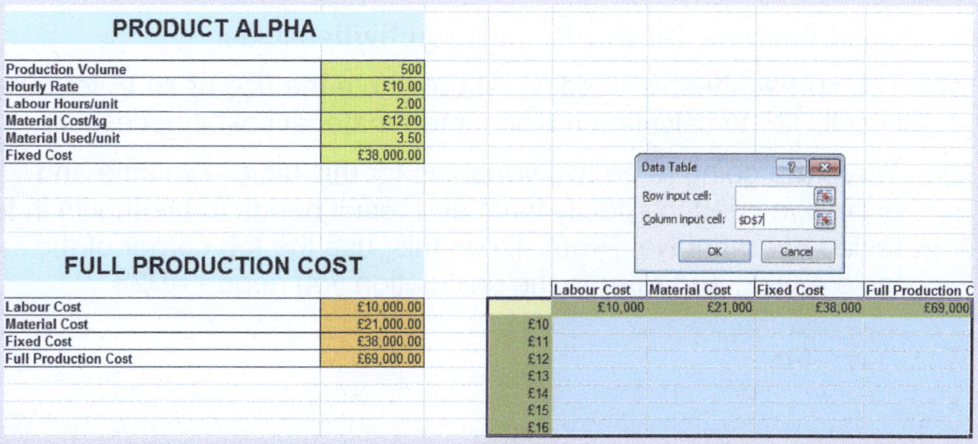

(g) The final table is populated – only the material costs and total costs change – this is because labour and fixed costs are unaffected by changes in material cost.

	Labour Cost	Material Cost	Fixed Cost	Full Production Cost
	£10,000	£21,000	£38,000	£69,000
£10	£10,000	£17,500	£38,000	£65,500
£11	£10,000	£19,250	£38,000	£67,250
£12	£10,000	£21,000	£38,000	£69,000
£13	£10,000	£22,750	£38,000	£70,750
£14	£10,000	£24,500	£38,000	£72,500
£15	£10,000	£26,250	£38,000	£74,250
£16	£10,000	£28,000	£38,000	£76,000

(h) Save the file in the **Solutions** folder as **Activity 22-1** and close it.

Activity 22-2

This activity shows the use of a two-input **data table**, following on from activity 22-1.

(a) Open the **Data Table 2** file in the **Activities** folder

(b) The spreadsheet is already set up – note the use of an **IF** formula in cell D25 to calculate a discounted material cost if necessary.

(c) There are going to be two variables for this table – volume and price. We need to specify what end result needs to be shown in the table – we want Net Profit. To do this, use the top corner of the table – G22, and refer to the calculation you need - **=D28**.

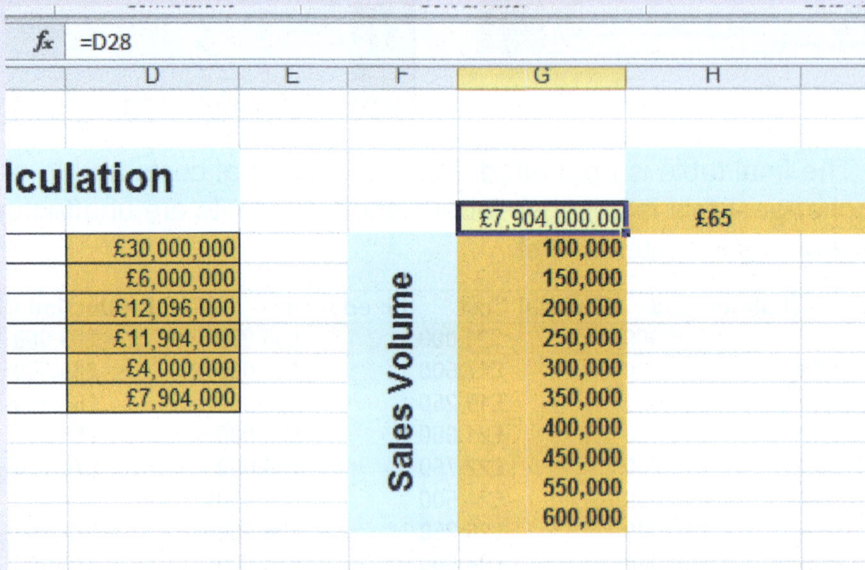

(d) Select the cells in the table (G22:L32), and select the Data Table function. The Row input is sales price – this is cell D5, the column is sales volume – D4.

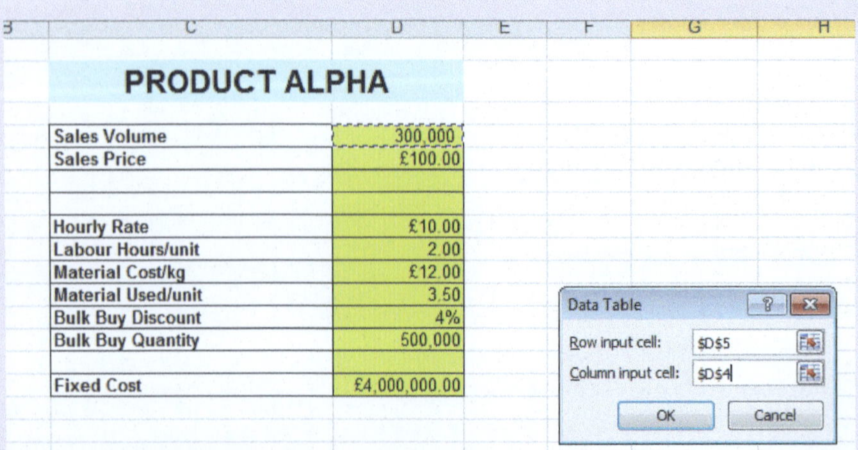

(e) The table is populated accordingly.

lation		Sales Price				
	£7,904,000.00	£65	£68	£75	£85	£100
£30,000,000	100,000	-£3,700,000	-£3,400,000	-£2,700,000	-£1,700,000	-£200,000
£6,000,000	150,000	-£3,298,000	-£2,848,000	-£1,798,000	-£298,000	£1,952,000
£12,096,000	200,000	-£3,064,000	-£2,464,000	-£1,064,000	£936,000	£3,936,000
£11,904,000	250,000	-£2,830,000	-£2,080,000	-£330,000	£2,170,000	£5,920,000
£4,000,000	300,000	-£2,596,000	-£1,696,000	£404,000	£3,404,000	£7,904,000
£7,904,000	350,000	-£2,362,000	-£1,312,000	£1,138,000	£4,638,000	£9,888,000
	400,000	-£2,128,000	-£928,000	£1,872,000	£5,872,000	£11,872,000
	450,000	-£1,894,000	-£544,000	£2,606,000	£7,106,000	£13,856,000
	550,000	-£1,426,000	£224,000	£4,074,000	£9,574,000	£17,824,000
	600,000	-£1,192,000	£608,000	£4,808,000	£10,808,000	£19,808,000

(Sales Volume)

You should also see that the profit for the current variables – price of £100 and sales of 300,000, is the same value shown in Cell D28.

(f) If you want to see a different result, for example contribution, change cell G22 to refer to the contribution calculation instead:

G22 =D26

	C	D
7		
8	Hourly Rate	£10.00
9	Labour Hours/unit	2.00
10	Material Cost/kg	£12.00
11	Material Used/unit	3.50
12	Bulk Buy Discount	4%
13	Bulk Buy Quantity	500,000
14		
15	Fixed Cost	£4,000,000.00
21	Net Profit Calculation	
22		
23	Sales Revenue	£30,000,000
24	Labour Cost	£6,000,000
25	Material Cost	£12,096,000
26	Contribution	£11,904,000
27	Fixed Cost	£4,000,000
28	Net Profit	£7,904,000

G	H	I	J
			Sales Price
£11,904,000.00	£65	£68	£75
100,000	£300,000	£600,000	£1,300,000
150,000	£702,000	£1,152,000	£2,202,000
200,000	£936,000	£1,536,000	£2,936,000
250,000	£1,170,000	£1,920,000	£3,670,000
300,000	£1,404,000	£2,304,000	£4,404,000
350,000	£1,638,000	£2,688,000	£5,138,000
400,000	£1,872,000	£3,072,000	£5,872,000
450,000	£2,106,000	£3,456,000	£6,606,000
550,000	£2,574,000	£4,224,000	£8,074,000
600,000	£2,808,000	£4,608,000	£8,808,000

(Sales Volume)

(g) If you look at the formulas in the table, they have curly brackets round them **{}** – these are called **array formulas**. They are very powerful, but not required as part of the SDST syllabus.

(h) Save the file in the **Solutions** folder as **Activity 22-2** and close it.

Activity 22-3

This activity shows the use of **Scenario Manager**, with some **Named Cells** and a few basic calculations.

(a) Open the **Scenario Manager** file in the **Activities** folder

(b) **Name** cell D2 as LabourRate and D3 as MaterialCost (see chapter 7).

(c) The formulas for the green cells (other than total variable costs) need to be populated. These are the Labour Cost per Unit, Material Cost per Unit, Contribution Per Unit, Total Contribution and Net Profit.

Note: contribution=selling price-variable costs.

(d) **Name** the three net profit results **Alpha_NP**, **Bravo_NP** and **Charlie_NP** respectively (cells D27, E27 and F27).

Charlie_NP | fx =F22-F25

	A	B	C	D	E	F	G
1							
2			Labour Rate per hour	£12			
3			Material Cost per kg	£14			
4							
5							
6							
7							
8							
9				ALPHA	BRAVO	CHARLIE	TOTAL
10			Hours in Production	2	3	4	
11			Material Quantity per unit	1	2	3	
12			Labour Cost per Unit	£24	£36	£48	
13			Material Cost per Unit	£14	£28	£42	
14			**Total Variable Costs**	£38	£64	£90	
15							
16			Selling Price	£77	£199	£143	
17							
18			**Contribution per Unit**	£39	£135	£53	
19							
20			Sales Volume	1000	400	1299	
21							
22			**Total Contribution**	£39,000	£54,000	£68,847	£161,847
23							
24							
25			Fixed Costs	30000	45000	28000	
26							
27			**Net Profit**	£9,000	£9,000	£40,847	£58,847

(e) The Scenario is ready to be set up. The idea is that we can show how the net profit results will change if the labour rate and material cost change to certain specified values. We could do this manually, but the Scenario Manager handles the changes quickly and presents them in a user-friendly way.

Select **Scenario Manager** from the **What-if Analysis** menu.

(f) Add the first Scenario – called 'Preferred'. The changing cells will be D2 and D3.

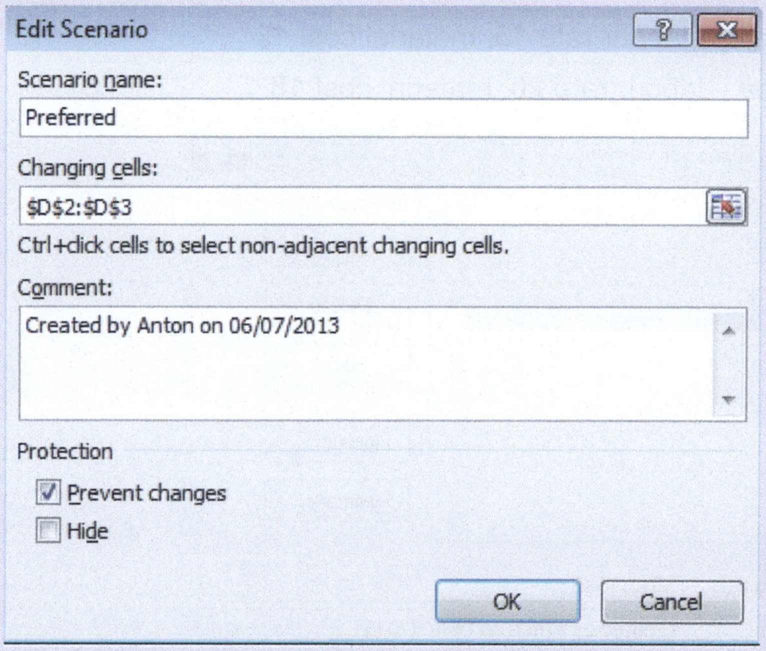

(g) After clicking **OK**, you will be asked to enter the values for the variables. Use 12 for the Labour Rate and 14 for the Material Cost. Notice that naming the cells makes this step easier – without the names you would be prompted for $D$2 and $D$3, and would have to work out what these meant.

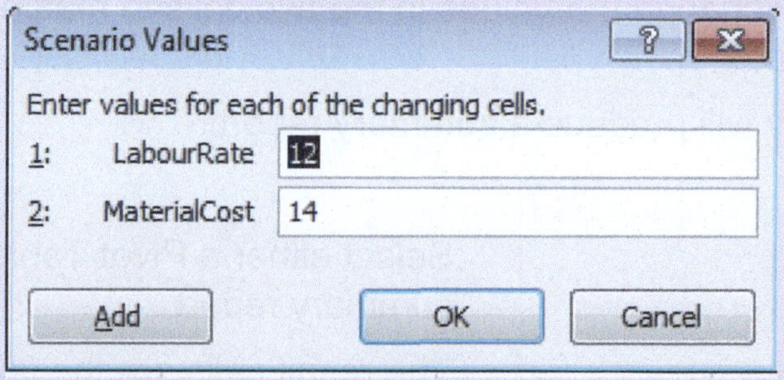

Click on **OK** – the first scenario has been entered.

(h) Add three more scenarios, as follows:

Unlikely – labour rate 13, material cost 15

Moderate – labour rate 16, material cost 18

Extreme – labour rate 20, material cost 18

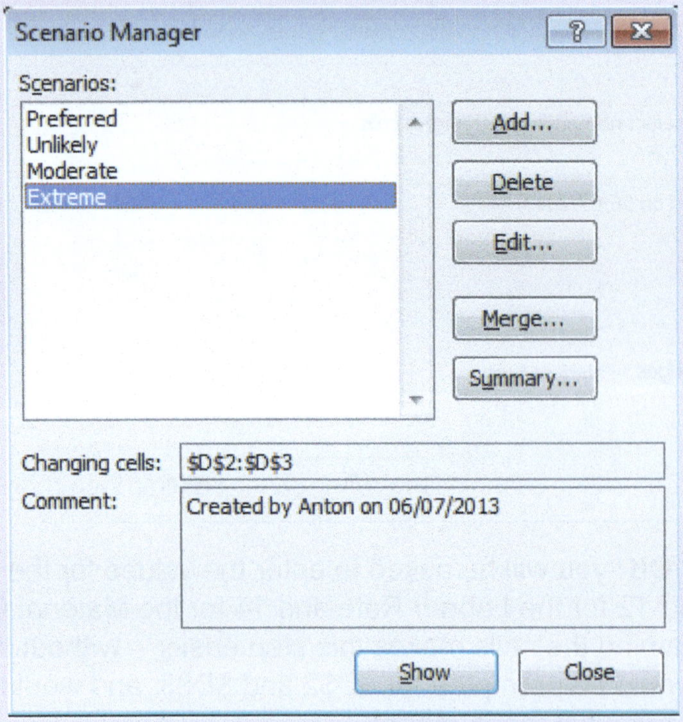

(i) Clicking **Show** will change the values in the two cells to match the scenario highlighted.

(j) Clicking **Summary** will produce a summary report.

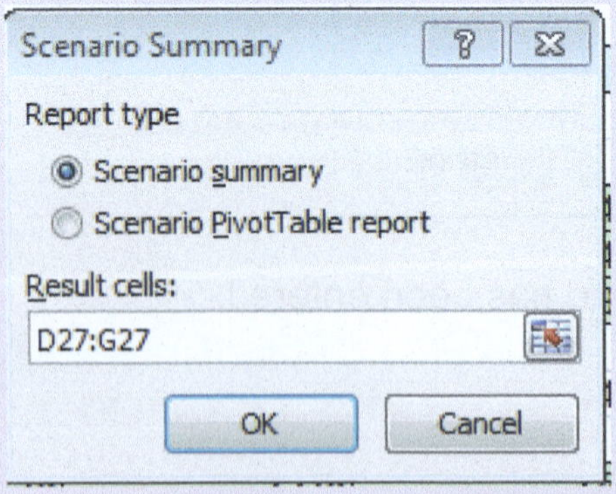

Select either a Pivot Table or summary report.

The result cells are the final results you wish to see – here the profit figures have been (correctly) selected by default.

(k) The final report is created on a new tab:

Scenario Summary	Current Values:	Preferred	Unlikely	Moderate	Extreme
Changing Cells:					
LabourRate	£12	£12	£13	£16	£20
MaterialCost	£14	£14	£15	£18	£18
Result Cells:					
Alpha_NP	£9,000	£9,000	£6,000	-£3,000	-£11,000
Bravo_NP	£9,000	£9,000	£7,000	£1,000	-£3,800
Charlie_NP	£40,847	£40,847	£31,754	£4,475	-£16,309
Overall_Net_Profit	£58,847	£58,847	£44,754	£2,475	-£31,109

Notes: Current Values column represents values of changing cells at time Scenario Summary Report was created. Changing cells for each scenario are highlighted in gray.

Again, note that the changing cells and result cells are shown in a user friendly way as we named them – otherwise the cell reference would be shown here, which would not be very useful.

(l) Save the file in the **Solutions** folder as **Activity 22-3** and close it.

Activity 22-4

This activity shows the use of **Goal Seek** in What-If Analysis.

(a) Open the **Goal Seek** file in the **Activities** folder

(b) We can use **Goal Seek** to find, for example, what material cost/kg would be required to give us a profit of £10,000 for a product.

(c) Select the Alpha Net Profit cell, D27, and launch Goal Seek.

(d) We wish to set cell D27 to a value of 10000 by changing D3.

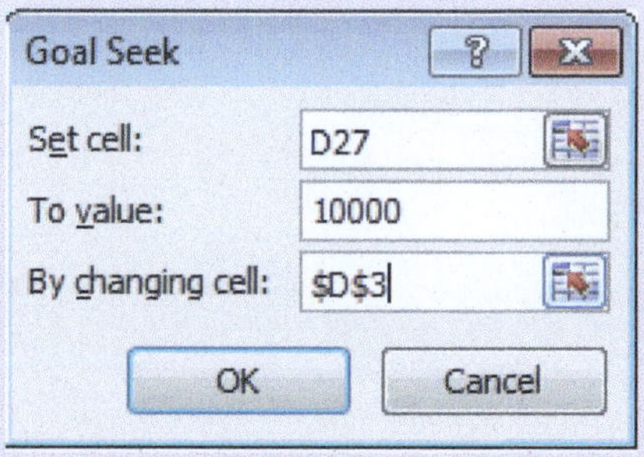

(e) A success message should be shown:

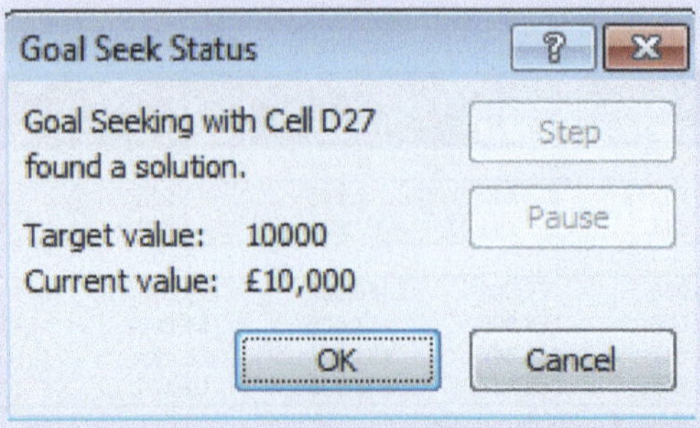

(f) Note that the material cost has been changed to give the required profit. Try other combinations. Remember, **Ctrl-Z** will still work after a Goal Seek, if you don't like the results.

(g) Save the file in the **Solutions** folder as **Activity 22-4** and close it.

Analysis tools

23

23.1 Introduction

This chapter will show you how launch an 'add-in' and to understand how to use analysis tools.

KNOWLEDGE

2.3 Select and use a range of tools and techniques to analyse and interpret data to meet requirements.

3.7 Use auditing tools to identify and respond appropriately to any problems with spreadsheets.

23.2 Installing analysis tools

Within Excel there is a selection of **Analysis Tools**. These tools do not come as standard on any menu and to use them you will need to activate an **Add-In.** These are found in the **Options** menu within the **File** tab.

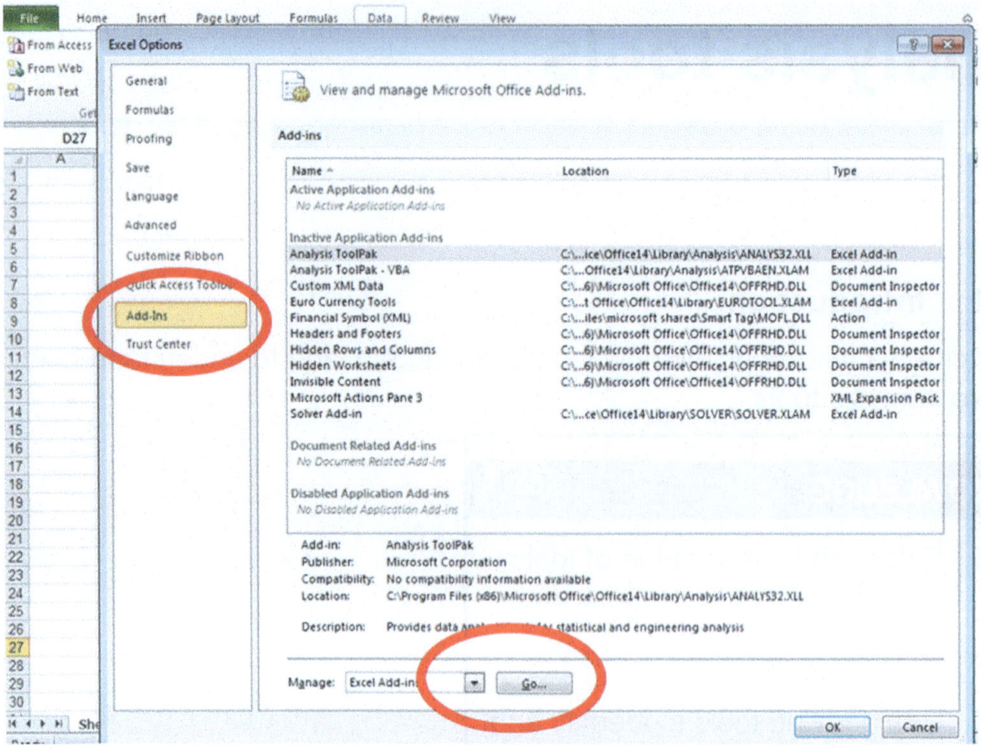

With **Manage Excel Add-ins** selected, click **Go**.

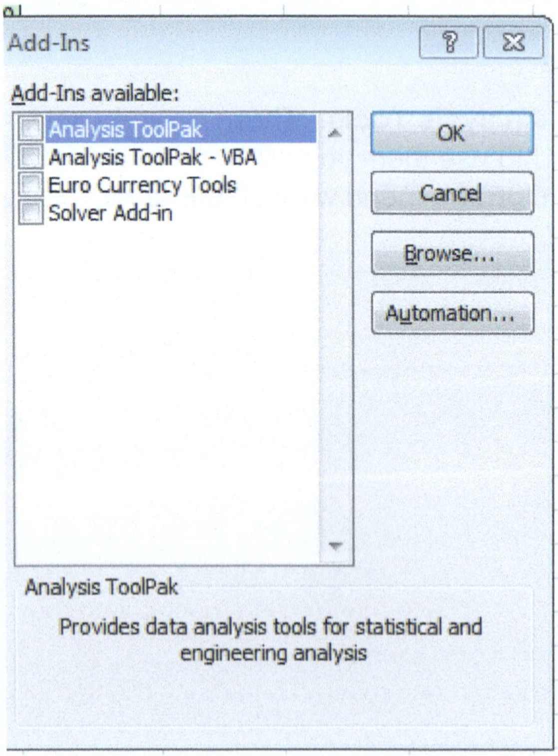

Select the Analysis ToolPak, and click OK.

23.3 Using analysis tools

There are lots of **Analysis Tools** but the ones you should be aware of are:

1 Histogram.

2 Moving Average.

3 Random Number.

4 Rank & Percentile.

5 Sampling.

Once the tools have been installed they can be accessed on the **Data** tab.

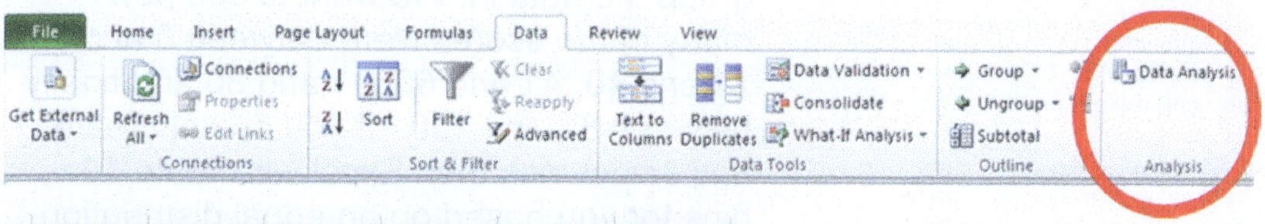

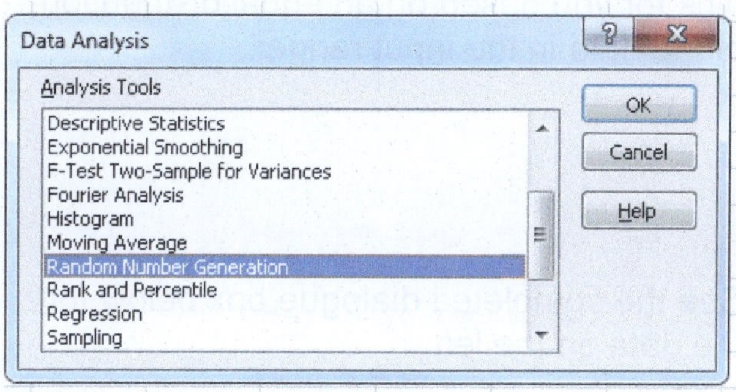

23.4 Histogram

You can analyse data and display it in a histogram (a column chart that displays frequency data) by using the Histogram tool of the Analysis ToolPak. The frequency of a particular data value is the number of times the data value occurs.

When the tool is launched you are presented with the following dialogue box:

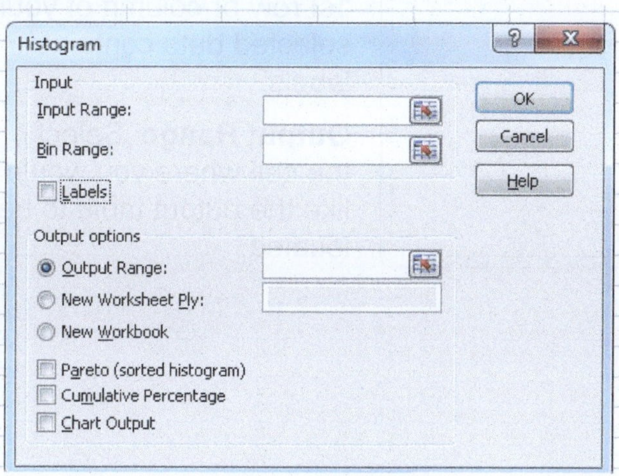

We can use a histogram to analyse how data groups together, for example the marks received from an exam.

	A	B	C
1	Student	Mark	Bin Range
2	Alice Cooper	76	20
3	Roy Rogers	97	40
4	Ray Sting	90	60
5	Tom Jones	98	80
6	Eric Clapton	36	100
7	John Lennon	31	
8	Eric Federer	100	
9	Roger Beckham	76	
10	Lowther Crouch	77	
11	Peter Defoe	100	
12	Ian Thorpe	79	
13	Will Buckley	81	
14	Serena Everitt	89	
15	Lionel Williams	74	
16	Henry Messi	98	
17	Diego Miller	98	
18	Andrew Maradonna	98	
19	John Strauss	74	
20	Rebecca Lewis	30	
21	Tony Storey	41	
22	Gordon Blair	83	
23	Tessa Brown	88	
24	Glenda Wyatt	85	
25	Sally Jackson	78	
26	Elizabeth Smith	95	
27	Bethany Price	84	
28	Georgina Whyte	95	
29	Wayne McCarthy	79	
30	Gareth Jones	46	
31	Sally Edwards	45	
32	Graham Gunnel	57	
33			
34			

Input Range: This is the data that you wish to include in the histogram, in this case the marks received. The data must be quantitative numeric data (such as item amounts or test scores).

Bin Range: In a histogram you can select a number of ranges or bins that you wish to group the data in. We want to see how many of the scores were between 0 and 20, 21 and 40, 41 and 60, 61 and 80 and finally between 81 and 100. If you do not create and select bins then Excel will create 10 bins for you based on an equal distribution of the data in the input range.

See the completed dialogue box below for the data on the left

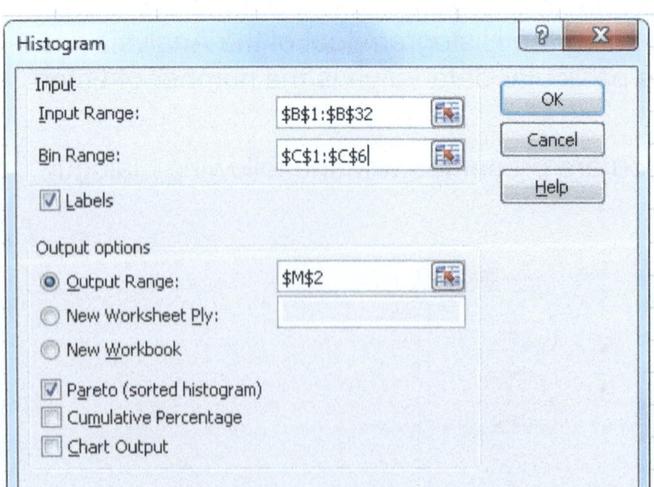

Labels: Excel will create suitable labels for the histogram; however, you should tick this box if the 1st row or column of your selected data contains labels.

Output Range: Select the cell where you would like the output table to be located.

New Worksheet Ply: If you wish for the output table to be in a new worksheet select it here.

New Workbook: If you wish for the output to be in a new workbook, select this option.

M	N	O	P
Bin Range	*Frequency*	*Bin Range*	*Frequency*
20	0	100	16
40	3	80	8
60	4	60	4
80	8	40	3
100	16	20	0
More	0	More	0

Pareto (sorted histogram): Select this to present data in the output table in descending order of frequency i.e. the most frequently occurring event will be shown first (see column O and P). If this check box is cleared, Excel presents the data in ascending order and omits the two columns that contain the sorted data.

Bin Range	*Frequency*	*Cumulative %*
20	0	0.00%
40	3	9.68%
60	4	22.58%
80	8	48.39%
100	16	100.00%
More	0	100.00%

Cumulative Percentage: Select this if you want Excel to create a cumulative percentage column in the output table.

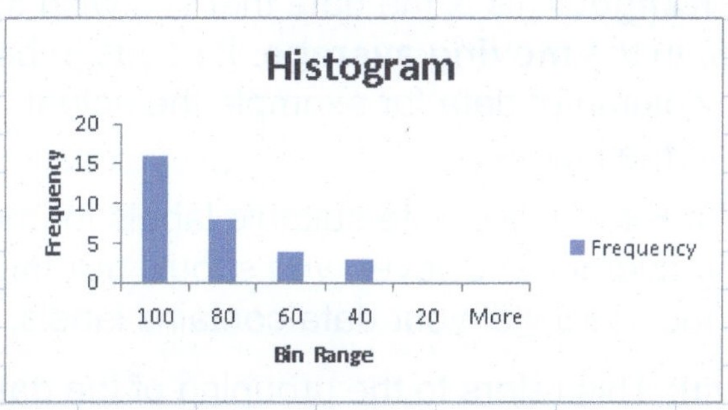

Chart Output: Select this if you wish Excel to create a chart. Excel will create an embedded chart. Once the chart has been created all the charting options seen earlier are available. The chart on the left has the Pareto option ticked.

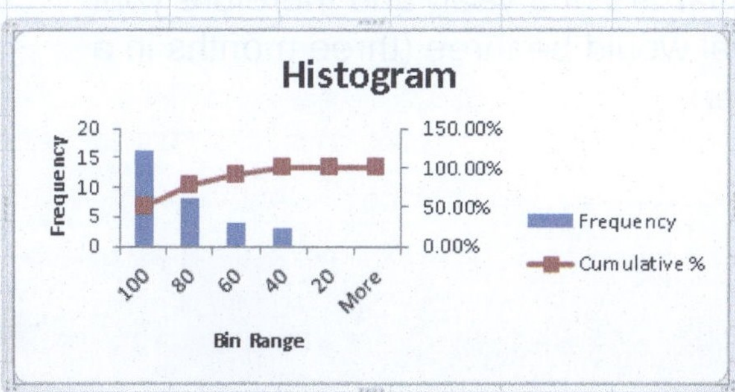

Excel can also create a cumulative percentage line on the histogram chart.

23.5 Moving average

A **Moving Average** is a series of averages calculated from time series data. By using moving averages, the variations in a time series can be eliminated leaving a 'smoothed' set of figures which is taken as the trend.

A moving average is used by accountants to smooth out fluctuations in numerical data over a time period, for example sales volumes over a year. It enables accountants to identify any trends in the data. When the tool is launched the following dialogue box appears:

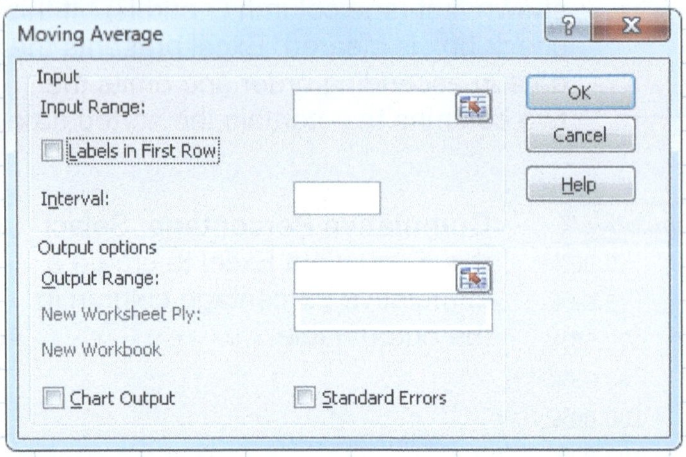

	A	B
1	Month	Actual sales
2	Jan	74
3	Feb	100
4	Mar	93
5	Apr	86
6	May	112
7	Jun	105
8	Jul	98
9	Aug	124
10	Sept	117
11	Oct	110
12	Nov	136
13	Dec	129
14		

Input Range: This is the data that you wish to include in the **moving average**. It needs to be a single column of data for example the actual sales in the image.

Labels: Excel will create suitable labels for the moving average; however, you should tick this box if the 1st row of your data contains labels.

Interval: This refers to the grouping of the data. For example you might be grouping your data into quarters of a year, and therefore your interval would be three (three months in a quarter).

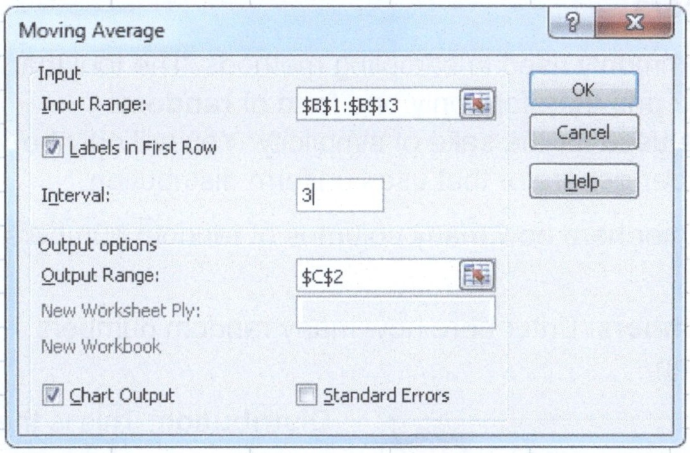

Output Range: Select the cell where you would like the output table to be. There is no option to put the output in a new workbook or worksheet.

	A	B	C
1	Month	Actual sales	
2	Jan	74	#N/A
3	Feb	100	#N/A
4	Mar	93	89
5	Apr	86	93
6	May	112	97
7	Jun	105	101
8	Jul	98	105
9	Aug	124	109
10	Sept	117	113
11	Oct	110	117
12	Nov	136	121
13	Dec	129	125
14			

Note: When the moving average is calculated the first 2 rows contain #N/A as it is not possible to calculate a moving average based on intervals of 3 with only 2 sets of data. The first value given is the average over the first 3 months and when moving averages is used as a forecasting tool the first value is usually positioned in the middle of the period it is averaging – see column D below.

	A	B	C	D
1	Month	Actual sales		
2	Jan	74	#N/A	
3	Feb	100	#N/A	89
4	Mar	93	89	93
5	Apr	86	93	97
6	May	112	97	101
7	Jun	105	101	105
8	Jul	98	105	109
9	Aug	124	109	113
10	Sept	117	113	117
11	Oct	110	117	121
12	Nov	136	121	125
13	Dec	129	125	
14				

Chart Output: Select this if you wish Excel to create a chart. Excel will create an embedded chart. Once the chart has been created all the charting options seen earlier are available.

Standard Error: Select this only if you want Excel to add a column of data showing the standard error. The standard error is the measurement of how far the values in the input range vary from an average calculation.

23.6 Random numbers

Random numbers are commonly used in sampling methods. The tool that Excel provides is complex and therefore only one form of **random number** generator will be used for the sake of simplicity. You will only be looking at a random number generator that uses uniform distribution.

Number of Variables: Enter here how many columns of random numbers you require.

Number of Random Numbers: Enter here how many random numbers you require in each column.

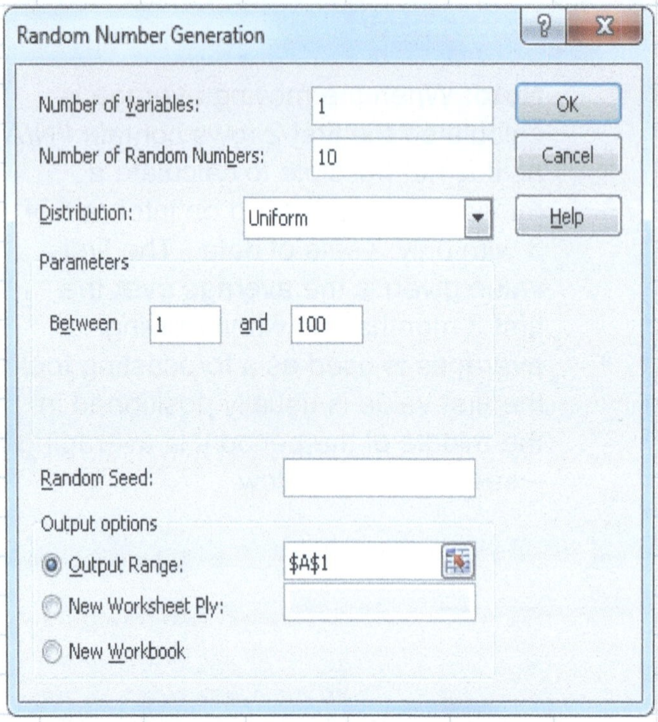

Distribution: This is the complex area of this tool. Different types of distribution are used for different purposes. We will use uniform distribution.

Parameters: Enter here a range between which you want the numbers generated.

Random Seed: A value can be entered from which the random numbers will be generated. This can be used to ensure that the same numbers are generated in the future.

	A
1	68.8984
2	43.68236
3	28.98056
4	60.22718
5	15.2486
6	22.80193
7	78.0893
8	46.50731
9	69.58425
10	63.318
11	

Clicking ok on the above dialogue box has produced the random numbers to the left. If the same box was completed again different numbers would appear as the Random Seed box is blank.

Output Range: Select the cell where you would like the output table to be located.

New Worksheet Ply: If you wish for the output table to be in a new worksheet select it here.

New Workbook: If you wish for the output to be in a new workbook, select this option.

23.7 Rank and percentile

The Rank and Percentile analysis tool produces a four column table that contains the ordinal and percentile rank of each value in a data set. You can analyse the relative standing of values in a data set.

- **Ordinal rank:** The numerical position in a series of data i.e. 1st, 10th, 23rd
- **Percentile rank:** The percentage of scores that are the same or lower than a given score.

When you launch the tool you get the following dialogue box.

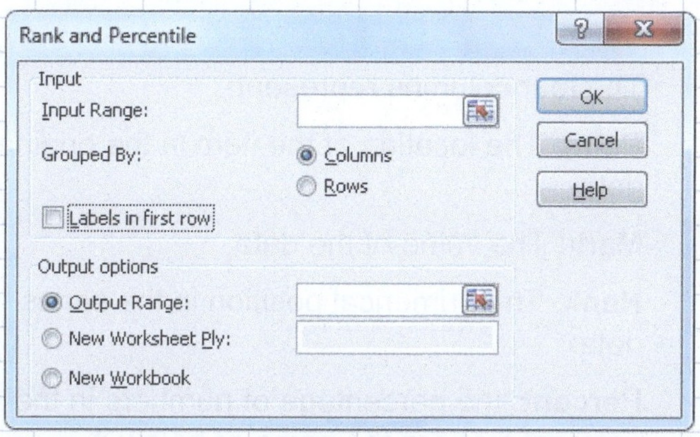

Input Range: The items that you wish to rank. For example a set exam marks

Grouped By: State whether the data is in a column or row and whether there are **labels** i.e. if there is a title to the column or row**.**

	A	B	C
1	Student	Mark	
2	Alice Cooper	76	
3	Roy Rogers	97	
4	Ray Sting	90	
5	Tom Jones	98	
6	Eric Clapton	36	
7	John Lennon	31	
8	Eric Federer	100	
9	Roger Beckham	76	
10	Lowther Crouch	77	
11	Peter Defoe	100	
12	Ian Thorpe	79	
13	Will Buckley	81	
14	Serena Everitt	89	
15	Lionel Williams	74	
16	Henry Messi	98	
17	Diego Miller	98	
18	Andrew Maradonna	98	
19	John Strauss	74	
20	Rebecca Lewis	30	
21	Tony Storey	41	
22	Gordon Blair	83	
23	Tessa Brown	88	
24	Glenda Wyatt	85	
25	Sally Jackson	78	
26	Elizabeth Smith	95	
27	Bethany Price	84	
28	Georgina Whyte	95	
29	Wayne McCarthy	79	
30	Gareth Jones	46	
31	Sally Edwards	45	
32	Graham Gunnel	57	

Output Range: Select the cell where you would like the output table to be located.

New Worksheet Ply: If you wish for the output table to be in a new worksheet select it here.

New Workbook: If you wish for the output to be in a new workbook, select this option.

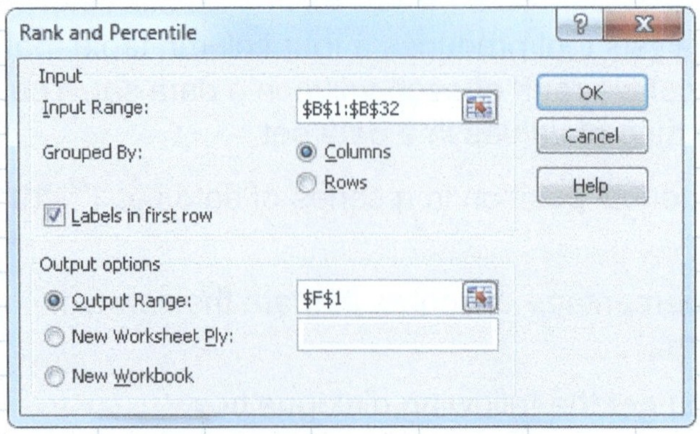

The information input into the dialogue box will produce the following results:

F	G	H	I
Point	*Mark*	*Rank*	*Percent*
7	100	1	97%
10	100	1	97%
15	98	3	87%
16	98	3	87%
17	98	3	87%
4	98	6	83%
2	97	7	80%
25	95	8	73%
27	95	8	73%
3	90	10	70%
13	89	11	67%
22	88	12	63%
23	85	13	60%
26	84	14	57%
21	83	15	53%
12	81	16	50%
11	79	17	43%
28	79	17	43%
24	78	19	40%
9	77	20	37%
1	76	21	30%
8	76	21	30%
14	74	23	23%
18	74	23	23%
31	57	25	20%
29	46	26	17%
30	45	27	13%
20	41	28	10%
5	36	29	7%
6	31	30	3%
19	30	31	0%

The four columns represent:

Point: The location of the item in the original data.

Mark: The value of the data.

Rank: The numerical position in the series data.

Percent: the percentage of numbers in the data-set that are the same or below it.

23.8 Sampling

The sampling tool creates a sample from a population by using the input range as the population. Sampling could be used if a number of exam papers or invoices needed to be audited.

	A	B	C
1	Student Number	Student	Mark
2	1	Alice Cooper	76
3	2	Roy Rogers	97
4	3	Ray Sting	90
5	4	Tom Jones	98
6	5	Eric Clapton	36
7	6	John Lennon	31
8	7	Eric Federer	100
9	8	Roger Beckham	76
10	9	Lowther Crouch	77
11	10	Peter Defoe	100
12	11	Ian Thorpe	79
13	12	Will Buckley	81
14	13	Serena Everitt	89
15	14	Lionel Williams	74
16	15	Henry Messi	98
17	16	Diego Miller	98
18	17	Andrew Maradonna	98
19	18	John Strauss	74
20	19	Rebecca Lewis	30
21	20	Tony Storey	41
22	21	Gordon Blair	83
23	22	Tessa Brown	88
24	23	Glenda Wyatt	85
25	24	Sally Jackson	78
26	25	Elizabeth Smith	95
27	26	Bethany Price	84
28	27	Georgina Whyte	95
29	28	Wayne McCarthy	79
30	29	Gareth Jones	46
31	30	Sally Edwards	45
32	31	Graham Gunnel	57

We want to sample 5 of these exam papers randomly to check the assessment is correct.

When the tool is launched you get the following dialogue box:

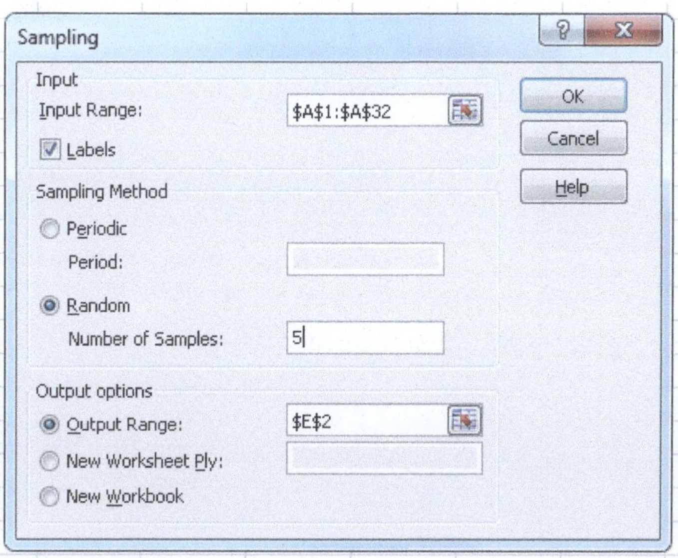

Input Range: The items in your population that you wish to pick your sample from. The input range should be numerical.

Labels: tick this box if your selected data has a heading

Sampling method:

- **Periodic:** This is where you choose to select every n^{th} value in your population, for example every 9th value.
- **Random:** This is where we allow Excel to choose our sample at random from the population.

Number of samples: How many items do you wish to choose from the population.

Clicking OK produces a list of student numbers to use to sample the exams:

E
Sample
22
29
10
20
4

INDEX